Cultural Atlas of
RUSSIA
and the Former Soviet Union

Editor Graham Speake
Art Editor Andrew Lawson
Cartographic Editors Olive Pearson, Sarah Rhodes
Picture Editor Linda Proud
Text Editor Jennifer Drake-Brockman
Index Ann Barrett
Design Adrian Hodgkins
Production Clive Sparling

For revised edition
Project Managers
Graham Bateman, Richard Watts
Editors Lauren Bourque, Helen Rappaport
Map Editor Tim Williams
Picture Research Claire Turner
Design Christopher Howson

AN ANDROMEDA BOOK

Planned and produced by Andromeda Oxford Limited 11–13 The Vineyard, Abingdon Oxfordshire, England OX14 3PX

Published by Checkmark Books, an imprint of Facts On File

Library of Congress Cataloging-in-Publication Data
Milner-Gulland, R. R.
    Cultural atlas of Russia and the former Soviet Union / by Robin Milner-Gulland with Nikolai Dejevsky. — Rev. ed.
      p.   cm.
    Includes bibliographical references and index.
    ISBN 0-8160-3815-5 (alk. paper)
    1. Former Soviet republics—Civilization.   2. Art, Russian. 3. Art, Soviet. 4. Former Soviet republics—Maps. I. Dejevsky, Nikolai J.   II. Title.
DK32.M62   1998
947—dc21   98-29263

Facts On File books are available at special discounts when purchased in bulk quantities for businesses, associations, institutions or sales promotions. Please call our Special Sales Department in New York at (212) 967-8800 or (800) 322-8755.

You can find Facts On File on the World Wide Web at http://www.factsonfile.com

ISBN 0-8160-3815-5

Origination by Scantrans, Singapore

Maps drawn and originated by Euromap, Pangbourne; Alan Mais, Hornchurch; Lovell Johns, Oxford; Cosmographics, Watford

Printed in Spain by Fournier A. Gráficas SA, Vitoria

This book is printed on acid-free paper

10 9 8 7 6 5 4 3 2 1

Frontispiece Country sports in 19th-century Russia, from J. Richter and C.G.H. Geissler, *Jeux et divertissements du peuple russe.*

Cultural Atlas of
RUSSIA
and the Former Soviet Union

by Robin Milner-Gulland
with Nikolai Dejevsky

Revised Edition

✓® **Checkmark Books**™
An imprint of Facts On File, Inc.

CONTENTS

Special Features

List of Maps

CHRONOLOGICAL TABLE

	800	900	1000	1100	1200
POLITICS AND RULERS	Ryurik ruler of Novgorod c.862 Oleg unites Kiev and Novgorod c.882		Princely conference at Lyubech 1097		Tatar rule established in Rus 1240

Christian relief from Georgia, 9th century

Mosaic from St Michael's, Kiev, 12th century

Ogaday, son and successor of Genghis Khan, 13th century

INTERNATIONAL RELATIONS	First Rus attack on Constantinople 860	First Russian treaty with Constantinople 911 Igor of Kiev makes treaty with Constantinople 944 Svyatoslav of Kiev sacks Khazaria 967			First Tatar raid 1223 Alexander Nevsky defeats Teutonic Knights 1242 Novgorod signs treaty with Hanseatic Leauge 1270
TERRITORIAL CHANGES			Yaroslavl founded 1025	Vladimir founded 1108 Moscow founded 1147	Nizhniy Novgorod founded 1221
RELIGION		Olga of Kiev baptized c.955 Christianity officially adopted 988/9	Boris and Gleb martyred 1015 First native Russian metropolitan elected 1051		
ART AND ARCHITECTURE			St Sophia, Kiev, begun 1037 St Sophia, Novgorod, begun 1043	Virgin of Vladimir icon c.1125 Dormition Cathedral, Vladimir 1158 (enlarged 1189) Church of the Savior, Nereditsa Hill, Novgorod 1198	St George, Yuryev-Polsky 1230 Transfiguration Cathedral, Tver 1285
LEARNING, SCIENCE AND LITERATURE	Cyrillic alphabet devised c.860(?)		Hilarion's *On the Law and the Grace* mid-11th century	*Instruction* of Vladimir II Monomakh c.1100 Primary Chronicle completed 1113 *Igor Tale* c.1187	

1300	1400	1500	1600	1700	1800	1900
Yury of Moscow obtains *yarlyk* from Tatars 1318 Dmitriy Donskoy defeats Tatars at Kulikovo 1380	Ivan III ends tribute to Tatars 1480	Ivan IV assumes title of "tsar" 1547 *Sudebuik* (law code) 1550 Fyodor I, last Ryurikid ruler, dies 1598	Time of Troubles begins 1605 Mikhail I, first Romanov tsar 1613 *Ulozheniye* (new legal code) promulgated 1649 Revolt of Stenka Razin 1670–71 *Mestnichestvo* abolished 1682	Peter I transfers seat of government to St Petersburg 1712 Gentry liberated from obligatory service 1762 Legislative Commission 1767 Pugachov rebellion 1773–75 Charter of Nobility 1785	Decembrist uprising 1825 Revolt in Polish provinces 1830 Emancipation of serfs 1861 First "To the People" movement 1873–74	First Duma 1906 February and October Revolutions 1917 Civil War 1917–20 USSR formed 1923 End of NEP, institution of five-year plans 1928 Great Purges 1936–38 Stalin dies 1953 Dissolution of USSR 1991

Boris Godunov's chain armor, late 16th century

Patriarch Filaret, 1553?–1633

Church of the Transfiguration, Kizhi, 1714

Lenin, 1870–1924

1300	1400	1500	1600	1700	1800	1900
	Lithuanians defeat Teutonic Knights at Tannenberg 1410 Constantinople falls to Ottoman Turks 1453 Ivan III closes Hanseatic depot in Novgorod 1494	Muscovy Company formed in London 1555 Commercial links established with Holland 1577	Treaty of Nerchinsk signed with China 1689 Peter I's Great Embassy 1697–98	Start of Great Northern War against Sweden 1700 Peter I defeats Charles XII of Sweden at Poltava 1709 Peace of Nystad 1721 First partition of Poland 1772 Second partition of Poland 1793 Third partition of Poland 1795	Treaty of Tilsit signed with Napoleon 1807 French invade Russia 1812 Outbreak of Crimean War 1853	Russo-Japanese War 1904–09 World War I 1914–18 Nonaggression pact with Germany 1939 Hitler invades USSR 1941 Hungarian uprising crushed 1956 Cuban missile crisis 1962 "Prague Spring" 1968 Invasion of Afghanistan 1979
Moscow annexes Nizhniy Novgorod and Suzdal 1392	Ivan III crushes Novgorod 1478	Vasiliy III annexes Pskov 1510 Moscow absorbs territory of Smolensk 1514 Ivan IV conquers Kazan 1552 Conquest of western Siberia 1582 Archangel founded 1584	Irkutsk founded 1632 Treaty with Poland confirms Russian possession of Kiev 1686	Site of St Petersburg captured from Swedes 1703 Annexation of Crimea 1783 Sitka founded as capital of Alaska 1799	Duchy of Warsaw becomes part of Russia 1832 Vladivostok founded 1860 Alaska sold to United States 1867 Building of Trans-Siberian Railroad begun 1891	Independence of Poland and Finland 1918 Independence of the Republics of USSR 1991
Metropolitan see transferred from Kiev to Vladimir 1300 Metropolitan see transferred from Vladimir to Moscow c.1321 St Sergius founds Trinity Monastery c.1340	Solovki Monastery founded 1429 Lithuanians set up rival Orthodox metropolitan in Kiev 1458	Church council supports "Josephites" 1503 Council of Hundred Chapters 1551 Patriarchate of Moscow established 1589 Union of Brest 1596	Nikon patriarch of Moscow 1652 Church council deposes Nikon but confirms reforms 1666–67 Archpriest Avvakum martyred 1682	Patriarchate abolished 1721 Dukhobor sect founded 1740–50		Reestablishment of patriarchate 1918 Church property confiscated 1922 Death of Patriarch Tikhon; no new patriarch elected 1925 Reestablishment of patriarchate 1943
Theophanes the Greek active in Novgorod 1378	Iconostasis of Annunciation Cathedral, Moscow 1405 Rublyov's Old Testament Trinity icon c.1410 Fioravanti builds Dormition Cathedral, Moscow, 1475–79	Archangel Cathedral, Moscow, begun 1505 Church of the Ascension, Kolomenskoye 1532 St Basil's, Moscow 1555–60 Smolensk kremlin 1596	"Marvelous Church" at Uglich 1618 Church of the Nativity in Putinki, Moscow 1649 Nikon's New Jerusalem begun 1658 Palace of Kolomenskoye 1667–70	Old Admiralty building, St Petersburg 1704 Rastrelli's Winter Palace, St Petersburg 1754 Falconet's *Bronze Horseman*, St Petersburg 1766–82	Admiralty building, St Petersburg, remodeled 1806 First Wanderers' exhibition 1871 *Mir iskusstva* (World of Art) launched 1898	Institute of Artistic Culture (Inkhuk) organized 1920 Lenin Mausoleum, Moscow 1929–30 Doctrine of Socialist Realism formulated 1934 Union of Artists founded 1957
	Trinity Chronicle early 15th century	First book printed in Moscow 1564	*Life* (autobiography) of Avvakum 1670s Slav-Greek-Latin Academy established in Moscow 1687	Russia's first newspaper published 1703 Academy of Sciences founded at St Petersburg 1725 Lomonosov's *Letter on the Utility of Glass* 1752 Moscow University founded 1755 Academy of Arts founded at St Petersburg 1757 Radishchev's *Journey from St Petersburg to Mosow* 1790	Karamzin's *History of the Russian State* 1816–26 Pushkin's *Yevgeny Onegin* 1823–31 Chaadayev's first *Philosophical Letter* 1836 Lermontov's *Hero of our Time* 1840 Gogol's *Dead Souls* 1842 Turgenev's *Fathers and Children* 1862 Tolstoy's *War and Peace* 1864–69 Dostoyevsky's *The Brothers Karamazov* 1879–80 Moscow Art Theater founded 1897	First issue of *Pravda* 1912 Sholokhov's *The Quiet Don* 1928–40 Artistic groups officially dissolved 1932 First congress of Union of Soviet Writers 1934 Eisenstein's *Alexander Nevsky* 1938 Sputnik I launched 1957 Pasternak's *Dr Zhivago* 1957 Gagarin first man in space 1961 Solzhenitsyn's *One Day of Ivan Denisovich* 1962

THE RULERS OF RUSSIA

Ivan IV

Vasiliy III

Peter I

Catherine II

In the period before 1547 the rulers of Russia were princes or grand princes; the title of tsar was adopted by Ivan IV in 1547, and that of emperor by Peter I in 1721.

Names in square brackets are those of regents. In many cases the succession passed between brothers or uncles and nephews, rather than from father to son, or by some other arbitrary arrangement; see notes. Many of the dates of the early reigns are doubtful.

Kievan line
862–79 Ryurik *semilegendary ruler of Novgorod*
879–913 Oleg *first ruler at Kiev (from c.882)*
913–45 Igor
945–64 [Olga] *widow of Igor*
945–72 Svyatoslav I
973–78/80 Yaropolk I
978/80–1015 Vladimir I (the Saint) *brother of Yaropolk I*
1015–19 Svyatopolk I
1019–54 Yaroslav I (the Wise) *brother of Svyatopolk I; divided the Kievan realm (1026–36) with another brother, Mstislav*
1054–73 Izyaslav I ⎤
1073–76 Svyatoslav II ⎟ *sons of Yaroslav I, who ruled Kiev in turns*
1077–78 Izyaslav I (*again*) ⎟
1078–93 Vsevolod I ⎦
1093–1113 Svyatopolk II *son of Izyaslav I*
1113–25 Vladimir II Monomakh *son of Vsevolod I*
1125–39 Mstislav I
1132–39 Yaropolk II ⎤ *younger brothers of Mstizslav I*
1139–46 Vyacheslav ⎦
1146–54 Izyaslav II ⎤ *sons of Mstislav I*
1154–67 Rostislav ⎦
1149–57 Yury Dolgoruky (i.e. Long-armed or Long-sighted) *younger brother of Mstislav I; overlaps with Rostislav; prince of Suzdal*
1157–74 Andrey Bogolyubsky *titular grand prince of Kiev, ruled from Vladimir*
1176–1212 Vsevolod III (Bolshoye Gnezdo; i.e. of the Large Nest) *son of Yury Dolgoruky; ruler of Vladimir-Suzdal*
1212–38 Yury II
1238–46 Yaroslav II *brother of Yury II; ruler of Kiev before moving to Vladimir*
1247–48 Svyatoslav III *brother of Yury II*
1249–52 Andrey II *son of Yaroslav II; prince of Vladimir*
1252–63 Alexander Nevsky *son of Yaroslav II; prince of Novgorod, subsequently Vladimir*
1263–71 Yaroslav III *son of Yaroslav II; prince of Tver*

Muscovite line
1263–1303 Daniil *youngest son of Alexander Nevsky; first prince of Moscow and (from 1302) of Pereyaslavl*
1303–25 Yury III (Danilovich) *grand prince of Moscow*
1325–41 Ivan I (Kalita; i.e. Moneybags) *brother of Yury III; "Grand Prince of Vladimir and All Russia," resident in Moscow*
1341–53 Semyon (Gordy; i.e. the Proud)
1353–59 Ivan II (Krasny; i.e. the Fair) *brother of Semyon*
1359–89 Dmitriy Ivanovich (Donskoy)
1389–1425 Vasiliy I
1425–62 Vasiliy II (the Blind) (*throne of Moscow claimed by Yury of Zvenigorod and successors in civil war 1425–50*)
1462–1505 Ivan III (the Great)
1505–33 Vasiliy III
1533–38 [Yelena Glinskaya] *widow of Vasiliy III, mother of Ivan IV*
1533–84 Ivan IV (the Terrible)
[*1575–76 Semyon Bekbulatovich khan of Kasimov, "parody tsar" installed by Ivan*]
1584–98 Fyodor I *last of Ryurikid dynasty*
1598–1605 Boris Godunov *brother-in-law of Fyodor I*

Time of Troubles

1605 Fyodor II *son of Boris Godunov*

1605–06 False Dmitriy I *claimed to be Prince Dmitriy (d. 1591), youngest son of Ivan IV; there were other subsequent pretenders*

1606–10 Vasiliy IV (Shuysky)

1610–13 Wladyslaw *tsar-elect, son of king of Poland; not crowned*

Romanov dynasty

1613–45 Mikhail Romanov *son of Fyodor Romanov, who later became Metropolitan Filaret*

1645–76 Aleksey Mikhaylovich

1676–82 Fyodor III ⎫   *Aleksey's children by Maria Miloslavskaya;*

1682–89 [Sophia]   ⎬   *Ivan V senior co-tsar with Peter I,*

1682–96 Ivan V   ⎭   *but with Sophia as effective ruler until 1689*

1689–96 [Natalya Naryshkina] *Aleksey's second wife and widow*

1682–1725 Peter I (the Great) *Aleksey's son by Natalya Naryshkina; co-tsar with Ivan V to 1696*

1725–27 Catherine I *widow of Peter I*

1727–30 Peter II *grandson of Peter I; son of the tsarevich Aleksey*

1730–40 Anna *daughter of Ivan V*

1740–41 [Anna Leopoldovna] *niece of Anna; mother of Ivan VI*

1740–41 Ivan VI *grand-nephew of Anna*

1741–62 Elizabeth *daughter of Peter I*

1762 Peter III *nephew of Elizabeth*

1762–96 Catherine II (the Great) *widow of Peter III*

1796–1801 Paul I *son of Peter III (?) and Catherine II*

1801–25 Alexander 1

1825–55 Nicholas I *brother of Alexander I*

1855–81 Alexander II

1881–94 Alexander III

1894–1917 Nicholas II *constitutional monarch from 1906*

Post-Revolutionary period

1917 (Feb–July) Prince Georgiy Lvov *prime minister in provisional government*

1917 (July–Oct) Alexander Kerensky *prime minister in provisional government*

1917–24 Lenin (Vladimir Ilyich Ulyanov) *chairman of the Council of People's Commissars*

1924–53 Joseph Stalin (Iosif Visarionovich Dzhugashvili) *secretary-general of the Central Committee of the Communist Party from 1922; effective sole power from 1928; from 1940 official head of government*

1953–55 Georgiy Malenkov *unofficial head of collective leadership after Stalin*

1955–64 Nikita Khrushchev *first secretary of the central committee*

1955–58 Nikolai Bulganin *official head of state*

1964–82 Leonid Brezhnev *first secretary of CPSU*

1982–84 Yury Andropov *first secretary of CPSU*

1984–85 Konstantin Chernenko *first secretary of CPSU*

1985–Dec, 1991 Mikhail Gorbachov *first secretary of CPSU*

1991– Boris Yeltsin *first President of Russia after the dissolution of the Soviet Union in December 1991*

Alexander I

Nicholas II

Joseph Stalin

Boris Yeltzin

PREFACE

"This book has been written and produced in remarkable times . . ." These words opened my preface to its first edition in 1989: in the years since then they have become even more apposite. It takes an effort to remember how recent and how astonishing were such late-Soviet events as the rehabilitation of "taboo" writers and artists, the institution of multi-party elections, the questioning of the bonds between the Union Republics, the reestablishment of such time-honored names as St Petersburg. These symbolically-resonant renamings, and the emergence of so many new sovereign states on former Soviet territory, would be enough to justify our revised edition in themselves. More fundamentally, the end of Soviet rule, and the beginning of a new, internationally-reorientated existence for Russia are a momentous historical punctuation-mark, making a clear-eyed look at the interwoven history, culture and geography of Russia and the new post-Soviet republics imperative. Visitors to Russia, students, business people and ordinary readers are likely to be as concerned as specialists to explore these matters – about which Western journalists and politicians often assume much but know little.

Coincidentally Russia has just experienced the greatest of its cultural anniversaries: the millennium of its official conversion to Christianity in 1998–9. Vladimir I's choice of religion set Russia on a cultural path which, with twists and turns—discontinuities, some believe—has led to the present. The social and political history that emerges from the centuries in between, though turbulent, is by no means a record of unmitigated oppression or hardship, as some seem to assume; Russia, while usually eccentric to the Western experience, was never wholly isolated from it and can demonstrate—positively as well as negatively—alternative possibilities within the European heritage.

The term "Russia" is not self-explanatory: what it has meant through more than a thousand years of changing circumstances—from Kievan Rus through Muscovy, the Russian Empire, the Soviet Union and the CIS—is indeed one of this book's themes. Geographical context is of the highest importance, and is provided in our first and last sections (in the latter, the new republics are treated individually). The bulk of our text is a narrative history from the earliest times to the present. It is both impracticable and undesirable to separate cultural from political or any other kind of history. But particular attention has been paid to the context of ideas in which Russian history has unrolled, to the Russians' self-image as a nation, and to the arts through which non-Russians generally make first contact with this culture, and which are its "public face."

Even a book-length text demands rigorous selectivity in coverage. This can be all to the good when it concentrates attention on what is most important, painful when interesting topics may be omitted or merely touched upon. That we do not systematically discuss Russian food, or chess, or folksong, does not mean we do not consider such topics significant parts of the culture: simply that history and geography have had to come first. Within Russian history, too, we have made choices of emphasis that need to be pointed out, even if unapologetically. On the grounds that the 19th and 20th centuries are likely to be far better known to non-Russians than earlier periods, we have tried to redress the balance somewhat towards the latter. In particular we have concentrated on that most crucial and ambiguous moment of Russian history, the reign of Peter the Great (and on the two centuries, 17th and 18th, between which his lifetime was divided).

This book is not all text: words, maps, diagrams, illustrations, and special features are interdependent. The special features play an important role in complementing the narrative visually and verbally on certain topics of particular interest. To produce such a volume has taken dedicated effort by many people. I must single out Graham Speake and Jennifer Drake-Brockman, a most discriminating copy-editor, who contributed the features on pp. 30–32. Dr Nikolai Dejevsky undertook the considerable task of contributing most of the political history on the period 1855–1988 onwards and wrote the features on pp. 138, 140, 166 and 170. Malcolm Day produced many expert map briefs and drafted parts of the last section.

For the rest, and indeed for the overall shape of the volume, I have to take responsibility. But to many colleagues I must express thanks for helping me on detailed queries (often without knowing they were doing so): among them are Professors A.A.M. Bryer, A.G. Cross, G.S. Smith and R.E.F. Smith and Drs D. Dyker, S. Franklin and S. Hackel; also members of my family. Above all I have profited by the support and comments of Professor Sir Dimitri Obolensky, as indeed I have throughout a friendship lasting decades.

Robin Milner-Gulland

PART ONE
THE GEOGRAPHICAL BACKGROUND

THE LAND AND THE PEOPLE

Any account of Russian culture through the ages should begin by evoking the circumstances and locations in which the history of this culture has unrolled. Russians may not have a unique status among peoples in their sense of self-identification with their land, but their awareness of the part it has played in shaping their destiny, sometimes as ally, sometimes as antagonist, has always been particularly acute.

For the past thousand and more years several constraints can be seen in the relationship of the people and the land of Russia. These tend to present themselves in the form of problems in whose resolution a positive aspect can emerge. (1) Russia is, and throughout history has been, large—very large on a European or even world scale: only evanescent empires of conquest have outreached it. This huge extent has generally entailed poor communications and the threat of ungovernability. (2) Russia is thinly populated, and this was true even before it added the vast emptiness of Siberia to its territory. (3) Russia is agricultural. The often precarious harvests of field and forest have been the prime source of its wealth (and cause of its difficulties). Even in the industrialized 20th century the rural population has been larger than the urban until the present generation. (4) Russia has lacked fixed frontiers. The unequivocal natural demarcations of seacoasts or high mountain ranges have been attained by Russians only very gradually, and through infiltration or conquest that has taken them far beyond their historic lands. Nor did the boundaries of the former Soviet Union or the Russian empire before it follow ethnic/linguistic demarcations at all closely. (5) Russia is astonishingly far north: even its great historic southern metropolis, Kiev (now modern-day Kyyiv), is on a level with the southern tip of Hudson Bay; St Petersburg is on the latitude of the Shetland Islands; nearly half of Russian territory is north of 60°, that is, on a level with Alaska, Baffin Island or Greenland. (6) Finally the Russian climate seems expressly designed to foil human habitation and activity. Winter lasts half the year or more, but the summer is actually often very arid, with rainfall slight and ill-distributed; vast tracts of desert are matched by even vaster tracts of waterlogged swamp.

The vegetation belts

The great overriding constant in Russian and Eurasian geography has been the natural division of the country's vegetation, following its climate, into a series of latitudinal bands running roughly from west to east across European Russia and well into Asia, unhindered by what on the map might look like the natural obstacles of the Ural Mountains, the Caspian Sea and several great river systems. This spectrum of seven long, often narrow zones, each continuing for literally thousands of kilometers, is closely related to soil type and in turn to geology and to climate. The latter becomes,

as might be expected, colder as one proceeds from south to north, but also from west to east until close to the Pacific seaboard, as a truly continental climate supersedes the somewhat more variable and comparatively temperate conditions of western and even central European Russia. The vegetation belts are of considerable importance to the economy and remain easily recognizable to the modern traveler, despite centuries or millennia of human interference and modification. The most basic distinction is between forest and grassland (or steppe). Each has presented its own difficulties and opportunities for exploitation. It is however worth dwelling briefly on all seven of the great vegetation zones and their distinctive traits.

The northernmost is tundra—the true Arctic waste, where summers are too short and cool for trees or exploitable grasses to grow. Though it fringes the entire Arctic Ocean coastline and part of the Pacific, it forms only a narrow strip in European Russia on either side of the White Sea entrance: in central Siberia however it stretches several hundred kilometers south from the Taymyr Peninsula. It was not, for obvious reasons, a place of permanent Russian settlement until very recently, yet it is not wholly hostile to life: it supports reindeer on its lichen, water-birds on its innumerable pools and summer swamps and fish and walruses in its seas—resources which for centuries the Russians, not to mention Eskimo peoples such as the Nentsy, have to some extent exploited. The soil beneath the tundra is permanently frozen; it would be wrong however simply to equate tundra with "permafrost," a frozen subsoil, since in parts of central and eastern Siberia permafrost actually stretches far further south, up to and beyond the Mongolian border.

South of the tundra, yet reaching in many places beyond the Arctic Circle, comes the most extensive zone of all: the coniferous forest belt. Stretching as it does from the Gulf of Finland to Kamchatka, not less than 1000 kilometers wide (sometimes double that), this, the "Hercynian Forest" of the ancients, is one of the mightiest features of our planet. The Russian term for it is taiga, which properly implies trackless or virgin forest, though geographers worldwide have adopted it to apply to the entire zone. In any case it has always been thinly, where at all, inhabited, with sparse settlements along its river systems developing around forts, monasteries and trading posts, and scattered non-Russian (mostly Finno-Ugrian) indigenous inhabitants living generally as hunters and gatherers. Where the forest is cleared, particularly in European Russia, some cultivation of hardy crops is possible, but the soil is usually poor and often swampy, the growing season short and chancy. Yet from these northern forests Russia has derived great wealth over the course of the last millennium, nowadays from the timber which is methodically exploited and exported, but in the past above all from the fur-

Tundra in summer: an Eskimo fishing settlement by the shores of the Arctic Ocean.

Overleaf Where taiga and tundra meet: a herd of reindeer on the move in the north of European Russia. Reindeer, which feed mainly on lichens, are a valuable resource for the peoples of the north where conventional livestock farming is impossible.

bearing animals whose luxuriant pelts were well adapted to the bitter cold.

The next two zones, very narrow by comparison with the taiga, can conveniently be treated together. First comes the mixed coniferous-deciduous forest: this fans out towards the western border, taking in all of Belarus and the Baltic states, linking up with the forests of central Europe. Here the firs, pines and larches of the north are interspersed with large stands of (chiefly) birch and oak: such trees, together with limes, characterize too the so-called wooded steppe, a narrow band running alongside the mixed forest across European Russia, then becoming wider beyond the Urals until fading out among the mountains of central Asia. With discontinuities, both zones can be traced subsequently along the southern fringe of Siberia to the Far East. Relatively inconspicuous on the map, these two zones have been of the greatest importance to Russia's historical geography. With a somewhat better climate and more fertile soils, they, unlike the taiga, have been cleared and tilled from the beginnings of Russian history, while still retaining a fair amount of exploitable forest land. Russia's three ancient capitals of Kyyiv (formerly Kiev), Vladimir and Moscow lie within these zones; they represent not only the agricultural heartland of the Old Russian state, but the corridor along which the Russians, in the 16th and 17th centuries, pushed eastwards to the middle Volga region, thence through the southern Urals and along the thin fertile strip of southern Siberia between forest and mountains—the line that was later to be taken by the Trans-Siberian Railroad—and reaching the Pacific Ocean with the mixed forests of the Amur valley.

The wooded steppe gradually gives way to the steppe proper, that most distinctively Russian landscape, almost treeless and very flat, though dissected in places by deep-cut river valleys and ravines. It covers much of Ukraine, from a little south of Kyyiv to the Black Sea, fringes the Caucasus, then continues as a rather broad band south and eastwards of the Urals and (in patches) to Mon-

golia. The steppe landscape is quite distinct from that of the forested zones, and to understand this distinction we need to go back to the ice ages. In European Russia the maximum extent of glaciation reached approximately as far as what is now the belt of wooded steppe. To the north of this the ice irregularly scoured the landscape, leaving sandy, clayey or gravelly surface deposits overlying the chalk and limestone (north of St Petersburg, older rocks) beneath, and creating many moraine ridges as it retreated: an undulating, sometimes hummocky landscape has resulted, with many scooped-out lakes and swampy hollows, among which rivers wander rather inconsequentially. Below the limit of glaciation, however, thick and fertile soils, including much windblown loess, have built up undisturbed.

The age-old steppe vegetation is the tall and luxuriant feather-grass, whose matted roots trap such moisture as is available in this thirsty region, and over millennia of growth and decay build up a splendidly rich layer of humus. This is the famous "black earth" or chernozem, the availability of which is Russia's greatest agricultural blessing. There also exist various less remarkable, but still useful related "brown" and "chestnut" soils. No blessing, however, comes unmixed, and where the natural grass has been plowed up in the more accessible steppe territories, dustbowl conditions can develop, soils can degenerate and drought is always a threat. Since the dawn of their history the steppe has been important for the Russians, yet they never managed to colonize it methodically until the last couple of hundred years (with Cossacks and runaway peasants as an "advance guard" during the Muscovite period). Not only were there natural obstacles—waterlessness (save in the few river valleys) and the considerable difficulty of breaking up the thick mat of grass-roots before the days of modern agricultural machinery—there were human impediments too.

The steppe is splendid horse country, and represented a natural highroad for mounted invaders from the east or south; any settlement was easy

prey for plunderers, and the horsemen could appear without warning and without giving time to mobilize defense. Not surprisingly, the Cossack outposts, when they were established, were semi-military in character. Even Kyyiv itself, in the wooded steppe, was not safe from the attentions of these mobile raiders, and the southward lines of communication along the great rivers (above all the Dnieper) were particularly vulnerable. Control and subsequently colonization of the European and Asian steppe were probably the most important preconditions for Russia's status as a great power.

South of the steppe come the last two zones: semidesert and desert proper. They are largely a feature of Central Asia, though they continue south of Siberia, but on Chinese and Mongolian territory. However, both also curl around the top of the Caspian Sea, down to Azerbaijan, across the Volga embracing Astrakhan, second most populous city of late Muscovite Russia, and into Europe. Semi-desert contains, among its boulder-strewn wastes and salt-pans (*solonchaki*), considerable patches of rough vegetation, and it has always been used by the grazing flocks of transhumant pastoralists. The desert proper, with its bare rock and in many places dunes—most notoriously the Kyzyl Kum, "Red Sands"—is inhabited only in its oases. Yet both zones contain small, but economically most important strips of highly productive land, where artificial irrigation or natural river valleys permit the cultivation of fruit crops, notably melons, and of cotton, the foundation of what is, by Asiatic standards, the considerable prosperity of Central Asia.

These seven great zones are those normally distinguished by geographers. There is another, however, stretching (though discontinuously) along the whole southern frontier of the region, that deserves mention, though it is in a somewhat different category since it is not primarily determined by any single type of vegetation. This is the zone of the great mountain ranges that historically have helped to set limits upon the Russians' expansionist urges. From west to east they include: the northeastern arm of the Carpathians; the limestone Yayla range in the Crimea; the main spine of the Caucasus, and to its south, beyond Georgia, the tangled uplands where Armenia, Turkey and Iran meet; the ranges separating Turkmenistan from Iran and Afghanistan; the very high and extensive Pamirs and Tien Shan ("Mountains of Heaven"); thereafter many other less continuous ranges that succeed each other along the border with Mongolia and Manchuria to the Sikhote-Alin overlooking the Pacific. Mountains indeed are characteristic of the whole of eastern Siberia beyond the Lena. The southern mountains of the former Soviet Union, as elsewhere, are favorable for livestock and timber exploitation; the precipitation they attract is important in the most arid parts of the country, watering in particular the fertile Transcaucasian republics and the great oases of Central Asia.

The only important range eccentric to the pattern described above is that of the Urals: relatively low, and without special agricultural significance, they nevertheless have been most important for centuries to Russia as a source of mineral wealth. Old Russia's territory touched on mountains only at its extreme southwestern corner (the

Carpathians) and extreme northeast (the Novgorod territory stretched to the foothills of the northern Urals): crossing the main passes in the Ural range (which they called "The Rock") in the late 16th century marked the first major expansion of the Russians beyond their traditional lands.

As a coda to any description of the great zones of vegetation that characterize Russia and the surrounding republics, mention must be made of its very small, but totally distinctive pockets of subtropical vegetation: in western Georgia (particularly Adzharia), in Azerbaijan, in Turkmenistan and on the southeast coast of the Crimea. They do not form any coherent zone or belt; indeed they are scarcely large enough to be noticed on most vegetation maps. Yet as normally frost-free areas they are remarkable in the context of this northerly country and have disproportionate economic significance. Citrus fruits are grown, while the largest of these pockets—at the extreme eastern end of the Black Sea, around Bat'umi in Adzharia—has rich tea plantations, and its hinterland actually represents a continuation of the subtropical rain forest of the

Above Where mixed forest meets wooded steppe: an early spring scene in a large nature reserve overlooking the Oka River in Ryazan province, southeast of Moscow. The spring thaw produces swamp-like conditions over huge areas of the country as invading armies from the Tatar hordes to Hitler's panzer divisions have found to their cost.

seemed limitless: there was always more untouched forest to clear and land for the sparse population to exploit. To wrest prosperity rather than mere subsistence from it, however, was hard. Slash-and-burn techniques would give reasonable crops from cleared forest for only a few seasons: then it was time to move on, letting the former clearances revert to scrub. Crop-rotation systems remained very primitive till recent times. Russian agriculture was traditionally extensive rather than intensive, and the Russian peasant gained a reputation among some Western observers and Russian historians (such as Klyuchevsky) for ravaging rather than husbanding the countryside. Such a judgment rests upon inappropriate comparisons with the very different circumstances of the advanced Western European agricultural regions. Actually the Russians were quite capable of applying careful and intensive methods when they wanted (as did Tsar Aleksey Mikhaylovich, a notable horticultural experimenter, in the 17th century), or where it was profitable (but the landless urban population was too small until modern times to support very much in the way of market gardening).

Peasants had to get what they could out of the land as fast as they could in the brief growing season. Certain factors operated on their side: the abundance of land, the long warm days of midsummer, the tradition of village cooperation in the heavier tasks. Ranged against them, however, were rather more: six months or so of iron-hard winter, with the consequent difficulties of keeping livestock; the fickle weather that would quite often deliver a drought in the growing season of early summer, but thunderstorms to knock down the crops at harvest time; long and difficult communications that made it hard to dispose of surpluses.

Right The mixed-forest zone of central Russia has long been hospitable to human settlement. The woman with her cluster of small livestock represents a timeless mode of peasant life.

Trebizond area. The Crimean "dry Mediterranean" coastal strip in the lee of the Yayla has long been an area of touristic importance as a winter and summer resort.

Humankind in the landscape

An account such as this may tend to emphasize the region's diversity: apart from at its mountainous southern fringes, however, its uniformity is more apparent on the ground. A modern geographer (D.J.M. Hooson) has rather picturesquely pointed out that "while in midsummer almost all Russians can be happy in shirtsleeves, in mid-winter it would be perfectly feasible to skate on the rivers from the Arctic to the Caspian, or sledge from Leningrad [St Petersburg] to Vladivostok"; "on no other comparable stretch of land has the climate been able to use such a broad brush." The consequences for the Russians through history have been clearly evident.

Once established as agriculturalists, well over 1000 years ago, on the European mixed-forest and wooded-steppe belts, their horizons must have

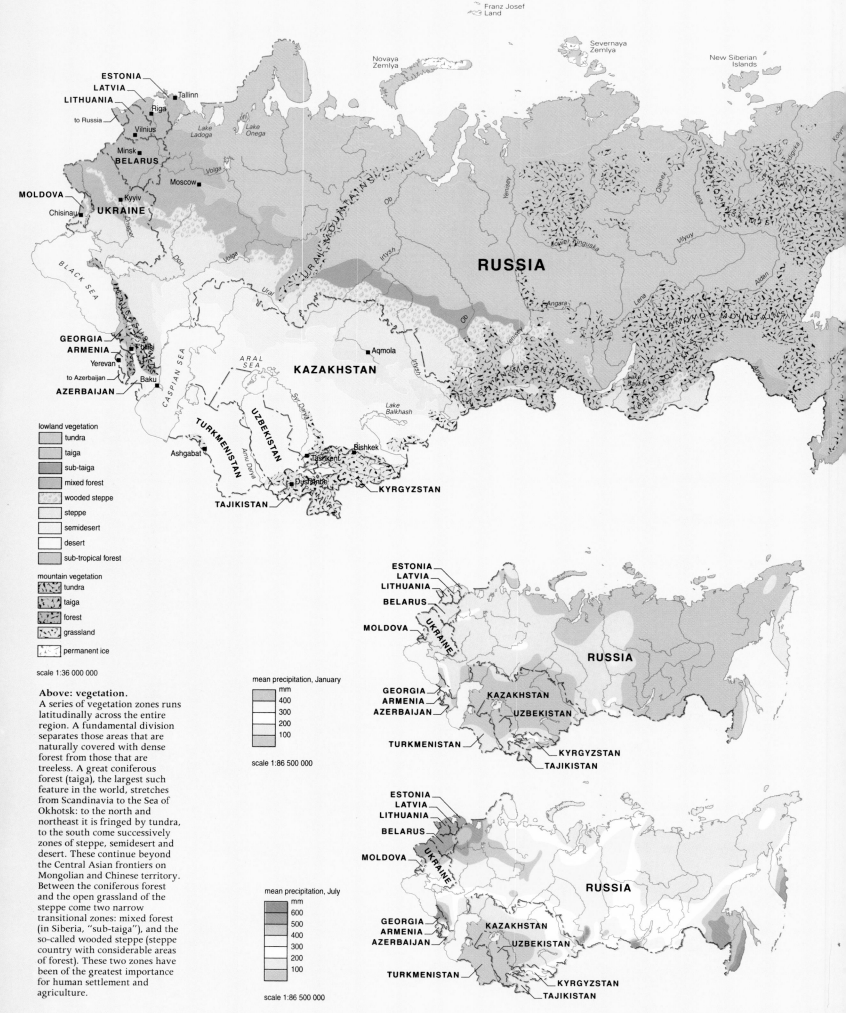

lowland vegetation

- tundra
- taiga
- sub-taiga
- mixed forest
- wooded steppe
- steppe
- semidesert
- desert
- sub-tropical forest

mountain vegetation

- tundra
- taiga
- forest
- grassland
- permanent ice

scale 1:36 000 000

mean precipitation, January

mm
400
300
200
100

scale 1:86 500 000

mean precipitation, July

mm
600
500
400
300
200
100

scale 1:86 500 000

Above: vegetation.
A series of vegetation zones runs latitudinally across the entire region. A fundamental division separates those areas that are naturally covered with dense forest from those that are treeless. A great coniferous forest (taiga), the largest such feature in the world, stretches from Scandinavia to the Sea of Okhotsk: to the north and northeast it is fringed by tundra, to the south come successively zones of steppe, semidesert and desert. These continue beyond the Central Asian frontiers on Mongolian and Chinese territory. Between the coniferous forest and the open grassland of the steppe come two narrow transitional zones: mixed forest (in Siberia, "sub-taiga"), and the so-called wooded steppe (steppe country with considerable areas of forest). These two zones have been of the greatest importance for human settlement and agriculture.

22

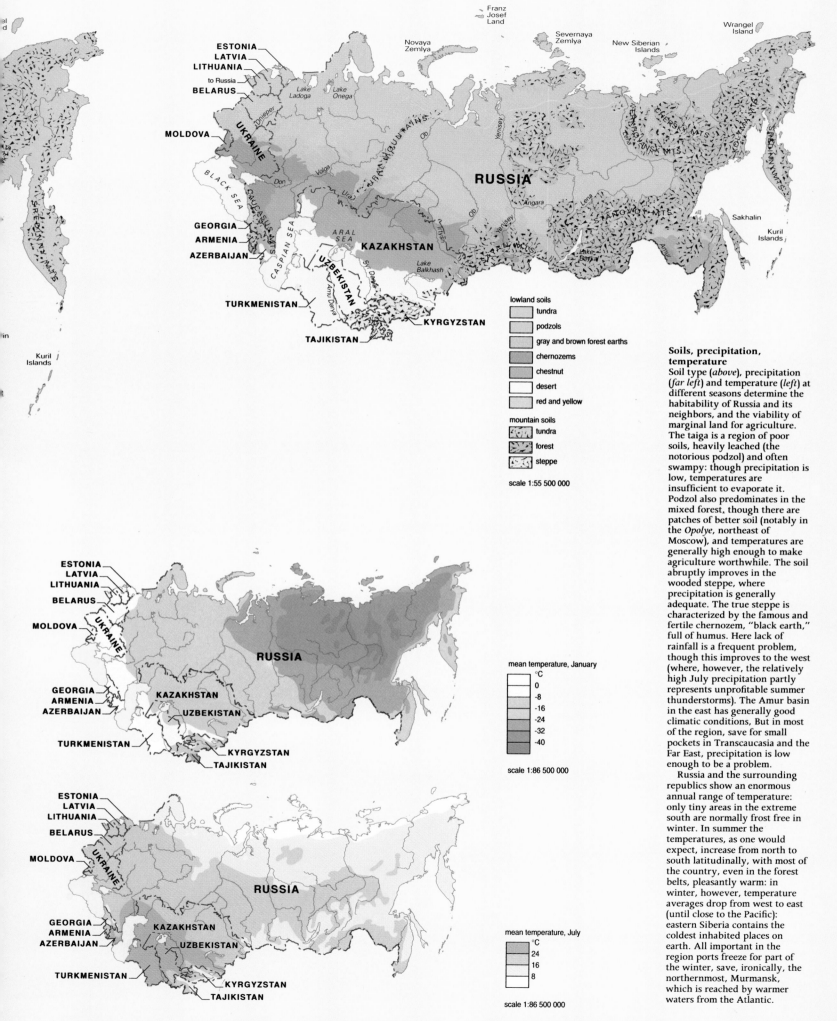

ESTONIA
LATVIA
LITHUANIA
to Russia
BELARUS

MOLDOVA
UKRAINE
Dnieper
Lake Ladoga
Lake Onega
Don
Volga
Ural
URAL MOUNTAINS
Ob
Yenisey
RUSSIA
CHERSKIY MTS
VERKHOYANSK MTS
KOLYMA MTS
SREDINNYY MTS

Franz Josef Land
Novaya Zemlya
Severnaya Zemlya
New Siberian Islands
Wrangel Island

BLACK SEA
CAUCASUS
CASPIAN SEA
ARAL SEA
KAZAKHSTAN
Lake Balkhash
Lake Baykal
Sakhalin
Kuril Islands
Angara
Lena
Amur
STANOVOY MTS
ALTAY MTS
Irtysh
Ob

GEORGIA
ARMENIA
AZERBAIJAN
UZBEKISTAN
Syr Darya
Amu Darya
TURKMENISTAN
KYRGYZSTAN
TAJIKISTAN

Kuril Islands

lowland soils
- tundra
- podzols
- gray and brown forest earths
- chernozems
- chestnut
- desert
- red and yellow

mountain soils
- tundra
- forest
- steppe

scale 1:55 500 000

Soils, precipitation, temperature

Soil type (*above*), precipitation (*far left*) and temperature (*left*) at different seasons determine the habitability of Russia and its neighbors, and the viability of marginal land for agriculture. The taiga is a region of poor soils, heavily leached (the notorious podzol) and often swampy: though precipitation is low, temperatures are insufficient to evaporate it. Podzol also predominates in the mixed forest, though there are patches of better soil (notably in the *Opolye*, northeast of Moscow), and temperatures are generally high enough to make agriculture worthwhile. The soil abruptly improves in the wooded steppe, where precipitation is generally adequate. The true steppe is characterized by the famous and fertile chernozem, "black earth," full of humus. Here lack of rainfall is a frequent problem, though this improves to the west (where, however, the relatively high July precipitation partly represents unprofitable summer thunderstorms). The Amur basin in the east has generally good climatic conditions, But in most of the region, save for small pockets in Transcaucasia and the Far East, precipitation is low enough to be a problem.

Russia and the surrounding republics show an enormous annual range of temperature: only tiny areas in the extreme south are normally frost free in winter. In summer the temperatures, as one would expect, increase from north to south latitudinally, with most of the country, even in the forest belts, pleasantly warm: in winter, however, temperature averages drop from west to east (until close to the Pacific): eastern Siberia contains the coldest inhabited places on earth. All important in the region ports freeze for part of the winter, save, ironically, the northernmost, Murmansk, which is reached by warmer waters from the Atlantic.

ESTONIA
LATVIA
LITHUANIA
BELARUS
MOLDOVA
UKRAINE
RUSSIA
GEORGIA
ARMENIA
AZERBAIJAN
KAZAKHSTAN
UZBEKISTAN
TURKMENISTAN
KYRGYZSTAN
TAJIKISTAN

mean temperature, January
°C
0
-8
-16
-24
-32
-40

scale 1:86 500 000

ESTONIA
LATVIA
LITHUANIA
BELARUS
MOLDOVA
UKRAINE
RUSSIA
GEORGIA
ARMENIA
AZERBAIJAN
KAZAKHSTAN
UZBEKISTAN
TURKMENISTAN
KYRGYZSTAN
TAJIKISTAN

mean temperature, July
°C
24
16
8

scale 1:86 500 000

23

Eventually the social system subjected the peasants to a landlord and officials, who tried to stop them moving and commandeered part of their labor or their cash. Their most constant antagonist, however, was the very soil they worked. In the forest belts this was likely to be podzol: a thin sandy or clayey soil whose minerals had been leached out, often to form an impermeable layer or "hardpan" a little below the surface, hampering drainage, impervious to anything but deep plowing (usually the peasant had neither time nor resources to do more than superficially furrow the soil with a light wooden *sokha*). With enough manure the soil could be improved, but few peasants could keep many animals through winter. In such marginal conditions, what is more, any experimentation with farming methods represented a life-or-death gamble; it is hardly surprising that landlords in the 18th and 19th centuries who wished to bring in improved methods, putative or real, ran up at best against a wall of "peasant obstinacy," which was at root commonsensical, at worst against arson or personal violence.

In view of all these problems faced by the mass of the Russian people, one can hardly be surprised even by as sweeping a verdict as that of Richard Pipes: "Their heavy reliance on farming under adverse natural conditions is perhaps the most single basic cause of the problems underlying Russian history." From such a judgment it is easy to pass to the censorious implication that the forest and steppe were made to support no more than a small scattering of hunters in the former, livestock-breeders in the latter; that the establishment of any unitary and populous Russian state was a mistake, founded as it had to be on settled agriculture; that at some stage in its history it should have fallen apart, and serve the Russians right for their pig-headedness.

It is important to note the relatively benign climatic conditions that prevailed across northern Europe in the early Middle Ages, when the Russians were consolidating their position in their land, and made marginal farming a more viable risk (conversely the "Little Ice Age" of the early modern period probably made its own contribution to the late Muscovite crisis). The foothold that the Russians established as early as the 9th century in the central mixed-forest belt is at least partly the consequence both of this climatic improvement and of a lucky geographical accident: the existence, well to the north of other such features, of a large isolated pocket of fertile "black earth." This is the *Opolye* (deriving from the word for "field"), a roughly oval area with a long axis of some 130 kilometers, located between the rivers Klyazma and Volga. At its center is one ancient city (Yuryev-Polsky), while others are ranged round its perimeter: Vladimir, Aleksandrov, Pereslavl-Zalessky, Rostov "the Great," Suzdal; Moscow is not far off. To this day the traveler notices the region's comparative treelessness and its numerous farming villages; nowadays it is specially noted for the quality of its cherries.

In general though the Russian peasant in the forest zone had to look beyond merely cultivating the land to reach a reasonable standard of life. Not only fish, that could be caught in winter too through the ice, but game birds and animals were a

Above The Aral Sea, which cuts across the frontier between Uzbekistan and Kazakhstan, and was once the fourth largest inland sea in the world, is now shrinking at an alarming rate. This beautiful saltwater sea, once rich in shoals of the highly valued sturgeon and other fish, is not only suffering some of the worst depradations of pollution but has also, since the 1960s, been drained of its waters for irrigation purposes at such an alarming rate that it has now been reduced to half its original volume. Its major northeastern port, Aralsk, is now stranded several miles inland from the Sea itself.

Left Central Asian desert: the Kara Kum ("Black Sands") in Turkmenistan. The wind blows the sand into shifting dunes (barkans) up to 20 m high.

significant part of the family's diet—unlike in Western Europe, where laws against poaching grew progressively more stringent. The forest would also yield honey (wild or domestic), berries, nuts and mushrooms, all suitable for winter storage. When distilling reached Russia in the late 16th century it served not only as a means for jollification but as a practical method of "preserving" any surplus of grain. Hunting could be a more seriously and lengthily organized activity, particularly at the fringes of the coniferous forest. But any excessive exploitation or considerable settled population would drive the precious fur-bearing mammals farther and farther away—where Russians found it worthwhile to pursue them over thousands of kilometers, and eventually in the 18th century even across the Bering Straits into Alaska.

In the often isolated Russian villages and the farms that in some regions would house a large extended family all activities and cottage industries necessary for an almost completely self-sufficient life—a school of self-reliance—would be carried on: baking, brewing, preserving, weaving sandals and baskets from bast (usually of birchbark), simple metalworking and the production of a vast number of articles from wood. Only the occasional itinerant pedlar, selling fine cloth, some metal items, woodcuts, icons and similar goods would bring news from the outside world.

The Russian people

Who then are these Russians, with whose history and culture this book is primarily concerned, and who from before the start of written records lived in parts at least of what we now consider "Russia"? How did a Russian state arise, from what origins, and who organized it? Perhaps unexpectedly, the early medieval Russians themselves were interested in such problems, and these last three questions are precisely those that the author of the Russian so-called Primary Chronicle, *The Tale of Bygone Years*, set himself in the first words of his great work (written probably in the years 1111–13). The answers that he gives as his narrative unfolds are sometimes purely speculative, sometimes unintentionally or deliberately misleading or full of gaps. Yet more often they are generally convincing, needing little revision or amplification even in the light of all the further knowledge amassed in nearly 900 years, and are the product of a recognizably keen historical intelligence.

To the Primary Chronicle as a source for history and as a literary work we shall return (see below p. 40). Here we are concerned with its description of the origin of the Russians. They are Slavs, related to those who "over a long period settled beside the Danube, where the Hungarian and Bulgarian lands now lie." Some tribes scattered along what we now regard as the wooded-steppe and mixed-forest zones to the east, mostly in defined territories along major river valleys. The chronicler several times names these tribes, about a dozen, whose territories correspond fairly closely to the principalities of the subsequent Kievan federation, and indeed are traceable in later administrative divisions of Russia. He is much interested in their customs and way of life, and as a good Kievan he

praises the mild and respectful habits of the Polyane tribe, the Kievans' own ancestors. Though divided, they retain a unified language, Slavonic; they "live separately," that is, independently, though some pay tribute to the Khazar kingdom of the steppe country (one tribe, the Vyatichi, was to do so until the later 10th century). The establishment of a more-or-less unitary Russian state took place in the mid-9th century when a group of Vikings, headed by a certain Ryurik (a name perhaps cognate with "Rorich" or "Roderick") assumed the government of Novgorod and north Russia, apparently by invitation, and his descendants extended their power southwards.

The chronicler does not hazard a guess as to the time scale over which this migration or infiltration of Slavs on to what is now Russia, and the coalescence of small clans into larger tribal units, took place. There is very little clear evidence. Unequivocal references to the Slavs on the territory of Southern Russia are found only from the mid-6th century onwards, in the writings of Byzantine, and subsequently also Arab, historians and geographers. It seems likely that a confederation of tribes known as Antes or Antae, who dominated the Pontic steppe (north of the Black Sea) as vassals of the Sarmatians until crushed by the Turkic Avars, were wholly or partly Slavonic. So too must have been the more northerly Venedi (from whose name derive modern forms such as "Wendish"). It is

quite possible that Slavonic tribes, probably (though not certainly) direct forebears of the Russians, occupied parts of Southern Russia many centuries before they were first mentioned in written sources by outsiders; some archaeological evidence points in this direction. To postulate a long and formative period of contact and cooperation with southern steppe peoples of Iranian stock (as does the much-read historian G. Vernadsky) goes far beyond any ascertainable facts. Yet there remains one not easily explained phenomenon: the indisputable existence in the early Kievan period (10th–11th centuries) of a single Russian outpost far to the southeast of any other Russian domains, the small principality of Tmutorokan on the Strait of Kerch, where the Sea of Azov debouches into the Black Sea. Was its establishment merely one of the consequences of the military expeditions of that greatest of peripatetic Kievan warriors, Prince Svyatoslav (960s), or a unique, hence precious remnant of an early Russian presence south of the great steppe, guarding the mouth of what an early Arab writer calls the "Slav River" (the Don)? Answers do not come readily, but what is certain is that Kievan Russians considered this area an important part of their realm, and devoted much ultimately unsuccessful effort to retaining it.

Up to this point we have referred to the forebears of the Russians as "Slavs," as members, that is to say, of a larger unit of people, linguistically

Languages of Russia and Northern Eurasia.
Well over 100 languages are spoken in the region, the majority of them by very small ethnic groups, and hence unrecordable on any save the most detailed maps. The greatest diversity is seen in the Caucasus, particularly in Dagestan on the northeast flank of the range. Two great language families, however, dominate the territory in question. The larger is the Slavonic, comprising the closely related Russian, Ukrainian and Belarusian. Native speakers of Russian extend from the Gulf of Finland to the Pacific; nevertheless they are now less than half the total population. The other family is the Turkic, most of whose recognized languages and dialects are intercomprehensible: it extends from Azerbaijan to Yakutia. Other non-Indo-European language families include the Finnic to the north and the Caucasian group to the south.

Wrangel
Island

Sakhalin

Kuril
Islands

Indo-European (with branch)
- Belarusian (Slavonic)
- Russian (Slavonic)
- Ukrainian (Slavonic)
- Latvian, Lithuanian (Baltic)
- Tajik, Ossetian (Iranian)
- Moldovan (Romance)
- Armenian (other)

Altaic (with branch)
- Azeri, Turkmen, Yakut (Turkic)
- Bashkir, Tatar (Turkic)
- Karakalpak, Kirghiz, Uzbek (Turkic)
- Kazakh (Turkic)
- Mongol, Tungus-Manchurian, Tuvan (other)

Caucasian
- Abkhaz, Chechen
- Dagestani languages
- Georgian

Uralic (Finnic, Ugric & Samoyedic branches)
- Estonian, Karelian, Komi, Lapp, Nentsy

Paleo-Siberian
- Chukchi, Gilyak, Koryak

 uninhabited or sparsely populated

scale 1:36 000 000

homogeneous, who during the middle centuries of the first millennium AD spread outwards from a fairly confined territory somewhere in east-central Europe to occupy, wholly or partially, a vast swathe of the continent, extending to the Elbe in Germany, to the Adriatic, to the Baltic, to beyond the Gulf of Corinth in mainland Greece, and into the wooded steppe, and perhaps the true steppe country eastwards. It is clear that in the course of this great migration, or rather these waves of migration, the Slavs split into three main branches: the Western, the Southern and the Eastern. Out of these, over centuries, the present Slavonic nations crystallized: Poles, Czechs and Slovaks (all, as well as some smaller groups, such as the Sorbs or Lusatians of East Germany, West Slavs); Bulgarians, Serbo-Croats and Slovenes (South Slavs); and the Russians (subdividing only from the late Middle Ages into Great Russians, Belarusians and Ukrainians) or East Slavs. This Slavonic expansion is poorly documented: evidently it did not have the suddenness or the military character of the great movements of barbarian peoples that alarmed and sometimes threatened the Romans and Byzantines.

The Slavonic languages

The Slavs, their three major branches and their subsequent subdivisions, are fundamentally to be defined not territorially, racially or politically but linguistically. The Slavonic group of languages forms one of the major components of the great Indo-European language family, whose speakers range from North India (Hindi and Urdu), through Iran (Farsi) and parts of middle Asia (Tajik), to Armenia, the Baltic (Lithuanian, Latvian) and virtually the whole of Europe. The Slavonic group stands on an equal footing with, for example, the Romance languages (derived from Latin), the Germanic (including English and the Scandinavian tongues) and also such solitary surviving representatives of ancient groups as Greek. By tracing back the evolution of the existing Slavonic languages and extrapolating to the period before documentation, linguists have without difficulty reconstructed a plausible "Common Slavonic" language from which the three major branches originated. Common Slavonic, incidentally, must have developed in proximity to the Baltic group (Latvian, Lithuanian, the extinct Old Prussian) with which it shares several significant features. Certain non-Indo-European languages (Finnish, Estonian, Magyar, Turkish, Tatar) have also adjoined the Slavs, apparently without affecting their linguistic structures. Some more conjectural detective work has attempted to fix a prehistoric "homeland" for the Slavs, chiefly on the basis of the distribution of plants that either have, or have not, Slavonic names: thus the word for "beech-tree" is not native in any Slavonic language. This homeland would appear to be somewhere in east-central Europe, perhaps around the upper Vistula (Wisla) in modern Poland. But even the proto-Slavs presumably came from somewhere. Problems connected with the spread of the Indo-European peoples are highly contentious. A modern theory, propounded by the archaeologist Colin Renfrew, sees the Indo-Europeans as the bearers of the settled agricultural way of life that during the Neolithic superseded hunting and gathering over most of Europe, spreading in waves from eastern Anatolia. It is a concept of particular interest in a Russian context, but it is largely untested and has been vigorously disputed.

The Indo-European language family overall has some rather distinctive characteristics that set it apart on the world linguistic scene: a highly developed grammatical system whereby discrete words—nouns, verbs, adjectives and pronouns—undergo a series of systematic changes (usually to their endings) to indicate their "agreement" with other words and/or their semantic function within the sentence; a pervasive and apparently arbitrary attribution of the category of "gender" to nouns; an elaborate set of verb forms distinguishing the manner (usually temporal) of an action. Modern Indo-European languages have mostly, in the course of their evolution, shed parts of this complicated web of interconnections—English more than any. The Slavonic languages, by contrast, have retained a remarkable amount of the pristine grammatical system. A most characteristic and interesting feature that distinguishes them from other modern European languages is their virtual abandonment of fine temporal distinctions through the tense of verbs (as in modern English and French) in favor of a different category, "aspect," based on the concept of the duration or completion of an action. It is not so many years since whole theories on the nature of the "Slav soul" used to be propounded on the basis of this rather fundamental grammatical point.

The modern Russian language, even after more than a millennium of separate development, is not remote from the other Slavonic languages either phonetically, grammatically or (with reservations) in vocabulary. These languages are much closer to each other than, for example, even English is to Dutch: it is probably as easy for one Slav to be understood in another's language as, say, for an Italian in Spain or a Dane in Norway. The awareness of this communality has always been important to Slavonic peoples, though it has not always led to undying affection between them. A certain inter-Slav solidarity has probably been fostered through the ages by a lurking sense of being, collectively, "outsiders" on the European scene, seldom if ever among the cultural or political leaders, aware since the days of the Germanic Ottonian empire in the 10th century of the covetous eyes of powerful neighbors. Sense of linguistic community is incorporated in the very word "Slav," which is cognate with *slovo*, word: its derivatives are found in the Slovenes who live at the head of the Adriatic Sea and, at the opposite corner of the Slav world, the *sloveny* who were the northernmost of the original Russian tribes, in the hinterland of Novgorod. Conversely, *nemets,* non-understandable, was and is the general Slav designation for "German."

The coming of literacy to the Slavs, and with it the development of a distinctive alphabet, was an event of prime historical importance to the Slavs as a whole rather than merely to the one nation in which it took place. This nation was Greater Moravia, in the 9th century the most powerful and best-organized Slav state that had ever existed, occupying at its maximum all modern Slovakia and the Czech Republic, most of what is now Hungary, large parts of Germany, Austria and Poland. It was soon to succumb to the Magyar invasion of the early 10th century and to disintegrate. In the middle of the century before, however, the Moravian princes made a momentous choice: to join the Christian world and to seek teachers and books from the Byzantine emperor. The Russian Primary Chronicler (working doubtless from a Moravian source) puts these words into their mouths: "Our nation is baptized and yet we have no teacher. We understand neither Greek nor Latin . . . we do not understand written characters nor their meaning: therefore send us teachers who can make known the words of the Scriptures and their sense." The Emperor Michael III sent to Thessaloniki, the second city of the Greek world, a point at which the Greek and Slav worlds meet. Two scholarly brothers, Constantine (later, as a monk, called Cyril) and Methodius, were dispatched with assistants as missionaries, since they were bilingual in Slavonic and Greek. An ambitious and speedy program of biblical and liturgical translation was put under way, traditionally starting at the first phrase of St John's Gospel, "In the beginning was the Word . . ." Use of the vernacular for the religious purposes of a newly converted nation was extraordinary, and remained high in the consciousness of all Orthodox Slavs through the Middle Ages.

Constantine-Cyril devised an alphabet for the new literature of his Slav converts. The curious thing is that we do not know for certain what alphabet that was. The Cyrillic alphabet, which in several variants is used in the Orthodox Slav countries to this day, is named after him. It is based closely on the Greek alphabet, with a dozen or so (the number has varied through time and according to location) additional letters invented to represent Slavonic sounds not found in Greek. Some of the earliest Slav manuscripts to come down to us are in Cyrillic (particularly those from Russia); others however use the very strange script known as Glagolitic, and it is this that many scholars believe St Cyril to have invented. A few of its letters seem to have cursive Greek or Hebrew models, some may have been adapted from medieval diacritics, but most are novel and elaborate creations. It is cumbersome to write and could have been first devised as a deliberately obscure "secret" script. Glagolitic soon became obsolete in most of the Slav world, but lingered on in Croatia, as a legacy, it seems, of the Moravian mission, till modern times.

Cyrillic on Russian soil, was written in the early Middle Ages in the beautifully clear-cut *ustav* (majuscule). There later developed a succession of cursive forms that get ever harder for the non-specialist to read. A fine tradition of manuscript illumination existed in Russia from the 11th century to the 16th, with its culminating moment around 1400. From the mid-16th century printed books appear in Russia, though few in number until the end of the 17th century. Two moments of change affected the Russian Cyrillic alphabet, coinciding with general political upheavals: in the early 18th century under Peter the Great the forms of letters were simplified and regularized, while some appropriate only to Greek were removed; further redundant letters were excised in 1918, leaving us with the alphabet in general use today.

Though the alphabet was the most obvious lasting result of the Cyrillo-Methodian mission for the Russians and other Orthodox Slavs, there was, and remains to the present, a profounder legacy affecting the very character of their language. The missionaries used for their translations—and soon, original compositions—the language they themselves spoke: the South Slavonic dialect of the hinterland of Thessaloniki—hence a type of Old Bulgarian, to which historians have given the name "Old Church Slavonic." The name is perhaps rather misleading: although in the circumstances of medieval society far the larger part of written literature was naturally religious in nature, this was by no means exclusively a church language, but a language for "high culture" in general; nor is it exclusively "old," since it has remained, even if not spoken save for ritual purposes, a living force through the centuries. It was the first multinational literary language of Europe apart from the ancient Greek and Latin, the first in European history to be deliberately so created, a point that many Slavonic writers were to cite with pride. As an international language it continued to be understood by Slavs while their nations and their vernacular tongues developed away from each other, and its use even

The Slavonic language family. The Slavonic languages form one of the major families within the Indo-European group. In prehistoric times a proto-Slavonic tongue, spoken somewhere in east-central Europe, divided into Eastern, Western and Southern branches, as the Slavs began their gradual expansion in these directions. Out of these branches grew the existing Slavonic languages, differentiating themselves gradually from about 1100 to 500 years ago: the Western in Poland, the Czech Republic, Slovakia and parts of eastern Germany; the Southern in the Balkans; the Eastern in Russia, Belarus and Ukraine.

West Slavonic
- Czech
- Polish
- Slovakian
- Sorbian

East Slavonic
- Belarus
- Great Russian
- Ukrainian

South Slavonic
- Bulgarian
- Macedonian
- Serbo-Croatian
- Slovenian

approximate limit of Slavonic-speaking areas, 800

approximate limit of Slavonic-speaking areas, 1500

spread to certain non-Slavs, most notably the Romanians. It is to this day the language of the Orthodox Church liturgy.

There are two main factors that make this of more than merely historical or ecclesiastical interest. First, the missionaries, in order to translate books of the New Testament and other spiritual works, had to devise an entire abstract vocabulary (mostly from Slavonic roots, following to some extent Greek patterns of word formation). Thus they opened the door for the enrichment of simple vernacular tongues with a whole new vocabulary of intellectual concepts. Secondly, because the Slavonic languages have remained fairly close—for a long time intercomprehensible, despite their separate development—Old Church Slavonic has never been sensed as "alien," hardly indeed as a separate language: rather as an archaic, time-honored, solemn, abstract or rhetorical version of one's spoken tongue. A good deal of Old Church Slavonic vocabulary remains identical with that of modern Russian; where there are differences, including in grammar, they are often of a simple and consistent nature. There is thus a radical difference between the role of "Slavonicisms" in Russian and that of "Latinisms" in English and other Northern European languages, which in other respects is a comparable case.

Modern Russian thus has innumerable "doublets"—words recognizably similar, but of East Slavonic (Russian) and Old Church Slavonic origin respectively, never merely synonymous but carrying greater or lesser differences in meaning, in usage or in stylistic "load." An interesting, still "productive" Old Church Slavonic element in Russian, known to everyone, is the termination *-grad* indicating a city (as in Volgograd); the Russian equivalent is *gorod*, town. A similar phonetic alternation affects the personal name "Vladimir," whose Old Russian (and modern Ukrainian) equivalent is "Volodimir," from which is derived the modern "familiar" form "Volodya." A characteristic Old Church Slavonic abstract formation is the well-known word *glasnost*, relating to Russian *golos*, voice. Throughout its history the Russian literary language has, with varying degrees of self- awareness and recognizability, mixed native Russian and Old Church Slavonic elements; in the mid-18th century a consistent attempt was made to codify these variables in terms of "high," "middle" and "low" styles—an attempt that soon broke down as too unsubtle a rigidification of an infinitely mobile system.

Russian has absorbed other outside linguistic influences besides those from Slavonic over its long history. To the earliest neighboring peoples of the Slavs in general and the Russians in particular—Germans in the west, Iranians in the southeast, Finnic peoples in the northern forests, even Norse Vikings who provided early Russia's rulers—only a tiny handful of words can be attributed. Much more significant are the Turkic elements that arrived partly through the Tatar invasion and period of rule (c. 1240–1480), partly with the opening-up of routes to the East in the 16th century. But even these were limited to certain areas of vocabulary, mostly to do with officialdom and trade. New techniques and cultural terms from Western European languages, often through the

intermediary of Polish, entered Russian in some quantity during the 17th century. With Peter the Great's deliberate reorientation of Russia towards the West after 1698 this trickle became a flood. Naval and military terms, titles, even place names were borrowed (often in rough-and-ready transliteration) from Dutch, German and English. As the century progressed French- and Latin-based words and expressions became very numerous, and more significantly much word formation and even syntax was produced with Slavonic word-roots on Western patterns (so-called "calques"). Both calques of this kind and transliterated words (generally, but not always, adapted to the exigencies of Russian grammar) have entered the language in vast numbers during the last century. The Western visitor to modern Russia is often surprised and pleased to find that a mere ability to decipher the Cyrillic alphabet (a skill quickly acquired) is enough to reveal that large numbers of words in street signs, newspaper headlines and elsewhere are familiar friends from the European "international" vocabulary.

Russia, like any long-established rural society, has plenty of dialect differentiation at village level: on a larger scale, however, the language is remarkably uniform over its vast range (far more so, for example, than English, German or Italian). Probably the early mobility of the Russian population (even, until the late 18th century, of the aristocracy) has been a contributory factor in this. Basically there are two main Russian dialects— "northern" and "southern"—that come together, or overlap, in a narrow mixed "central" belt. The most general and obvious differences concern the pronunciation of vowels and certain consonants: the central dialect, which is the basis of modern standard Russian, takes some features from each.

It would be neat if the dialect distinction corresponded with the forest/steppe divide: to some extent it does, with the central belt (that includes Moscow and St Petersburg) representing the mixed forest, but in fact the dialect division slopes southwards as it goes further east, thus giving a much larger (though less thickly populated) area, including most of the Volga basin and Siberia, to the northern division. The southern dialects not surprisingly share some features with the Ukrainian language, to which they are transitional. Until the late Middle Ages, indeed, what were to become Muscovite (or "Great") Russian, Ukrainian and Belarusian were the fundamental dialect divisions of Russian (or East Slavonic): differentiation into what are now regarded as separate languages came with the political division of Russia after the Tatar conquest and consequent absorption of Ukraine and Belarus into the Polish-Lithuanian state. A form of early Belarusian was in fact the chancery language of the medieval Lithuanian principality. But their status as independent languages was recognized in the case of modern Ukrainian and Belarusian only with their development of self-sufficient literatures and the general rise of nationalistic awareness in the early 19th century, and was given official recognition only after the Revolution. None of these three great branches of the East Slavonic peoples can lay exclusive claim to the Old Russian heritage, as their propagandists might energetically try to do so.

Scythian Gold

Scythian gold was the stuff of Greek legend. The story of Jason and the Argonauts told how Greek adventurers sailed the ship *Argo* from Iolcos in Thessaly to the land of Colchis at the far eastern end of the Black Sea in order to obtain a fabulous golden fleece. Modern researches, including a voyage from northern Greece to the republic of Georgia in a replica of a Bronze Age ship, have indicated a core of possible historical truth in the legend. Interestingly, contemporary Georgian prospectors, searching for alluvial gold in the rivers of the north Caucasus, know an extraction technique using a sheepskin to trap the minute granules as they are washed downstream.

The Scythians appear above the horizon of history with the information recorded by the Greek historian and traveler Herodotus, writing in the mid-5th century BC. Herodotus gives an especially graphic account of the funeral ceremonies conducted by the Scythians for their dead kings, and archaeological investigation of the huge mounds raised over their graves has corroborated much of his narrative. Early Scythian barrow (*kurgan*) burials occur particularly in the Kuban steppe north of the Caucasus; later ones are concentrated in the Crimea and along the lower reaches of the Dnieper in the Ukraine. This last area became the heartland of a Scythian kingdom that reached its peak in the 4th century BC defying even Alexander the Great, before being gradually overrun by Sarmatian nomads.

Scythian art evolved in a distinctive style suited to the circumstances of these warlike nomads. Favored motifs were animals—both real and fantastic—that symbolized strength, speed and ferocity. Perhaps the most popular were griffins, fabulous creatures of Asiatic folklore, whose mythical role was as guardians of gold mines and treasure. The animals' outlines were often grotesquely contorted and parts of one animal merged with another to create weird imaginary beasts, as in the case of the griffin which combined the head and wings of an eagle with the body of a lion. This so-called Scythian Animal Style showed both Near Eastern and, later, Greek influences.

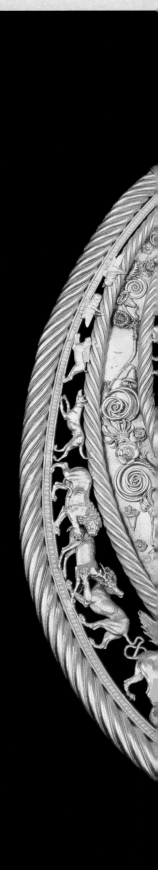

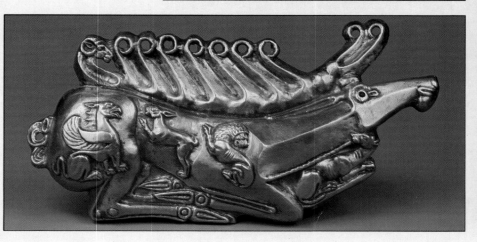

Right A shield plaque in the shape of a recumbent stag from a 4th-century burial at Kul Oba, near Kerch, in the Crimea. The outline of the stylized stag is strongly reminiscent of a much earlier Scythian shield plaque (known as the Kostromskaya stag from its find spot in a late 7th-century grave in the Kuban area) and demonstrates the staying power of favored motifs in Scythian Animal Style. The animals on the stag's body are however much more realistic, in a style showing Greek influence.

Above A gold plaque of the 4th century BC depicts two Scythians drinking from the same rhyton (cup) to confirm an oath of blood brotherhood. The participants in the ritual slashed their fingers to draw blood, which they collected in a vessel filled with wine; they then drank the mingled liquid. This was a popular subject in Scythian art, and several stories attest the seriousness of the obligations imposed by ritual brotherhood.

Opposite top Two Scythian nobles are depicted on the side of a silver parcel-gilt ritual bowl. Despite the apparently relaxed poses, both have weapons ready to hand: the man on the left casually rests his hand over his *gorytus* (case for bow and arrows); the man on the right seems to be reaching for his sword.

Opposite center This comb (early 4th century BC) was found in the Solokha barrow in the Ukraine. On its crest a mounted Scythian warrior, backed up by a foot soldier, is poised to thrust his spear at an unhorsed opponent.

Left A masterpiece of Greco-Scythian goldsmithing of the 4th century BC, this pectoral was discovered in a mound south of Dnepropetrovsk in 1971. Its outer register depicts animals in their wild and ferocious aspect: pairs of griffins attack horses, lions maul a stag and a boar while hounds pursue hares. The inner register shows animals beautifully observed in their domesticated roles, with a mare suckling her foal and a cow her calf. One of the four human figures milks a ewe; another holds an amphora, possibly containing milk from the ewe on her right. In the center two men make a sheepskin shirt; despite their domestic preoccupation, their *goryti* are close by—reminders of the Scythians' famed and feared prowess as equestrian archers.

The Peoples of the Steppe

The earliest human inhabitants of the steppe were already advancing over the land before the last Ice Age. Paleolithic and Neolithic remains are widely distributed across Russia and its neighboring republics. As the Neolithic gave way to the Bronze Age, agriculture became widespread in the chernozem zone. The best-known culture of this period (4th–3rd millennia BC) is named after Tripolye, south of Kyyiv (Kiev); its sites have yielded the earliest evidence for the domestication of the horse—probably at first for meat.

The use of horses for riding, evident on the steppe from the late 2nd millennium BC, brought about the rise of societies based on mounted nomadism. The nomads' mobility gave them a priceless advantage over the settled farmers whom they could raid without fear of retaliation. The migratory pressure of the nomads was remarked (c.675 BC) by the earliest known Greek to penetrate the steppe country, Aristeas of Proconnesus, who observed that the peoples there "continually encroached on their neighbors."

Cultural continuities can be traced right across the steppe through the different nomadic peoples, whatever their ethnic origins. At the opposite end of the Scythian world, the graves (5th–3rd centuries BC) at Pazyryk, preserved by permafrost in the Altay mountains in western Siberia, contained items that corroborate Herodotus' description of the Scythians.

Left A leather appliqué decoration from a saddle, found in a 5th-century BC barrow grave at Pazyryk. The contorted silhouettes of the deer and its attacker are typical of the vigorous, stylized form of nomadic art that reached its apogee in Scythian Animal Style.

Left A finial in the shape of a griffin's head; it holds the head of a deer in its beak. Finials with animal motifs like these were common in the ancient steppe cultures and may represent clan totems.

Right A leather flask from Pazyryk. It is made of four pieces of leather stitched together with sinews and is decorated with appliqué work, also of leather. The stylized plant motif indicates the flask's use as a container for herbs or seeds.

Above A swan worked in felt. A group of these birds, whose design strongly suggests Chinese influence, formed part of the appliqué decoration of the funeral cart cover. The cart was dismantled and buried with the occupants of the grave. Although robbed in antiquity of any precious metals, the ice-filled Pazyryk tombs have preserved remarkable textile remnants showing influences from both China and Iran, including by far the oldest known pile carpet.

Above A man's headdress made of felt over which a fine layer of leather has been applied. A leather piping strengthens the edges and an ornament of thick leather has been sewn to the crown. Both practical and decorative, headdresses of similar shape, with long side flaps, are still in use against the biting cold of the steppe; the felt would also have offered some protection against head wounds in battle.

PART TWO
HISTORY

RUS

The early tribes

Documentation of the inhabitants of the land that is now Russia begins with Herodotus in the 5th century BC. He and subsequent ancient historians were interested in what lay north of the Black Sea littoral on which there were already long-established Greek colonies. The people beyond were the Scythians, nomads who had conquered the steppe country apparently around 700 BC and had in part settled along the great river valleys. They grew grain which they exported, along with slaves, wax and other commodities, to the Greek colonies. They, or at least their ruling class, were of Iranian stock, and therefore in Greek eyes barbarians, but over the course of several centuries they established a *modus vivendi* with the Greeks, in which Scythians became partially Hellenized. The beautifully made grave goods (mostly objects of personal adornment) that have been found in the numerous burial mounds of the steppe country testify to this mixed culture. The cultural mingling and the trading connections persisted when the Scythians were displaced by another Iranian nomadic people, the Sarmatians, around 200 BC. Their federation of tribes eventually seems to have included a strong Slavonic element, though the detailed history is uncertain.

From the 3rd century AD, a disturbed period in the history of the south Russian lands ensues. In Obolensky's words: "the picture we obtain from the written sources is that of a bewildering procession of tribes and nations which every few centuries succeed each other on the steppes, only to sweep each other off the map." (Some were to settle permanently elsewhere than in the Russian steppe: there are still Avars in the Caucasus, Magyars in Hungary, Turks in many parts of the Eurasian landmass.) It is best, perhaps, to distinguish the successive broad groupings of peoples involved. (1) In the early 3rd century an eastern branch of the Germanic speakers, the Goths, migrated southeastwards to the Black Sea coast, and some settled there. (Others moved westward to menace the Eastern Roman Empire, overwhelming the Emperor Valens in 378 near Adrianople.) There was still a residual Gothic population in the Crimea till recent times. (2) The Huns, who moved across the steppe and deep into Europe in the 4th to 5th centuries, achieving under Attila a particular reputation for ferocity, are hard to categorize ethnically: they seem to have included Turkic, Mongol and Finno-Ugrian elements. (3) Thereafter, with the solitary exception of the Finno-Ugrian Magyars in the 9th century, whose language is distantly related to Finnish and Estonian, all invaders from the east were Turkic peoples. Their differing fates depended on where, how and for how long they succeeded in turning from a mobile to a settled existence.

Early successors to the Huns were the Bulgars, whose territories subsequently split into two parts,

quite remote from each other. The better-known group followed the Black Sea coast to modern Bulgaria, where in the 7th century they formed a warrior elite amid the recently settled South Slavs. The resulting ethnic mix produced a powerful Balkan state, Slav-speaking within a few generations, sometimes an ally but more often an irritating rival to the Byzantines right up to the Ottoman conquest at the end of the 14th century. This Bulgaria was Christianized in the 9th century by followers of Cyril and Methodius, an event that had an impact on the early Russian state, which was in close contact with its South Slav neighbors. The other "Bulgaria" was established in what is now east-central Russia, at the very important junction of waterways where the Kama flows into the middle Volga. Its capital was a city not far from modern Kazan known as Great Bulgar. It too survived with vicissitudes until the late Middle Ages. Unlike their cousins in the Balkans, these Bulgars converted to Islam at an early date and remained for centuries the only Islamic people in direct contact with the Russians.

Meanwhile another Turkic people with Mongol admixture, the Avars, occupied the Pontic steppe and Danube valley from the mid-6th century, before collapsing suddenly two-and-a-half centuries later. They came within the Russian Primary Chronicler's horizon of historical consciousness, and he quotes as a proverb the phrase "disappeared like the *Obry* (Avars)." Their eclipse was due to the rise of yet another Turkic people: the Khazars. The Khazar state, to which many of their neighbors, including the Volga Bulgars and some East Slavonic tribes, were tributary, was centered on cities at the lower reaches of the Volga (Itil), of the Don (Sarkel) and of the River Terek at its approach to the Caspian Sea (Samandar). They showed a strong instinct for geopolitics. Despite an expanse of desert at the center of their territory, agriculturally productive river valleys threaded their way through it, and these were also among the most vital trade routes in the Near East. The ancient portage between the Volga and the Don, which approach to within 60 kilometers of each other near modern Volgograd, was theirs; so was the whole "isthmus" between the Caspian and Black Sea, and the Kuban steppe to the north of the Caucasus.

This region was of great strategic significance, as the Byzantines (who tried to keep on good terms with the Khazars) well understood. It was the Khazars who in the 8th century suffered and blunted the eastern thrust of the two-pronged Arab Islamic assault on Europe (the simultaneous westward invasion through Spain met with more success). The Khazars brought peace, stability, an "international" outlook and religious tolerance. The last point brings us to the unique feature of the Khazar state. When, probably in the 9th century, its ruling class decided to adopt one of the world's developed

Above This gold coin, carrying an image of a bearded satyr, comes from the ancient city of Panticapaeum, on the site of modern Kerch, and dates from about 360 to 340 BC. Kerch commanded the "Cimmerian Bosphorus," a narrow waterway giving access to the Sea of Azov, the mouth of the River Don and the Scythian-dominated steppe. Greek colonies on the Black Sea—trading in corn, slaves, gold and other commodities— date back to preclassical times. Kerch is on the Crimea, which remained a Greek outpost till the late Byzantine period; opposite it the early Russian principality of Tmutorokan flourished in the 10th and 11th centuries.

Right: Eastern Europe and the Byzantine world in the 10th century.
A number of powers, mainly of Turkic origin, successively established themselves along the steppe belt that separated Kievan Rus from the Byzantine empire. The largest and most powerful was Khazaria, which controlled the important Don-Volga trade route and the strategic neck of land north of the Caucasus. The Byzantines, always diplomatically astute, took care to maintain good relations with the Khazars. For a long time the Khazars brought peace and stability to the region, but in the 960s Prince Svyatoslav of Kiev challenged the Khazars' right to tribute from some East Slav tribes. His successful campaigns through Khazaria and later westwards against the Danubian Bulgars brought huge swathes of land into his realm. His removal of the Russian capital southwards to Pereyaslavets unnerved the Byzantines who forced him to retire to Kiev; en route he was ambushed on the Dnieper and killed by steppe nomads.

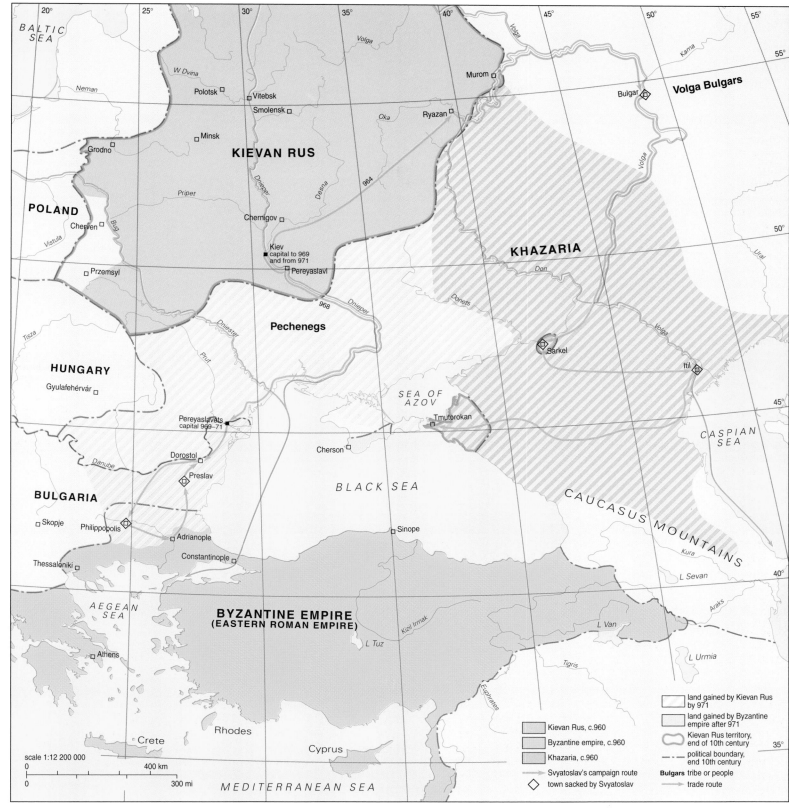

	land gained by Kievan Rus by 971
	land gained by Byzantine empire after 971
Kievan Rus, c.960	Kievan Rus territory, end of 10th century
Byzantine empire, c.960	political boundary, end of 10th century
Khazaria, c.960	**Bulgars** tribe or people
Svyatoslav's campaign route	trade route
town sacked by Svyatoslav	

religions, it was to neither of the obvious alternatives—Christianity or Islam—that it turned, but to Judaism: the only such conversion of a non-Jewish nation in history. Various historians, including Arthur Koestler, have speculated that the large Jewish population of Eastern Europe in later centuries was partly a legacy from Khazaria.

By the 9th century the circumstances were right for the coalescence and political development of the East Slav tribes into a great nation: Kievan Russia. This happened within a triangle of disparate cultural-political forces, to each of which the nascent East Slav nation reacted differently. The

southeastern corner of this triangle was represented by the Khazars. Their *pax Khazarica* stabilized the turbulent steppe frontier, but their imposition of tribute and controls on trade was evidently resented by the Slavs. The southwestern corner was represented by the Byzantine Empire, which from the early 9th to the mid-11th century was at the height of its early-medieval glory. Constantinople, its capital, was more than just the major entrepôt of east Mediterranean trade: it was the greatest city of the world, the metropolis of Christianity, where, if anywhere, it was thought that God's kingdom on earth might be realized.

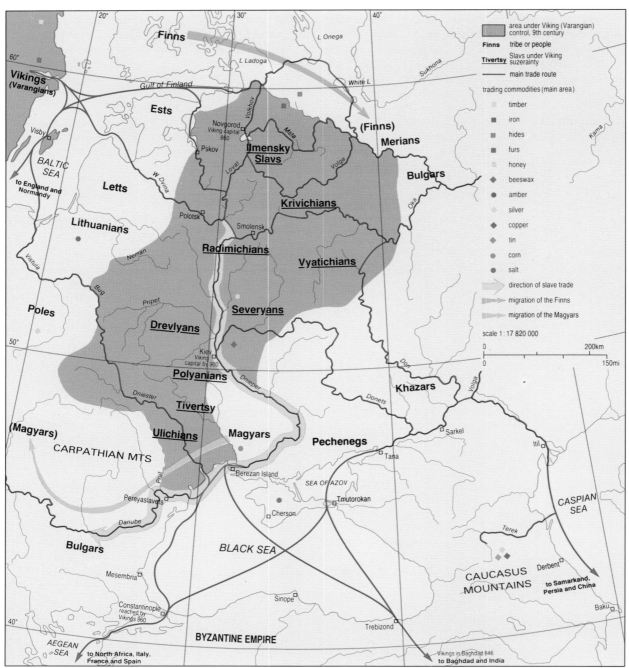

Russia and the Vikings.
The amazing expansionist urge that led the Scandinavian peoples (Vikings) in the 9th and 10th centuries to colonize many parts of northern and western Europe had profound effects too in eastern Europe. By the early 9th century adventurers from Sweden had crossed the Baltic in search of trade routes first to Samarkand and China (via the Volga), then to the Byzantine empire (via the Dnieper), exploiting too the resources of the northern lands through which they passed (amber, honey, beeswax, slaves, furs). The number of Viking settlers (known to the Russians and Greeks as "Varangians") seems not to have been large, and relations with the local Slav and Finnic peoples were usually cooperative.

The descendants of the semilegendary Ryurik established themselves as the ruling dynasty of a more-or-less unified Rus first at Novgorod (860s); by 900 the capital had shifted southwards to Kiev. Though the Ryurikids and their retainers (*druzhina*) were soon Slavicized, contacts with Scandinavia persisted until the 12th century, while intermarriage with the royal houses of central and western Europe was normal. The career of a mid-11th-century Viking, Harold Hardradi, could thus embrace service in the imperial bodyguard at Constantinople and marriage to the daughter of Yaroslavl the Wise as well as an attempt to seize the throne of England.

This was the great age of Byzantium's missionary endeavor, closely linked with diplomatic and military efforts to secure its northern frontier. Trade, religion and politics brought the early Russians into the orbit of Byzantine interest. The Russians alarmed the Byzantines with a series of freebooting raids on the empire and the City itself from the 9th to the 11th century, but more constructively they established the famous trade route down the River Dnieper and thence to Constantinople. It is memorably described by Emperor Constantine Porphyrogenitus of Byzantium in the mid-10th century, and from a different perspective in the Russian Primary Chronicle.

The coming of the Vikings

The third corner of the triangle was occupied by the Vikings to the north and northwest. The history of their penetration into Russia is unclear and controversial. Vikings (in Russian sources "Varangians"—compare Norse *Vaeringjar* and Anglo-Saxon *waerengs*, wanderers) had crossed the Baltic by the start of the 9th century, and perhaps much

earlier: what they were after was trade. A famous passage in the Russian Primary Chronicle describes their trade route to Constantinople: "There was a way from the Vikings to the Greeks . . ." This way led from the Gulf of Finland, up the short River Neva to Lake Ladoga, south along the Volkhov to Novgorod and Lake Ilmen, up the Lovat to the Valday Hills, across a portage to the headwaters of the Dnieper (flowing from the great source of Russian rivers, the Okovsky Forest), down the Dnieper to the site of Kiev. Constantine Porphyrogenitus continues from this point: assembling at Kiev, the flotilla took the Dnieper downstream in the high water after the spring thaw; where the river breaks through an outcrop of metamorphic rocks in the southern Ukraine a series of rapids had to be circumvented; reassembling at an island, the flotilla passed down the Black Sea coast to the "Great City" of Constantinople (to the Vikings "Miklagarth," to the Slavs "Tsargrad," City of the Emperor). How they got back, upstream, is passed over in silence. In Constantinople they sold their cargoes of furs, wax, honey, amber and slaves.

There is something rather strange about the geography of this great Viking trade route. If the Vikings simply wanted to get from Scandinavia to Byzantium, it is scarcely credible they should add many hundreds of kilometers to their journey by going via the Gulf of Finland. The Vikings, no fools when it came to orientating themselves, can only have established a route along the Neva in consequence of already having depots set up in that area: certainly at Aldeigjuborg (Russian Ladoga), probably already at Novgorod and Staraya Russa (at the other end of Lake Ilmen). It is clear, in fact, that the first sorties of the Vikings on the farther shores of the Baltic led them not south, but eastwards: to the upper Volga, through Bulgar and Khazar territory, to the Caspian. The natural magnet in that part of the world was the Islamic caliphate, whose center of gravity had shifted east, to the newly founded capital city of Baghdad, in the early 8th century. The most obvious route from the Gulf of Finland to the Volga passed via Lakes Ladoga and Onega, the White Lake (Beloozero) and the Sheksna; almost as good (though by more turbulent rivers) is the more southerly route via Novgorod, then either the River Msta and the portage at Vyshniy-Volochek to the Tvertsa, or through Lake Seliger. The northern route would scarcely, if at all, pass through territory then inhabited by Slavs; the southern route impinged upon the land of the *Sloveny*.

The Viking turn to the south is certainly bound up with the development of Novgorod (literally, "New Town") as a strongpoint and trading post. There is no record of bloodshed and terror, and it seems that a deal between Vikings and Slavs was struck at an early stage. The Primary Chronicle tells a curious story of how the Vikings were first ejected, then invited back by a coalition of Slav and Finno-Ugrian tribes to "bring order" to the land. This they did, for a time at least, but they were not (as was once widely believed) great bringers of culture too. On the contrary, early Russian law, religion, literature and language bear at most only slight and haphazard traces of Viking influence. There cannot have been much colonization. Place names of Scandinavian origin (ubiquitous in eastern England) are virtually nonexistent in Russia: by contrast north-central Russia is full of place names derived from Finno-Ugrian, including even *Moskva*, Moscow, itself. The well-known personal names Igor, Oleg and Olga, however, are Scandinavian and associated with the Viking dynasty; even Vladimir, thoroughly Slav in form, has a perhaps fortuitous resemblance to Valdemar.

The Vikings certainly found the Slav tribes in the process of civilization; they called the land Gardariki (realm of enclosures or of cities), presumably from the numerous towns or fortified citadels they encountered there. What the Vikings brought, or encouraged, were military, political and commercial skills. Hoards of Anglo-Saxon, Byzantine and Arab coins found all over Eastern Europe bear testimony to their commerce. Their extraordinary mobility broadened horizons. A perhaps surprising aspect of the Viking-Slav partnership was that Russia was then in closer touch with the whole of the rest of Europe than at any time till the end of the 17th century. Kievan princes and princesses married into all the royal houses of Europe.

The word "Rus" itself, appearing generally at this period, and referring both to a land and to its people, needs some explanation. Serious historical questions about the origins of Russia have tended to focus too narrowly on the etymological derivation of its name: since the modern controversy about it erupted in the mid-18th century, much nationalistic emotion, pro- or anti-Slav, has surrounded what has come to be known as the "Normanist" issue. Even for the Primary Chronicler in the 12th century the matter had political significance, affecting the legitimacy of the dynasty under whom (and for whom) he wrote and the status of his city of Kiev: "these particular Varangians were known as Rus, just as some are called Swedes, and others Norsemen, English and Gotlanders . . . on account of these Varangians, the Russian land received its name." The most striking independent testimony to this comes from Constantine Porphyrogenitus, who lists the "Russian" and the "Slavonic" names of the cataracts over or around which the Dnieper trade route had to pass: the "Russian" names turn out to be Scandinavian linguistic forms, the "Slavonic" early Russian (they are among the earliest written specimens of Russian words). Certainly, therefore, there were well-informed people in the 10th century and later who equated Russians and Varangians.

A very early and most curious story in a Western source (the Bertinian Annals) recounts how in 839 some "Russian" envoys from the Khazar *kagan* arrived at the court of Louis the Pious at Ingelheim, via Constantinople; on being interrogated they turned out to be Swedes. The Finnish word for Sweden, *Ruotsi*, is brought in as evidence; so too is the name of a stretch of Swedish coastline, Roslagen. Yet "Rus" as a term for Viking or Vikings is unknown in the Viking lands. The "anti-Normanist" case, apart from some Chronicle ambiguities, concentrates on evidence that the Greek "Rhos" and similar forms were known in the south before Viking penetration. Also, "Rus" tended to be applied in early sources to southern Russia, around Kiev, and not to the Novgorod area where the Vikings arrived. Near Kiev there is a river with the significant name of Ros.

There are some curious complications. Arab sources, generally geographically reliable, give certain strange items of information: "Russia is an island, around which is a lake, and the island in which they dwell is a three days' journey through forests and swamps . . ." (Ibn Rusta, early 10th century). The Byzantines apocalyptically equated "Rhos" with a sinister prince mentioned (through a translation error) in the prophecy of Ezekiel, which perhaps accounts for the otherwise odd change of vowel from "Rus," and certainly for their fright when Russian raiders appeared at their walls in 860 AD. What is beyond doubt is that the name came into general use to describe a new entity in the Europe of 1100 years ago, a state, its land and population, whose Slav basis and Viking admixture were inextricably fused, together with Estonian and Finnish elements (known to the Old Russians as Chud, Merya, Ves). This entity quickly advanced in cultural terms beyond the level of any of its previous component parts. When the first treaty between Russia and Byzantium came to be written in 911, it seems that it was written down in

two languages, Greek and Slavonic, though most of the Russian signatories' names can be identified as of Scandinavian origin. Those Norsemen permanently resident in Russia were becoming culturally Slavonicized.

Sources for Kievan Russian history

In general, the history of premodern societies yields, as we go back in time, proportionately less and less of the material remains and general quality of "everyday life," while information is still available about political events, official decrees and so on. With Kievan Russia things are not so straightforward. The copious state archives that in many Western countries stretch back to the early Middle Ages have not survived, not only because of Russia's turbulent history but because of the extreme susceptibility of its largely wooden cities to fire. Later copyists have fortunately reproduced and preserved a few official documents: the first written law code, church statutes, two very early treaties. Gaps remain at several crucial points: the early organization of the church, the succession system of the Kievan rulers and, most notoriously,

the manner in which Viking settlers established themselves in, or were invited into, Old Russia. But in certain limited areas a great deal can confidently be said about early Russian life.

First, there are material remains. Standing buildings from pre-Tatar Russia number only a tiny proportion of the surviving Romanesque buildings of Italy, France or England, yet they include a handful of remarkable churches whose architecture, pictorial decoration and even graffiti can yield up information about Old Russia, its wealth, ideology and external contacts. On the secular front, modern archaeology, developed systematically only in the Soviet period, has revealed immeasurably more about Old Russian cities, their architecture and way of life (in some cases with the baneful assistance of Hitler's bombs). Domestic artefacts, grave goods, coins (including Arabic, Byzantine and Western European) have turned up in considerable numbers. But one area of recent archaeological discovery in Russia has produced a cache of objects so abundant, unexpected and revealing of the life of early Russia as to put it in a class of its own.

The generally unfavorable geographical

conditions of the Russian forest zone—short summers, acid soils, poor drainage—mean that several anciently inhabited sites are situated on what amount to peat bogs with a permanent water table not far below the surface. The northern metropolis of Novgorod is the classic example of such a location. Wooden objects that find their way into the ground are excellently preserved in this environment, although much care is needed in their conservation once they are exposed to air again. Since in the forest zone wood was the normal material not only for house-building but also for a wide range of domestic utensils, for shoes, for the paving of roads, for fortifications, the excavations in such areas have given us a remarkably comprehensive view of the conditions of early Russian life. Novgorod has proved particularly favorable not only because of its soil conditions, but because of its decline after the Middle Ages (hence little disturbance of the archaeological record) and the wholesale reconstruction, accompanied by careful investigation, that has been necessary as a result of World War II. A well-validated dendrochronology assists dating; up to 25 layers of wooden paving have been found superimposed on the sites of some ancient streets. It was in this context that around 1950 numerous small and tightly rolled strips of ancient birch-bark began to emerge. When it was realized that they bore traces of scratched writing they were painstakingly unrolled and, where possible, deciphered. Thus Novgorod began to make its unique contribution not just to our evidence about medieval Russian life, but to world archaeology of the last half-century. So astonishing did the discovery and its implications seem in the atmosphere of the last years of Stalin that some Western historians were skeptical, suspecting a hoax in the spirit of Russian nationalistic chauvinism. Any such doubts however have long been stilled.

The birch-bark documents, in Cyrillic characters inscribed with a stylus (*pisalo*), using the vernacular Old Russian language, are brief personal letters or notes, most often concerning money transactions, debts, legal claims, landholdings and family matters. By now several hundred have been published, and a Soviet expert (D. Yanin) estimates that over 20 000 may still lie in the Novgorod subsoil. Very recently the first examples in Latin, Runic (Scandinavian) and Greek scripts have been discovered, while a number of specimens have now been identified from half-a-dozen other ancient Russian cities as far south as Smolensk. This was a society in which, contrary to what was until recently supposed, literacy was widespread and taken for granted (the "throwaway" character of the documents is significant), at least in the milieu of urban traders. The purposes of these documents were evidently various. They do not seem to have been primarily connected with local bureaucratic administration. Though the majority are late medieval, some go back to the early days of Christian Rus, and if inscriptions on other objects (wooden tally-sticks, ceramic fragments) are taken into consideration, Russian literacy can be shown to predate the conversion to Christianity.

Literary sources

Despite the lack of official documents, the literary sources for knowledge of Kievan Russia are in fact rather rich, and of course are not limited to what archaeologists have managed to uncover. From the late 10th century the newly converted and newly educated nation took readily to the forms of medieval literature as they had developed in the Christian East Roman empire of Byzantium. Not surprisingly, the religious element predominates. Ideological intentions can be discerned in a remarkable piece of religious rhetoric, the *Sermon on the Law and the Grace* by the first Russian metropolitan of Kiev, Hilarion (mid-11th century); Grand Prince Vladimir Monomakh's *Instruction* to his children (c. 1100) reads as if it were a piece of autobiography; and the beginnings of certain idiosyncratic paths that the Russian Orthodox Church was to take can be traced in the various *Lives* of two of Russia's first martyrs, the Princes Boris and Gleb (d. 1015). In some works towards the end of the Kievan period the secular impulse overwhelms the religious: for example, the learnedly witty *Supplication of Daniel the Captive* and above all the most remarkable relic of Kievan literature, the anonymous *Tale of the Armament of Igor* (or *Igor Tale*, c. 1187). This work, in highly rhythmic prose crammed with effectively deployed rhetorical devices, is also a powerful vehicle for contemporary political messages. It has the peculiar interest that it seems to be a written, indeed highly literary, adaptation of the age-old unwritten forms of the oral heroic epic. Such epic poems, known as *byliny*, were recited and reworked through the centuries until they were transcribed in the last couple of hundred years; in many cases they refer back to the Kievan period and evidently preserve much archaic material.

All such works, as primary documents of their time, tell even if indirectly or unintentionally of their society and its concerns. It should however

Left: Eastern Europe and the Mediterranean in the mid-11th century.
Until the turn of the millennium the Christian patriarchates of Constantinople and Rome—the future Orthodox and Roman Catholic churches–competed to win converts among the pagan peoples of the Slavonic world. By the mid-11th century the spread of Christianity across this region was virtually complete and in the future would lead to strong antipathies: the Orthodox-Catholic dividing line, even if subsequently somewhat blurred, remains an important cultural boundary on the map of Europe to this day. Of the non-Christian peoples, the Volga Bulgars remained for centuries the only Muslims in direct contact with Russia; the Lithuanian ruling class remained pagan until dynastic union with Poland (1385).

Right This is the first birch-bark document to be identified and deciphered from Novgorod excavations in 1951, by A. Artsikhovsky. It is still one of the longest known, with 13 lines of incised script; it lists village feudal dues payable to one Foma, and dates from the 14th century. These "throwaway" documents, preserved in the anaerobic environment of peat bog, were so unique and unexpected a discovery that it took time for their authenticity to be accepted outside Russia. Now many hundreds have been published (some from other ancient sites), and thousands more still lie in the Novgorod subsoil. They testify to widespread literacy among urban townsfolk.

ЗУНАКТРЕ · АШЕХОЩЕШН Ѡ ЕСНОУ ІОСТОАТІ · СОПРАВЕДЛН
ЧМН̑ · ПОКРТИСА · ВОЛОДНМН̑РО · КЕПОЛОЖНМЛЅ СРДЦЕВО
ЕМ̑ · РЕКАПО РАДОУЕ ЩЕМАЛО · ГОТАИСПЫТА ТНѠ ВСБ
ВЕРА · ВОЛОДНМН̑РО ЖЕСЕМОУ Ѧ АДЫНЛНО ВЛАСТН НW ПОСТН
СЫСЕ ПТНА ПЕ ЛНС ЛА —

Left In the elaborate process of Vladimir I's conversion to Christianity in the 980s, as recounted in the *Tale of Bygone Years*, a central episode was Vladimir's audience with a "Greek [i.e. Byzantine] philosopher"—here depicted in the early 15th-century Radziwill Chronicle. The philosopher summarized the tenets of the faith at considerable length, then displayed an icon of the Last Judgment. Apparently still unconvinced, Vladimir then sent emissaries to report back on various religions; at Constantinople they were struck by the beauty of Greek Orthodox ritual. Vladimir then demanded the emperor's sister in marriage; it seems that reason, aesthetics, politics and prestige all played a part in his decision.

be noted that all those mentioned have come down not in contemporary manuscripts, but in often defective later copies (in the case of the *Igor Tale* the sole late-medieval manuscript was destroyed in the 1812 fire of Moscow). One work above all, while being a far from negligible literary achievement, is of such a sustained historical value that it eclipses any other fundamental source. This is the so-called Russian Primary Chronicle—to use the chronicler's own words, the *Tale of Bygone Years* (*Povest vremennykh let*). Old Russia has left an abundance—greater than from any other medieval nation—of historical chronicles, produced in all important and many obscure places up to the early 18th century. Chronicles were not kept and updated as a diary or similar record might be, though they would doubtless partially derive from notes of such a nature. Rather they were compiled afresh on the basis of as many earlier chronicles as could be collated and of any additional material available, as the result of a special commission, perhaps from a new ruler, perhaps to celebrate a great occasion. Monasteries were the main but not the sole center of such activity. The aim of any chronicle was, roughly speaking, to link the events of one's city, monastery or principality with universal history. To this end almost all later chronicles began with much the same integrated narrative, recounting the course of world and Russian history from biblical times up to the early 12th century: the *Tale of Bygone Years*.

Taken as an independent entity, this Primary Chronicle is a work whose significance to our knowledge of Russia and to the Russian national consciousness can scarcely be matched by any comparable work, not even by the Anglo-Saxon Chronicle, which is probably its closest rival in these respects. Any educated Russian will recognize many quotations from it. Without it, know-

ledge of the origins and early development of Russia would be impossibly fragmentary: the odd nuggets of information or hearsay in, for example, Arab geographies, Byzantine histories or Icelandic sagas have a value in adding to, confirming and modifying the Primary Chronicle account, but could not alone provide any sort of a coherent tale. For the discussion of any event in medieval Russian history the account in the Primary or other, later chronicles is almost bound to be the point of departure.

The Primary Chronicle, save for its first few pages, is set out in the form of separate entries for individual years, measured from the supposed creation of the world in 5508 BC. But it is not the mere annalistic record this format might suggest. It is a huge compendium of diverse materials: Byzantine, Russian and probably Scandinavian; religious and secular; learned and folkloric. At several points there are self-contained narratives several pages long, such as the stories of the death of Oleg and of the blinding of Vasilko; at others, entire documents, legal or literary, are inserted (the two famous treaties of 911 and 944, the "Speech of the Greek Philosopher" to Prince Vladimir I, the "Testament" of Vladimir Monomakh). There are diverting anecdotes, sententious digressions, edifying ruminations, notes on signs and portents, summaries of the lives of individual princes, saints and monks inserted, sometimes appropriately, sometimes inappropriately, under a given year. Yet this encyclopedic work is shaped by an underlying purpose: the uncovering of Russia's identity and historical destiny. The chronicler himself boldly states his intentions in his first sentence: "These are the narratives of bygone years regarding the origins of the land [i.e., nation] of Rus, the first princes of Kiev and from what source the land of Rus emerged."

Right: Kievan Russia.
The East Slavs who settled along the major river valleys of what are now European Russia, Belorussia and the Ukraine coalesced into a dozen or so large tribal units with many enclosed settlements. To the Vikings, this land was Gardariki, "land of towns (or enclosures)." Under the leadership of Oleg, the Viking Ryurikid family captured Kiev in the 880s, opening up the north-south trade route from the Baltic via the Dnieper to the Black Sea. This was the birth of Kievan Russia; the largest country of early-medieval Europe, it was by no means economically or culturally backward.

The prince of Kiev (later termed "grand prince") was considered senior member of the royal house, whose junior princes ruled (with frequent changes of location) in other cities: Chernigov was considered second in importance, Pereyaslavl third. (The independent existence of some of the principalities, for example, Turov-Pinsk, has been doubted by some historians.) There was an unexpected Kievan outpost at Tmutorokan on the Black Sea. Though strong Kievan princes (notably Vladimir I, Yaroslav the Wise, Vladimir II Monomakh) could maintain the integrity of the whole realm, persistent local traditions of independence asserted themselves during less forceful reigns. The lower Dnieper region and Kiev itself were vulnerable to attack from tribes such as the Pechenegs to the east, and in the mid-12th century Kiev yielded primacy to Vladimir in the northeastern forests.

The surviving version of the Primary Chronicle was written in the 1110s, but the chronicler based himself probably on a lost original of the 1050s. Byzantine Greek historians, notably George Hamartolos whom he cites by name, helped him to establish a secure chronological framework. From the reign of the Byzantine Emperor Michael III (842–67) the chronicler has precise, if not always accurate dates for the events he records, and arranges his material accordingly. This reign marks a crucial stage in the history of the Slavic peoples: it witnessed the great Christianizing mission of Cyril and Methodius to Moravia (see p.28) and the irruption of the Russians into European history with the raid (860) of Askold and Dir on Constan-

tinople. For what happened before then, in Russia at least, the chronicler is dependent on undated and mythologized oral sources, but he is not daunted: in a single highly interesting "essay" he takes us from the biblical account of the division of the world among the three sons of Noah, to the territories of the Slavs and their tribal divisions, to an account of the land of Russia itself, its geographical and ethnic situation, to the foundation of its main cities and to the establishment of a ruling dynasty of Viking origin in a unified state.

Kievan Rus in history
At its zenith, around the turn of the millennium, Kievan Russia (Rus, as it was known to its inhabi-

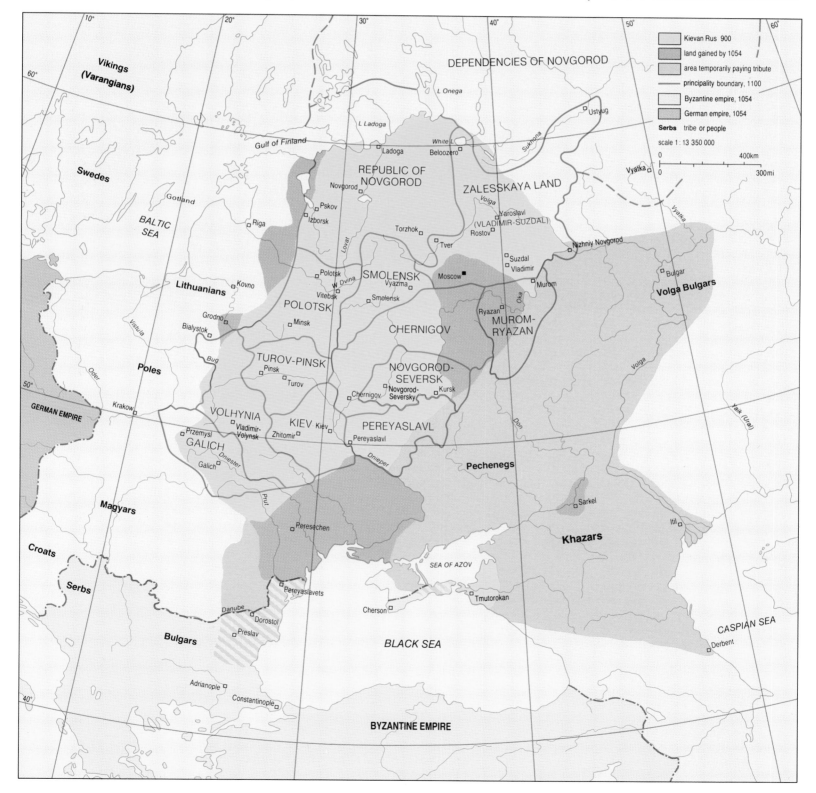

tants) was the largest state of early-medieval Europe, and by no means isolated from the rest of Europe culturally or politically. It had a recorded history of nearly 400 years, ending with the Tatar conquest of 1237–40. This history can be taken to begin with the attack on Constantinople by the Kievan rulers Askold and Dir (18 June 860), or perhaps a little later, with the forcible unification of Kiev with Novgorod by Oleg around 882. Culturally it is easily subdivided into a "pagan" and a "Christian" period by the official conversion to Christianity of 988/9. From the political point of view a dividing line can be drawn at 1132–35, when a more or less unitary state seemed rather suddenly to fall apart into more than a dozen component parts, with the role of Kiev itself as capital shortly to be usurped by Vladimir.

A more shadowy division of Kievan history can be made around the middle of the 11th century. Culturally Russia "came of age" in the long and prosperous reign of Yaroslav (1019–54); a learned Russian, Hilarion, was astonishingly chosen as metropolitan (head of the Russian Orthodox Church) in 1051; a national consciousness was beginning to be forged with the probable first compilation of a comprehensive Russian chronicle; the "Great Church" (St Sophia) of Kiev was completed. It happens that from that time onwards many architectural and literary relics of Kievan Russia survive, from before it very few. But at the same period future political difficulties can be sensed with the uneasy division of Yaroslav's heritage among his sons after his death in 1054, and with the appearance of a new enemy in the steppe country, the Polovtsians or Cumans.

To understand the history of Kievan Russia is to understand the polarities and tensions that underlay it and gave it both its dynamism and its weaknesses. Some are the geographical factors that have haunted all Russian history: the contrast between forest and steppe, between the exploratory and sedentary ways of life. Some are geopolitical: particularly the tension between the forcibly linked partners, Novgorod and Kiev, who respectively controlled the northern and southern parts of the trade route that was the axis of the first Russian state, the "way from the Vikings to the Greeks." Some are national: between the native Slavs and Scandinavian incomers, and between the different tribes with their varied customs. Some are social, as during the Kievan period clan relationships gave way to a strongly differentiated class structure and eventually to an approximation to feudalism. Perhaps the greatest tension—as is only to be expected in a huge territory with difficult communications—is between centralizing, unifying forces on the one hand and centrifugal provincialism on the other, a tension that is still far from resolved in the 20th century.

Kievan Russia projected an image to later ages of comparative peace, stability and prosperity, yet, like most states at most times, it existed and flourished in an atmosphere of incipient or actual warfare. Most of its non-Russian neighbors posed a military threat at one time or another, but the most strength-sapping and unrelieved menace came at the southern steppe frontier, to which Kiev itself was dangerously exposed. Year after year the Pechenegs and subsequently the Polovtsians ambushed and eventually terminated the trade convoy southwards to Constantinople and disrupted settled agricultural life. Kievan history begins with Rus as tributary to one great steppe power (the Khazars) and ends with conquest by another (the Tatars or Mongols). Even more fatally, early Russia was sapped by internecine civil war, sometimes on a trivial level, sometimes a fight to the death. Such civil strife, resulting normally from rivalries, greed or feuding within the ruling dynasty, became the more deeply ingrained in Old Russia as its branches proliferated after the reigns of Vladimir I and Yaroslav: it would take until the late 15th century for a permanent solution to the problem to be found in ruthless centralization under Moscow. Meanwhile the more farsighted among the Kievan Russians were not slow to make a connection between each type of chronic and debilitating warfare. Agreement among the princes to sink their differences would free them to apply their efforts cooperatively in beating back the raiders from the steppe. This is the ideological subtext of the late-Kievan *Igor Tale;* politically, it was most successfully, though briefly, realized under the influence of Vladimir II Monomakh at the beginning of the 12th century.

The Kievan princes and Christianity

The early rulers of Russia are shadowy figures; in particular the founder of the dynasty, Ryurik (unattested in any source before the *Tale of Bygone Years*) seems to belong almost wholly to myth. The next princes of Kiev—Oleg (d. 913), Igor (d. 945), Svyatoslav (d. 972), Yaropolk (d. 978 or 980) and St Vladimir (978 or 980–1015) for all that their recorded doings are wrapped in a good deal of folklore, gradually take on clearer outlines as historical personages. Though they "ruled" Russia, in the sense of being able to impose their will through force of arms, it was only slowly that they began to govern in any methodical way, and that Russia became recognizably a "state" rather than merely their realm, or their field of exploitation.

Presumably, however, the Vikings' East Slav subjects were quite capable, within the limits of tribal society, of arranging justice, religion, agriculture and perhaps trade according to custom. Long before the Vikings arrived, Byzantine sources (Procopius, Pseudo-Maurice) speak of the Slavs' "democracy": "everything which involves their welfare, whether for good or ill, is referred to the people." Quite early in the Kievan period, as the main towns began to attract a significant population, a rough-and-ready democratic institution emerged in the form of the popular assembly or *veche*. In some cities, notably Novgorod, its power grew to such an extent that from the early 12th century the role of the prince became marginalized: the Novgorod princes were thereafter regarded as little more than military commanders, to be hired or fired at will by the citizens. It seems clear that social differentiation, the concept of landownership and similar preconditions for a medieval rather than tribal or clan society were developing among the Slavs, irrespective of the Viking presence. The political heritage of the latter in Russia has had a baneful aspect: the great gulf between the interests of the rulers and the ruled, the exploitative relations of the one towards the other. Sometimes this was overcome by statesmanship or the influence of more sophisticated political and religious ideas, but it reappeared often in Russia's history, particularly in the way that "patrimonial" authority was exercised in the Muscovite state.

The first moves in the direction of systematically organized government seem to have been taken by Olga, widow of Igor, who was regent of Russia for some 17 years during the childhood of her son Svyatoslav. She regularized tax gathering, pacified the rebellious Drevlyane tribe (who had killed Igor for his arbitrary exactions) and established a network of fortified posts. She was also a Christian convert, and made a visit to Constantinople, of which we have a Byzantine account. Svyatoslav however was a remarkably different character: the epitome of the pagan Viking wanderer-warrior, even though he bore a thoroughly Slavonic name. For a hundred years the ruling dynasty and its band of retainers (*druzhina*) had used Kiev not only as a trading depot for the annual southbound flotilla, but also as forward base for occasional far-ranging raids of plunder throughout the Black Sea area and even beyond. Svyatoslav, placing princely relatives to look after the main Russian cities in his absence, devoted his reign to a series of such exploits, becoming doubtless the most successful Russian military commander till Suvorov 800 years later.

In the mid-960s, learning that a Russian tribe still paid tribute to Khazaria, Svyatoslav sacked the Khazars' cities and destroyed their power for ever. Then he turned westwards, incited rather rashly by the Byzantines to attack Bulgaria. For a few years he was ruler of a colossal empire, successor to all the ephemeral steppe-country powers: it seems that he and two or three subsequent Kievan grand princes even adopted the Khazar rulers' title of *kagan*. The Balkans suited Svyatoslav, who announced in 969 that he was shifting his capital from Kiev to Pereyaslavets on the lower Danube: "since that is the center of my realm and all merchandise is brought there: gold, silks, wine and various fruits from the Greeks, silver and horses from Hungary and the Czechs, and from Russia furs, wax, honey and slaves." But after a couple of years a new, militarily skilled Byzantine emperor, John Tzimisces, forced him and his retinue to retreat to Kiev. At the Dnieper cataracts he was killed by the Turkic nomad Pechenegs, an ominous irony, since it was precisely his destruction of Khazar power that would enable the dangerous steppe peoples to harass the southern flank of the Kievan state for the remainder of its existence.

Svyatoslav was last of his kind, though the ruling dynasty sporadically kept up contacts with Vikings overseas till well into the next century. Even before his time it would seem that the composition of the *druzhina* was ethnically mixed: while the signatories to the 911 treaty with Byzantium were overwhelmingly Scandinavian, those to its successor of 944 include a significant proportion of identifiable Slavonic and even one or two Estonian names. A new commitment to the Russian land is already visible in the reigns of his sons Yaropolk and Vladimir. Having overthrown Yaropolk after a somewhat confused civil war, Vladimir refused to allow his retinue to sack Kiev, sent some to serve in Constantinople and gave others grants of land,

while establishing his capital as one of the great cities of Europe. With the consequent flourishing of the Kievan realm the question of the choice of a state religion posed itself in an acute form. The time was ripe: paganism was on the retreat throughout northern and central Europe, and Vladimir's neighbors, the Poles, accepted Christianity in the 960s. Vladimir resolved the issue in 988/9 by pledging his adherence and that of his people to Christianity on the Byzantine pattern, what has come to be called the Orthodox Church.

Curiously, Byzantine sources are silent on the events of 988/9, while speaking glowingly of the reported conversion of the Russians in the 860s, over a century before. The circumstances are unclear, but in some way the aftermath of the raid on Constantinople in 860, led by Askold and Dir, had resulted by 867 in the official adherence of their followers to Christianity. When Oleg seized Kiev around 882 paganism must have been reinstated, but there was a Christian presence—indeed a church—there in the first half of the 10th century, even before Olga's conversion. Olga may have tried to establish an autocephalous (independent) church organization, and to have played off the Eastern and Western branches of Christendom. In any case a would-be bishop, Adalbert, arrived in Kiev from the German Emperor Otto I in 962, only to encounter the pagan reaction when Svyatoslav assumed power and to retire home embittered.

Vladimir, understanding that a centralized and developed religion was a prerequisite of civilized states in the world he knew, first instituted a synthetic pantheon of the various pagan deities of the Russian lands, to whom he set up idols. Their chief was to be Perun, god of thunder. Other gods appear to have had Oriental antecedents. This artificial religion proved unsatisfactory, and soon Vladimir carried his investigations farther. The Primary Chronicler recounts the whole process at understandably great length, and with embellishments that have a mythical ring. Emissaries came from various lands to expound their faiths in Kiev: Islamic Bulgars (from the Volga), Germans, Jews (from Khazaria), Greeks (from Byzantium). The "Greek Philosopher" summarized Christianity at considerable length and finished by unveiling an icon of the Last Judgment; this should have clinched the matter. But, according to the chronicle account, Vladimir then summoned his elders, reported his conversations and sent 10 "good and wise men" to experience the faiths at first hand.

In the responses, first by Vladimir, then by his investigators, a note of surely intentional comedy can be heard. The Islamic version of paradise sounds good, but the prohibition of alcohol is too much, and, anyhow, the Volga Bulgars stink. The Germans are drab. The Jews are losers, without a homeland, the Khazars having been routed by Svyatoslav 20 years before. But in a Greek church, the 10 report, "we did not know whether we were in heaven or earth. For on earth there is no such splendor or beauty, and we are at a loss to describe it. We only know that God dwells there among men . . ." Even this powerful aesthetic argument, much quoted to this day, did not finally decide the issue. Vladimir's advisers preferred a more pragmatic argument: "If the Greek faith were evil, it

This rare gold coin from the reign of Vladimir I (978/80–1015) shows the prince with a heraldic emblem above his shoulder: the inscription reads "Vladimir and this is his gold."

would not have been adopted by your grandmother Olga, who was wiser than anyone.'' Even then Vladimir delayed. He went off to capture the vital Byzantine city of Cherson in the Crimea and demanded the emperor's sister Anna in marriage: all ended happily when he accepted baptism, got his princess and handed back Cherson as the bride price. This extraordinary and protracted drama ended with Vladimir's return to Kiev and a mass baptism in the Dnieper.

The acceptance of Christianity on the Byzantine model as state religion was not just a confessional choice. A medieval religion was a ''package deal'' involving many elements. Vladimir's Russia was importing, together with a doctrine, the abstract literary language in which that doctrine could be expressed, the literature and ''high culture'' (including much that was ultimately of classical origin) that already existed in the language; an architecture adapted not just to different purposes, but employing new materials (masonry, mosaic); an art of enormous theological as well as aesthetic import; a whole new music; a sophisticated political theory, involving not just the ruler's responsibility to his subjects but his international status; certain aspects of law; and an educational system. The Chronicler describes how, immediately after founding churches and establishing a clergy, Vladimir ''began to take the children of the best families and send them for instruction from books,'' to their mothers' distress. Literate personnel were needed quickly, and it seems the already Christian and Slavonic Bulgarians obliged; many early manuscripts in Russia are of Bulgarian origin.

It is easy to see what Byzantium stood to gain from the transaction—even at the price of a ''purple-born'' (imperial) princess, a rare privilege for the Russian ruler. Many souls would be brought into the Orthodox fold, not just to their own benefit but to that of the Constantinopolitan patriarchate. A warlike and barbarous people would be at least civilized and become imperial allies, taking their place in the hierarchy of peoples headed by the empire, the ''oikoumene'' or ''Byzantine Commonwealth.'' For Vladimir things must have looked more of a gamble: not only was there a risk of social upheaval, but by adhering to Byzantine Christian ideology he was also to some extent reducing his own unfettered sovereignty. But the benefits of joining the international family of civilized nations evidently outweighed these other worries.

Vladimir and Novgorod

Vladimir I's long reign is the ''classic'' age of Kievan Russia, the moment when everything, or most things, went right. Much of the surviving oral epic folk poetry of Old Russia (the so-called *byliny*) is set in the court of Vladimir the ''Bright Sun'' (*Yasnoye solnyshko*). When he died, confusion set in, as his numerous sons battled for supremacy. Two, Boris and Gleb, were murdered at the instigation of their elder brother Svyatopolk (reigned 1015–19). Consciously choosing non-resistance to evil, they became celebrated as the first Russian martyrs. Eventually (1026) the two most powerful brothers, Mstislav and Yaroslav, established a diarchy, dividing Russia between them along the line of the River Dnieper; with Mstislav's death (1036) Yaroslav, a tough and probably ruthless survivor, reigned alone until his own death in 1054. This was

Below In the late 15th century Russian icons began to portray complex scenes without traditional iconographic models, and sometimes to have publicistic purposes. A singularly interesting subject in view of Russia's political history is one that became popular in Novgorod when the ancient city's independence was under threat from Moscow. It depicts an earlier, 12th-century medieval skirmish in which the Novgorodians drove back the army of Suzdalia (the Vladimir Land, predecessor to Muscovy) with the miraculous assistance of a cherished icon, the ''Virgin of the Sign.'' The narrative unfolds in three stages: in the middle register, shown here, we see the icon, unharmed, repelling enemy arrows from the city walls.

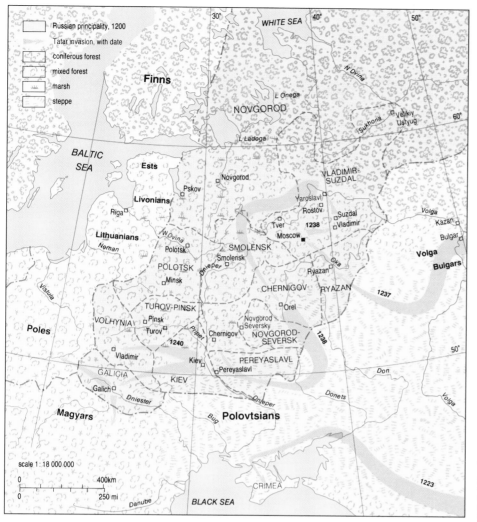

Above: Russia on the eve of the Tatar conquest.
Internecine warfare among the Kievan princes and the increasing frequency of incursions by steppe nomads such as the Polovtsians drove many Russians northwards in the 12th century to seek the natural shelter of the forest zone. A demographic and political shift away from the old capital, Kiev, was taking place. Novgorod had long been the great entrepôt of Baltic trade and now the town of Vladimir (founded 1108) grew rapidly as a center of trade. The Vladimir-Suzdal land enjoyed good river communications with both Novgorod and, via the Volga, with the Volga Bulgars and the East; it seems to have been developed in deliberate imitation of the Kievan land (there are many placenames in common). The older capital no longer traded down the Dnieper and was eclipsed economically in the south by Galicia and Volhynia.

Kiev's second golden age. Yaroslav (known as "the Wise") fostered building, the arts, literature and learning, and drew up the legal code known as *Russkaya pravda*—a rich source of social information (and controversy). A Russian intellectual, Hilarion, was appointed metropolitan in 1051, apparently without due reference to Constantinople. The "Great Church" of Kiev, St Sophia, was built and adorned with mosaics and frescoes, including a representation of Yaroslav's family. It survives to the present, as do fragments of the "Golden Gate" of the city.

In his testament Yaroslav adjured his numerous family to heed the eldest brother, Izyaslav, but again confusion followed. The inability of the Ryurikid dynasty to work out any effective succession system is puzzling. Presumably the realm was perceived as belonging to the princely family as a whole. Princes frequently shifted their seat of power, even over a distance as great as from Tmutorokan to Novgorod, so that a vast game of musical chairs seems sometimes to have been in progress. There was certainly a hierarchy of principalities (Chernigov was the second city of Kievan Russia, southern Pereyaslavl the third), and some historians have postulated a succession system from brother to brother, with everybody moving up one place on a senior prince's death. No written evidence exists for this, and it cannot have been more than a rough-and-ready principle. There was always the temptation for branches of the royal family to put down roots and found a local dynasty. This was acknowledged in a conference of

princes held at Lyubech in 1097, where the princes said to one another: "Why do we ruin the Russian land by quarreling? The Polovtsians plunder our country and rejoice that we wage war among ourselves. Let us rather hereafter be united in spirit and watch over the Russian land . . ."

Such unity proved fragile in practice, but was best achieved in the reigns of Vladimir II Monomakh (1113–25), who was brought to power by a popular uprising in Kiev, and his son Mstislav (1125–39). Vladimir II, who is sometimes confused in folklore and epic with his great predecessor, was half-Greek, son of a Byzantine princess of the Monomachos family. He himself married Gytha, daughter of the King Harold of England who was killed in 1066. He was architect of the Lyubech conference and other inter-princely accords and was a tireless defender of all Russia's borderlands, in particular managing to get the upper hand over the Polovtsian steppe raiders. He was also a lawgiver and a man of learning, and his so-called *Testament* (or *Instruction*), a compendium of autobiography and good advice addressed to his sons, is one of Russia's most fascinating medieval documents. Vladimir and Mstislav could do no more than hold Kiev's problems at bay, and the highly poeticized account of a disastrous expedition by Prince Igor of Novgorod-Seversk (the *Igor Tale*, c. 1187) looks back sorrowfully to the days of princely cooperation.

Vladimir II traveled widely and paid close attention to all parts of the Kievan federation. He founded or refounded a stronghold and city on the River Klyazma in northeast Russia, to which he gave his own name, Vladimir. This soon superseded its ancient neighbors Suzdal and Rostov as capital of the *Zalesskaya zemlya* ("Land beyond the Forest," usually if confusingly known as the Vladimir-Suzdal principality). Russians had been thin on the ground in this distant region, but the foundation of Vladimir marks the beginnings of a demographic and political shift that was to have the most lasting consequences for Russian history. The region, centered on the fertile *Opolye* (see p.24) between the great rivers Volga and Oka, turned out to be one of the most suitable areas in the forest zone for colonization. It seems to have grown phenomenally in the 12th century. Its many eastward-flowing rivers fed into the Volga and provided trade links in one direction with the Bulgars, and thence with the Caspian and Georgia and Armenia; in the other, by a choice of easy portages it was linked to Novgorod, gateway to the Baltic. With the decline of the Dnieper route from Kiev to Constantinople, Russia was reorientating itself.

This was made brutally clear when Andrey Bogolyubsky, who succeeded to the grand princely throne in 1157, did not take up residence in Kiev but announced that Vladimir would be his capital. He remained titular "Grand Prince of Kiev," but, after sacking the city in 1169, he installed his younger brother in the older capital. Even in its decline Kiev remained ecclesiastical capital, until in 1300 the metropolitan too took up residence in Vladimir. Among the 12th-century cities established in the wake of Vladimir was Moscow, traditionally founded by Andrey's father Yury Dolgoruky (the "Long-armed" or "Long-sighted") in 1156. The site was actually inhabited earlier, as excavations of the

45

Above The greatest artistic glory of Vladimir Russia, in the final century before the Tatar conquest, is a small group of churches in fine white limestone that represents the culmination of early Russian architecture. The St Demetrius Cathedral (1194) at Vladimir is extraordinary for the tapestry of low-relief carving, both ornamental and figurative, on its exterior walls: inside are some fine (probably Byzantine) frescoes.

Left The icon of the "Virgin of Vladimir," the palladium of Vladimir and Moscow Grand Principalities, is of the iconographic type known as "Tenderness," subsequently very popular in Russia. It is Byzantine of the early 12th century—an early and outstanding example of the softening of stylistic rigidity in the direction of portrayal of emotions. Only the face and hands are original: the rest is late medieval overpainting. There are marks from the elaborate silver casing (*oklad*) that was subsequently applied to this, as to most other old icons.

Europe. Its real "head of state" was not its prince, but its almost independent archbishop, and the city styled itself "Lord Novgorod the Great." It came to control a vast tract of northern Russia, sometimes fancifully called the "Novgorod empire." There were few other towns in this agriculturally unproductive region, but Novgorod had a "younger brother" to its west, the ancient city of Pskov. This too was a well-located trading center, which also developed a *veche* culture and asserted its individuality to such effect that in the 14th century it was to achieve independence.

The transplanted Byzantine culture of Kievan Russia flourished, sometimes developing rather individual characteristics, to which the vernacular folk culture often contributed elements. Apart from the chief secular literary works (see above pp. 39–41), there was also a rich religious literature, including several versions of the *Lives* of Sts Boris and Gleb, and the varied and vivid tales collected in the *Paterikon* of the Kiev Monastery of the Caves. This establishment, the greatest religious foundation of early Russia, was also a focus of learning, where the legendary monks Nestor and Sylvester compiled the *Tale of Bygone Years*.

The great buildings of Kievan Russia, though not numerous, form an impressive legacy of its culture. The foundations of Vladimir I's large and ornate Tithe Church in Kiev are known from excavation. The even greater St Sophia (1037) is almost wholly preserved, though outwardly obscured by baroque accretions. Chernigov, Smolensk, Polotsk and Pskov all preserve important early buildings. Predictably, the most remarkable collection survives in Novgorod, including its own severe and monumental St Sophia (1043). As the Kievan period progressed the exterior of buildings, previously almost unadorned, tended to be treated more delicately, with, for example, patterned brickwork or pilaster strips. The roofline and drum took on a pyramidal silhouette. Inside, all churches (and doubtless too the palace architecture of which little is known) were plastered and painted in fresco. Occasionally in Kiev mosaic was used, but for this imported specialists, not to mention a glass factory, were needed, making it prohibitively expensive. The surviving Kievan frescoes, mostly fragmentary, are monumental and rather linear in manner, at least until the mid-12th century. There is a precious relic of secular art in the paintings of the staircase towers of St Sophia, Kiev, showing scenes from the Hippodrome in Constantinople.

Half-a-dozen astonishing churches of the later 12th and early 13th centuries, in Vladimir and nearby, are perhaps the finest works of art to survive from Kievan Russia. All save the Dormition Cathedral in Vladimir itself are quite small, but their fine proportions are enhanced by beautiful white limestone masonry. They are like sculpted caskets, and the impression is heightened by the remarkable low-relief sculpture that adorns them. On two, St Demetrius, Vladimir (1194) and St George, Yuryev-Polsky (1230), almost the entire external surface of the building is covered by a profusion of architectural, vegetable, animal and human carving of unknown origin. The chronicler, tantalizingly, merely observes "God sent craftsmen from all the lands to Andrey (Bogolyubsky)," leaving unexplained the buildings' mystery.

waterside of the Moskva River have revealed. The first name of the settlement was in fact Kuchkovo, after the local landowner.

The disintegration of Kievan Russia became evident in its last century of existence. Even in southern Russia the Kiev land was losing its economic leadership to the united principalities of Galicia-Volhynia in the far southwest. Polotsk, in the northwest (the heart of what was later to be Belorussia) was well placed for trade down the Dvina towards western Europe. Its separate identity was emphasized by the establishment of its own dynasty of princes from Vladimir I's time on; however, its powerful late 11th-century Prince Vseslav (reputedly a werewolf) made a strong bid for the Kiev throne. Smolensk, too, had western trade links and revived in the 12th century.

The most independent and politically interesting of the Russian lands was Novgorod, which remained to the end of the Kievan period and beyond the great entrepôt of Baltic trade. It clearly had special status and privileges from a very early period. In its later subordination of its princes and the growth of its assembly (*veche*), Novgorod turned in effect into an oligarchic city-state, not dissimilar from those in Italy and parts of northern

St Sophia, Kiev

The "Great Church" of Constantinople, built (532–37) under Justinian in substantially the form that has survived to this day, was dedicated to *Hagia Sophia*, "Divine Wisdom." In the early 11th century the newly converted Russians used the same dedication for cathedrals in three major cities: Kiev (1037), Polatsk (1044) and Novgorod (1043), in south, west and north Russia respectively; St Sophia, Kiev, was grandest, as befitted the capital. Half-abandoned after the Tatar invasion, it was fully restored by order of Ivan V and Peter I in the 1680s. The exterior is almost wholly baroque: inside, the 11th-century building, with its fine mosaics and frescoes, remains largely unchanged. Built by order of Yaroslav the Wise, the cathedral had a group portrait in fresco of Yaroslav's family in the central nave, and still contains his magnificent marble tomb. Even now, it is more numinous with the spirit of early Rus than any other place.

St Sophia, Kiev, built in 1037–39, is one of the handful of great middle-Byzantine churches that are among the glories of East European art. Though thoroughly Byzantine in concept and in its comprehensive internal scheme of decoration, it is in some respects quite individual, and looks forward to specifically Russian architectural developments. It has 13 domes—an unparalleled number—on rather tall drums, grouped in such a way (on stepped side aisles) as to give a strongly pyramidal outline when we imagine it without its present baroque accretions. The domes were helmet-shaped rather than semicircular in section. The pictorial scheme unusually integrates mosaic and fresco: the former, as befits its cost and prestige, in the more "heavenly" parts of the building: main dome and main eastern apse. Broad internal upper galleries were for the use of the grand prince, his family and retinue: domed staircase towers that were soon added led to the palace. Externally, the patterned brick and stone courses would not originally have been plastered.

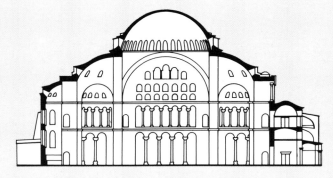

Above Hagia Sophia of Constantinople exercised a lasting fascination on eastern Christians—yet its only direct architectural successors, curiously, are the great Ottoman mosques. However it anticipates most subsequent Byzantine and Russian churches in making great play with dazzling light and darkness, with large and small spaces, with what is revealed and concealed, with simplicity and complexity, with the straight and the curved.

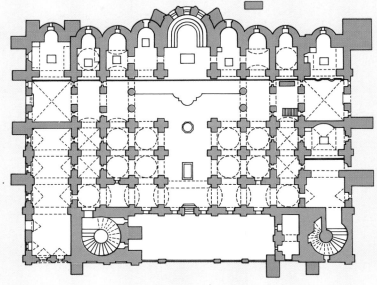

Left The ground plan of St Sophia, Kiev, is an elaborated version of the "cross-in-square." Probably five naves were originally intended, surrounded by arcaded galleries; by the early 12th century the latter were enclosed to make extra naves, and further galleries added (eventually also enclosed). A building surprisingly broader than long resulted.

Details of the main dome of St Sophia, Kiev. The domes of Orthodox churches rest on masonry drums that tended to be built higher and narrower as time went on. The transition between drum and the piers or walls on which it stood was effected either through the crude bridging squinch or the far more elegant pendentive. The dome itself is always occupied by the Pantokrator or Almighty (*above*); immediately below him there is a circle of archangels (*below*). Between the windows of the drum there were usually representations of the twelve apostles; on the pendentives often the four evangelists.

MUSCOVY

The Tatar invasion

The end of Kievan Russia came suddenly and catastrophically, though not without warning. In 1223 armed horsemen appeared on the southeastern steppe frontier. The Polovtsians, Russia's old nomadic enemies, warned the Kievan authorities, but there was little time. A Russian army was hastily raised by three princes (all, coincidentally, called Mstislav) and marched into the steppe country to give battle. On the bank of the Kalka River, after a dogged fight, they were overwhelmed. The prince who led them was killed, despite a safe conduct, an ominous sign: these people made war by different rules. Then the invaders left, their reconnaissance completed, leaving the shocked Russians to wonder who they were, whence they came, whither they departed and what they purposed.

The people in question were the Tatars, and 14 years passed before they reappeared. In 1237 they descended unexpectedly on the Ryazan land, destroyed the city of Ryazan so thoroughly that when it was refounded it was on a different site, sacked several towns including Moscow and Vladimir, headed towards Novgorod and then turned back eastwards: the swampy conditions of the spring thaw were unfitted for their cavalry. In 1240 a new

assault was aimed at the southern cities, Chernigov and Kiev. It is with this event that Tatar rule in Russia is generally taken to begin.

The Tatars, or Mongols as they are more often called outside Russia, were a confederation of clans living in the land still known as Mongolia, a treeless region whose harsh climate is unfavorable to settled agriculture but adequate for horses. As transhumant pastoralists they lived in tents, had no towns until the 13th century, and were well equipped for a mobile existence. All the men bore arms, so their military potential was disproportionate to their meager numbers. Their explosive impact on the outside world was initiated by Temuchin (1167–1227), who united the Tatar clans, gathered together the people in a great Kuriltay (popular assembly) in 1206, was given the new title Genghis (Chingis) Khan, and embarked on world conquest. Genghis Khan centralized the Tatar army and administration, partially feudalized the clan system, established stringent discipline and set out on his career of conquest. In 1215 Peking fell. Then came the turn of Central Asia, Persia and the Transcaucasian lands: it was a battle-hardened force that traveled up through Azerbayjan to victory on the Kalka.

Below: **Russia and the Asiatic world, 13th–14th centuries.** Contacts between Russia and its Asiatic neighbors have fluctuated through the centuries according to political circumstances. Since before recorded Russian history began, the River Volga and the Caspian Sea have been important links connecting Russia and the Scandinavian world with the Middle East. From early times, too, there was east-west movement across the steppe: not so much a trade route (though some detours of the silk route pass that way), the steppe was more an unobstructed highway for nomadic or migrant raiders and invaders on horseback. The last such great movement, cataclysmic for the Kievan lands as for settled states over a vast swathe of Eurasia from China to the Balkans, was that of the Tatars, whose leader Genghis Khan embarked on world conquest at the end of the 12th century. Kiev fell to the Tatar general Batu in 1240. Thereafter the Golden Horde ruled Russia until 1480 from its capital at Saray on the Volga.

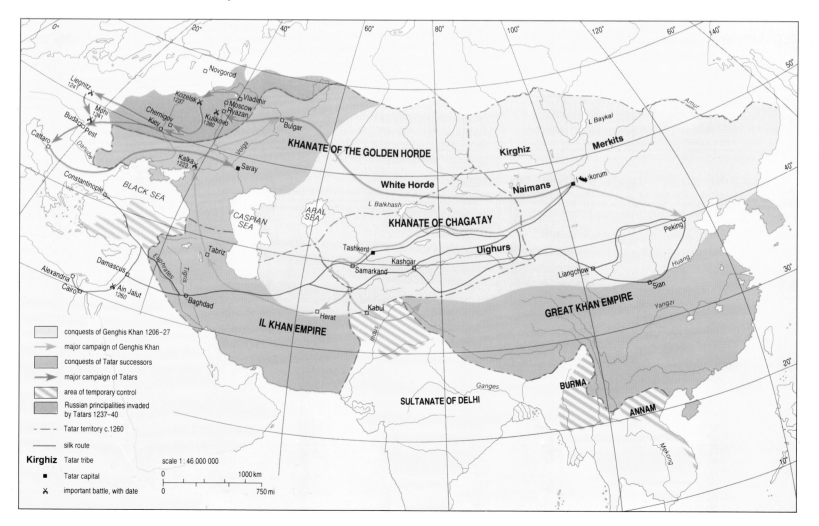

conquests of Genghis Khan 1206–27
major campaign of Genghis Khan
conquests of Tatar successors
major campaign of Tatars
area of temporary control
Russian principalities invaded by Tatars 1237–40
Tatar territory c.1260
silk route
Kirghiz Tatar tribe
Tatar capital
important battle, with date

scale 1 : 46 000 000

Right Genghis Khan (d. 1277), the great ruler who united the Mongols (Tatars) and set them on their path of world conquest, is here represented in a Persian miniature of the 14th century. He is seen enthroned in a stylized nomad tent in a garden, surrounded by his retinue which includes his sons Ogaday and Juchi. Ogaday was Genghis's immediate successor; Juchi's son Batu devastated Russia in 1237–42. The Mongol dynasty in Persia lasted from 1256 to 1344; Tatar rule in Russia is reckoned to have lasted from about 1240 to 1480.

Above Yaroslav Vsevolodich was grand prince of Vladimir at the time of the imposition of Tatar rule. He succeeded his brother Yury who was killed in a major battle against the invaders in 1238. This donor-portrait of him comes from the church on Nereditsa Hill outside Novgorod and dates from around 1246, the year of his death. The Nereditsa church itself dated from 1199 and had a complete set of frescoes, unique in Europe, but, like several other early Novgorodian churches, it was destroyed in World War II; it has been rebuilt, but the paintings were nearly all lost.

What did the Tatars want? Plunder, obviously, and power; but beyond these it was, surprisingly, not territory that they sought—certainly not agricultural land for their own use—but people, and the skills people brought. Manpower could be exploited *in situ* through efficient taxation, as generally was the case in Russia, or else by impressment into the ranks of Tatar soldiery, bureaucracy and craftsmen. Large numbers of Turkic people thus quickly became assimilated into Tatar society, with consequent linguistic mingling (such "Tatar" words as have passed into Russian vocabulary are usually Turkic in origin). To some extent the Tatars settled as a ruling elite in the lands they first conquered, but this scarcely happened in Russia. A strong awareness of national

tradition bound the Tatar leaders together despite the vast extent of their empire; all had to travel back to Karakorum in Mongolia when death occasioned the election of a new Great Khan. But gradually the far-flung regions of the Tatar realm became more or less autonomous, sometimes in rivalry with each other. For most of its Tatar period Russia was ruled not from Mongolia or Peking, but from Saray, the new city established on the lower course of the Volga (at that time well beyond settled Russian territory) by the rulers of the western branch of Tatar dominion, the Golden Horde. The Horde controlled not only central, southern and eastern Russia, but the steppe country from Siberia to the western shores of the Black Sea, much of central Asia and Caucasia.

There are no statistics to estimate the loss of life caused by the Tatar invasion, but the destruction of cities, forced levies of manpower and financial exactions were an economic and social catastrophe, while sudden and total military defeat at the hands of the infidel was a great psychological trauma. The only Russian principalities that escaped devastation were those that submitted and paid tribute without offering resistance, notably Novgorod and Pskov. Daniil of Galicia, in the extreme southwest, attempted to rally Western European assistance, offered obedience to the pope and received a crown—but no armies. The consequence was a devastating Tatar raid in 1260, and tight control thereafter. Yet though the Tatars were Russia's overlords, they did not rule there as they ruled in China until 1368. Political authority remained, as before, in the hands of the princely families. The Tatars at first stationed a small number of *baskaki* (overseers) in the Russian towns, but presumably the vast majority of Russians, almost all the rural population in fact, never set eyes on any Tatar or experienced any change in legal or social status.

For the princes and their retinues the situation was very different. Their patent to rule (*yarlyk*) was dependent on undertaking the humiliating and hazardous journey to a Tatar capital—sometimes to Karakorum, a monstrous distance, usually to Saray, which was bad enough. From such a journey the prince, if his loyalty was suspect, might never return. At any moment the Tatars might launch a punitive raid. This did not need to happen very often. The princes, understandably if not very nobly, acted as the khan's agents, generally suppressing discontent occasioned by tax-gathering methods, levies or censuses among the populace.

While from one point of view Russia can be seen as enslaved by an alien and merciless conqueror, from another it was business as usual, with the Tatars a considerable but occasional menace. But, as reflected in the surviving literature of the time, the Russians had difficulty in coming to terms with their loss of sovereignty. Any given defeat could be recorded and bitterly regretted as a sign of God's displeasure; the permanent overlordship of infidels was another matter, passed over in silence or alluded to in terms more adequate to the steppe skirmishes or inter-princely feuding of the previous age. Later, of course, a whole historical-ideological theory of the "Tatar yoke" would be constructed, involving the image of Russia as a sort of European punchbag, absorbing dazedly the vicious onslaught of barbarians and thereby protecting the progress of Western civilization, at its own expense. There is some measure of truth in this picture, yet it does not really correspond to how things looked to Russians at the time.

Alexander Nevsky and the Kievan legacy

Tatar domination meant different things at different times and in various circumstances, while Russian responses were far from uniform. The interpretation of such responses can be a minefield, and nowhere more so than when we consider the figure of St Alexander Nevsky, eldest surviving son of Grand Prince Yaroslav of Vladimir, himself Prince of Novgorod, aged about 20 at the time of the invasion. In summer 1240, when the second great Tatar assault was being unleashed on Cherni-

gov and Kiev, Alexander defeated the Swedes, who were already much interested in territorial expansion on the far side of the Baltic, beside the River Neva, whence his honorary surname "Nevsky." Later he became the patron saint of St Petersburg, built almost 500 years afterwards near the site of this victory. In April 1242 Alexander fought his other great battle, partly on the frozen Lake Peipus. The so-called Teutonic Knights, semireligious crusading military orders of German origin, bent on conquering the Orthodox lands and bringing them into the Catholic fold, had been working their way up the Baltic and had reached Pskov. In the "Battle on the Ice" Alexander's forces destroyed a mixed army of Germans and local Estonians, and the Knights advanced no farther. Subsequently Alexander submitted to Batu, leader of the Golden Horde, thereby averting any Tatar assault on Novgorod. The Tatars later placed him on the throne of Vladimir.

Within a couple of generations Alexander had become a legend, was canonized in the 14th century and was made the subject of a heroic biography. The First Novgorod Chronicle makes him more than life-size: "His stature exceeds that of other men, his voice is like a trumpet . . . his strength is like the strength of Samson; God has given him the wisdom of Solomon and the courage of the Roman caesar Vespasian . . ." His heroic image was evoked under Stalin in World War II, not only in Eisenstein's famous film, but in, for example, the attaching of his name to a tank corps raised from the donations of Orthodox believers. Some modern historians have looked with a beadier eye at contemporary sources that treat Alexander's campaigns in a more matter-of-fact way, observing that the victory over the Swedes was no more than another skirmish in a centuries-long process of boundary definition. They also rather damningly point out that Alexander's submission to the Horde was more the result of political maneuvering and ambition within the princely family than of military necessity; had he made common cause with his brothers, Alexander would have had a good chance of successfully resisting Tatar occupation of the forest zone. Whatever bargain Alexander struck with the khan, it brought advantages not just to him personally, but to Russia, in mitigating the harsher aspects of Tatar rule, and to the Orthodox Church, which was even permitted to set up a diocese at the Tatar capital of Saray in 1261.

Folklore hauntingly allegorized the lost glory and independence of Kievan-Vladimir Russia in the legend of the Invisible City of Kitezh, which rather than fall to the infidel sank below the waters of its lake, to reemerge in better times. It is the subject of one of Rimsky-Korsakov's most spectacular operas. Sophisticated literature lamented the conquest in several works, of which the most memorable is the fragmentary *Tale of the Ruin of the Russian Land*, which starts with the most idyllic and poetic of apostrophes to Old Russia: "O brightly brilliant and splendidly adorned Russian land! Many beauties have made you marvelous . . ." The bright image of Kiev has inspired Russian nostalgia many times since, while the cultural and political attempt to resurrect its heritage can be observed as early as the 15th century.

Above Frescoes of the glorious progenitors of the Moscow line of grand princes adorn the Archangel Cathedral (1505) of the Moscow Kremlin, the last and externally the most ornate of the series of great buildings that were commissioned to enhance their new independent capital by Ivan III and his son Vasiliy. This fresco depicts Alexander Nevsky, Prince of Novgorod, who was canonized in the 14th century (hence his halo). In 1240 he defeated the Swedes, and in 1242 the German Teutonic Knights, in battles whose significance was subsequently built up (as was Alexander's own personality) to heroic status. He made a probably unavoidable accommodation with the Tatars, who later had him installed as grand prince in Vladimir.

Right Mount Athos is a precipitous peninsula projecting 70 kilometers into the Aegean Sea east of Thessaloniki. Remote today, it was in the late Middle Ages the religious heart of the Orthodox world, a "monastic republic" (as it still is), meeting place of many nationalities: Russians, Bulgarians, Serbs, Romanians and Georgians, as well as Greeks, had monasteries on the "Holy Mountain." The Russian monastery of St Pantaleimon, shown here, is an ancient foundation, but now looks a rather anonymous conglomeration of 19th-century buildings: under the last tsars it was deliberately enlarged, and accommodated thousands of pilgrims. All Athonite monasteries are fortress-like, picturesquely huddled round their main church.

Tatar rule

The trauma of the Tatar conquest healed slowly as generations passed and Tatar power became an accepted fact of Russian life, however unwelcome. In the Russian lands there was an intensification of certain trends already visible in Kievan days: notably the relentless subdivision of the large principalities into ever-smaller appanages (in the absence of primogeniture) and the generalized feuding between them, exacerbated by the desire to seek Tatar favor. Considerable significance attached to acquiring the *yarlyk* or patent to the title of grand prince of Vladimir from the khan, with whom the grand prince alone had the right of direct dealing, and for whom he acted as chief tax gatherer and law enforcer. From the early 14th century onwards the rulers of Moscow, formerly a somewhat insignificant subdivision of the Vladimir principality, were most often successful in this. At the same time they managed to reverse the usual trend by increasing rather than diminishing their territory. For this reason we generally associate the 14th and 15th centuries with the rise of Moscow. This was not the only political process at work in the historic Russian lands at the time, however, and indeed Moscow's rise is matched by the simultaneous rise in west Russia of that large and remarkable, if often-forgotten, medieval state, the Grand Duchy of Lithuania. Meanwhile Novgorod enjoyed a silver age of prosperity and cultural activity in the 14th century. For a time around 1400 it looked as if the old Kievan federative system might be restored. It would be far too deterministic to regard the rise of Moscow as inevitable, or as the only proper destiny of Russia.

Tatar conquest, accompanied by the widespread destruction of cities and consequent disruption of commerce and industry, must have forced much of Russia back to a subsistence economy. Building activity, a normal indicator of surplus wealth, stopped, as far as is known, from the 1240s to 1280s. Kiev itself was particularly hard hit, "reduced almost to nothing" as the papal envoy Plano Carpini noted on passing through in 1246. Loss of skilled manpower to the Tatars was significant, but actual loss of life was probably slight compared with the huge disaster of the Black Death a century later. This reached Russia from the West in the 1350s and became endemic for many decades. In none of these matters are precise statistics available. Nonetheless Russia began recovering from the effects of the conquest fairly quickly. It was in the Tatars' interest to encourage trade, and they soon issued decrees to ensure free passage to merchants. Even if they let others rule on their behalf, they were keen to order and to enumerate their subjects, instituting censuses (far from popular) and an efficient post-horse service to impose their notions of discipline even at a distance.

Church life and the monastic movement

A notable phenomenon in 14th-century Russian culture is the blossoming of the Orthodox Church. The conditions for this were partly supplied, rather surprisingly, by the Tatars. They exempted the church, with its lands and all its servitors, clerical or lay, from the exactions and conscription that the rest of society suffered. The Tatars, who were themselves shamanistic pagans at the time of the conquest and long afterwards, followed Genghis Khan's example of tolerance towards the various developed religions they encountered, perhaps for superstitious reasons. Their own choice of religion depended on where they were. In Mongolia they remained pagans. Many in the west toyed with Christianity, until in the early 14th century the Golden Horde as a whole adopted Islam. Despite comparative Tatar benevolence, the church in this period became more strongly identified with the Russian nation than before; it remained an all-Russian institution at a time of political fragmentation and demoralization. It has been quite recently demonstrated that there must have been an agreement between the Russians and the patriarchate in Constantinople, whereby the metropolitans of Kiev (resident in Vladimir, and afterwards Moscow) were chosen alternately by each partner. The Byzantines were much weakened politically, and between 1204 and 1261 were under occupation by the Western European adventurers of the Fourth Crusade. Byzantium was no longer in the dominant position it had held in the 9th and 10th centuries. Yet it was still capable of generating religious ideas to grapple with the challenge of Islamic successes and of several heretical movements.

A general mood of heightened spirituality suffused the whole Orthodox Church in the 14th century, finding its most remarkable expression in the theological movement called Hesychasm (literally, "quietism"). Drawing upon and elaborating certain practices of earlier Church Fathers, this recommended disciplined repetitive prayer and spiritual exercises that might, with God's grace, put the individual in direct contact with the divine energy. After bitter wrangling Hesychasm was ratified as Orthodox doctrine at church councils by the mid-14th century, and it remains so to the present. It had considerable effect on late-medieval art and literature.

The church was important as a link between Russia and the wider world. There was considerable movement, including some revival of trade, between Russia and the east Mediterranean lands in the 14th and early 15th centuries, no longer using the Dnieper, but normally via the River Don and the Crimea. Pilgrims and church delegations traveled to Constantinople (where their graffiti have recently been identified in the galleries of St Sophia), but the great spiritual powerhouse of the Orthodox was the monastic republic of Mount Athos in the northern Aegean, where the Russian monastery of St Panteleimon still exists. Here books were translated and copied, icons painted and ideas exchanged. Emissaries too traveled in the other direction: senior Byzantine churchmen several times went to Moscow and the other Russian lands in effect to beg for alms, usually so as to repair the buildings of Constantinople—a striking testimony to the 14th-century revival of Russian prosperity and comparative Byzantine indigence.

It could have been one such emissary who reported back to the patriarch that the Grand Prince Vasiliy I was saying, "We have a church, but no emperor," and leaving the latter out of official prayers. Patriarch Antonios sent a long letter of rebuke, pointing out that church and empire were inseparable. One of the classic statements of Byzantine political ideology, it was written in the 1390s when the empire itself had been reduced to little more than the City and a few islands, with the Ottoman Turks already sweeping all before them. The Russians apparently accepted the rebuke, and it was only after 1448, a decade after the Council of Florence had patched up a union between Eastern and Western churches, causing grass-roots outrage, that they cautiously took the destiny of their church into their own hands, appointing their own metropolitan without reference to Byzantium. Prior to that, the Byzantine patriarchate had had the awkward task throughout the 14th century of deciding between the rival claims of northeast Russia (Vladimir/Moscow) and the Grand Duchy of Lithuania (which in mid-century annexed Kiev, historic seat of the metropolitan) to represent Russia. Lithuania probably had a considerably larger population of Orthodox believers, but its ruling class were still pagans, the last pagan nation in Europe. After much wavering, Constantinople decided for Moscow, and the Lithuanian rulers joined forces with Poland and accepted Catholicism in 1385, though they set up a rival Orthodox metropolitan in Kiev in 1458. Subsequent Russian cultural history was radically influenced by these events.

The most interesting and important development in Russian church life of the Tatar period was, however, purely internal to the country. This was the so-called monastic movement: the founding of numerous monasteries and hermitages in ever-remoter parts of the northern forests. Before 1300 the major monasteries had been in or near towns, closely associated with the princely courts. A complete change of pattern was instigated by Sergius of Radonezh (c.1321–91), later considered one of Russia's patron saints. He came from a family of boyars (aristocrats) in Rostov, dispossessed as a result of pressure from Moscow during his childhood. As a young man he sought out a refuge from the world in trackless forest northeast of Radonezh; his "wilderness," symbolically rather than physically remote, soon attracted other hermits. Against his will he was persuaded to organize his hermitage into a monastery, of which he became abbot. The town of Sergiyev Posad (Zagorsk under the Soviet regime) grew around it.

Sergius's monastery, dedicated to the Holy Trinity, became before his death the leading intellectual center of resurgent Russian culture. Its early monks founded remoter monasteries, and from these remoter ones still were established. It has been estimated that nearly 200 arose in the century 1340–1440, reaching eventually to the White Sea and the Urals. Peasant colonists followed: not surprisingly the Moscow grand princes did their best to profit by the whole process. Ideologically the friendship between Sergius and Grand Prince Dmitriy Donskoy stood the latter

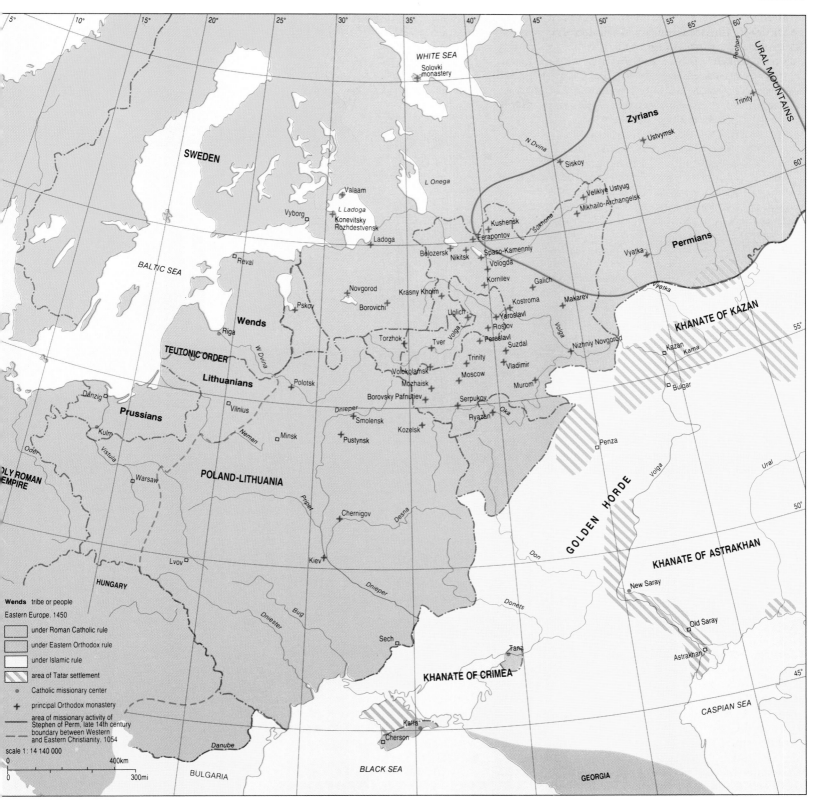

Wends tribe or people

Eastern Europe, 1450

- under Roman Catholic rule
- under Eastern Orthodox rule
- under Islamic rule
- area of Tatar settlement
- • Catholic missionary center
- + principal Orthodox monastery
- —— area of missionary activity of Stephen of Perm, late 14th century
- – – boundary between Western and Eastern Christianity, 1054

scale 1: 14 140 000

400km

300mi

in good stead at a crucial moment, whether or not Sergius actually blessed Dmitriy's successful military challenge to the Tatars. Another friend and contemporary of Sergius was St Stephen of Perm, whose single-handed missionary activity managed to convert the Komi people (Permians) to Orthodox Christianity. In imitation of Sts Cyril and Methodius he devised them an alphabet and a literature. Muscovite centralization extirpated both a few generations later, and an icon of the Trinity carrying Permian script is a unique surviving relic.

The story of Moscow's aggrandizement is complex, but its general outlines are clear enough. Its

family of resident princes begins with the youngest son of Alexander Nevsky, Daniil. From the start, the dynasty was concerned to add to its territory, whether by peaceful means (purchase, marriage, inheritance) or force. In or about 1318 Prince Yury Danilovich married the sister of the khan of the Golden Horde, receiving the title of grand prince. Thereafter his successors tenaciously struggled to keep the title in their own family. Moscow had tough rivals. Lithuania too was growing fast and intervening frequently in central Russian politics. Novgorod was at the height of its commercial power. The chief opposition, however, came from another newcomer to the political scene, the city of

Tver on the upper Volga. The struggle for supremacy, with the sometimes bloody involvement of the Tatars, continued well into the 15th century. Support from the church was a factor that raised Moscow's prestige: from about 1328 the metropolitans resided there, while the wise and courageous Metropolitan Aleksey acted as regent during the minority of Prince Dmitriy Ivanovich. The latter, who inherited the principality in 1359 at the age of nine, later found fame as Dmitriy Donskoy. The surname alludes to the headwaters of the River Don, where on Kulikovo Pole (Field of Snipe) in 1380 Dmitriy led an army from an alliance of principalities into battle against a large Tatar force sent to punish him for several acts of insubordination. Mamay, the Tatar commander, expected help from the Lithuanian ruler Jagiello, but it arrived too late, and he was comprehensively defeated.

Two years later another Tatar army under Tokhtamysh sacked Moscow. Dmitriy continued to pay tribute and was confirmed as grand prince. The Tatars mounted occasional highly destructive raids and remained Russia's nominal overlords for another century, but their grip had obviously loosened. The Golden Horde was demoralized, and Russian independence under Moscow's leadership could only be a matter of time. An internecine civil war in the Moscow royal house, lasting for the entire second quarter of the 15th century, marks the last public eruption of the sort of ''uncle-nephew'' generational conflict that so bedeviled the princely succession in Kievan days. Generally the Moscow dynasty was fortunate enough to enjoy uncomplicated father-to-son inheritance. It also produced long-reigning monarchs. From 1359 (disregarding civil war claimants) six rulers in succession (Dmitriy, Vasiliy I, Vasiliy II, Ivan III, Vasiliy III, Ivan IV) enjoyed reigns that spanned 225 years (30, 36, 37, 43, 28, 51 years respectively), a rather astonishing record in turbulent and disease-ridden times.

The arts of early Muscovy

From the cultural point of view 14th- to 15th-century Russia tends to be overshadowed by the glories of the Kiev and Vladimir heritage. Yet the Tatar period, once the initial shock was over, was no dark age. Building activity restarted on a modest scale before the opening of the 14th century, and as the century progressed a considerable number of churches appeared, particularly in Novgorod. Moscow acquired walls under Dmitriy Donskoy, and a small number of early Muscovite buildings survive from about 1400. These buildings pick up the traditions of the elegant white limestone architecture developed in Vladimir 200 years earlier, though less monumentally and without the external figurative sculpture of some Vladimir buildings. Certain pre-Tatar tendencies in the direction of increasing the visual impact of rooflines were greatly developed, with an interestingly varied effect of pyramidality. Domes were probably still helmet- rather than onion-shaped. External walls are articulated by the application of small arcades, stringcourses, decorative gables, pilasters and other devices that have a purely aesthetic effect, since they no longer correspond with internal structure.

The visual arts flowered magnificently in

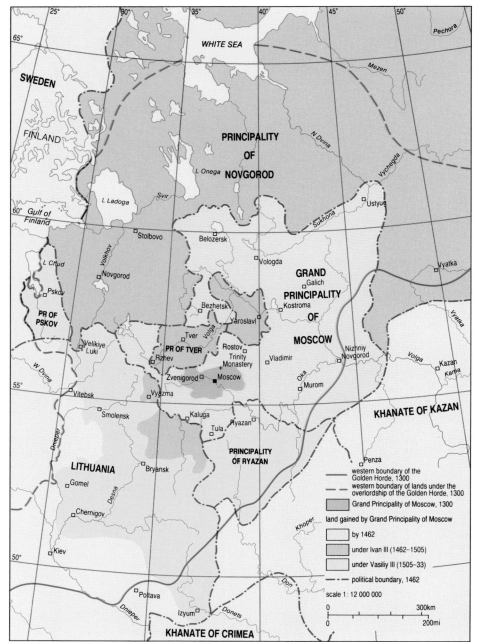

another area: painting. The first half of the 15th century is rightly considered the golden age of the Russian icon. Though earlier medieval art had generally been anonymous, individuality began to assert itself, and from about 1400 the names of several of the best practitioners are known. In particular the life and work of the monk Andrey Rublyov (c. 1370–1430) have in the 20th century been resurrected from myth. We can also grasp the distinct artistic personalities of Rublyov's older contemporary Theophanes the Greek (Feofan Grek, a lay Byzantine expatriate) who worked in Novgorod and in 1405 with Rublyov in Moscow, and of his last important successor, Dionisiy (late 15th century).

Few icons survive from Kievan Russia: those that do mostly display a static, uncluttered monumentality. In the early Tatar period Russian art, thrown back on its own resources, shows a ''folk'' quality, with expressive, plastic distortions and simplifications of figure style and clear, unnaturalistic colors. When Russian culture revived in the late 14th century its art was able to draw on both these aspects of its past, but also on renewed inter-

Left: Moscow and the "gathering-in" of the Russian lands.

Moscow was founded in the mid-12th century (though its site was inhabited earlier); with the decline of Kiev the central and northeastern forest zone was being rapidly opened up to Russian colonization. After the Tatar invasions of 1237–40 Moscow, at first a minor subdivision of the Vladimir principality, began the process of territorial aggrandizement and rise in power that led to the consolidation under Ivan III (1462–1505) of the centralized Muscovite realm. In the 14th century Moscow rulers "gathered in" adjoining principalities by conquest, cajolery, purchase or inheritance; the metropolitan of Kiev and All Russia moved first to Vladimir, then to Moscow, increasing their prestige; Moscow's princes were generally successful in acquiring the title "grand prince" from the Tatars. Stiff opposition to Moscow's ambitions, however, came from the Grand Duchy of Lithuania (later united with Poland), from Novgorod and from Tver (both subdued by Ivan III). The principalities of Pskov and Ryazan were allowed to continue as buffer states to the west and southeast respectively, but they too were absorbed into the Muscovite realm in the first quarter of the 16th century. The reasons for Moscow's success have been much debated by historians, though inconclusively; its location at the heart of the Volga-Oka river system is often cited, though Tver, Vladimir and other cities would seem as well or better situated.

Right The earliest accurate plans of Moscow date from the end of the 16th century; some are copies from a lost original traced by Fyodor, son of Boris Godunov. A similar, though not identical, map was made for Sigismund III, king of Poland, who in 1610–12 expected to make Moscow his own capital. This is one of the variants of Sigismund's map. The Moskva River is shown flowing from top to bottom left (west to east), with its tributaries, the Neglinka (flowing round the Kremlin: it is now piped) and the Yauza. The concentric quarters of the city are all fortified. In the middle of the map is Red Square with market rows (6) and the church of Basil the Blessed. Among features of interest indicated are public bath houses on the Moskva and the Yauza (13). South of the Moskva is the quarter of the *streltsy*, with the tsar's great garden (14) opposite the Kremlin; the physic garden adjoins the Kremlin's northwest wall.

national contacts, above all with Byzantium. There were certainly also contacts with the South Slavs (Serbians are known to have worked in Novgorod) but none can be proved with Western Europe. The best painters of the late-medieval Orthodox lands seem to have sought a tender expressivity, though in the case of Rublyov combined with *gravitas* and a pure and monumental line. There seems to be a truly classical impulse at work here, whether looking back to the nobility of Kievan art or through recent Byzantine models to a sort of refined Hellenistic legacy. The painters of 15th-century Russia seemed to share a common interest in unnaturalistic but often dramatic effects of light, notably in scenes such as the Transfiguration and the Descent into Hell; it is reasonable to see in this an effect of Hesychast mysticism.

Icon painters had singular opportunities in the early 15th century as a result of the development of the iconostasis, a wooden screen closing off the altar area of a church and clad with tiers of icons, often life-size or greater. The central tier (the "Deisis") represented holy figures interceding with Christ on behalf of the worshipers. The iconostasis as a gallery of representations of saints compares with the great sculpted portals of Western medieval cathedrals, while the opening and closing of its central doors enhance the drama of the liturgy. The impact of the whole ambience is increased by the frescoes covering all interior walls and ceilings. Good 14th- to 15th-century examples of these survive, though fragmentarily, in Novgorod (World War II took a heavy toll here), and include paintings by Theophanes. There are wall paintings by Rublyov in the Dormition Cathedral at Vladimir. A small number of very fine illuminated gospel books

of the period have been attributed to the circles of both artists.

Inevitably, the literature of the period, distanced by its language, cannot have the immediacy or universality of the great icons, but it is not negligible. Chronicle writing continued to flourish: a notable example is the early 15th-century Trinity Chronicle compiled in St Sergius's Trinity Monastery, a comprehensive work that attempts to speak from an all-Russian perspective. Grand Prince Dmitriy Donskoy of Moscow inspired two unusual works. One was a highly poeticized *Life*; the other, extant in several versions, celebrates the victory at Kulikovo in 1380 and is usually called *Zadonshchina* ("What happened across the Don"). This work quotes and skillfully adapts the *Igor Tale* of 200 years before.

The finest writer of the time is known to us by name: Yepifaniy Premudry (Epiphanios the Wise), a monk who personally knew St Sergius and wrote his *Life*, and that of Stephen of Perm, soon after their deaths, doubtless with a view to bringing about their canonization. Both works are long (over 100 pages) and intricate in construction: unfortunately all extant variants of the *Life of Sergius* have been demonstrably reedited and tampered with in the interests of Muscovite propaganda in the 15th century, but the *Life of Stephen* is intact. Yepifaniy describes his own literary method as "braiding of words," and though set out as prose, the *Life*, or much of it, is probably best read as poetry—full of rhythmic and sonorous devices, rhyme and alliteration, neologisms, rhetorical figures, structural echoes. The effect is highly emotionalized yet it and the *Life of Sergius* also pack much interesting factual narrative into the texture. Both works are

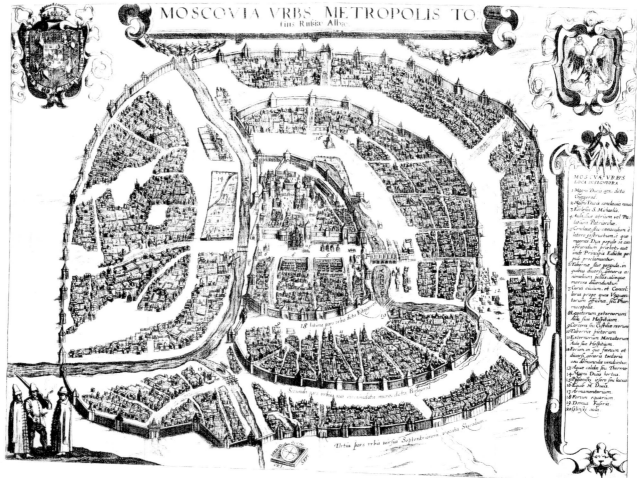

really highly elaborate verbal "icons," whose purpose is to move the emotions and the soul, and so to instill veneration. It has been a commonplace of Russian literary histories to ascribe this remarkable manner of writing to South Slavonic immigrants into Russia, refugees from the Ottoman conquest of the Balkans. Though some such immigrants are known, notably the learned Metropolitan Kiprian, and though they certainly influenced a movement towards the refurbishment of Church Slavonic as a pan-Slavonic literary medium, Yepifaniy's style and concept of literature have turned out on analysis to be highly original and, as it emerges, inimitable: his methods were simply vulgarized by his successors, notably the 15th-century immigrant Pakhomy the Serb. These two *Lives* are undoubtedly the best literary relics of the short but productive period (roughly, the reigns of Dmitriy Donskoy and Vasiliy I), that represents what D. S. Likhachov has termed the Orthodox "Pre-Renaissance." It is possible to view this as the "Sergievan" period of Russian civilization, centered on St Sergius's Trinity Monastery, before Moscow finally tightened its grip on all areas of Russian cultural as well as political life, and brought all possibility of any full Renaissance to a halt.

Ivan III and the triumph of Muscovy

Muscovite Russia—known in the West as Muscovy, and implying the free, unitary Russian state with Moscow as its undisputed capital—was the creation of one man: Grand Prince Ivan III, sometimes known as "the Great." Yet even a great mover of historical events can be very much a child of his times; it is far from clear that Ivan thought in categories that differed essentially from those of his predecessors and contemporaries, or that he saw the novel implications of the goals he strove so hard to achieve. It is very hard to say anything definite about his motives, beliefs or personality: the evidence that survives is generally of a most formal or official kind. He was at least tenacious, since he does not seem to have wavered in his aims even when he had to move slowly and circumspectly towards their realization. We can also guess that childhood experience of civil war left a legacy of suspiciousness. There was a long-drawn-out dynastic crisis towards the end of his reign, when Ivan's favor was withdrawn from his eldest surviving son, Vasiliy, in favor of his grandson by an earlier marriage, Dmitriy, but later restored. Historians have floundered in the interpretation of this important power game. Did Ivan vacillate? Behave capriciously? What personal factors were involved? Did Vasiliy, Dmitriy and their respective mothers represent identifiable social or religious factions? The evidence is simply not there.

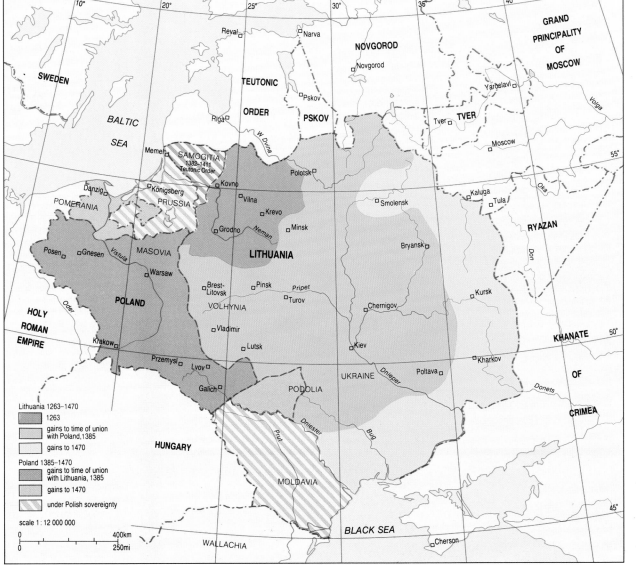

Left: West Russia: the growth of Poland and Lithuania.
At the same time as Moscow was increasing in power in the 14th and 15th centuries, its arch-rival, the Grand Duchy of Lithuania, was expanding over huge tracts of land to the west. Lithuania grew from a confederation of pagan tribes formed under King Mindovg (d. 1264) to fight off the Teutonic Knights who were advancing on Lithuanian territory through eastern Prussia. In the century following the Tatar invasions of 1237–40, the old south Russian principalities such as Kiev and Chernigov fell easy prey to Lithuanian expansionism under energetic empire-builders such as Gediminas (ruled 1316–39), who took Kiev in 1321 and founded his own capital of Vilnius two years later. Algirdas (ruled 1345–77) bequeathed to his son Jagiello an empire covering over 900 000 square kilometers and containing many Orthodox Christian subjects.

Under the Union of Krevo (1385) Lithuania made a dynastic alliance with Poland and officially accepted Roman Catholicism. The confessional difference further exacerbated the antagonism between the Orthodox Muscovites and their acquisitive western neighbors. Ivan III's protracted struggle with Lithuania eventually turned the tide in Moscow's favor at the start of the 16th century, though both Kiev and Smolensk remained within Lithuania's borders for some years more.

Map legend:

Lithuania 1263–1470
- 1263
- gains to time of union with Poland, 1385
- gains to 1470

Poland 1385–1470
- gains to time of union with Lithuania, 1385
- gains to 1470
- under Polish sovereignty

scale 1: 12 000 000

0 — 400km
0 — 250mi

Above Muscovite embassies excited the unbridled curiosity of Western Europeans, who were much taken with their participants' fine robes, outlandish hats and unfamiliar manners. This early woodcut (1576) by Michael Peterle shows an ambassadorial procession of boyars to the Austrian Emperor Maximilian II, followed by merchants carrying furs. Members of Russian embassies generally had no cash, and maintained themselves by fur sales as best they could while abroad.

In the event Vasiliy succeeded to the throne, and continued his father's policies. He was in turn succeeded by Ivan IV "the Terrible," who put his stamp on the 16th century as his grandfather had on the 15th. Between them, over a total of 94 years, the two Ivans established a society whose institutions were so powerful that even the extinction of the Ryurikid dynasty in 1598, and the subsequent anarchy of the "Time of Troubles," did not prevent its reinstatement under the Romanovs in 1613—as a complete anachronism on the European scene, since times had moved on—and its survival for another century. Peter the Great was paradoxically the last great Muscovite ruler in both his major goals and many of his methods, and genuinely admired his strong-minded Muscovite predecessors.

Ivan III's fundamental aim was the restoration of his full patrimonial authority as Grand Prince "of all Russia" (often mistranslated in the West as "of all the Russias"), which implied vigorous attention to the strength, security, independence and prestige of his realm. These in their turn had many more implications: a protracted struggle against the expansionist pretensions of the Grand Duchy of Lithuania, by this time in dynastic alliance with Catholic Poland; the ostentatious upholding both of Orthodoxy and of his own sovereign title; careful diplomacy with foreign powers that might lend their weight to the struggle; the concentration of all forces in the non-Lithuanian territories (that is, northern, eastern and central Russia) into the hands of the grand prince; the casting off of the last vestiges of subjection to the Golden Horde; the marshaling of all sections of society into the purposeful organism that historians have called the Muscovite "service state." This was a considerable agenda, even for a reign of 43 years.

The Golden Horde proved the least of Ivan's worries. Russia's 240-year subjection to the Tatars ended not with a bang, but a whimper: what might have been a bloody showdown in the autumn of 1480 ended with a Russian and a Tatar army confronting each other across the River Ugra, southwest of Moscow, and, after staring at each other for

some days, simply going their separate ways. Ivan ceased to pay tribute to the Horde, but did not stop gathering it from his countrymen, merely diverting it to his own purposes. Several decades before the non-event on the Ugra the Moscow princes had already been subverting Tatar power by taking "dissident" Tatar nobles into their service, with or without conversion to Orthodoxy. Ivan III's father, Vasiliy II, had even set up a small vassal Tatar principality at Kasimov on the Oka, ruled by Kasim, a descendant of Genghis Khan. In certain respects the Muscovite rulers apparently saw themselves as heirs to the khan (just as some Kievan rulers had been dubbed *kagan*). In a bizarre episode in Ivan IV's reign, a Kasimov ruler, Semyon Bekbulatovich, would officially (if jocularly) be made tsar of Russia for a few months in 1575–76.

The crushing of Novgorod

Ivan III faced a much tougher and more invidious task in settling accounts with those of his Russian compatriots who did not accept his title to supreme authority over the Russian lands, or whom he at least perceived as a threat to his supremacy. Chief among them were the Novgorodians and Tverians, or at least their ruling circles. The suppression of Novgorod in 1478 is the most notorious single act of Ivan's reign. Novgorod's political situation had long been a balancing act. Although acknowledging the theoretical supremacy of the grand prince —and hiring as its own princes members of the Ryurikid family—the Novgorodians maintained complete practical independence through their development of city-state institutions and efficient management of their huge territories. In the *veche* or assembly (which anybody could summon by the ringing of a great bell) the citizens held ultimate authority, but this large and argumentative body could not make day-to-day decisions. These were left to an oligarchic council and elected officials: the mayor, the head of the city militia and the archbishop (also a city appointment).

In the earlier part of the Tatar period Novgorod, with its wealth, geographical seclusion and smooth

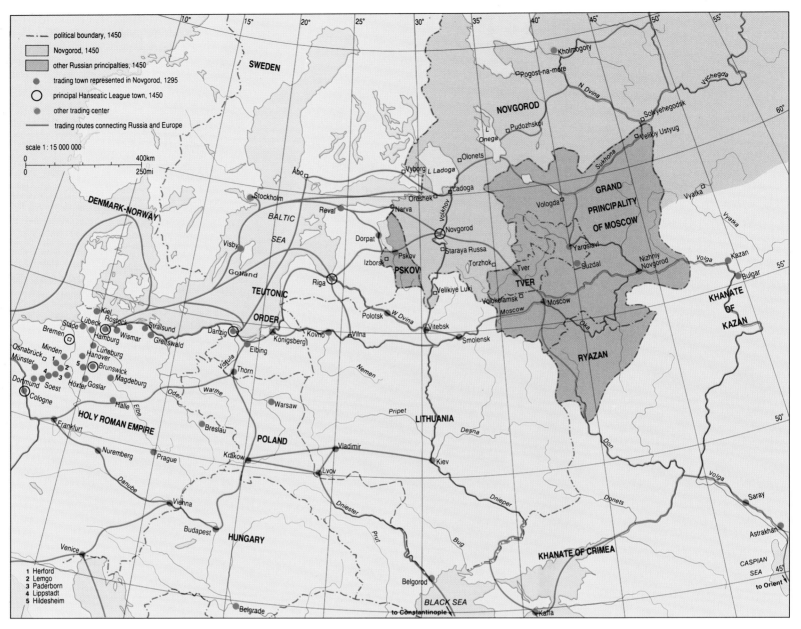

functioning, must have seemed unassailable. By the mid-15th century the situation was dangerously fluid. With the slackening of the Tatar grip and the polarization of the Russian heritage between Moscow and Lithuania, Novgorodian aloofness was becoming harder to maintain. Vasiliy II made a demonstration of authority in 1456 when he scored a military victory over the city and fined it for backing the wrong side at a late stage of the Moscow civil war. Thereafter Novgorod could not treat independently with foreign powers and had to use the grand prince's seal. Nevertheless it preserved its institutions, and it seems that neither Vasiliy II nor, at first, Ivan III intended to extinguish them.

However, as so often in city-states, rivalry between the wealthiest families (from whom the mayor usually came) and the mass of townsfolk was becoming steadily greater. The economic position too was shaky: the Hanseatic League, of which Novgorod was the important eastern terminus, was by now siphoning off ever more of the profits of Novgorod trade, since Novgorod merchants had largely stopped shipping their goods. Simultaneously the bottom had dropped out of the European squirrel fur market. Above all, Nov-

gorod, still richer and probably more populous than Moscow (a figure of 30 000 inhabitants is the usual estimate), had two great handicaps: it could neither reliably defend itself, nor feed itself. For its army it had only its imported prince and his retainers, together with a small city militia. As for food, the Novgorod climate (adequate only for growing flax and hemp) was marginal even for the hardy cereals, rye and oats. In the frequent years of bad harvests, Novgorod was fatally dependent on grain shipments from middle Russia, which could be cut off by whoever controlled the rivers and portages.

In the years after 1456 the Novgorodian leaders, notable among them the tough-minded Marfa Boretskaya, widow of a mayor, made the fatal mistake of parleying with Lithuania. Ivan sent a punitive expedition in 1471, but gave the city a last chance to recognize his authority. Equivocation and panic sealed the Novgorodians' fate. Ivan proved to be extremely touchy about the exact title by which the Novgorodians would recognize him, and when slighted besieged the city in 1478, demanded the abolition of all its separate institutions, and hauled off the *veche* bell to Moscow. He exiled the archbishop, who was replaced subsequently by a Moscow strongman, Gennadiy, and confiscated large amounts of church land.

In addition to these confiscations, some thousands of the better-off Novgorod citizens were forcibly deported during the 1480s to other parts of Russia. They were replaced by a smaller number of Ivan's servitors, whose somewhat larger estates were intended to be sufficiently remunerative for them to equip themselves for military service. Most significantly, they were not granted outright title to the land, as had been normal up to then (a tenure known as *votchina,* patrimony), but only for their lifetimes, and conditionally upon their satisfactory performance of duties. Some 1·2 million hectares were disposed of in this manner, and the new system, known as *pomestye,* was quickly extended. Under Ivan III's successors even *votchina* holders had to serve, under threat of expropriation: they were better off than *pomestniki* only insofar as they could sell their land or bequeath it in their wills. In Muscovy there was only one true, unconditional *votchina* left: Russia itself, over which the ruler had what the Romans termed *dominium,* unfettered right of disposal.

The system of land tenure in 15th-century Muscovy may seem arcane, yet it is the chief foundation of the practices and one of the foundations of the ideology—of the Muscovite realm, a source of both its strengths and its weaknesses. It affected the attitudes of the tsars towards their lands and subjects up to Nicholas II. It equally affected their attitude to the international scene and promoted the arrogance for which the Muscovite monarchy was also noted. A letter from Ivan IV to Queen Elizabeth of England (1570) complains that he had assumed she was truly sovereign, "but now we perceive that there be other men that do rule," that is, that she recognized that her subjects had rights. The use of land, that apparently limitless resource in a state otherwise far from wealthy, as reward for service long outlived Muscovy, continuing throughout the 18th century. Moreover the exploitation of the land—for trapping, mining, manufacturing, distilling, salt-working and so on—was also generally regarded as a royal prerogative, even if farmed out into private hands.

It was not only because of the consequent institution of *pomestye* that the sack of Novgorod is a great punctuation mark in Russian history. Novgorod represented "the possible other case," an authentic part of Russia that shared the same Kievan and pre-Kievan antecedents as its rivals Muscovy and Lithuania, yet grew into a society more attractive than either to modern minds: it commanded the loyalty rather than the fear of its citizens, was freedom-loving, relatively democratic, famously resourceful and hardworking, tolerant in its law code and penal practice, artistically prolific. It was also a "window on the West," like its successor St Petersburg, past whose site Novgorod merchants once used to sail. Ivan III closed the shutters by ejecting the Hanseatic merchants in the 1490s. The suppression of Novgorod was ruthless in itself, though understandable in terms of Ivan's fear of Lithuanian power, but it was made more ominous by the forced deportations that accompanied it. In Muscovy human life and dignity were held cheap, and people became adjuncts to the land; in such an atmosphere the gradual institution

of serfdom during the 16th century could take place almost unnoticed. It started with the occasional, then regular, abrogation of the peasants' traditional right to change their employment during the two weeks around St George's day in November; the motive was to ensure that land would have the necessary hands to work it.

With the sack of Novgorod the "gathering-in" of the Russian lands became more like a mopping-up operation. Tver, Moscow's old rival, capitulated in 1485: its last independent prince had turned desperately to Lithuania, while his boyars, sensing the need to salvage what they could, flocked to Moscow. Ivan, whose first wife had been a Tverian princess, treated it relatively leniently. There remained two other lesser city-states with free institutions that followed the Novgorod pattern. One was Pskov, an ally of Moscow, on which it relied for military support against the German Baltic colonists. The other, a remarkable offshoot of Novgorod's farthest domains, was Vyatka, a large but thinly populated land of hunters and freebooters in the far northeast, with traditions as libertarian as Novgorod's, if not more so. The Vyatkans were quite ready to make common cause with their neighbors, the Kazan Tatars, against Moscow, and Ivan suppressed them, again with deportations, in 1489. At the end of Ivan III's reign only two independent Russian lands remained: Pskov, the buffer-territory to the west, and a truncated principality of Ryazan, performing the same function at the eastern steppe fringe. Vasiliy III finished them off in 1510 and 1520 respectively, deporting Pskovians and the *veche* bell as his father had done in Novgorod, if less brutally, despite Pskov's traditional friendship with Moscow.

Lithuania was a harder nut to crack. Ivan moved cautiously and craftily. At one stage he married off his daughter to the Lithuanian grand duke, apparently in the hope of establishing a political and religious foothold in the Lithuanian court. He regained several border territories, though not the chief prize of Smolensk. The continued existence of an independent Lithuania was, however, a greater danger to the Muscovite political system than mere questions of territory would suggest. The oldest and most stubbornly maintained right of the upper class of the Old Russian principalities was that of free service: at a moment's notice the servitor was entitled to transfer his allegiance to another prince. With the "gathering-in" of Russia there was no one but the Moscow grand prince left to serve, except for Lithuania, Moscow's deadly rival. Not surprisingly, from Ivan III's time departure from Moscow's service began to be regarded as treason. Suddenly the aristocrats of Russia found themselves as defenseless as peasants or even slaves against the ruler's whims. There was no "feudal contract," as in Western Europe, whereby the stronger as well as the weaker party pledged himself to observe certain obligations. It is significant that Western Europeans in 16th-century Muscovy often particularly noted the self-abasement of the boyars and service class generally before the ruler. A late and most dramatic defection from Muscovy took place in the 1560s, when Ivan IV's successful commander and personal friend, Prince Andrey Kurbsky, went over to Lithuania. This event, which gave rise to a long correspondence between

Novgorod was a crucial trading post between Viking, Slavonic and Finnic peoples from the 9th century, if not earlier. The name means "New Town," "new" perhaps in comparison with the older settlement of Ladoga. Between the 12th and 15th centuries Novgorod enjoyed effective independence as the northernmost of the great European city-states, more or less democratically ruled, controlling vast tracts of northern territory as far as the Urals; this so-called "empire" was exploited for the fur trade by the five *kontsy* ("ends" or "wards") into which the city itself was divided. Major trade routes ran from Novgorod eastwards to the Volga basin, southwards to Kiev (and ultimately Constantinople) and westwards to Sweden and the lands of the Holy Roman empire. Novgorod was the terminus of the Hanseatic League and had its own important entrepôt on Gotland (where probably Novgorodian fresco paintings survive). Two Novgorod cities—Pskov to the southwest and Vyatka in the east—became independent in the late Middle Ages until forcibly incorporated, like Novgorod itself, into Muscovy.

Ivan the Terrible

The image of Ivan IV "the Terrible" (Russian *Grozny*, properly "Awe-inspiring") has for many people been formed by Eisenstein's movies (1943–46). This is no bad thing: Eisenstein, working under an autocrat— Stalin—who partly modeled himself on Ivan, matches Ivan in his ambiguities, his mixed nobility and grotesquerie, suppressed panic and laghter.

Ivan encompassed rational political aims (particularly the strengthening of the Muscovite service state by an assault on the old aristocracy and promotion of new men) through increasingly irrational and unpredictable means as his long reign (1533–84) progressed. An extraordinary "masquerade" quality characterized his actions and self-image (there are remarkable parallels with Peter I). Full of ill-directed intellectual energy, he produced copious correspondence in an inimitable histrionic style. Foreigners were impressed by his learning and quick wit. Despite the real psychological and physical damage he did to Russia, his folk image is generally admiring, as upholder of Russia's interests, unity, traditions and piety. But his Muscovy was already a rigid, ideologically hidebound, unprogressive and hazardous place, outwardly excessively ordered, underneath simmering with discontent.

Above Ivan IV's great state seal. The crowned double-headed eagle is of Byzantine origin. representing Old and New Rome; on it is superimposed a shield with the Moscow emblem of St George. Twelve seals of principalities incorporated into Muscovy, together with the Orthodox cross, surround it; the inscription round the rim records Ivan's full titles.

Right In 1564 Ivan IV suddenly withdrew to the small town of Aleksandrov, 100 kilometers northeast of Moscow, and threatened to abdicate. He made his resumption of rule conditional upon being able to punish his enemies at will and to set up the *oprichnina*. The central corps of *oprichniki*, when not out devastating the countryside, lived a pseudo-monastic life centered on Aleksandrov. In this contemporary drawing they are shown feasting in the presence of the tsar, as they did every morning at 10.

Above A miniature from the illustrated chronicle of Nikon (15th century), shows the building of a new palace in Moscow to house Ivan IV's *oprichniki*. The tsar himself monitors progress from inside a fancifully depicted Kremlin.

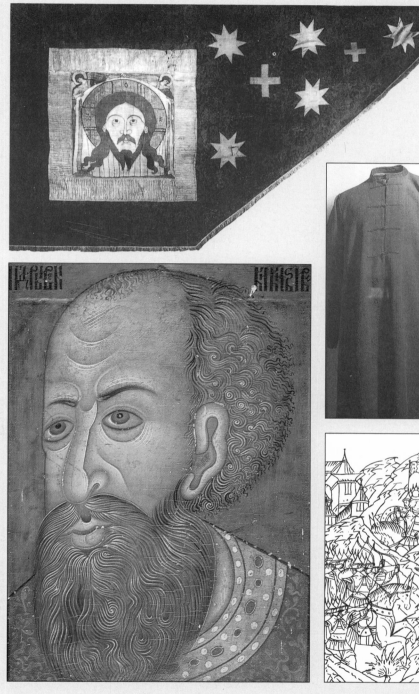

Below The main banner of Ivan IV's troops at the siege of the city of Kazan: it can also be seen depicted imaginatively in the background of the miniature of the siege (*bottom right*). It carries a representation of an icon of the face of Christ—the traditional "first icon."

Above Portraits of individuals, usually commemorative, are known in Russia from the later 16th century; they are at first completely within the traditions of icon-painting, though some attempt at individualization is made. This iconic depiction on a wooden panel of Ivan IV (probably early 17th century) is now in Copenhagen.

Above right The capture of Kazan (1552) was the most significant military success of Ivan IV's early years. Kazan was the most powerful successor state to the Tatar Golden Horde: its strategic location on the middle Volga made it the gateway to south and east, its capture opened up Siberia and the Urals to Russia. This miniature shows Ivan's new force of *streltsy* using firearms against the Kazan Tatar cavalry, with the city to left; Ivan and his mounted retainers are in the background.

Top One of the strangest and socially most disruptive episodes of Ivan IV's reign was the creation of a separate "realm-within-the-realm," the *oprichnina* ("place apart"; 1564–72). A parallel administration was set up and the *oprichnina* handed over to a mounted force, the *oprichniki*, empowered to destroy the tsar's enemies. In parody of monks, they dressed uniformly in black: this is one such surviving garment.

the two, probably helped to unbalance Ivan's personality. It signalled the total subjection of the boyar class, which had grown in numbers with the absorption of so many old principalities into Moscow and might well have proved a counterweight to autocracy.

Orthodoxy and heterodoxy

A series of religious and ideological problems, issues and initiatives accompanied the birth of the Muscovite system; these were generally interlinked. Two serious heresies arose, in the late 14th and late 15th centuries: the "Shearers" (*Strigolniki*) and "Judaizers" (*Zhidovstvuyushchie*). Both spread from Novgorod, suggesting possible connections with Western European pre-Reformation movements, though the influence of the eastern Bogomils may have also reached Russia from the Balkans. Both seem to have been rationalistic and anti-hierarchical, but beyond that it is hard to characterize their beliefs, since both were suppressed and are known largely from their opponents' attacks. The second was the more successful movement, even gaining a foothold in Moscow in the grand prince's entourage. In the spirit of the times, it was eventually dealt with more harshly, its leaders being burned after long hesitation on Ivan's part. Gennadiy, the tough Muscovite archbishop of Novgorod, had urged Ivan to follow the example of the Spanish Inquisition. More peaceably, he commissioned the first full Russian Bible to counter the heretics' scriptural knowledge.

The Orthodox Church proper meanwhile had its own problems and was developing its own idiosyncrasies. Some of these were a legacy from the great eremitical and monastic movement initiated by St Sergius in the 14th century. Its tradition of contemplative Hesychast spirituality was articulated and carried farther by some notable figures in Ivan III's and Vasiliy III's reigns: these include St Nil Sorsky ("of the Sora River," d. 1509), his successor Vassian Patrikeyev and their followers the "Trans-Volga Elders" (with hermitages in the northern forests). They were dubbed "Non-Possessors" from their argument that monasteries should be free of worldly encumbrances. An opposing position was held by St Joseph of Volokolamsk (Iosif Volotsky, d. 1519); it supported the integration of monastic and everyday life, church patronage of the arts and large landholdings (the wealth from which would allow the monasteries to perform good works). These two divergent positions sharpened into a conflict that had a political dimension, since "non-possession" implied separation of religious and secular affairs, while the "Possessors" saw the ruler as protector of the church, and the latter as closely enmeshed with the state. In 1503 a church council decided in favor of the "Josephites," the Possessors; this is not surprising in view of the whole drift towards centralized autocracy of the Muscovite state, in which the "Non-Possessors," spiritual opters-out, were an anomaly. Subsequently their followers were persecuted, yet their general spirit was harder to eradicate. Much that remained individualistic about Russian Orthodoxy, such as the many wandering "holy men," including the "fools in Christ" who become prominent in the 16th century, is outside the "Josephite" tradition.

Some historians see the Russian Church as no more than an arm of government, completely controlled by the ruler after 1503, a situation termed by Toynbee "Caesaropapism." The concept is not really valid: the Russian ruler never took a "high-priestly" role, and in the last resort could face sanctions by the church, however closely it would normally cooperate with him. At the height of Ivan IV's irrational terrorism, the Metropolitan Philip courageously reproached him, and lost his life for it; actually ecclesiastical leaders seem more often to have exercised an influence in Muscovite state affairs than vice versa. But clearly Ivan III saw himself in a special role as protector of Orthodoxy, if not from choice, then through circumstances. Constantinople had fallen to the Turks in 1453. When Russia threw off the Tatars, it became the only important free Orthodox nation. From Ivan's viewpoint the religious threat from the West was equally serious: the breach between the two halves of Christendom, hugely widened with the crusaders' sack of Constantinople in 1204, was made obvious to all by the failure of the Council of Florence in the 1430s, both events leaving a legacy of great bitterness.

With the fall of Constantinople a bizarre theory, apparently hatched in the Slavonic Balkans, became current in Russia: that Moscow had become the "Third Rome" (to supersede Constantinople, "New Rome"), "and a fourth there shall not be"; it would represent the convergence of all the Christian realms and "shine to the ends of the earth." This formulation of the doctrine comes in a famous letter of 1515 from the monk Filofey of Pskov to Vasiliy III, but many decades before that it had been applied to Moscow's rival, Tver. In any case Ivan and Vasiliy soon started building up their outward and visible signs of prestige, from the emblem of the double-headed Byzantine eagle to the propagation of texts that purported to give their dynasty a Roman pedigree and Byzantine regalia. Increasingly elaborate and comprehensive titles were adopted, culminating when the young Ivan IV became the first Russian ruler to be crowned "tsar": the title, deriving from "Caesar," was previously used in official Russian sources to refer to the Byzantine emperor and Tatar great khan. Further prestige accrued to Ivan III from his marriage, after the death of his first wife, to Zoe (renamed in Russia Sophia) Palaiologina, niece of the last Byzantine emperor, Constantine XI. Since the bride had been brought up in Italy, the Vatican took considerable interest in the match; but Ivan, concerned to recover his own patrimony, was deaf to blandishments, even when they suggested an anti-Turkish alliance that might have put him on the throne of a reconquered Constantinople.

The Italian connection, however, produced a still visible result: the rebuilding of the main structures of the Moscow Kremlin in appropriately grand style. Muscovite builders, who had had plenty of experience over the previous century, started the construction of the greatest Kremlin cathedral, dedicated to the Dormition, but they mixed the mortar badly, and there was a collapse. Ivan called in a team of experts from Pskov, who diagnosed the trouble and stayed to design several buildings in the Moscow area. The Dormition itself, however, was entrusted to the Italian engin-

eer "Aristotele" Fioravanti, who remained in Russia from 1475 to 1479, went to study the great 12th-century Dormition Cathedral in Vladimir and succeeded in designing a building that, while grandiose and novel in several respects, was thoroughly Russian in conception and detail. Other Italians arrived over the course of the next 30 years, and we can still see their handiwork in the Faceted Palace, the brick walls with their swallowtail Italianate battlements and, last of all (1505 onwards), the grand Archangel Cathedral with its High Renaissance detailing but Byzantine ground plan.

Ivan IV "the Terrible"

A break with Byzantine architectural precedent was marked by one of the greatest, or most astonishing, of Muscovite buildings, the Church of the Ascension at the royal palace of Kolomenskoye outside Moscow: it is a great brick spire, probably representing a reinterpretation in masonry of a wooden design. It was built in 1530 to celebrate the birth of an heir to the long-childless Vasiliy III, the future Ivan IV "the Terrible" (*grozny*, properly "Awe-inspiring"). His father died when Ivan was three, and his mother, Yelena Glinskaya, was declared regent. A chaotic period ensued, in which the child-tsar was endangered and humiliated, his mother died, possibly poisoned (in 1538) and his boyars proved themselves self-seeking and unreliable. It is curious that Ivan's great predecessor, Ivan III (during the Moscow civil war), and later Peter I, also had similarly alarming, maybe traumatizing experiences in childhood. Each was highly, perhaps morbidly suspicious in later life of treasonable plots, and it is not unreasonable to see a cause in the early violence and uncertainty that surrounded them.

Ivan IV's long reign is the most characteristically "Muscovite" of periods: Moscow's centralization of Russia's resources under a regime of, apparently, complete stability was most clearly realized during it. Yet it was also, much of the time, a period of prolonged crisis, and Russia took a couple of generations to recover from its effects. It is hard to ascribe this crisis to anything other than the tsar's own personality, though he would have blamed his untrustworthy servitors. The course of the reign, sometimes intricate or mysterious, is clear enough on a large scale: it had a "good" half and a "bad" half, of roughly equal length, with the division coming in the early 1560s. Although we can get a far better idea of Ivan's personality than of any of his predecessors', it is still hard to judge how far this dislocation in his reign is the result of mental unbalance, or how far the threats he perceived almost everywhere had any rational basis. His reign began with superabundant promise, ending in failure and disillusion on almost every count.

In 1547 Ivan suddenly decided the time had come for his coronation, a ceremony of great pomp. His personal rule began, and he made his first and happiest marriage to Anastasia, who came from a family that was later to play such a significant role: the Romanovs. With a council of enlightened advisers, including the Metropolitan Makariy, he instituted a series of reforms and had them approved by a popular assembly, the *zemskiy sobor*. They included promulgation of a law code (1550) and a great church council (1551). Then

Above Italian architects and engineers worked on a variety of structures in the Moscow Kremlin over the course of 30 years. The last and most ornate of these was the Cathedral of the Archangel Michael (1505), burial church of the tsars. It was designed by Alevisio Novy ("the New"), who also worked for the Crimean khan at Bakhchisaray on his way. It popularized various Renaissance exterior decorative motifs in Russia; heavy cornices, pilasters with capitals, scallop shells in gable ends. The portals (this is the north doorway) are elaborately carved in low relief on limestone. Inside, the cathedral remains Old Russian in its forms.

Left The smallest of the main Kremlin cathedrals, that of the Annunciation, was rebuilt in the mid-16th century after a fire. Some experts believe that two tiers of the fine icon screen may have been saved and reassembled from the building painted in 1405 by Theophanes and his team (including Rublyov). The screen is here glimpsed from the surrounding gallery through the west portal, of carved and painted limestone in the manner of Alevisio (and even more elaborate); the floor is of semiprecious stone from the Urals.

came regularization of the gentry's service requirements and a reorganization of the army, including the inauguration of an up-to-date corps of musketeers, *streltsy*.

In the wars that followed, the Russians achieved some remarkable successes. The two Tatar relict kingdoms controlling the Volga, Kazan and Astrakhan, fell in 1552 and 1556: not only did Ivan thus greatly increase his territory and prestige, gaining two populous cities with their fisheries, trade and agriculture, but he opened the doorway to Siberia and the east. In 1558–63 considerable gains were made in the west against the Germans of the Livonian Order (successors to the Teutonic Knights) and it seemed only a matter of time before Russia would have unfettered access to the Baltic. Meanwhile Ivan recruited foreigners to work in Russia, and in 1553, by a remarkable stroke of fate, encountered Richard Chancellor, captain of an English ship washed up on the coast of the White Sea while seeking a northern passage to the Indies. Trade links with England through what soon became the great Russian port of Archangel, at the mouth of the Northern Dvina, were set up: cities between Archangel and Moscow, such as Yaroslavl, prospered. To exploit this windfall, the English established the first ever joint-stock company, and they retained for years a near-monopoly of Russian trade. The 16th-century English trading house and embassy in Moscow has recently been unearthed.

The style and atmosphere of Ivan's reign changed dramatically after the sudden death of Anastasia in 1560. Ivan was shattered and thought she had been poisoned. He broke with his council and turned on those closest to him with great savagery. Prince Kurbsky and some others wisely defected abroad. Ivan's character, studious, intelligent and eager as a boy, became more and more subject to fits of rage and equally unpredictable remorse, prone to superstition, blasphemy and extreme piety. In 1564 the most remarkable episode in his reign began. First, without warning, he retreated to a monastery in the small town of Aleksandrov, 100 kilometers northeast of Moscow. He then wrote to the metropolitan, abdicating the throne, denouncing his aristocracy but praising the common people. The bluff, if such it was, worked: a stunned populace begged him to resume the throne, on whatever conditions he might set. This he did, on condition that he could punish whomsoever he wished and set up a separate realm-within-the-realm, to be managed at his own discretion.

This extraordinary institution, known as the *oprichnina,* "the place apart," was a mosaic of estates, towns and even parts of Moscow, interlocking with the *zemshchina,* "country," in a giant jigsaw puzzle, with parallel administrations. Little is known of the workings of this scheme, for lack of surviving documents, but it is notorious that Ivan instituted in the *oprichnina a* reign of terror, manned by a force of bullies known as the *oprichniki* charged with destroying the tsar's enemies. Among many acts of savagery, the worst was the massacre of the Novgorodians (descendants in the main of Muscovite settlers drafted in by Ivan III) on an unfounded rumor that they were negotiating with Poland. In 1572 the *oprichnina* was abruptly

abolished, probably because of a devastating raid the previous year by the Crimean Tatars, who had even reached an unprepared Moscow. Meanwhile the war in the west dragged on, going from bad to worse. Sweden joined in, and eventually, by treaties in the early 1580s, Russia had to give up its gains of 20 years before. All hope of a port on the Baltic was lost until the time of Peter the Great.

On Ivan IV's death in 1584, probably from poisoning, his second son Fyodor came to the throne. Fyodor was pious and unassertive, but his chief minister and brother-in-law, Boris Godunov, of partly Tatar descent, was a "new man" of great ability. Fyodor's reign at last saw some military successes again. Domestically it was notable for the upgrading of the head of the Russian Church to the rank of patriarch, on equal terms with the five ancient patriarchates (Rome, Constantinople, Antioch, Alexandria, Jerusalem).

Fyodor, the last of the Ryurikid dynasty, died childless in 1598, and the country faced an unprecedented succession crisis. Another son of Ivan IV, Dmitriy, had indeed survived him, but died in 1591 at the age of nine in the out-of-the-way town of Uglich. To this day the circumstances of his death are completely unclear, but at the time rumors started that Boris, ambitious to gain the throne himself, had had Dmitriy murdered. Since Boris could not at that time have known that Fyodor would die without heir, the rumor is *prima facie* improbable, but it was to have disastrous consequences for Russia. Boris was duly elected to the vacant throne, to the annoyance of old boyar families such as the Shuyskys. The subsequent events are well known from Pushkin's play and Musorgsky's opera. Boris's reign (1598–1605) witnessed a series of disasters, in particular crop failure and famine. Though he attempted enlightened measures (which included sending a batch of students to Western Europe, one of whom settled in England and became an Anglican country parson) and revived building activity, he could not retain popular support. A pretender claiming to be the miraculously saved Dmitriy appeared in Poland, and advanced upon Moscow with a motley army that grew despite defeats. Boris suddenly died, his young son, Fyodor II, was lynched and "False Dmitriy" was acclaimed tsar. This was the beginning of nearly a decade of the Time of Troubles *(smuta).*

The Time of Troubles

Dmitriy, whether or not he believed in his own authenticity, proved a capable ruler. However, the Moscow boyars, for whom he had served his purpose in toppling Boris's family, no longer supported him, and he made the mistake of marrying a Pole, Marina Mniszek, occasioning widespread unpopularity. He was unseated in a boyar rebellion, killed and his ashes fired from a cannon in the direction of Poland. Vasiliy Shuysky became tsar (1606–10) but without much general support. In the last year of his reign, before he was deposed by a Moscow assembly, Russia was in turmoil, with no acknowledged authority. Only the soldier Prince Skopin-Shuysky could hold the country together, but he died suddenly. The next couple of years saw Swedish and Polish claimants for the throne. A second "False Dmitriy," bizarrely recognized as

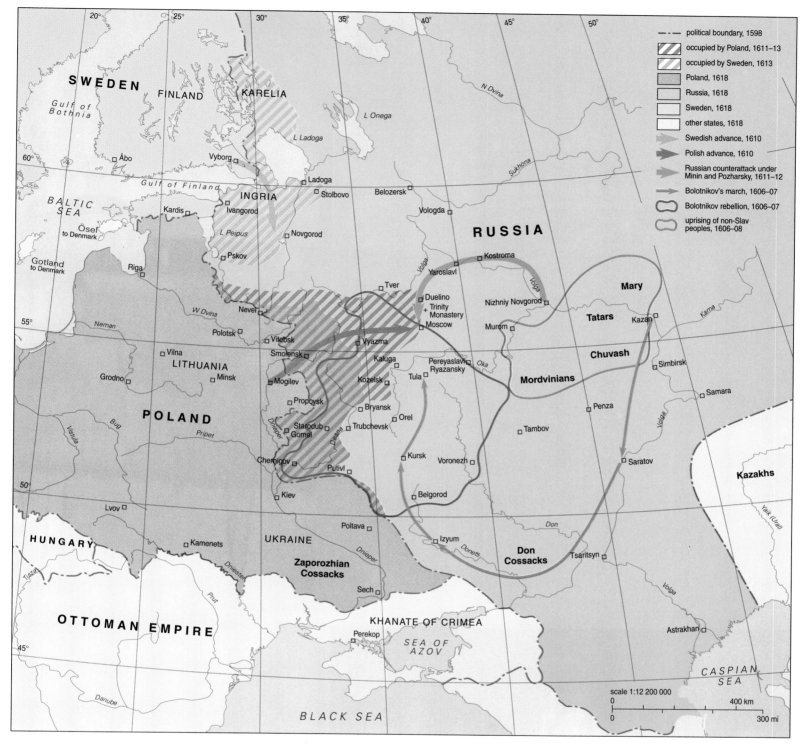

Left A stylized portrait of Boris Godunov (tsar 1598–1605) with regalia. Boris—of partly Tatar descent, and not from a traditional boyar family—was one of the "new men" who emerged in Ivan IV's reign. He was a capable chief minister to Ivan's unassertive heir, Fyodor I (1584–98). Elected tsar on the extinction of the Ryurikid dynasty, he proved a well-intentioned, intelligent but unlucky ruler: crop failures brought famine and popular discontent. Boris revived building activity (completing the great Kremlin belfry) and sent students abroad, anticipating Peter I.

authentic by Marina Mniszek, set up an alternative court and government at Tushino, just outside Moscow. He was the most successful of several pretenders. In 1610–12 a Polish garrison held Moscow: armed bands, particularly of Cossacks, roamed and terrorized the countryside. Only the great walled monasteries, notably St Sergius's Trinity Monastery, were strongholds of Russian resistance to anarchy.

Instead of falling apart completely, Russia rallied and met the challenge. It became obvious that national unity and the election of a generally acceptable Russian tsar were needed, and it was leaders of the church, the last remaining respected Russian institution, who sent out this appeal. The Russian response centered on the eastern city of Nizhniy Novgorod, where Kozma Minin, a butcher with remarkable organizational abilities, gathered a

people's army. Commanded by Prince Dmitriy Pozharsky, it ejected the Poles and created conditions in which a *zemskiy sobor* could elect a new tsar. A relative of Ivan IV's popular first wife, sixteen-year-old Mikhail Romanov, too young to have been compromised in the factionalism of the Time of Troubles, was chosen for the throne. His father, who had been forced under Tsar Boris to become a monk, was at the time a prisoner of the Poles. When a truce was negotiated he returned as the newly elected Patriarch Filaret, and became the guiding light of his young son's reign. So ended the Time of Troubles, an exhausting and devastating period, with no one social group emerging as clear "winners," but leaving behind it a strong image of the need for national unity, and a terror of anarchy and foreign intervention, that the Russians have never forgotten.

The Trinity Monastery of St Sergius

Among the great monasteries of Old Russia the Trinity Lavra (or Monastery) of St Sergius, 70 kilometers northeast of Moscow at Sergiyev Posad (Zagorsk in the Soviet period), is doubtless the most remarkable. Its large and picturesque ensemble has preserved some of Russia's greatest artistic treasures; it witnessed crucial events in Russian history; it is still an important Orthodox Church center.

Nowadays it stands by one of the great highways of Russia, but when young Sergius (born c.1321), Russia's future patron saint, retreated here from nearby Radonezh the area was trackless forest. Sergius's settlement attracted other hermits and peasant colonists, and he reluctantly accepted the position of abbot at the head of an organized monastery. By his death (1391) this had come to hold a unique position in Russian spiritual (and even political) life, as the mother foundation from which over 100 houses and hermitages were founded in ever-remoter regions of the forest zone, blazing a trail for colonization.

In the 15th century the Trinity Monastery served as an all-Russian cultural metropolis, patron of art and literature, standing above the fragmented principalities; here was compiled the best late-medieval chronicle. In 1408 it was destroyed in a Tatar punitive raid; thereafter it was rebuilt in stone, with the Trinity Cathedral that still stands. Dating from the 1420s (so within memory of Sergius's life-time), it is the earliest surviving structure at Sergiyev Posad. Each subsequent age added churches, refectories, domestic quarters, towers. Its massive walls withstood a prolonged siege during the Time of Troubles, and provided Peter I with refuge in the crisis of 1689.

Right The first view of the Trinity Monastery that meets the eye after the road or rail journey from Moscow is dramatic. Above a small valley tower the 16th-century walls, strong enough to stand an 18-month siege in 1608–10. Beyond them rises an extraordinarily picturesque skyline of the main monastic buildings—each stylistically different, blending harmoniously and vivaciously. The major buildings seen here (*central group*) are: the refectory, one of the largest and strangest "Moscow Baroque" buildings; the belfry, designed by D. Ukhtomsky (1741 onwards), that dominates the undulating countryside for miles around—freestanding and partly openwork, like many such in Russia; the great Dormition Cathedral (1550s onwards)—like much "official" Muscovite architecture a simple five-bay whitewashed cube, derived loosely from the Kremlin Dormition, relieved by its unforgettable blue and gold domes.

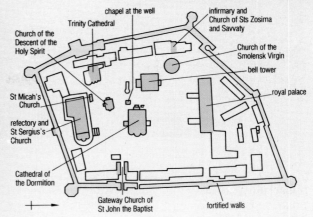

Far left The interior of the small Trinity Cathedral. The great iconostasis of the later 1420s rivals that of the Kremlin Annunciation as the most important that exists. Painted under the general direction of the elderly Rublyov, it shows a stylistic diversity testifying to the varied potential of Russian art before Muscovite centralization absorbed and homogenized local schools (notably that of Novgorod). Beside the central "royal doors" stood the most revered of Russian icons, Rublyov's *Old Testament Trinity* (see p. 72): it has been replaced with a facsimile since the original was put in the Tretyakov Gallery. The frescoes have not yet been cleaned, though it is assumed that those of Rublyov's period have not survived.

Left Two picturesque small churches in Sergiyev Posad: the Presentation of the Virgin and St Paraskeva-Pyatnitsa (both 16th century). The attractive curved roofline, so typical of pre-17th-century Russian churches, was often later replaced by a cheaper flat roof, and (as here) sometimes restored in modern times.

Above Among the smaller structures within the Trinity Monastery are this 19th-century (stylistically eclectic) open rotunda above the holy spring, and the elegant round well-chapel in the Moscow Baroque manner of the late 17th century. Over them looms the cliff-like wall of the central Dormition cathedral, beside which is the burial vault of Boris Godunov and his family.

Left Worshipers with candles inside the main Dormition cathedral. The roomy interior suggests the Moscow Dormition Cathedral, but at Sergiyev Posad there are fine 17th-century frescoes in Yaroslavl manner, bright and rather small-scale.

69

Novgorod the Great

RUSSIA

Novgorod, near the northern fringes of Old Russian settlement, was agriculturally marginal—only flax and hemp grow well there—but splendidly located for Baltic trade and the exploitation of the forest zone. Its name means "New Town" (there are several others, notably Nizhniy Novgorod "Lower New Town"); its formal title was "Lord Novgorod the Great." Founded by the 9th century, Novgorod was the main Viking foothold in early Russia and dominated trade between the Baltic, middle Russia and (via the Volga) the Near East. It developed in Kievan times into an independent city-state, controlling vast northern territories, until forcibly incorporated into Muscovy (1470s). It was also the easternmost base of the Hanseatic league, which it supplied with furs, salt, wax and honey. Politically it was administered through local assemblies, culminating in the oligarchic city *veche*, which was empowered to choose officials—even the prince. Its real head of state was its archbishop. After Ivan IV sacked it (1570s), it rapidly declined; its role was later taken over by St Petersburg.

Novgorod had a rich culture. Its cycle of *byliny* (oral epic poems) reflect merchant life. It produced several important chronicles and other literary works. A distinctive school of icon painting flourished in the 14th and 15th centuries; it is stylized, very linear and clear toned, featuring the brilliant cinnabar often called "Novgorod Red." Novgorod's early brick and stone churches (St Sophia, 1043) are craggy, monumental, externally plain. The city's churches provided an amazing gallery of stylistically diverse fresco painting, though much was lost during World War II.

Left A wooden board with the old Russian alphabet incised upon it. It could he fixed to a wall as a study aid in teaching. Both literary culture and basic literacy flourished in Novgorod. The former led to a profusion of chronicles and hagiography, produced largely in clerical and monastic scriptoria. The latter permitted a high volume of business documentation and personal correspondence, recorded with telegraphic conciseness by styli on birch-bark strips.

Right This hypothetical reconstruction shows Novgorod as it may have appeared in the late 15th century; the town plan dates to the 12th century. The city was divided in two by the River Volkhov. The near half is the Cathedral Side, while the far half is the Trade Side. The riverbank citadel on the Cathedral Side housed the cathedral, archbishop's court and city assembly chambers. The Trade Side was the commercial district. Residential quarters centered on parish churches.

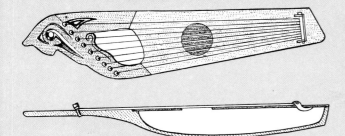

Left The *gusli*, a stringed musical instrument, made of wood, was popular in Novgorod. It could vary in size from 20 to 70 cm in length, and could have between three and eight strings. The peg end was carved with traditional decorative motifs. *Gusli* were used to accompany recitation of oral epics.

Right This metal reliquary cross probably belonged to a Novgorodian cleric. It is hinged at the bottom, with a pendant loop at the top for pectoral wear. The crucified Christ has the Mother of God to his right, St John the Evangelist to his left and St George above.

The Great Age of Russian Art

When Russia received Christianity from Byzantium in the late 10th century, an important part of the culture transplanted onto Russian soil was the early medieval art that Byzantium had brought to a level of great sophistication. For the Orthodox Church, icons (images of holy personages or events) were an integral part of worship and theology, testifying to the reality of the Incarnation. Characteristically icons were painted in tempera on wooden panels, though they may be of other materials, and the fresco wall paintings (occasionally mosaics) with which early churches were always adorned are equally "iconic."

After the Tatar conquest building activity, and with it painting, revived gradually during the 14th century. First Novgorod, then increasingly Moscow were the major patrons; but the political fragmentation of the time led to productive artistic activity in many smaller places. Contacts with the Mediterranean world revived: Serbian painters worked in Novgorod; the learned Greek Theophanes (in Russian Feofan) worked both there and in Moscow. But home-bred talents made this the great age of Russian painting: notably the monk Andrey Rublyov (c.1370–1430). He is first recorded as one of the painters of the Moscow Annunciation Cathedral in 1405. He was evidently aware of new stylistic currents in Byzantine art of the time—and also conveys the Hellenistic impetus behind Byzantine art generally. A notable development of the period was the multitiered iconostasis (icon screen), giving unprecedented opportunities for panel painters.

Far left School of Theophanes the Greek: *Virgin of the Don*. From fragmentary frescoes in Novgorod, the iconostasis of the Kremlin Annunciation Cathedral and a few works, like this one, attributed to Theophanes or his followers, we can assess his highly individual style: stark, dramatic, painterly, unnaturalistically highlighted. The influence of Hesychast mysticism on his art is probable.

Above left Three splendid icons, discovered in a woodshed at Zvenigorod, west of Moscow, in 1919, can be safely attributed to Rublyov at the height of his powers. The central icon of Christ exemplifies the mingled gravity and gentleness of Rublyov's finest images. It derives from—though surpasses—the very linear late Byzantine manner certainly known in Moscow of the 1390s from the imported Vysotsky tier of icons.

Left The so-called *Old Testament Trinity* was painted in memory of St Sergius when the Trinity Monastery was restored after the Tatar raid of 1408. The scene is the Hospitality of Abraham (Genesis 18): three pilgrims, recognized as angels, are given a meal by Abraham and Sarah.

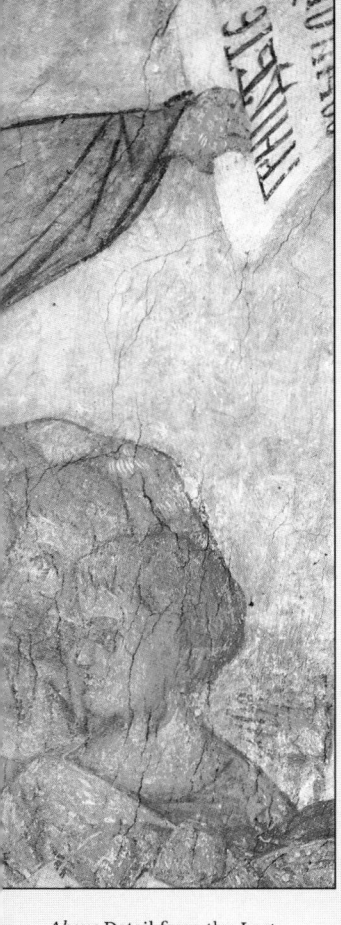

Above Detail from the *Last Judgment* wall painting by Andrey Rublyov and Daniil Chorny in the Dormition Cathedral, Vladimir (1408). In the 15th century some of the great pre-Tatar monuments were restored: chronicles record the work of Rublyov and associates at Vladimir, from which parts of a large iconostasis and a fresco cycle have survived. Particularly noble—comparable with the contemporary work of Masaccio in Florence—are the almost classical figures in the scene of Sts Peter and Paul ushering the righteous into Paradise, part of which is seen here.

Right The last significant figure of the great age of Russian painting was Dionisiy, who with a team of artists painted the Moscow Dormition Cathedral in the 1480s; his and his sons' subsequent frescoes in the Ferapontov Monastery near the White Lake (1500) are splendidly preserved. His manner is light, linear and delicate, but rather stiff and bloodless compared with Rublyov's. The icon *In Thee Rejoiceth . . .* represents a hymn to the Virgin Mary, and is characteristic of the rather complex and abstract iconographic scenes that became popular after about 1450.

THE LAST CENTURY OF OLD RUSSIA

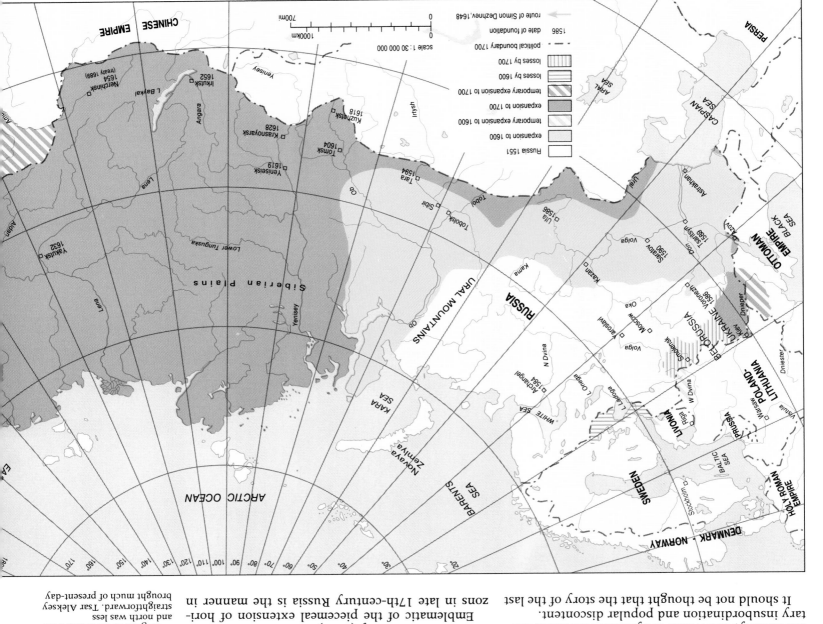

Muscovy under the early Romanovs

The Muscovite state, with its basically medieval system of government, way of life and artistic culture, was revived almost in defiance of the march of history, with the ending of the Time of Troubles and the establishment of the Romanov dynasty in 1613. It survived for nearly another century, but its apparently unshakable, timeless stability turned out to be subject to disruptive factors that in the second half of the 17th century led step by step to its end. Two generally sensible rulers whose long reigns spanned more than half of the century—Mikhail Romanov (tsar 1613–45) and his son Aleksey Mikhaylovich (tsar 1645–76)—gave validity and durability to the traditional order, but its crisis was perhaps all the worse when it erupted, spasmodically but violently, during the last quarter of the century, in a welter of dynastic confusion, military insubordination and popular discontent.

It should not be thought that the story of the last period of Muscovy is simply one of decline, still less of ruination. Already easily the largest country in the world in terms of territory, though not of population, Russia was beginning—after the debilitating wars of the 1650s and early 1660s—to achieve a modest prosperity. The chief visible legacy of this prosperity is in the considerable quantity of late 17th-century buildings still to be found in Moscow itself, in several great monastic ensembles and in some provincial towns, notably Yaroslavl and Archangel. Measures to modernize Russian life—what would later be thought of as "Westernization"—were, however uncertainly and unsystematically, being undertaken. With them came a greater need for literacy and even for European-style higher education: this period sees the establishment in Moscow of the so-called Slav-Greek-Latin Academy (1687).

Emblematic of the piecemeal extension of horizons in late 17th-century Russia is the manner in

The expansion of Muscovy in the 16th and 17th centuries.
The most spectacular expansion of the Russian lands took place in the last century of Muscovite rule. The successful campaigns of Ivan IV against Kazan and Astrakhan in the 1550s were followed up in the later 16th and 17th centuries. Once the Russians were across the Urals, the vast Siberian plains with their extensive river systems and easy portages were open to explorers seeking to extract "fur tribute" (*yasak*) from the sparse population. In 1648 the Cossack adventurer Simon Dezhnev became the first known person to sail through what later became known as the Bering Straits.
Progress to the south, west and north was less straightforward. Tsar Aleksey brought much of the present-day

which each of the arts began to absorb into itself disparate "modern" elements, assimilating them more or less successfully into medieval patterns. Thus literature acquired the new form of syllabically based verse, coming ultimately from France via Poland; church music, notably in the reign of the highly musical Fyodor III (tsar 1676–82), underwent fundamental changes, particularly in the field of harmonization; icon painting moved towards secular portraiture, itself a new genre (known to Russians as *parsuna*, a derivative of the Latin "persona"); wall painting particularly of the Yaroslavl School became saturated with picturesque detail, often of secular inspiration, and sometimes of Western iconographic origin. In architecture, pediments and other reminiscences of the classical order system were grafted on to Old Russian forms, and secular building in stone and brick rather suddenly acquired an importance and dignity it seems not to have had before: the tsar's new palaces and a few great houses (notably that of V.V. Golitsyn in the 1680s) are imbued with Western notions of comfort and privacy. A quite new art form—literary drama—had already established a toehold in the Russian court during Aleksey Mikhaylovich's last years.

Several factors from the mid-17th century onwards facilitated these developments. The first is the absorption into Muscovy, partly through war, partly by voluntary submission, of much of what is now Ukraine and Belarus, including the ancient capital, Kiev. These historic Russian lands, though well on the way to the linguistic differentiation that has since led to the recognition of independent Ukrainian and Belarusian languages, had remained largely Orthodox in religion, and supplied Muscovy in the last third of the 17th century with a number of churchmen, intellectuals and artists, not to mention simple builders and craftsmen, who had grown up in the post-Renaissance, in effect Western, society of the Polish-Lithuanian commonwealth, and had in many cases undergone a humanistically based Jesuit education.

Despite late medieval Russia's seclusion and xenophobia with regard to the rest of Europe, foreigners were no novelty in 17th-century Muscovy; hundreds, eventually thousands, of Westerners were at any given moment resident in Moscow, living in their own suburb after 1652 and playing a vital role, particularly in military matters. Western books, too, found their way into 17th-century Moscow libraries. Intermarriage, though rare, was not unknown: Artamon Matveyev one of the most powerful figures in the later years of Tsar Aleksey, married Mary Hamilton from Scotland, and it was in this thoroughly Westernized household that the tsar's second wife, Natalya Naryshkina grew up. To her influence Aleksey's growing taste for things Western in his last five years is usually attributed. As it happens, Aleksey, in his Polish and Swedish wars of the 1650s, was the first tsar to cross Russia's western frontier. It is interesting, perhaps surprising, that each of the three *de facto* Russian rulers immediately preceding Peter (Aleksey, Fyodor, the regent Sophia), though far from rejecting either traditional religion or regal ceremonial, were in their various ways' "Westernizers," concerned, however cautiously, to widen Russia's cultural horizons.

Expansion and diplomacy

The political history of Muscovite Russia during its last century of existence is largely a story of how a centralized autocracy, unwilling in general to change its ever more antiquated principles and methods, coped with huge internal stresses. External politics were of secondary importance; Russia was little known, and of small diplomatic interest, to the nations of Western Europe, and it played no part in the great settlement of European frontiers and religious claims at the Peace of Westphalia (1648), unlike its then still powerful neighbors Sweden and Poland.

This picture of non-involvement can be modified in some important respects as Russia expanded territorially to the west, the south and the east. Westwards, the chief friction was with Poland-Lithuania. In the immediate aftermath of the Time of Troubles, an exhausted Russia negotiated a 14-year truce with Poland; when it ran out, inconclusive fighting broke out again, chiefly over the great fortress-city of Smolensk. Tsar Aleksey was more successful: the anti-Polish Cossack-Ukrainian popular revolt of 1648 and his own campaigns of 1654 onwards brought the "left-bank" Ukraine (that is, east of the Dnieper), with the cities of Smolensk and Kiev, into Muscovy. Later there was talk of a Romanov candidate for the elective throne of Poland, which interested even the papacy, ever hopeful of bringing Russia into the Catholic or Uniate fold. Aleksey educated his children in Polish and Latin, regretting his own lack of languages.

Southwards too, Muscovy's settled territories crept on, over the "Wild Field" ("*Dikoye pole*") of the nearer steppe, towards the Black Sea. In the southern territories the key population of this thinly settled area was that of the independent Cossacks, some already landed agriculturists, some still mobile freebooters. Russians by origin and language, the Cossacks were mostly content to place themselves under the tsar's protection so long as their ancient rights were guaranteed, but their often over-adventurous harassment of Turks and Persians brought Muscovy headaches rather than advantages. Several times in the 17th and 18th centuries the fortress-city of Azov, at the mouth of the Don, gateway to the sea, was captured from the Turks, only to be lost again.

Eastwards, Muscovy made far more spectacular advances in the 17th century. Early in his reign Ivan IV had conquered Kazan and Astrakhan, gateways to the East. The gentle passes through the Urals presented no barrier. Once across, Russians had ahead of them a great plain intersected by a river system that could take them with easy portages to the vicinity of Lake Baykal. The merchant Stroganov family, empowered by Ivan to exploit Siberia, hired a band of less than 1000 men, mostly Cossacks under Yermak, who in the 1580s captured the western Siberian khan's citadel of Isker on the River Irtysh. They established nearby the new Siberian capital of Tobolsk, nowadays a comparatively insignificant and out-of-the-way place since the railroad bypassed it to the south. The forward momentum of the Russian fur-seeking explorers was extraordinary. In 1632 Irkutsk, near Lake Baykal, was founded, and in the 1640s the Russians pushed on through mountainous territory to the

Ukraine and Belarus (Belorussia) under Muscovite rule, and the push southwards towards the Black Sea continued slowly. Attempts to expand north-westwards into the Baltic regions met with strong resistance from Sweden, which would ally itself with Poland-Lithuania against the common enemy; permanent conquest of these lands would have to wait until the time of Peter the Great.

Amur river basin and the Pacific Ocean. Simon Dezhnev, another Cossack, sailed down the Kolyma River to the Arctic Ocean and thence to Anadyr by the northeast passage round the far tip of Siberia, through what were later named the Bering Straits. In the Amur valley, however, the Russians found a more considerable settled population of Manchurians who owed allegiance to China: eventually Chinese forces resisted the Russian advance, and by the Treaty of Nerchinsk (1689)—the legacy of which has caused contention even into the later 20th century—the Russians withdrew to the north of the Stanovoy range, still maintaining the possibility of access to the Sea of Okhotsk.

All this expansion, however, caused few ripples in the wider context of international relations, and 17th-century Russia remained largely shut off from any but its most immediate neighbors. This is illustrated in the practice of Muscovite diplomacy. Embassies were often exchanged between Russia and Western European powers, notably England, its leading trading partner since the mid-1550s, when an "Ambassadorial Department," or Foreign Office, was set up in Moscow. Muscovite diplomacy tended however rather to hinder than to expedite its own purposes. While the no-nonsense, mercantile and bourgeois Northern European states generally wanted practical negotiations, Muscovy viewed such contact first of all from a ceremonial standpoint. English and other Western embassies in Muscovy had to put up with mysteriously delayed or circuitous travel arrangements, endless and incomprehensible speeches, the attentions of numerous guards, civil servants and customs officials, highly formalized feasts with an excess of "grosse meates and stinking fish" (Jenkinson, 1557), and ultimately audiences in the Kremlin, sanctified by the tsar's presence, that were uncomfortably ritualistic in nature. From a Muscovite point of view. Westerners were mysteriously recalcitrant and discourteous, grumbling continually about such harmless matters of protocol as dismounting upon meeting the senior official at the Russian frontier.

Russian envoys in the West attempted to export their own protocol, which did not go down well. They were poor negotiators, since they had to stick closely to inadequate briefs and could not take unauthorized initiatives. Their intelligence about what was going on abroad was utterly inadequate. The methodical Tsar Aleksey eventually put the gathering of information on a sounder, if still fairly primitive footing, but in the 1650s he still valued an embassy to Venice in terms more of the fascinating tales of foreign customs it brought back than of hard results.

Crisis and church schism

The internal crisis of late Muscovy expressed itself throughout the 17th century in violent explosions of civil disorder. The most notable of these were: (1) Bolotnikov's rising in 1606–07 (the first of many whose heartland was the recently settled, turbulent wooded-steppe lands of the south) that threatened Moscow and came close to toppling Tsar Vasiliy Shuysky; (2) a series of rebellions during the 1620s and 1630s in Ukraine directed against Poland, and culminating in 1648 with Bogdan Khmelnitsky's successful "liberation" of the Cos-

sacks; (3) the Moscow uprisings of 1648 (the Salt Revolt) and 1662 (the Copper Revolt), both of which put Tsar Aleksey in grave personal danger; (4) the Novgorod bread riots of 1650; (5) the huge popular uprising in the Volga and Don regions led by the Cossack Stepan (Stenka) Razin in 1670–71; (6) the mutinies of the Moscow *streltsy* militia in 1682 and 1698. In the first decade of the next century there were to come the Bulavin rebellion on the Don (1707) and what amounted to a national war of independence by the Turkic Bashkirs, lasting several years. In addition, from the 1660s onwards there was a perpetual grumbling rebelliousness connected with the schism in the church (see below, p. 77–78).

Rebellions were of the most varied nature: some urban, some rural; some associated with a clearly defined social group, some not; some involving Russians, some non-Russians, some mixed; some well led, some anarchic; some with a positive program, some without. They originated in the north, the south, the east and the west of Russia, though it was the southern and southeastern borderland that was particularly notorious in this respect. Some put forward pretenders, often pretty implausible, to the Russian throne. All sprang from popular grievances, fears or ambitions: taxes, shortages, inflation, social and religious innovations, national oppression, the exactions of landlords or the general severities of serfdom and of the service state.

In the circumstances it seems rather remarkable that the state was able to survive at all. However it

Tsar Aleksey receives foreign ambassadors. The illustration is from *Journey to Muscovy* (1660) by a German, Adam Olearius, which is one of the fullest, best-informed and best-illustrated accounts of late Muscovy. Among the details Olearius has noted are the double-headed imperial eagles on the tsar's throne and the sharply differing styles of dress worn by the tsar's attendants and the Western European visitors.

Aleksey Mikhaylovich (tsar 1645–76). This anonymous painting by a Western artist of the second Romanov tsar apparently derives from a portrait from life. European-type portraiture appeared in Russia for the first time, as far as is known, in the later 17th century.

managed to outlive not only peasant and military revolts, but the longest lasting and most intractable of its difficulties, the religious crisis (though its implications were also social and intellectual) whose manifestation was the Great Schism. This split in the Russian Orthodox community, which led to the disaffection from the official church of perhaps half the population of Russia and a situation close to civil war, has often seemed to outsiders a rather grotesque and uniquely Muscovite business, whereby a monstrous legacy of antagonism and bloodshed was occasioned not by any serious doctrinal differences but by ritualistic and formalistic squabbles. Notoriously, there was the question of whether one should cross oneself with two fingers or three. The schism's most heroic figures were precisely those who were most benighted and backward-looking. Altogether it has seemed the deplorable but natural consequence of a superstitious, hidebound and intellectually inert religious culture.

The background to the Great Schism is that of a new self-consciousness and self-examination in the Orthodox Church, aware in the 17th century not only of its particular mission but of its international standing and general credibility. The question of relations with Catholicism on the one hand, and with the new Protestant churches on the other, would not go away. Many of the tsar's new Ukrainian subjects were, as a result of the Union of Brest (1596) Uniates, in communion with Rome; yet precisely those northern European countries with which Russia conducted most trade and on which it relied for immigrant skills were the strongholds of Protestantism. The Orthodox clergy had the worrying task of defending their own faith in debate when, in the early 1640s, the Danish prince Valdemar seemed likely to marry Tsar Mikhail's

daughter Irina (he refused to convert, and the wedding was eventually called off). When the ritual habits and dubiously translated service books of the Muscovite church came under scrutiny during Tsar Mikhail's reign, it was clear they were aberrant when juxtaposed with Greek Orthodox texts and practice.

The foreground to the schism was a grass-roots movement of renewal in the Russian church known as the "Zealots of Piety." Its senior figure, the future Patriarch Nikon, was born in 1605, his ally and bitter enemy-to-be, the Archpriest Avvakum, in 1620/1. Both came from humble families in the deeply provincial middle-Volga area. The third element in a tense triangle of personalities, Tsar Aleksey himself, was significantly younger, being born in 1629. Nikon, a man of commanding presence, became a monk—and so eligible for elevation to bishop—after the deaths of his children and the retreat to a convent of his wife. Avvakum remained a member of the married "white" (that is, parish) clergy until forced to enter a monastery in 1666. The zealots wished to revivify and purify the Russian church, to extirpate laxity in its ritual and counteract *dvoyeveriye* (survival of pagan customs alongside Christianity) that was still endemic in the countryside. They found a receptive ear in the young and pious Aleksey, whose chaplain Stephen was one of the leading members. The tsar summoned several members of their group to officiate in Moscow; Nikon achieved speedy preferment, first (1648) to the metropolitanate of Novgorod, then (1652) to the patriarchal throne. He had, or rather seemed to have, an almost complete hold over Aleksey, who promised to obey him in spiritual matters and granted him the title of a regent, "Great Lord" (*Velikiy gosudar*), when he himself left for the wars.

Nikon, by nature imperious, assured and impatient of delay, immediately on becoming patriarch put in hand reforms to ritual and prescribed revised service books, starting with the Psalter, the biblical book with which all Russians were most familiar. An uproar of dissent followed, largely from his erstwhile zealot companions. The fact that these reforms followed Greek models was no reassurance; the Greeks after all were contaminated with Latinism (many of their books were printed in Venice), and God had deprived them of their city of Constantinople. A variety of means was used to try to silence objectors, at first persuasive, but as the century progressed more and more coercive. Avvakum was exiled, first to Tobolsk, then on a lengthy and distant expedition to Dauria (eastern Siberia) and finally to the Arctic north at Pustozyorsk, where he compiled his *Life*. In 1682, having consistently refused to retract, he was burned at the stake.

Nikon meanwhile was scarcely popular with any section of society, though he commanded reluctant obedience. From Aleksey's point of view Nikon had admirably succeeded in bringing order to the Russian church and to its books, yet showed disturbing signs of claiming special status, perhaps superior to the tsar himself. A curious and significant early (1652) sign of this was his insistence on moving the relics of the Metropolitan Philip from the northern Solovki monastery to Moscow. Philip had been martyred for resisting Ivan the Terrible, a predecessor whom Aleksey revered. Nikon clearly wished to emphasize Ivan's offense; Aleksey saw the occasion as one of reconciliation.

For half-a-dozen years, however, tsar and patriarch cooperated closely in a remarkable late manifestation of the Byzantine ideal of *symphonia* (harmony); omens of discord seemed negligible. Indeed, this harmony had a lavish visible manifestation in the great monastic foundations that tsar and patriarch jointly sponsored, culminating late in 1657 in Nikon's extraordinary project known as New Jerusalem, 60 kilometers west of Moscow near the modern town of Istra. In the summer of 1658 however things were clearly going wrong. Nikon did not cooperate with Aleksey in the politically sensitive matter of church authority over the newly acquired Ukrainian territories. Thereafter relations went quickly and publicly to the bad. Nikon, in a gamble reminiscent of that taken by Ivan IV when he withdrew to Aleksandrov, left Moscow for his citadel-monastery of New Jerusalem, abandoning his patriarchal duties without abdicating his title. A cat-and-mouse game, lasting to the mid-1660s, ensued. Aleksey, though appalled, kept his nerve and called Nikon's bluff: in the end, lacking popular or clergy support, Nikon needed the tsar more than the tsar needed him.

It was intolerable to the tsar that the situation remain permanently unresolved. The only solution was to try the issue before a council in which non-Russian Orthodox authorities could participate and give disinterested judgment. Aleksey appealed to the four traditional Eastern patriarchates: Constantinople and Jerusalem refused to get closely involved, but Antioch and Alexandria fortunately agreed, and at the end of 1666 the council got under way. In its personnel, its spirit and in the arguments adduced this remarkable event was entirely Byzantine: doubtless it was the last major political event in European history of which this is true. The clinching point came from the Byzantine canon law book (*Nomokanon*): "Whosoever troubles the emperor and disturbs his empire has no defense." Nikon was formally deposed from office, reduced to the status of an ordinary monk and exiled to the north.

Strangely enough, this was not the end of all contact between tsar and former patriarch: Aleksey even sent Nikon gifts, but did not receive the formal blessing he sought. Nikon outlived Aleksey and was permitted to return to New Jerusalem, as Aleksey had desired, but died on the way back; his cell-church (*skete*) still stands, having survived the general destruction of the monastery in World War II. In the 1680s, after Nikon's death, a hagiographic *Life* was written by one of his disciples; in his old age as a monk Nikon was credited with healing powers.

The deposition of the patriarch was only the first and indeed briefest task of the church council of 1666–67; it had to choose a new incumbent and generally to bring order, as the tsar so much desired, to a disorientated church. In the years immediately before, with Nikon removed from Moscow and Aleksey desperate for solutions, it seemed as if the "Old Believers," as they came to be known by the orthodox (in Russian *starovery*, *staroobryadtsy*), might find accommodation with

the new order. Avvakum came briefly back from Siberian exile to Moscow and met with abundant signs of the tsar's favor. The new service books, though in use for a decade, were not yet compulsory. Nikon's downfall in 1666 looked like a triumph for the anti-reformers, but caused yet further strains, since some of those churchmen who condemned Nikon personally disapproved even more of dethroning a patriarch.

Even in Nikon's absence, the council however proceeded to back the liturgical reforms, behind which of course the tsar had thrown his own weight, and condemned the ignorance of the councils convened by Ivan IV. This was too much for Avvakum and other Old Believers, some of whom—notably the widowed Boyarinya Feodosiya Morozova—were in high places: they refused all compromises, courting—and in many cases subsequently achieving—punishment, exile and even martyrdom. The crucial sticking point was usually the sign of the Cross, a clearly public gesture, made many times each day and serving as much, say, as a military salute to identify one's loyalties. It was not amenable, as liturgical changes might be, to silent inner reservations.

Tsar Aleksey behaved, if not tolerantly, then at least with some mercy and understanding towards the schismatics whom he had partially provoked. In subsequent reigns things got worse for them. To the threat or reality of military force against them several Old Believer communities responded by mass suicide, immolating themselves by setting fire to their wooden churches. Peter I doubled taxation on Old Believers; his successors put them under punitive legal disabilities. Only under Catherine the Great were these disabilities reduced and an attempt, apparently at Potemkin's instigation, made at reconciliation. The schismatics soon divided and subdivided among themselves. The dominant faction, from which many further sects were born, were the "Priestless" (*Bezpopovtsy*), who held that, since no bishop had renounced the church reforms, there could be no further valid ordinations; their views resulted in a communal religious life remarkably different from that with clergy to celebrate the liturgy.

Old Believers in the next two centuries provided Russia with many of its hardiest colonists, traders and free peasants, as well as many rebels; by the mid-19th century there was a very prosperous Old Believer merchant class. In contrast, the closed nature of some Old Believer communities has led to the bizarre phenomenon of remote Siberian villages where old sectarian battles are continually refought on the paper of manuscripts copied and recopied in peasant scriptoria, a 17th-century way of life surviving into the late 20th-century in one or two parts of the region. The extraordinary durability, communality and steadfastness of the schismatics command respect, but beyond that modern historians have not come near to agreeing what to make of the whole phenomenon.

Political structures

The absolute claim to power of the tsar may have continued unshaken throughout the last Muscovite century, and indeed into the new age of Peter I, but the system of government did change, even if not very obviously. No one person of course could

Right: Russia in the reign of Tsar Aleksey.
Aleksey was more successful than his predecessors in expanding the frontiers of Muscovite Russia. His campaigns of 1654 onwards, on the back of the popular uprising led by the Zaporozhian Cossacks against their Polish overlords, brought "left-bank" Ukraine into the Muscovite realm. Support for the Cossacks made inevitable a confrontation with Poland and the resulting war lasted until 1667, when the Treaty of Andrusovo confirmed Russian possession of the land on the east bank of the Dnieper, a small area on the west bank around Kiev and the province of Smolensk.

Aleksey's reign however was dogged by social unrest as awareness grew of a polarization between tradition and modernization; rebellions broke out in many parts of the country, affecting various sectors of society. Peasants from nearly every quarter, but particularly the south and southeast, rose up, often in support of Cossack initiatives, and the Turkic Bashkirs waged what amounted to a national war of independence. Although all this together gives the impression of a nation on the verge of anarchy, grievances were largely unrelated and posed no combined threat to the existing constitution.

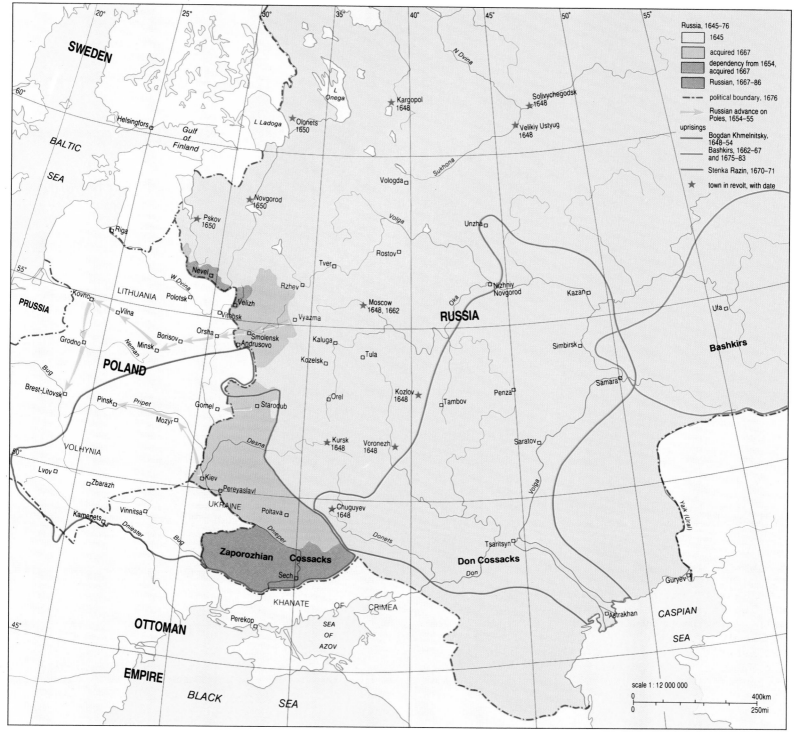

Russia, 1645-76
- ☐ 1645
- acquired 1667
- dependency from 1654, acquired 1667
- Russian, 1667–86
- ·—·—· political boundary, 1676
- ⇨ Russian advance on Poles, 1654-55

uprisings
- Bogdan Khmelnitsky, 1648–54
- Bashkirs, 1662–67 and 1675–83
- Stenka Razin, 1670–71
- ★ town in revolt, with date

scale 1 : 12 000 000

0 — 400km
0 — 250mi

take all the decisions needed to manage Russia single-handed, and in fact Muscovy was governed by the tsar in council, the council being the "Boyar Duma," an assembly of notables that seems to have been in permanent session, on call at all times in the Kremlin. The standard formula for the opening of a decree was "The tsar indicated and the boyars assented . . . ." Such boyars were, of course, performing a specialized kind of state service for the tsar, rather than representing separate interests in the manner of a parliament, but as there are no surviving minutes of their debates it is impossible to know how far any incipient pluralism developed or might have developed.

Even more tantalizing is the role of the other great advisory body, the *Zemskiy sobor* (Assembly of the Land). Such assemblies, summoned for a particular purpose, included representatives of various estates: boyars, servitors, clergy, townsfolk and on occasion even peasants. Sometimes they took crucial decisions: such an assembly put Mikhail Romanov on the throne and brought the Time of Troubles to an end. In the first half of the 17th century assemblies met frequently, debated issues of peace or war, probably took some decisions on finances. Early in Aleksey's reign a great assembly was summoned to bring order and codification to the chaotic legal system; it is quite unclear how far the tsar "used" the assembly, or the assembly used the tsar, or how far they fruitfully cooperated. But the work was efficiently done, for the great *Ulozheniye* or Code of 1649 was quickly promulgated. It was the first officially to recognize the already existing institution of serfdom, but also the first to proclaim the principle of "equal justice for all."

In the second half of the century, however, convocations of the assembly sharply declined as Aleksey's administration became more centralized and better organized. In 1682, we are told, "a host of men of all ranks from the whole of the Muscovite state" ratified, or maybe instigated, the arrangements for the regency that followed; this seems to refer to such an assembly, and if so it was the last known one, since Peter the Great had no use for it and it is never recorded as having met again. Perhaps its distant descendants were the great Legislative Commission of 1767 and Gorbachov's Communist Party Congress of 1988.

On a lower, day-to-day level Russia was administered through an array of fifty-odd "offices" (*prikazy*). Some, like the Ambassadorial Department mentioned above (p. 76), dated from well back in the 16th century; others dealt with new territorial acquisitions such as Siberia and the Ukraine and were set up in an ad hoc way, frequently overlapping in function. The local self-government of provincial towns, encouraged, perhaps surprisingly, by Ivan IV, disappeared with the Time of Troubles. Large provinces were run by royal governors or "representatives." These were basically tax-farmers who delivered up income to the treasury while enriching themselves at the local expense, a completely medieval arrangement known to Russians as *kormlenie* (literally "feeding"). In this autocratic but disorganized state system it is not surprising that a succession of efficient "strong men" emerge and exercise "prime ministerial" power throughout the 17th century, from the "new man" Boris Godunov at its start to Menshikov at its end (even more humbly born); others included the two Patriarchs Filaret and Nikon, Boris Morozov, Ordyn-Nashchokin, Artamon Matveyev, V.V. Golitsyn.

Dynastic turmoil

The end of Muscovy—and simultaneously of "Old Russia"—came with another protracted crisis, this time of dynastic origin. At the time of Aleksey's death there survived, out of his 16 children by two marriages, three boys and six girls; ultimately four of them were to rule. Despite the endemic Russian uncertainty about the royal succession system and the relative newness of the Romanov dynasty, it was clear who the heir apparent was, since Aleksey had had his eldest surviving son Fyodor ceremonially "presented to the people" and crowned as his successor. But Fyodor was known to be in delicate health; he was intelligent, pious, well read and artistic, but unassertive and still very young. He died at the age of 20 after six years' reign, his wife and only child having predeceased him. There developed a fight to the death (literally, for some of those involved) for the spoils of the realm between various boyar family groupings headed by the Miloslavskys, Aleksey's first wife's family, to which Fyodor belonged, and the Naryshkins, family of the widowed Natalya, mother of the future Peter the Great, who was still under four years old at his father's death. Under Fyodor a precarious balance was held, though the vengeful Miloslavskys were dominant, and the major political figure of Aleksey's time, Artamon Matveyev (former guardian of Natalya Naryshkina), was exiled.

Fyodor III (tsar 1676–82): a typical late 17th-century "iconic" portrait by a Russian painter, B. Saltanov. Fyodor, a child of Aleksey by his first marriage to Maria Miloslavskaya, succeeded his father at the age of 14, but he was sickly and died at 20, leaving no descendants.

Dramatic events erupted at Fyodor's death without an heir. Next in succession was the 16-year-old middle brother, Ivan (a Miloslavsky), but he was mentally retarded, or, at least, defective in speech, and could not rule alone. His half-brother, Peter, was ten, evidently bright, healthy and a budding future ruler. Tensions between the boyar groupings were matched, if not exacerbated, by the general tensions in society. At the center of these tensions, as it transpired, was the Moscow-based militia, some 20 000 strong, known as *streltsy* (musketeers). Founded in the mid-16th century as an up-to-date army, by the 1680s they were a force of dubious value, only semi-professional (they engaged in trade and agriculture when not campaigning), under-educated and prey to rumor, potentially mutinous and uncertain of their loyalties, anachronistic compared with foreign-officered standing troops, irregularly paid, inclined to the Old Belief, suspicious of foreigners, with their own ambitions and anxieties about the preservation of their privileged status.

The *streltsy* were one element bidding to fill the power vacuum after Fyodor's death; the other was one rather unexpected member of the royal family. Fyodor died on 28 April 1682: the patriarch instantly proclaimed young Peter tsar, with his mother Natalya regent. Matveyev was already on his way back from exile. The politically inexperienced Natalya made the mistake of ordering 16 *streltsy* colonels to be flogged. Rumors circulating among the *streltsy* that both Fyodor and Ivan had been poisoned by the Naryshkins provoked them into a riot. Matveyev returned and took his seat at the head of the boyar council on 15 May, but by that evening he had been brutally lynched by *streltsy*, and for three days the murderous hunt for Naryshkins was on. Ten-year-old Peter with his mother, prisoners in the Kremlin, though spared by the rioters, witnessed some of the killings.

The outcome was a modification to the succession arrangement, proclaimed on 26 May, whereby Ivan and Peter were to be joint tsars. The unexpected figure who eagerly filled the power vacuum was their 25-year-old Miloslavsky sister, Sophia. Well educated, unlike other Muscovite women but like the other children of Tsar Aleksey, she saw her chance with considerable perspicacity; in the crisis-ridden atmosphere she was proclaimed regent. Not only was she the first woman to rule Russia since Olga in the 10th century, she was not even the senior princess of the family (Yevdokia was seven years older, Marfa five). But she was quick-witted and decisive and had the support of the leading Russian statesman V.V. Golitsyn. At first decrees were issued simply in the names of the curious child diarchy of Ivan V and Peter I: a throne that still survives in the Kremlin Armory Museum has a double seat and a small "prompt window" behind, presumably for Sophia's whispered instructions or answers. Soon Sophia was using grander titles such as "Great Sovereign" (curiously, there were no special terms for "regent" or "regency" in the Russian of the period), and was portrayed in grand regalia, devising special ceremonies appropriate to a queen.

Meanwhile Ivan V was married at 17, and fathered a string of daughters, one of whom, nearly 40 years later, would come to the throne as the Tsaritsa Anna. Peter, though at 16 he was still little interested in government, seems to have been nudged by his supporters and family into attending the boyar council from 1688; in January 1689 he too married, and late that summer moved against his half-sister, objecting to her presence in ceremonies and denouncing her in a remarkable letter to his co-tsar Ivan: "And now, sovereign brother, the time has come for us to rule the realm entrusted to us by God . . . It is disgraceful that in our majority this shameful person should rule the state in our stead." Sophia lived out the rest of her days, until 1704, in the Moscow Novodevichy Convent.

Squeezed as they are between the long and eventful reigns of Aleksey and Peter, Fyodor's and Sophia's periods of rule often get no more than a passing mention from historians of Russia, yet they have considerable interest. "Westernization" took some steps forward, though still hesitantly, in both. Just before he died Fyodor made a political decision of considerable symbolic and some practical significance: he abolished *mestnichestvo*, the ranking system whereby boyars would only accept service positions equal to or above those held previously in their families, and according to their status within their families. It was a constant source of quarrels and inefficiency and often had to be temporarily suspended in time of war. Fyodor's dramatic gesture not only in abolishing the system, but also in burning the great manuscript books (*razryadnye knigi*) in which the whole rigmarole was recorded, thus preventing its return for ever, opened the door for Peter's service meritocracy.

The single figure most responsible for ending *mestnichestvo* in the last months of Tsar Fyodor, and thereafter the dominant politician during the regency of Sophia, the outstanding Russian of the 1680s, in fact, was Prince Vasiliy Golitsyn. Head of the Old Russian equivalent to the Foreign Ministry, he was Sophia's favorite and *de facto* prime minister. Foreign policy in fact loomed larger in the 1680s in Russia than had ever previously been the case, and the period deserves note as one of peace in comparison with the expensive Polish war of Aleksey and the lengthy northern wars of Peter. The atmosphere in Moscow under both Fyodor and Sophia was distinctly pro-Polish: Poland, still powerful and prosperous, offered the most readily accessible models of cultural progress and what we would now call Westernization. In 1685 Sophia's government concluded an important treaty with Poland; from the Russian point of view most significantly it confirmed in perpetuity what had been the temporary acquisition of Kiev.

The Polish alliance, however, had unwanted and disastrous complications. For the first time in its history Muscovy was brought into an alliance of European states that carried military implications. The last great thrust of Ottoman expansion had brought the Turks to the outskirts of Vienna in 1683, and Russia was drawn into war against an Ottoman empire with which it had no specific quarrel. An Ottoman vassal-state existed north of the Black Sea: the so-called Crimean Tatars, Turkized remnants of the Great Horde, who had irregularly harassed the Muscovite state for over 200 years. A reluctant Golitsyn had to launch and lead two large expeditions against the Crimean Tatars in 1687 and 1689. Neither could force the Perekop isthmus into the Crimea itself, nor indeed make any gains that could plausibly offset their considerable human losses. Both were presented in Moscow however as triumphant victories, and it is probable that no one factor so discredited Sophia's rule (and strengthened Peter's hand when, immediately afterwards, he instigated the showdown that terminated her regency) as this double defeat and cover-up. As for Golitsyn, he lived out the rest of a long life (until 1714) in exile after Sophia's downfall. Thus Russia lost, at the outset of Peter's reign, the person who represented the best hope for a gradualist and perhaps painless approach to Westernization.

Golitsyn was a man of great erudition and intellect, well read and fluent in several languages, totally at home in Western European company, humane and farsighted. Among his achievements were the mitigation of the severer parts of the criminal code, the opening of the Slav-Greek-Latin

Top A gold coin of about 1682 shows the crowned figure of the Tsaritsa Sophia, regent to her younger brother Ivan V and their half-brother Peter I. The joint tsardom of the two young half-brothers under the regency of their older sister was an arrangement reached in response to the succession crisis that erupted on the death of Fyodor III. Another gold coin of the same period (*above*) shows the two child tsars with the emblem of the double-headed eagle. Seven years later Sophia's probable designs upon the throne led to her forcible retirement to a convent at the instigation of Peter, then 17 years old. Peter and Ivan then ruled as nominal co-tsars until Ivan's death in 1696.

Academy and the impetus he gave to the rebuilding of central Moscow, so often ravaged by fire, as a city of brick and stone rather than wood. His own great pedimented house, which survived in Moscow into the 20th century before being wantonly demolished, was noted for the taste and opulence of its furnishings, though his own preferred way of life was modest, even spartan. Golitsyn was unusual among Muscovite political figures in aiming not merely at the establishment of good order and the strengthening of hallowed institutions; he envisaged the development and education of his society, its economic growth and financial stabilization, freedom of religion and even the end of serfdom.

Culture and the arts in transition

Late Muscovite culture seems to have had a self-consciousness and at times an aridity about it that has given it mostly rather a bad press, both then and later. Travelers' accounts, though certainly not uniformly hostile to the Muscovites, reacted more critically than ever before to the limitations of their religious and general outlook and to the absolutism of their state system. Occasional individual Muscovites also raised critical voices. Grigoriy Kotoshikhin, a civil servant in the Ambassadorial Office, fled Muscovy and entered Swedish service in 1666. He wrote a most valuable, because detailed, though also strongly hostile account of Russian society and government. Despite his contention that "The men of the Russian state are arrogant by nature and untrained in all things, because they do not and cannot receive a good education in their country," Kotoshikhin and others nonetheless somehow obtained sufficient education to scrutinize their own condition.

Only in the last half-century has a reassessment of late Muscovite culture been made in terms not merely of its impoverishment and backwardness, but also of a complexity that increased as the 17th century proceeded, intellectual strivings and, on occasion, aesthetic achievements. In particular, the so-called Moscow Baroque period, which reached its height in the 1680s, has attracted much recent attention. To one of the greatest modern cultural historians, D.S. Likhachov, this period represents the belated Russian equivalent of the Renaissance, although it should be noted that this implies depriving the subsequent Petrine period of such a role. Some interesting "Renaissance" figures of many-sided cultural significance indeed emerged in, and helped to shape, this period.

The chief of these was Simeon of Polotsk (1629–80), a West Russian of wide Latin-based education, both theological and secular. He came to Moscow in 1664, was influential in court circles, becoming tutor to the royal family, and almost single-handedly established a new Russian literature largely on western Baroque, particularly Polish models. His copious writings include secular odes and shorter poems introducing a syllabically based metrics usually now considered to fit rather awkwardly with the strongly stress-accented Russian language. He also wrote plays on biblical subjects and an influential rhymed translation of that favorite among the Russians of all biblical books, the Psalter. But despite Simeon's activities and those of some of his circle, notably Silvester Medvedvev

(1641–91), adviser to and historian of the regent Sophia, himself executed subsequently at Peter's orders, there are no giant intellects at work, on surviving evidence, in this "Russian Renaissance."

Folklore and the vernacular arts flourished, and were at times able to interact with, or revivify, the rather stilted, ossified forms of "sophisticated" art. One literary masterpiece emerged from such an interaction, and from the social and personal circumstances of crisis in which Muscovy dissolved: the *Life* of the Archpriest Avvakum, written by himself and dating from his incarceration in a northern monastery in the 1670s. To take the hallowed religious genre of the *vita*, the saint's life, and to turn it into autobiography, was a daring conceptual leap, even more daringly accomplished. It was officially unpublishable in Russia till after 1861. It is significant and paradoxical that Avvakum's *Life* is, despite its individuality and complete stylistic originality, a last flare-up of Muscovite culture, not at all a product of the new Westernizing trends of its time.

Plenty of 17th-century prose writing has come down to us: historical accounts of that turbulent age and secular tales, fictional and semi-fictional, fantastical, parodistic and picaresque. Such works only catch fire as literature when, as with Avvakum, the full, albeit still rather chaotic resources of the Russian language are employed to surprise and influence the reader emotionally. A fine example is the *Tale of the Siege of Azov*, written by a participating soldier in the 1640s, weirdly blending the dry and factual manner of the military tale with highly rhetorical, folk-influenced purple patches. Even more remarkable is the *Tale of Woe and Misfortune* (*Povest' o Gore-Zlochastii*), a highly metaphoric and poeticized variant of the theme of the Prodigal Son, pursued through life by a personification of Woe. Generally, though, the most readable 17th-century Russian literature, often not closely datable, is anonymous poetry, more or less suffused with the spirit of folklore: in particular the so-called "spiritual verses" (*dukhovnye stikhi*), deriving from biblical and apocryphal stories, are refracted in the prism of Russian folk-consciousness and popular religious concepts.

Musical life of the period is an elusive topic. From what was noted down we might assume that nothing but unaccompanied church music existed, though in this area too, large changes had occurred by the end of the century under the influence of polyphonic Kievan chant. V. Titov set Simeon Polotsky's popular rhymed translation of the Psalter to music in 1680. Beyond that, of course, there was folk music, some of it, naturally, instrumental. Yet we can also be sure that Western European music too was performed in 17th-century Moscow—though how much, how well and in what circumstances are matters of conjecture. In 1648, for example, the Moscow rioters destroyed several cartloads of Western musical instruments. Even earlier, in the 1630s, the Holstein diplomat Olearius remarked casually in his well-known travel notes that Nikita Romanov, kinsman of the tsar, was "a friend of German music." By the 1670s Tsar Aleksey was watching the ballet *Orpheus* probably to the music of Schütz, the greatest German composer of the time; three-year-old Peter had his own clavichord.

The Patriarch Nikon in ceremonial dress, depicted in an early 19th-century drawing.

Western immigrant portraitists and engravers (not, admittedly, of the first quality) are frequently recorded as plying their trade in Russia in the 17th century; native Russian painting mostly stayed within the medieval territory of icons and frescoes, though tentatively reaching out into the iconic secular portraiture known as the *parsuna*. The same Patriarch Nikon who is reported to have personally destroyed icons that seemed too sensuously painted was realistically depicted together with his attendants by a Dutch portraitist. However, Western-inspired mannerisms took ever firmer root in the court icon workshops of 17th-century Moscow, with more emphatically modeled faces and limbs, architectural backgrounds using Renaissance perspective and slick handling of the paint imitative of, and occasionally in fact employing, oil pigments.

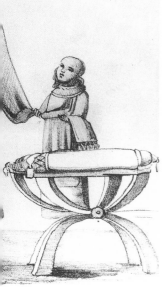

A great deal of 17th-century Russian painting survives. Much is perfunctory, but it varies greatly in quality, and the most skilled practitioners of the time were considerable artists; it is characteristic that in this last stage of medieval Russian art we often know them by name. The most important is that of Simon Ushakov (1626–84). From 1664 he was head of the major artistic workshop of late Muscovy, based on the Armory building in the Kremlin. He could handle secular subjects in a Western manner (he engraved the title page for Simeon Polotsky's translation of the Psalter) but is remembered above all for the numerous icons he and his team produced. The most interesting are those that delve into new subject matter, particularly with political import: one in particular, *The Planting of the Tree of the Muscovite State*, is a highly unusual work, incorporating depictions of Tsar Aleksey and his family with 20 medallion portraits of his great predecessors, arranged like fruits on a vine surrounding an icon-within-an-icon of the Virgin and Child. Some late 17th-century icons have a finicky delicacy derived from the earlier Stroganov School, incorporating much naturalistic detail; they unexpectedly, though accidentally, evoke the world of Western International Gothic of around 1400—it too the last bright flare-up of an over-refined art. This delicacy is seen to best effect, however, in the frescoes of the school centered on Yaroslavl, brilliantly hued and swarming with miniature figures; they are at the opposite extreme from the muted, uncluttered monumentality of early Russian wall painting. Most secular painting of the period, incidentally, is lost, giving us an unbalanced view of the whole artistic scene. Much elaborate, sometimes over-ornate but always splendidly crafted metalwork survives: icon casings (*oklady*), book covers, railings, metal folding icons, enameled and damascene objects.

Late Muscovite architecture

The art that thrived above all others in the last century of Muscovy was building. The 17th century begins with Boris Godunov's attempts to equip Muscovy with a monumental architecture that would pick up where Ivan III and Vasiliy III left off a century before. The most prominent heritage of this is the present form of the great Moscow Kremlin belltower, "Big John" (*Ivan Velikiy*, not named as is often thought after Ivan III or "Great," but after St John Climacus), while the

most spectacular, until its demolition in the early 19th century, must have been his planned new town, Borisov Gorodok, near Mozhaysk, which had the tallest of all "tent" churches (at least 73 meters). Under Tsar Mikhail there was a gradual renewal of building activity after the interruption and destruction of the Time of Troubles: a memorial to this grim period is the most elegant of "tent" churches, the triple-spired "Marvelous Church" at Uglich (1618; properly called the Church of the Assumption in the Alekseyev Monastery). By the 1630s a Moscow merchant, Grigoriy Nikitnikov, was rich enough to build the Trinity in the Nikitniki, adjoining his own house: it is a calculatedly picturesque and asymmetrical agglomeration of varied spaces, highly decorated inside and out, baroque in spirit though Old Russian in its forms. More regularized, at least outwardly, is the Terem Palace in the Kremlin, also built mostly in the 1630s by Bazhen Ogurtsov.

The most spectacular building of Tsar Aleksey's reign is (or was, until it was largely destroyed in World War II—it is now under restoration) the Patriarch Nikon's monastery of New Jerusalem (1658 onwards). Nikon was a keen builder: he disapproved of ornate Muscovite accretions and patronized a rather severe architecture based on the traditional Byzantine five-domed cubical church. He declared that "tent" churches were uncanonical, yet at the center of New Jerusalem there stood one of the largest and most daring derivatives of the type, surmounting the Cathedral of the Resurrection. Nikon had ordered from Palestine an inlaid wooden model of the Church of the Holy Sepulcher to use as his prototype; this model still survives. Many Belorussian workmen assisted in the construction of New Jerusalem, and there is a significant infiltration of elements of the Western order system into its architecture. Its great tent-like rotunda collapsed in the 18th century and was reconstructed in its final form by the major mid-18th-century architect Rastrelli. The last and most astonishing "tent" church in Moscow was the Church of the Nativity in Putinki (1649): its six calculatedly irregular flèches greeted travelers on the Novgorod road at the entrance to the city.

The opposite approach, from the southeast along the Moskva River, led past the old royal estate of Kolomenskoye, and here Tsar Aleksey commissioned and planned the most extraordinary Russian building of the age: the great wooden palace of 200 or more rooms—an anthology of the wood-builder's art, a fairytale jumble of disparate and picturesque elements—built to royal specifications in only three years (1667–70). This was the tsar's favorite place of relaxation during his second marriage, but it fell into disrepair in the St Petersburg era and had to be demolished a hundred years later. Luckily Catherine II had a large model of the palace made, which can still be admired.

Building activity reached its climax in the often ignored period of Fyodor III's reign and Sophia's regency. This was the time of the flowering of the Moscow Baroque, in whose extremely distinctive structures Western and Old Russian elements are so teasingly balanced that they cannot be categorized as ancient or modern. Churches are often in several diminishing stories, with centralized ground plans and rich ornamentation along the successive rooflines; belltowers are of openwork construction; fortress-towers have surprisingly dematerialized, lacy strapwork battlements; domestic buildings, of which for the first time many survive, have richly ornate window surrounds.

In this short era, barely a quarter-century long, the art of colored ceramic architectural decoration, which had been an occasional resource in Russian, as in Byzantine, architecture since the 15th century, if not earlier, reaches a splendid climax in the domes of the Kremlin palace church known as the Savior behind the Golden Grille (1680) and in the astonishing small Moscow palace called the Krutitsky Teremok, completely faced in polychrome tiles. Outside Moscow the age left many monuments in country estates, towns, fortresses and monasteries, particularly on the great trade route northeast to Yaroslavl and beyond. Here, at Rostov on the edge of Lake Nero, the Metropolitan Iona Sysoyevich built in the 1670s and 1680s the strangest of ecclesiastical follies: an entire Kremlin, a miniature city, all of a piece—a nostalgic anachronism in its time (Iona was a covert supporter of Nikon), marvelously preserved to the present.

But this was above all the age of Moscow itself, a huge city of perhaps quarter of a million people, many times more populous than any other in the realm. Until well into the 19th century it had a sprawling, village-like quality: outside the Kremlin its fundamental organization was into *slobody*, usually translated "suburbs" but here more appropriately "quarters," where specialized trades or merchant activities were carried on. Hints of the old wood-built *slobody*, clustered round their local church, survived into 19th-century Moscow and even, in the many street names referring to trades, up to the present.

The village-like quality of Old Moscow was enhanced by the way in which the residences of the service and aristocratic class were more like miniature estates than town houses: they had their own outbuildings, gardens, orchards and private churches. Relics of such complexes survive in two or three places in Moscow today, notably the Krutitsky Palace and the Bersenevka house. Herds of cattle wandered at dawn and dusk through Moscow streets to pasture outside the city limits during the day; every courtyard house had its flock of poultry. By day the central squares, especially the market area around the present-day GUM store, constituted a huge emporium, the center for the trade of half a continent.

Tsar Aleksey: the last Byzantine?

The turbulent, contradictory last age of Muscovy is hard to sum up. It remains, to Russians as to Westerners, an exceedingly remote age compared with the 18th century that immediately followed, an age in which medieval qualities (the unquestioned religious basis of life, its dominance over secular elements of culture, an absence of the very concept of progress, rigidity of behavioral norms) predominate. Memorable as many of the figures of the age are, we have to admit to bafflement if we try to look deeply into their motives or personalities: as so often with medieval people, the evidence just is not there, even in the cases of men like Nikon and Avvakum.

One exception to this can, however, be noted, and it is a most important one, since it is Tsar Aleksey himself. Here we have a figure whose extensive private archive, down to marginal doodlings, has survived, one who in addition was commented upon by innumerable observers from many cultural backgrounds. It may confidently be asserted that he can be known as no other personality from Old Russia is knowable. What emerges from a modern study of the evidence is a remarkably emblematic ruler for the final half-century of medieval Russia one who was by disposition and by conscious choice the last ruler of truly Byzantine mentality in Europe. He was Byzantine not just in his great devotion to religious observance, his Grecophile sympathies, his conviction of the high calling of his tsardom, his elaboration of symbolically charged royal ceremonial: he also had the

Rostov the Great, northeast of Moscow: the so-called Kremlin, built at the end of the Old Russian period by the Metropolitan Iona Sysoyevich in the 1670s and 1680s. Splendidly preserved, it is seen here from the frozen Lake Nero.

personal qualities of powerful human understanding, political subtlety (bordering on deviousness), a sense of God-given righteousness but above all passion for order and harmony characteristic of the ideal Byzantine ruler.

Aleksey had a sense of Russia's national interests that flowed from his own enthusiasms. A keen gardener, he put large-scale experiments in agriculture and manufacture under way on his estates; he was passionately enthusiastic and well informed about geography at a time when Russia was hugely expanding. His way of life, despite some modifications in his last five years, was still thoroughly medieval, revolving around lengthy ceremonies of court and church. His chief relaxation, an age-old occupation of rulers, was hunting and in particular falconry. Yet backward-looking as he may seem, part of his greatness was that he was flexibly

minded, able to widen his field of vision and learn from mistakes. He was one of the most revered of Russian rulers, with a reputation for sanctity and gentleness, despite his disciplined firmness and occasional strong temper. The adjective *tishayshiy*, "most-gentle," that was attached to him in his lifetime and since has usually been taken to reflect his personal qualities, though it is in fact a Russian version of the title *serenissimus* or its Byzantine equivalent *galenotatos*. More than anyone else he formed the nostalgic image of the ideal tsar in the popular imagination. In any case he had a great and usually underestimated effect on his son Peter— and it is the same Peter to whom we owe our unique opportunity to know Aleksey, since it was he who ordered the preservation and cataloging of his father's private papers, many years after his death.

Wooden Buildings of Northern Russia

Nowhere is the creative genius of the common people in Russia more immediately evident than in the wooden architecture of the forest zone. Throughout the Old Russian period stone and brick were reserved for occasional use in churches, monasteries and a few important town houses: wood was overwhelmingly the predominant constructional material, even for fortresses and palaces. The climax of domestic wooden architecture came as late as 1667 in the large and picturesque royal palace built for Tsar Aleksey at Kolomenskoye: it was still in use in the 1760s, and when it was demolished a model was made of it.

The age-old Russian log house (*izba*) is based on a simple square module that could be, and usually was, prefabricated and put up with great speed. Logs were always laid horizontally, their ends often lapped. Insulation would be provided by close-packed wadding; but wooden buildings would still "breathe," and were considered healthier to live in; wooden living rooms often surmounted a brick foundation story used for storage. The development of a spectacular folk church architecture in wood, using the simplest tools, is shrouded in mystery. Since wood is vulnerable to fire and decay the earliest surviving churches are late medieval. Yet we know, for example, that a wooden cathedral with "13 heads" (domes?) was built in 10th-century Novgorod.

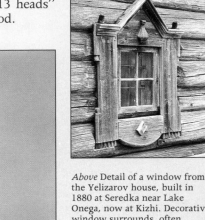

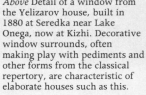

Above Detail of a window from the Yelizarov house, built in 1880 at Seredka near Lake Onega, now at Kizhi. Decorative window surrounds, often making play with pediments and other forms from the classical repertory, are characteristic of elaborate houses such as this.

Left Among several wooden buildings that have been dismantled and reassembled at Kizhi in recent years is the small and simple church of St Lazarus from the Murom Monastery on Lake Onega. This is thought to be the oldest surviving wooden church in Russia, built before the monk Lazar died in 1391. Three square cells of successively diminishing area represent narthex, nave and sanctuary, each having a differently pitched roof, with the nave rising highest; there is no foundation story.

Below The greatest treasure house of wooden architecture is at Kizhi, an island on Lake Onega in the far north. Its two spectacular churches are dedicated to the Transfiguration (1714) and the Intercession (*Pokrov*; 1764). Here the latter is seen from the shingled domes of the former. Both are highly elaborate showpieces: Kizhi was an important parish and trading post. Its renowned carpenters, working largely with axes, "followed their eye," needing no blueprints. The Intercession rises in an octagon above a cube: each rib of the octagon supports a decorative dome, with one more in the middle and another on the apse. The Transfiguration, a steep (38-meter) tiered pyramid, has the staggering total of 22 domes; it resembles a vast Christmas tree. It was built on the virtuoso "twenty-walled" plan: an octagonal core with four side-projections producing a cross. Its builder, Nestor, supposedly flung his axe into the lake, saying "There was not, is not and will not be such a one."

Top left The interior of the Church of the Intercession, Kizhi. There is a relatively low false ceiling, and a fine iconostasis, with carved and painted "royal doors" in the middle. Here the successive tiers of the iconostasis, working upwards, are: locally revered icons; feast-day icons (the "twelve major feasts" from the Gospels); the Deisis (the Virgin, the Baptist and other figures interceding with Christ on behalf of humanity); the Prophets.

Left Several wooden buildings from outlying places have been collected at Suzdal, Novgorod, Kolomenskoye and elsewhere. These 19th-century wooden windmills now stand at Suzdal.

Above Schematic drawings showing techniques of wooden building. The *kub* (cube) form of roofing (*top*), achieves the transition from a square of walling to an onion dome. Unable to reproduce most of the curved forms of masonry with logs, the carpenters resorted to a variety of ingenious solutions to arrive at equivalent aesthetic effects. Diminishing stories of varied cross-section were popular from the 17th century (as, indeed, in the Moscow Baroque). Small onion domes—purely decorative elements—are traditionally covered in silvery aspen shingles. Two widespread methods of securing the corners of buildings are lapping (*center*) and dovetailing (*below*).

PETER THE GREAT

Russia's new age

Well before the end of Peter the Great's reign it was made quite clear that Muscovy had expired: as the French civil servant Liboy, assigned to accompany Peter's second personal embassy to the West in 1717, reported: "Allow me to remark that the term 'Muscovite' or even 'Muscovy' is deeply offensive to all this court." It is of interest incidentally that these two names are purely Western European usages, with no Russian equivalents; to the tsars their domain was Rus, replaced (under Polish influence) with the Latinate form Rossiya, just as the very title *tsar* became, in official though of course not popular terminology, the Latin *imperator* (emperor). The moment that marked the end of Muscovy was the transfer of the seat of government in 1712 to Peter's newly founded city with its ostentatiously un-Russian name, St Petersburg. Even thereafter, however, Moscow continued to be considered Russia's alternative capital, as if both cities and what they represented were competing for the populace's spiritual allegiance.

Peter—despite his no-nonsense reputation—was highly aware of the symbolic dimension of words, gestures and behavior. From quite early in his reign (c.1698) his actions, however apparently impulsive, systematically aimed to reinforce the sense of fundamental change in Russia signaled by the new nomenclature of which the examples quoted above are only the most prominent. Foreigners were certainly impressed: Voltaire, not one to be lightly taken in, wrote in the middle of the century: "The establishment of this empire is perhaps Europe's greatest event after the discovery of the New World."

The chronological framework of Peter's early life —until, in his later twenties, he began to take on the role of reformer and "Westernizer" of his society—falls into a series of strongly demarcated compartments relating directly to political circumstances. He was born in May 1672, the eagerly awaited and much-loved only son of Tsar Aleksey's second marriage, to Natalya Naryshkina, at the palace of Kolomenskoye outside Moscow. While Aleksey was still alive Peter spent much of his time there and at other out-of-town royal residences, and on Aleksey's death in 1676 Natalya and her children were allocated rooms in the Kremlin. The first great, and horrific, dislocation came to Peter's life when his half-brother Fyodor III died in 1682. The events that immediately followed have already been described (p. 80). Peter's family largely withdrew from Moscow to the old royal hunting lodge at Preobrazhenskoye, some five kilometers to the northeast beside the little River Yauza. It is notorious that thereafter Peter hated and feared the Kremlin and what he took it to represent.

Already highly practical, inquisitive and experimentally minded, Peter spent his teenage years at Preobrazhenskoye acquiring various technical skills and, quite literally, playing soldiers. He

Peter I (tsar 1682–1725). Peter the Great was painted or sculpted many times: this, the earliest grand portrait of him, was made at William III's suggestion by Sir Godfrey Kneller, when Peter arrived in England with the Great Embassy in January 1698. Kneller may have sketched Peter earlier, in Holland. Formal as it is, the young tsar nonetheless considered it an admirable likeness, and many copies were made of it.

formed children's regiments named after Preobrazhenskoye and Semyonovskoye (an adjoining village), whom he drilled and engaged in mock battles. As time went by, his "soldiers" became older and their exercises more realistic; Sophia, presumably sensing no threat, authorized their use of arms and ammunition. Peter's boy regiments developed into the elite force of the new Russia, while among his playmates were some—notably Alexander Menshikov, who was of humble birth— that became his close subsequent friends and collaborators. His greatest enthusiasm of the time, and one that never left him thereafter, was kindled by the chance discovery in a shed of a sailing boat, Western European in design, supposedly a gift sent by Queen Elizabeth of England to Ivan IV a century before. Peter had it repaired and floated it on the Yauza; since the tiny river could not accommodate his efforts to tack it against the wind, he transferred his nautical endeavors to Pereslavl-Zalessky, a small ancient town some 160 kilometers northeast of Moscow on the finely situated Lake Pleshcheyevo. Peter's original boat was transported to St Petersburg where it later acquired "iconic" status as the centerpiece of a curious shrine in the Peter-Paul Fortress.

Early in 1689 the 16-year-old Peter was married to Yevdokiya Lopukhina, a wedding arranged by his mother and disastrous for all concerned— particularly for the unfortunate heir, Aleksey, that it produced. In late summer of that year came another crisis and turning point in Peter's life. Informed (on the basis of a misunderstanding) that the Moscow *streltsy* regiments were, at Sophia's instigation, about to move threateningly against Preobrazhenskoye, Peter and his immediate entourage fled in the middle of the night and established themselves in the strongly fortified Trinity Monastery some 70 kilometers northeast of the city. There he precipitated a showdown with his half-sister by sending letters demanding that the *streltsy* colonels and foreign mercenary officers should come in person to pledge their loyalty. He also sent the remarkable missive, quoted earlier (p. 81), to his co-tsar Ivan denouncing Sophia as a usurper. Peter's initiative caused shock and consternation in Moscow, particularly among the foreign officers who were genuinely uncertain whom they should obey. The decisive move was made by the veteran Scot, General Patrick Gordon (1635–99), who sensed the indecision of Sophia's government and went to Peter. Sophia's chief ministers had no choice but to follow. Sophia was forcibly retired to the Novodevichy Convent on the outskirts of Moscow. Gordon was to save Peter's throne for him again in the abortive *streltsy* rebellion of 1698.

It is a seldom-noticed irony that the regency of one woman (Sophia) was replaced by that of another (Peter's mother Natalya). But, unlike Sophia, the Tsaritsa Natalya was politically passive and unskilled. The country was ruled by a boyar oligarchy much influenced by the xenophobic and anti-progressive Patriarch Ioakim, and several years of reaction against anything foreign or innovative followed. Ivan V performed most ceremonial duties: Peter's attentions were focused upon shipbuilding at Archangel, Russia's only seaport.

It is surprising in view of what was to come that for many years Peter was the candidate favored as

ruler among the conservative (though not Old Believer) group in late 17th-century Russia—both the Orthodox xenophobes around the patriarch and the major boyar families whose position was undermined by the abolition of *mestnichestvo* under Fyodor III. Peter with his boats and war games seemed obviously content to leave politics to others. He had, however, the bad habit of consorting with Western Europeans in the Foreign Quarter, situated at only strolling distance from Preobrazhenskoye (particularly with the Dutch, but also, for example, with the Scot Gordon and the Swiss Lefort). It was not that Westerners offered him some sort of vision of higher civilization (far from it, given the reputation for dèbauchery of the Foreign Quarter). What he found there were experts of a sort in the skills and technologies that fascinated him; he also found an alternative, unbuttoned and carnivalistic way of life.

Tsaritsa Natalya died, to Peter's great sorrow, in 1694. Ivan V died in 1696. Peter seems always to have got on amicably with his brother and treated him punctiliously as co-tsar. Now he was left as sole ruler, and events began to move rapidly. In 1695, without specific cause, he decided to make another attempt to capture the Turkish fortress of Azov, key to the south. Not only had two unsuccessful expeditions against the Turks' vassals, the Crimean Tatars, been the undoing of Sophia's government; the Turks and Tatars continued to be a menace to the Ukrainian borderland, making frequent slave raids. Russia made regular payments to the Crimean Tatars (and did so till 1700); Peter was stung by a scornful missive from the patriarch of Jerusalem pointing out that this meant the Russians were as good as tributaries of the Turks. Peter

A mid-18th-century view of the main channel of the River Neva in St Petersburg. The nearest building on the left (south) bank is the Imperial Winter Palace, before its reconstruction in its present form (1754). Beyond it (middle distance) is the vast Admiralty building, its wings enclosing shipyards. Its great gold spire (1732) is still a prominent landmark in St Petersburg, though now enclosed in an open colonnade added by the neoclassical architect A. Zakharov when he remodeled the whole building in 1806. On the opposite (north) bank are the old Academy of Sciences building and the Menshikov Palace.

led the first campaign in person; it ended disastrously, though as Golitsyn's had been, it was presented in Moscow as a triumph. Peter decided on a second campaign in 1696, and had a fleet of galleys to control the River Don built at Voronezh in a matter of months. The second campaign took Azov, largely through Gordon's military experience, though it was to be given up again 15 years later. It is no accident that these military adventures, marking the transition from war games to life, also marked Peter's rather belated accession to practical power.

Azov fell in July: the Russian forces reached Moscow in triumphal procession (the tsar marching alongside other naval commanders) during October. At once Peter announced the forced drafting of thousands of laborers and *streltsy* to Azov, the construction of Russia's first naval base on the coast below the estuary of the Don at Taganrog and a massive, expensive and (as it turned out) overhasty program of shipbuilding. Foreign shipwrights started arriving within weeks. In November Peter announced the names of more than 50 Russian noblemen who were commanded, irrespective of their own wishes, to go as students of navigation and related skills to Venice, the Dalmatian coast, Holland and England—the first of many who would study abroad thereafter. Most were young, but the oldest, Peter Tolstoy, was 52. They were to pay their own expenses and to return with a certificate of competence. Peter, characteristically, devised their syllabus himself. In December a busy half-year reached its remarkable conclusion with the announcement that the tsar's "great ambassadors and plenipotentiaries" (including, as it later turned out, Peter himself) would shortly depart on a "Great Embassy," to a variety of Western European states,

The Great Embassy

Peter's Great Embassy was a colossal undertaking. The retinue numbered over 250, including trumpeters and court dwarfs; among them the tsar, whose incognito was to be preserved on pain of death, was simply known as "Peter Mikhaylov." In his absence from Moscow, which could scarcely have been expected to go unnoticed, a three-man regency council nominally held power. The real boss, however, was a figure no less alarming than Peter himself: Prince Fyodor Romodanovsky, governor of Moscow, first Russian head of a secret police force. The so-called Preobrazhensky Office that Romodanovsky headed was so effectively secretive that we do not even know when and how it was set up; it performed its grim task so well that such treasonable plots as came to public knowledge in Peter's time may well strike us now as pathetically ill organized or unthreatening. Romodanovsky also played a stranger role, one that bore more directly on his position as *de facto* regent of Russia. He was nothing less than "alternative tsar," semi-officially titled "Prince-Caesar" by Peter and unofficially called by him "king" or "lord" (*gosudar*); several of the best 18th-century sources (Kurakin, Shcherbatov, Golikov) testify to this masquerade, that parallels Ivan IV's enthronement of Semyon Bekbulatovich (see p.59).

In Romodanovsky's case the "prehistory" to his remarkable status lies in the last and most realistic (though still formalized) "mock battles" that were the culmination of Peter's war games at Preobrazhenskoye in the early 1690s, in which Romodanovsky, commanding the Preobrazhensky regiment, was preordained victor (since Peter and foreign soldiers were among his "subordinates") over I. Buturlin's Semyonovsky regiment (with its complement of *streltsy*). All this, although generally ignored by historians, is worth recounting for the insight it gives into the less obvious reaches of Peter's mentality, where childhood experiences and diversions shaded uninterruptedly into adult concerns, where masquerade could turn into ceremonial and vice versa. The week before the departure of the Great Embassy was marked by an ominous portent of what would come at its end. A colonel of the *streltsy*, Ivan Tsykler, discontented at being posted to Azov, had grumbled too outspokenly with some conservatively inclined boyars. Romodanovsky's department scented a plot; the upshot was an execution staged in the most bizarre and gruesome circumstances.

The Great Embassy was not, as often seems to be thought, primarily a sort of fact-finding mission or Russian equivalent to the Grand Tour. It had a quite specific diplomatic purpose: to interest the Western powers in an anti-Turkish alliance that could help Peter carry forward his gains at Azov, perhaps (via Kerch) into the Black Sea. In this it was wholly unsuccessful, even though Austria had been fighting for its life against Turkey in the 1680s and Venice was a traditional Mediterranean rival of the Ottomans. The Western powers had quite enough on their hands in countering the growing pretensions of Louis XIV's France to want a renewal of war on another front. When the Austrians finally made peace, Russia's interests were disregarded, to Peter's lasting bitterness.

During the embassy, however, another and greater war, that was to last 20 years and permanently change the map of Europe, was hatched in a quite casual manner. In the course of his progress through northern Europe Peter picked up hints that other countries were dissatisfied with the power and territorial aggrandisement of Sweden, a nation that had played so prominent a part in the Thirty Years' War. The Swedish "empire" (successor in this respect to the Teutonic Knights) stretched round the whole eastern Baltic, blocking Russia's access to any west-facing port. New possibilities began to take shape in Peter's mind. It so happened that early in its progress the embassy had passed through Swedish territory, stopping at Riga. There a sentry, unaware of "Peter Mikhaylov's" identity, had challenged him on the fortress battlements. Both the head of the embassy, Lefort, and Peter himself knew that the man was only doing his job. But this trivial incident was to be the preposterous pretext for Peter's declaration of war in 1700.

In general, the obscure purposes and unusual nature of the Great Embassy caused embarrassment to several of the nations through which it passed. There was the particular problem of how to deal with Peter, whose presence was an open secret but whose incognito had to be preserved. He expected, and usually received, royal honors while remaining unencumbered by time-consuming protocol. Sophia, Electress of Hanover, contrived to sit with

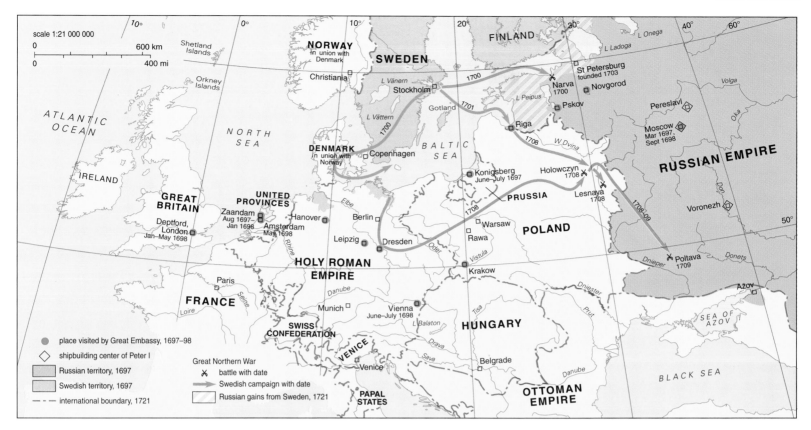

scale 1:21 000 000

● place visited by Great Embassy, 1697–98

◇ shipbuilding center of Peter I

Russian territory, 1697

Swedish territory, 1697

– – – international boundary, 1721

Great Northern War

✕ battle with date

→ Swedish campaign with date

Russian gains from Sweden, 1721

Peter I's Great Embassy and Northern War.
The Great Embassy to western Europe, including visits to Prussia, the United Provinces (Holland), Great Britain and Vienna, was symbolically a break with past Muscovite traditions, which were characteristically xenophobic. The primary ostensible purpose of the embassy, which lasted 18 months, was to instigate an alliance against the Turks, from whom Peter had recently captured the fortress town of Azov. This gave the landlocked Russians their longed-for opportunity of access to the Black Sea, with all that that implied in terms of naval potential; hence Peter's interest in the shipbuilding and dockyards at Deptford and Zaandam.

During the Great Embassy Peter conceived the bolder notion of a war against Sweden, which controlled the eastern Baltic lands, blocking Russia's access to western trade. After an initial defeat at Narva, Russian forces managed to hold a post on an island that was to become the heart of Peter's new capital of St Petersburg. With Charles XII of Sweden fighting Prussia and Poland as well, Peter was able to consolidate his hold on the east Baltic coast as far south as Riga. Important Russian victories at Lesnaya and Poltava finally contained the menace of Sweden, although the war dragged on for some years more until the Treaty of Nystad (1721) confirmed most of Russia's gains.

him at dinner and left a celebrated description of him. She praised his good looks, quick-spiritedness and repartee, but wished his manners were "a little less rustic"; he was "a prince at once very good and very bad," who "if he had received a better education, would be an exceptional man," with "great qualities and unlimited natural intelligence."

The embassy, naturally, attracted much attention and provided the first obvious demonstration of what those who knew Peter well in Russia must already have realized: his insatiable, almost manic enthusiasm for doing things himself. His greatest efforts were of course devoted to shipbuilding and related skills, at Zaandam in Holland and Deptford near London, but he also, as it were in passing, learnt watch-mending skills and, when delayed unexpectedly at the East Prussian port of Pillau, took a certificate course in gunnery. Among the skills he developed in Russia were boot making, woodcarving (a constant, time-consuming and probably therapeutic diversion) and, notoriously, the pulling of teeth—woe betide any of his subjects who mentioned their toothache in his presence. It was an ancient tradition that every ruler should learn a trade: this one, with characteristic arrogance or exuberance, evidently wanted to learn them all.

Revelry accompanied the embassy's progress through Europe, reaching its spectacular climax with a great masked ball in Vienna. It is notorious that, when the entire embassy had been accommodated for some months in the fine house of the diarist John Evelyn at Deptford, there was a huge repair bill (footed by the English government): it seems that the Russians particularly enjoyed driving wheelbarrows through holly hedges. What could Laetitia Cross, a leading London actress who moved in with Peter at Lord Carmarthen's suggestion, have made of it all? Carmarthen, a brilliant

seaman and drinking crony of Peter's, landed an immensely valuable tobacco supply monopoly in Russia. His offering of £28,000 in cash kept the embassy going when it was draining the Moscow treasury almost dry (it eventually cost 26 million roubles). The encouragement of a tobacco industry in Russia brought, conveniently for Peter, both financial and ideological rewards: tobacco was considered a grossly sinful substance by the Orthodox Church hierarchy. On a more systematic footing Peter recruited approaching 1000 foreign officers, technicians and experts to work in Russia, and sent home many shiploads of varied purchases.

A specter at the feast, Romodanovsky's messenger arrived hotfoot for Peter as the embassy was packing up to leave Vienna for Venice. To the surprise of his hosts Peter and his retinue left north-eastwards rather than southwestwards, heading home through Poland. Romodanovsky's alarming news was that four regiments of *streltsy*, ordered to march from Azov to the western borderland to make the Russian presence felt during the election of a new Polish king, had disobeyed orders and turned towards Moscow. Peter sent a command that the rebellion should be suppressed with the utmost severity. Soon afterwards another message confirmed that the rebels had been defeated and disarmed, largely thanks to the Russian army commander Shein and to General Gordon's cool-headedness. Thus Peter, instead of hurrying the remainder of his homeward progress, could stop for several pleasant days at Rawa with the new Polish king Augustus and plot war against Sweden. Nevertheless his arrival in Moscow on 25 August 1698 was sudden and unheralded. The date (Old Style) deserves to be mentioned, although among modern historians only Boris Uspensky seems to have noted its significance: a week before New Year's Day (until 1700, reckoned as 1 September) of 1699, the year in which Antichrist was expected by eschatologically minded Russians to appear. Even they could scarcely have expected the mayhem and bloodletting that was about to be unleashed.

Peter's return

If in the previous three years Peter had been remarkably and creatively active, now he appeared to be destructively so. On his first full day home, he suddenly, without warning, began to hack the beards off the boyars attendant on him with a dry razor. This was rather more than a practical joke: beards were considered by the Orthodox as a symbol of man's God-given dignity. Soon the entire service class was subjected to this facial metamorphosis: peasants and clergy were exempt from it, and an instantly visible chasm was opened up between the very appearances of upper and lower classes. This was strengthened when Peter began to snip off the long sleeves of traditional Russian dress, and eventually to forbid it to his servitors. In the end beards were permitted on payment of a quite substantial tax (certificated by "beard tokens"), but made no significant comeback till the mid-19th century. Next Peter summarily retired his unloved, uncomprehending and unwilling wife Yevdokia to a convent at Suzdal (where she continued to regard herself as tsaritsa), parting her peremptorily from their eight-year-old son Aleksey, whom he handed over to one of his sisters. Meanwhile in mid-September Peter's settling of accounts with the *streltsy* began.

The leading figure in the protracted and ghastly process that followed was Romodanovsky, and its central location was Preobrazhenskoye, the "counterfeit capital" of Peter and his intimates (they even gave it the garbled Germanic name of "Plezpurkh," that is, "Pressburg"), the locus of the new regiments that were rendering the *streltsy* humiliated and obsolete. Fourteen special interrogation chambers were constructed, and each weekday batches of *streltsy* were taken for torture and questioning. This whole exercise in mass cruelty produced no significant information of the sort Peter desired—either of a plot in high places or of the active participation of his incarcerated sister Sophia, whom he personally questioned. Soon executions began, both at Preobrazhenskoye and in the city itself.

Much has been written about this reign of terror, since Johannes Korb, a member of a recently arrived Austrian embassy to Russia, kept a detailed and much-quoted diary of what he witnessed and the rumors he heard. It seems highly probable that the tsar made leading members of his circle participate in the bloodshed, whether or not he did so himself. A repulsive symbolism characterized some events, as when priests who had blessed the *streltsy* were executed on a cross-shaped gibbet with the court jester in clerical robes acting as hangman.

Korb and other contemporary commentators, it should be noted, did not question that the *streltsy* were rebels who deserved an unpleasant fate. But Korb's diary caught a note of panic and terror, of the tsar's vengeful overreaction, and later Peter tried to suppress its publication in Austria. There were two great waves of executions, in the autumn of Peter's return and after Lent in the following

Left Peter began, without warning, to cut the beards of his boyars as soon as he returned from the Great Embassy in 1698. He then extended the ban on the wearing of beards to the entire gentry and merchant class (but not to the peasants and clergy). Russians regard beards as a symbol of God-given dignity, and the humiliation of losing them was particularly intense for the traditionalist Old Believers (one of whom is shown suffering it in this contemporary woodcut). In 1705 Peter permitted beards again on payment of a tax: tokens (*below*) were issued for this, certifying "the money has been paid," but few took advantage of this expensive concession.

spring, with a total of some 1200 victims. This was only a small fraction of the *streltsy* class as a whole, but reprisals did not end there: some (mostly those under 20) whose lives were spared were mutilated and exiled, while the victims' wives and children were sent to beg in the countryside. The other *streltsy* regiments, fearful and discontented, were in the next few years disbanded and forcibly settled in remote parts. The episode traumatized Russian society, however, out of all proportion to the actual number of victims: it seemed as if by his bloody gesture a tsar was now signaling that he would wage ferocious war against a whole traditional and sanctified culture.

Perhaps Peter's action did save his throne and the country's stability, as he himself thought. Yet even afterwards large and desperate rebellions were to break out. The second most populous city in Russia, Astrakhan, was the scene of an uprising in 1705 into which were fed varied ingredients: Old Believer resentment, *streltsy* bitterness, heavy burdens of taxation, the authoritarianism of Peter's governor (who was beheaded by the rebels), Orthodox apprehensiveness and wild rumor. It was said that the young women of the city would all be forcibly married off to Germans (on a single day 100 married to avoid this fate), and that the wigs the governing classes now wore were idols that the pious folk would have to worship. Behind all this was the more widespread belief that foreigners were infiltrating and taking over the land, that the true tsar had died while abroad and that "Peter" was a German imposter—such a rumor was heard in Moscow even before the return of the Great Embassy.

There is another aspect of Peter's personality and its lifelong activity that needs to be discussed and that was made indeed shockingly public at the same period. This is Peter's involvement with a group of cronies, partly overlapping with his inner circle of state advisers, headed by Romodanovsky, who gave themselves the name of "All-jocular Synod" (*vseshuteyshiy sobor*: alternatively *vsepya-neyshiy* "All-drunken"). Orgiastic carousing took place in a context that parodied church rituals, with mock dignitaries and mock ceremonies that sometimes, notably in the winter of 1698–99, became destructively public. What is important about this club, apart from its scandalous shock-value in a traditionalist society, is that Peter himself found it important. He was at the center of its activities, making out its "statutes," devising its rituals, from before the age of 20 to his death. Historians have interpreted the significance of this "synod" in diverse ways, or have avoided interpreting it save as horseplay or relaxation (its name has been softened into "the Jolly Company"). That the public hooliganism associated with the mock synod reached its climax in the winter of 1698–99 is doubtless connected with the fearful vengeance on the *streltsy* that was simultaneously in progress. The tensions of the time seem to have somewhat unbalanced Peter, and commentators noted thereafter an alarming facial tic that frequently distorted his features at times of stress.

If Peter had been, as some writers imply, indifferent to religion or even atheistically inclined, the mock synod's activities could have been dismissed as simply tasteless buffoonery. Actually this was far from the case. His writings continually invoke divine approval, he quotes the Bible frequently, his library was full of religious books, he even enjoyed singing in church. When, during the first wave of reprisals against the *streltsy*, the Patriarch Adrian (Ioakim's successor, elected in 1690 against Peter's wishes) tried to appeal to Peter's sense of mercy, he was rebuffed, according to Korb, with a remarkable speech in which he told the Patriarch "Know that I reverence God and honor his most holy Mother more earnestly perhaps than thou dost . . . ." The mock synod was, to put it simply, an adventure in blasphemy, from motives one can only guess. Peter's actions were interpreted by some as an attempt to live up to the role of Antichrist which so many of his subjects assigned to him, particularly in his "usurpation" of the role of patriarch after Adrian died in 1700 and was not replaced. Peter's chief clerical apologist Feofan Prokopovich explicitly saw him as *pontfex maximus*, high priest. Foreigners did not quite understand this: sensing his dissatisfaction with the Orthodox hierarchy, they tried to interest him in Catholicism, Protestantism, even Anglicanism and the Society of Friends (Quakers). But the blasphemer cannot do without the object of his blasphemy.

The Great Northern War

The year 1700 marked another moment of transition in Peter's reign. The internal terror was for the moment over and done with. A peace treaty with Turkey meant the cessation of tribute payments to the Crimean Tatars. But a more protracted, dangerous and financially draining war was

One of the bloodiest episodes in Russian history was the suppression of the *streltsy* (musketeers), some of whom staged a brief rebellion in 1698 when Peter was away on his Great Embassy. After his return, in late 1698 and early 1699, some 1200 rebels were interrogated and executed by hanging or beheading in or near Moscow. The secretary to the Austrian embassy, Johannes Korb, left the best-known account of this reign of terror; the illustration of the mass executions is taken from his *Diary of a Journey to Muscovy* (1700)—with an inaccurately depicted Moscow in the background. Though the victims were only a small proportion of the 20 000 or so *streltsy*, the force as a whole was doomed.

declared the same year: the Great Northern War against Sweden, that eventually established Russia as a force to be reckoned with on the European stage. The eastern Baltic provinces that formed part of Sweden's empire were full of discontent; Sweden had overreached itself and was generally disliked or envied in northern Europe; its new king, Charles XII, was still a teenager. But Sweden proved to be no pushover and more than once dealt Peter nearly mortal blows. First the fighting centered on the old fortress-city of Narva, where modern Estonia and Russia meet on the Gulf of Finland. Almost at once the Russian army besieging it was crushingly defeated by a much smaller Swedish force. Thereafter, fortunately for Peter, instead of advancing into Russia Charles XII turned to deal with Augustus the Strong.

In the breathing space Peter's forces recuperated sufficiently over the next couple of years to move in on the easternmost and least populous of Sweden's Baltic provinces, Ingria. This was, as Peter proclaimed, ancient Russian territory, vital as a trade route, despite its inhospitability, to the Novgorod state in the Middle Ages, and its recapture was a declared war aim. Here, in Charles's absence in Poland, Peter's forces met with success, taking back the old Russian towns Yam and Koporye, and in May 1703 knocking out the two Swedish fortresses on the great River Neva that connects Lake Ladoga with the Baltic. A few miles downstream from the only Swedish town on the river, Nyenskans, the Neva fanned out into a low-lying delta, too prone to flooding to tempt inhabitants, through which it found its way to the Gulf of Finland. Here, immediately after the capture of Nyenskans, Peter took part for the first time in his life in a successful naval engagement, capturing some Swedish vessels that came to relieve the town. Suddenly Russia once again had direct territorial access to the Baltic and the West. Peter marked the occasion by establishing a fort on Hare Island, a small patch of land near the head of the delta: so St Petersburg was born. During the 17 years of fluctuating fortunes that marked the remaining course of the war, Peter hung doggedly on to this vulnerable patch of coastline, and long before the war was over the Peter-Paul Fortress on Hare Island was the heart of his new capital city.

As the Northern War continued, Charles XII (reckoning Augustus to be his more threatening opponent) slowly consolidated his grip on Poland, while Russian forces raided the ill-defended Baltic provinces. Peter desperately reorganized and trained his numerous but inexperienced and undisciplined armies in an attempt to match the Swedish fighting machine. More and more money that the treasury scarcely knew how to find was pumped into the military effort, rising at times to over 90 percent of the state income. Everything imaginable was taxed, from bath-houses to coffins. Eventually, in 1718, the fundamental land or household tax of Muscovite Russia was done away with, and a poll tax on all adult males of the peasant and working class, to be collected by landowners, was substituted. This squeezed three times as much revenue out of the unfortunate populace as the taxes it replaced; regularized conscription for life of peasant soldiers was also instituted: both

were among Peter's more lasting innovations. Great levies of forced labor were raised for the tsar's public construction works: fortresses, canals and, more and more demandingly after 1703, the building of St Petersburg on its swampy, chilly and unhealthy estuary.

Apparently unworried by his east Baltic reverses, Charles XII meanwhile applied ever greater pressure on the combined armies of Poland and Saxony. This was a grim time for Peter's Russia: the treasury was empty, the army still semi-trained, and a series of great popular revolts broke out in quick succession: the Astrakhan and Bulavin (Cossack) rebellions and the Bashkir civil war. This decade culminated nevertheless in Peter's most famous success, the battle of Poltava (1709), that routed Charles's army and is indeed usually considered one of the great punctuating events of European history. The first major Russian victory, maybe the one that decided the war, took place however the year before (1708). Charles, having dealt with his westerly opponents, moved gradually east into Belorussia, keeping the Russians guessing as to where he would aim his next blow. Subsequent historians have blamed him for not heading directly towards Moscow. In the event he swung his armies south, towards the richer lands of the Ukraine, where the hetman (Cossack leader) Ivan Mazepa had secretly gone over to his side. This extended his supply lines, leaving him all too dependent on the arrival of a vast reinforcement of over 12 000 troops with a large baggage train. In September 1708 a roughly equal Russian force managed to intercept the Swedish reinforcements at the village of Lesnaya and comprehensively defeated them, the first time skill rather than numbers had brought Russia victory. Peter called this first true victory "the mother of the battle of Poltava."

The battle of Poltava was hard fought but over in half a day. Charles, badly wounded in the foot, escaped southeastwards with a few hundred followers, helped by Mazepa. Peter was hit by gunfire but remained unscathed. Charles's only hope, thin as it seemed, was to survive, reach Ottoman territory, reactivate the old hostility of the Turks and their strongly anti-Russian dependants the Crimean Tatars against Peter, restart the war with his tiny army and somehow make his way across the breadth of Europe to his northern homeland. All this, incredibly, he managed, though it took him five years. Meanwhile it was Peter's turn to overstretch himself. Only two years after Poltava, pursuing the dream that for over 200 years intermittently haunted Russian rulers—of an uprising of Balkan Christians against the Turks, under Russian leadership—Peter almost succumbed on the River Prut in Moldavia. Forced, in the face of defeat, to sue for peace on almost any terms save losing Petersburg, he, like Charles before him, escaped by the skin of this teeth. Skillful negotiation by his diplomat P. Shafirov, who was of Jewish origin, bribery of the pasha, perhaps instigated by his wife Catherine, and more importantly differences between the local and central Ottoman authorities, the Crimean Tatars and the Swedes let Peter off the hook, at the expense of Azov and some other forts and, to his bitter regret, the southern fleet he had built up.

In 1717 Peter made his second journey to the West, this time choosing (partly because of the recent death of Louis XIV) to visit France. This canvas by L.M.J. Wersent shows Peter at Versailles, holding up the child monarch Louis XV. Diplomatic results of the visit, again seen as an embassy, were negligible.

After Poltava the exhausted Swedes would have been as happy as the Russians to make peace. Charles XII's survival however ensured that the war dragged on, but after the Prut it was comparatively undramatic. The Russians gradually consolidated their Baltic gains, occupied Finland, won more naval engagements and finally sent raiding parties into Sweden itself. Charles was killed in Norway in 1718, and eventually the Peace of Nystad (1721) secured Russia's new territory, though, curiously, Peter had to purchase Livonia (the larger part of modern Latvia). Nystad was probably the crowning moment of Peter's life—literally so, since to celebrate it he was proclaimed emperor, "Father of the Fatherland" and "the Great." After it, Peter neither enjoyed the fruits of peace nor found that Russia itself ran smoothly. In 1722 he started a war against Persia, making some territorial gains that ultimately could not be held. It was, however, in these last few years of his life that many of the institutional changes for which his reign is remembered were made. Notable among these was his ordering of his entire "service class" according to a table with corresponding columns of ranks (for army, guards, navy and civil service), originally 14 in number, representing a ladder of promotion up which the servitor had to proceed step by step; the top eight rungs conferred hereditary nobility.

The succession drama

In 1717, 20 years after the Great Embassy, with the critical stages of the Northern War past, Peter made his second journey to Western Europe, this time to Holland and France. Again there were diplomatic motives: with the War of the Spanish Succession over and Louis XIV recently dead, it seemed a good moment to strike commercial and military bargains with the still enormously powerful and prosperous French. Once again his diplomacy bore little fruit, though a vague treaty of friendship was signed, and specialists, though fewer than before, were recruited to work in Russia.

Again, too, a crisis involving real or perceived treason erupted dramatically on his return. This time the central victim was his own son Aleksey, a quite intelligent but shallow, confused and indolent character. The divergence of their personalities had long been apparent: Aleksey was not only, and with reason, scared of his dominating parent, but handled their differences quite wrongly, alternately submissive, obstinate and evasive. Several missives that passed between them survive, helping to chart a complex and truly tragic story. When in 1716 Peter sent an ultimatum threatening Aleksey with retirement to a monastery (echoing his mother's fate), the latter went abroad and simply disappeared for many months. He resurfaced in Austria, whose diplomatic relations with Russia were poor. The Austrians were in a quandary: would Peter use force to get his son back? They permitted the experienced and unscrupulous envoy Peter Tolstoy to interview him: on a spurious promise of safe conduct Aleksey was unwise enough to return. He had been a focus for the hopes of malcontents in high places, and Peter sensed a dangerous plot. Aleksey and those who were supposed to have helped him, were sentenced to be executed for treason; before the sentence on Aleksey was confirmed, however, he died in prison, doubtless as a consequence of the current methods of interrogation.

Aleksey's death was a relief, and Peter hardly pretended otherwise. His infant son Peter (Pyotr Petrovich) by his second—in Orthodox eyes questionable—marriage to Catherine was the new heir. But the child soon died, to Peter's misery, and by a trick of fate his only grandson, the last male in the Romanov line, was another Peter (Pyotr Alekseyevich), son of the ill-fated Aleksey. There is another curious twist in this family saga. When Catherine (born Marfa Skavronskaya in Livonia) converted to the Orthodox Church, Aleksey had stood godfather to her, so that she was "reborn" into Orthodoxy as Yekaterina Alekseyevna: to many believers Peter's subsequent marriage to her was the grotesque symbolic blasphemy of marrying his "granddaughter."

After the crisis there was a dynastic problem: since so much in the "Petrine revolution" clearly depended on the tsar's person, how could a worthy inheritor of his title be guaranteed? In the secularized state God's grace was scarcely to be relied on. In any case Peter promulgated a law that each ruler could nominate his or her successor. He did not avail himself of it, and legend recounts that just before he died he managed to scrawl on a paper the words "I leave all . . ." without getting farther. To whom? "To the people," some later guessed. Be that as it may, he had not long before his death had Catherine crowned empress with lavish ceremony, suggesting a conscious evocation of the Byzantine system of crowning one's heir in one's lifetime. She was tough, sensible, not over-subtle and a loving interpreter of Peter's wishes; she was unlikely arbitrarily to dismiss his favorites or have any disturbingly innovatory ideas of her own. An *ad hoc* council of Peter's servitors—notably Menshikov, who stood to gain or lose much—started to press her claim to rule even before Peter had breathed his last, but the clinching factor was the support of the Guards regiments. These regiments had been Peter's own first creation and the focus of his power: they were henceforth to have a deciding voice in all accessions to the throne until that of Alexander I in 1801.

The legacy of Peter

How are Peter and his reign to be summed up? The problem is almost too enormous to grapple with, since it is perhaps the central problem of all Russian history. Here we can limit ourselves to a few comments and conclusions, viewed from four angles: that of military success and concomitant territorial acquisition; of domestic reform; of Westernization; and of legacy to Russia and the world. Naturally, these aspects are interlinked.

Peter's reign saw only small gains of territory compared with those of his grandfather Mikhail (across Siberia), of his father (into Poland and Ukraine) and of his 18th-century successors (into Central Asia, and subsequently southwards to the Crimea). Yet those small gains were crucial, and not only because they enabled St Petersburg to be

founded. By taking over the east Baltic provinces Peter made himself heir, in a sense, to another empire, that of Sweden, and in the process incorporated some sizeable non-Slavic national groups —Letts and Estonians, with some Jews and a German upper class. These, when added to the scattered Finnic, Turkic and Palaearctic people and the various Caucasian groups and Persians around the Caspian, made Russia by 1725 a remarkably multi-ethnic empire. Peter's constant warring impoverished and exhausted the country, but it did at least make it secure and provided the basis for some fairly long peaceful interludes in the rest of the 18th century; the same is true of his development of a fleet, however minor its impact at first. Despite his recruitment of foreign officers he actually assisted the Russification of the army, as well as its greater efficiency. But the militarization of society was the price paid, and the new Guards regiments acquired at times controlling political power.

Peter's reforms flowed out of the military and politico-economic situations in which he found himself, and also out of his personal dislikes and enthusiasms. After the turn of the century, however, and particularly in the last decade of his life, they began to have a more ordered character, implying a vision of a properly run society. Many recorded remarks and letters testify to his concern with the common good of Russia, to be manifested in its prosperity, orderliness and international glory. There was nothing particularly subtle, let alone revolutionary, in this, but it was pursued with a tenacity and assiduousness that made it extraordinary; Peter would work for months drafting regulations and decrees personally, rising to work normally at 4 a.m. Particularly interesting is the habit in his later years of prefacing decrees by explanations for them in terms of public benefit. It seems that he was the first ruler of Russia to have, or anyhow to express, a clear concept of the state as an entity separate from and superior to the current ruler. A famous instance is the exhortation he is reported to have delivered to his troops on the eve of Poltava, urging them to think not of "Peter" but of "Russia."

The Petrine reforms modernized the way society was administered and, to point up differences with Muscovite practice, brought in a new nomenclature. The 50-odd government departments (*prikazy*) yielded to a much smaller number of "colleges" or ministries, more clearly demarcated from each other. The committee of each was to contain at least one foreign expert. The old Boyar Duma, or permanent council of notables, had no place in the new order; still less had the Assembly of the Land. Instead, a "Ruling Senate" was set up, at first to govern when Peter was away fighting: its real boss was his own supervisory official, the procurator, who was to be the tsar's "eye and proxy." The church, deprived of its patriarch, was to be governed by the synod, in effect another department of state, chaired by a layman. The structure of society itself was not so much changed as more starkly, probably less organically delineated. Beards and Russian clothes marked out the peasant class, but so did payment of the poll or "soul" tax, which homogenized the various lower social groupings that had characterized the old system.

Above This engraving from Johannes Korb's *Diary* shows ships that Peter the Great had built at Archangel. This town, situated where the Northern Dvina flows into the White Sea, close to the Arctic Circle, was Muscovy's only direct point of access to the sea until the site of St Petersburg was captured from the Swedes in 1703. Archangel was established in the 1580s to cope with the growing volume of trade first with England, then with Holland and other countries. The Archangel shipyards expanded Peter's interest in shipbuilding which dated from his activities at Lake Pleshcheyevo in the early 1690s.

Below A page from *Vedomosti* (30 November 1723), a gazette founded as Russia's first newspaper; it was edited at St Petersburg and carried reports from abroad. The page shown here describes the conclusion of a state visit by King George I of England to Berlin. Note the clear new ''civic'' typeface introduced by Peter and the view of the Neva at St Petersburg in the vignette above.

As for the upper class, its ability to evade or ameliorate the conditions of state service was curtailed. Peter's simple social principle was that all must serve according to their capability, the tsar most of all; he once pronounced that ''a noble is he who is useful.'' Certainly part of Peter's aim was to set up what we would now call a meritocracy, and the Table of Ranks, through which theoretically any person of sufficient talent could progress, formalized this aim. A few low-born servitors (Menshikov, Yaguzhinsky, Shafirov) did manage spectacular careers, yet the top rungs of the ladder mostly still continued to be occupied by members of the great old families: Golitsyns, Golovins, Dolgorukys, Sheremetyevs and their like. There was undoubtedly an increase in social mobility, but it would be hard to claim that any large segment of society felt itself ''more free.'' Serfdom was if anything tightened up, while the impressment of hundreds of thousands of peasants into military or labor forces was a cruel hardship. There is one sterling exception: women's participation in society was improved, at least in the upper classes, and arranged marriages were officially forbidden. A subtler increase in mental freedom, at any rate, came from the growth in education that Peter, at first clumsily, propagated; promotion in service was conditional upon passing examinations, and at one stage it was forbidden even to issue marriage licenses to those who failed.

Did Peter's reforms add up to—or ultimately promote—Westernization (a term, incidentally, he and his contemporaries did not use)? A gloss of ''foreignness'' was deliberately applied by Peter to most of the products of his reign: to the organization of government bodies, to rank titles, to the educational syllabus, to the conduct of social gatherings, to the names of towns and palaces, to the styles promoted in architecture and painting. Sometimes things Western had a glamor for Peter and his associates that sprang simply from their not being Muscovite. Very often, however, one senses that the prime merit of Westernization for Peter was shock-value, emphasizing to the mass of the population the spirit of newness that his propagandists assiduously promoted.

Nevertheless there are also those who claim plausibly that Peter had a ''modern mentality'' (which in the context would have to mean Western). His world was no longer statically medieval: he was aware of historical progress, of the rise and fall of great nations, of the possibility that Russia's turn for greatness had come, or could be made to come. The desires for increased trade and for military success were scarcely ''modern'' or Western in themselves, but the active encouragement of capitalistic commerce and the intense interest in the natural sciences were so. An opening up of horizons, a sense of new possibilities, much as in the post-Renaissance West, was part of the Petrine atmosphere. Yet here too ambiguities lurk. There was greater access to information, admittedly, and a sort of public newspaper was published from 1703, yet there was unprecedentedly tight control on the expression of divergent views, and Peter was more concerned with the dissemination of propaganda (particularly abroad) than with the free flow of knowledge. The gates of Russia were thrown open to foreign experts (among whom were not a few second-rate adventurers), and they were offered huge salaries and opportunities; on arrival they tended to find they were no longer, as they naively thought, selling their skills in a free market, but absorbed into the peripheries of the service state, dependent on the whims, patronage and politicking of grandees. The service state itself, spruced up under Peter into a fine vehicle for the self-realization of absolutism, was essentially a thoroughly ''unmodern'' concept. Peter lived more than half his life in the hard 17th century, and is to be compared with figures such as the English Stuarts, the French Louis XIV or the Prussian Friedrich Wilhelm I—awkward, obsessive and obstinate figures, still curiously remote from modern understanding.

Peter's legacy to his country seemed to many later Russians all-pervasive, for better or worse or both. He could inspire fanatical devotion in some of his followers, to an unhealthy degree when his portrait could even be set up as an ''icon.'' There is something curiously unedifying about the spectacle of Feofan Prokopovich, the West Russian churchman who became Peter's leading intellectual propagandist, almost deifying the ruler who had abolished the patriarchate. The more specific or concrete legacy could be seen in the Russian fleet and in the new city of St Petersburg, but more deeply, if less tangibly, it concerned attitudes to power and its exercise, the Russians' self-image and their image abroad, their understanding of how things should get done and what sort of picture they (and others) have built up of Peter and his exploits.

However we evaluate Peter's reforms, we can hardly deny the strength of his personal example. The tireless worker, of simple (though not ascetic) personal tastes, on easy terms with even his humblest acquaintances—all this makes for a powerful image and impressed non-Russians greatly. An unpublished English manuscript describes a merchant's impression of the tsar's approachability in Archangel: ''He's no proud man, I assure you, for he'll eat or be merry with anybody . . . He invited all the nasty tars to dinner with him.'' He was one of the first great political voluntarists of modern times, one of those believers in the power of will and effort to change the world. Such strongmen normally believe that ends justify means, and the means usually involve cruelty. Peter, though able to be cruel, was not sadistic: except in the case of the *streltsy*, he did not apply the death penalty frequently, indiscriminately, or without warning.

Yet memories of the harsh effects of an unbending will lingered on, and became fused (as with Ivan IV) with the great achievements, as if somehow glory and cruelty were inseparable. This was well expounded by Alexander Pushkin in the early 19th century, most memorably in *The Bronze Horseman* (a poem haunted by the powerful ghost of Peter) but also in the epic *Poltava*. The effects for Russia were not, on the whole, for the best. Nor were other aspects of the Petrine cult: the ''deification'' of pure power in the person of a tsar no longer under divine sanction and the belief in the efficacy of a single superhuman or monstrous effort to make everything suddenly new and better. But the period, however much it cast a shadow on subsequent Russian history, has assuredly become a potent source of myth.

The Russian Baroque

The cultural impact of the West on Russia, the strength of the latter's native traditions, the sometimes uneasy but often exciting hybridization that resulted are strikingly evident in the great baroque buildings of Russia. A period of under a century (1680s–1760s) saw a rapid evolution of style that produced some of the most characteristic, varied and (to the visitor) surprising works of Russian architecture.

At least three "Baroques" should be distinguished. They share a striving for polychrome decorativeness: walls of pastel hues, details picked out in white, tiling, gilding, elaborate window surrounds. "Moscow Baroque" flourished quite briefly, largely in the joint reign (1682–96) of the young tsars Ivan V and Peter I, under the patronage of a few leading families— Naryshkins, Golitsyns, Sheremetyevs, also the regent Sophia—but not only in Moscow. It is very idiosyncratic: effectively the last stage of Old Russian architecture, with abundance of applied Western detailing, probably culled mostly from architectural textbooks. "Petrine Baroque," associated particularly with the early years of St Petersburg (though originating in Moscow), was comparatively modest and sober. Finally, the late Baroque, often called "Elizabethan" from the reign of Elizabeth (1741–62), is known primarily through the vast, breathtaking palaces of Rastrelli, but is actually a much wider phenomenon. Ukrainian Baroque also deserves mention: a Central European offshoot, it probably played a part in the formation of the Moscow style, but has distinctive forms. Baroque yielded rather suddenly to a severe and elegant neoclassicism.

Above left The Intercession Church (c. 1693) in the Moscow suburb of Fili exemplifies Moscow Baroque church architecture. A Naryshkin foundation, it rises pyramidally in stories of varied cross-section on a centralized, quatrefoil plan. The manner suggests the work of Yakov Bukhvostov, the best Moscow builder of the time.

Left B.F. Rastrelli (1700–76), son of the immigrant Italian sculptor C.B. Rastrelli, worked in or near St Petersburg and for Bühren in Courland. His influence became pervasive in Elizabeth's reign. The Great Palace at Tsarskoye Selo (renamed Pushkin) stands with the Winter Palace (both 1750s) as Rastrelli's masterpiece. Its seemingly endless, rippling facade was intended to be glimpsed through a belt of mature trees. Characteristic "Elizabethan" gilded domes crown the chapel.

Right Few domestic houses have survived from Peter the Great's time. The Kikin Palace, near Smolny in Leningrad, is a rare example, though much restored since it was built in 1714 for A.V. Kikin. He was one of Peter's closest servitors, but advised the Tsarevich Aleksey to flee abroad and was executed in 1718. Of the five houses Kikin owned in Petersburg this was doubtless the grandest, yet it is still architecturally unassuming, like much Petrine building. Characteristic are the pilaster strips, symmetrical projecting wings and naively cheerful pediments. Other survivors are a couple of wooden cottages where Peter stayed; his modest Summer Palace; Menshikov's rambling palace on the Neva; a house on the Bersenevka in Moscow. Drawings by the adaptable Swiss architect Trezzini, for Petersburg "model houses" for various social classes, are known.

Above Though Moscow Baroque appeared rather suddenly, it had a prehistory. In the 17th century Western motifs occur, notably in decorative window surrounds; an extremely ornamental mannerism and concern with effect enters much Muscovite architecture. An incomparable anthology of Moscow Baroque is the Novodevichy Convent that guarded the southwestern approach to the city. The main cathedral is a plain 16th-century "official" building; otherwise almost everything was planned or built in the regency of the Tsaritsa Sophia (1682–89). Sophia herself was subsequently incarcerated here. The stout walls and towers are crowned with insubstantial strapwork. There are two gatehouse churches on different plans, characteristic domestic buildings (seen here) and a splendid belfry of diminishing stories.

99

THE EMPIRE AFTER PETER

The mice and the cat

An energetic and autocratic ruler with a strong sense of mission, such as Peter, is likely to be much exercised over the question of how to ensure a worthy successor to carry on the good work. In Peter's case this led to the agonizing collision with his son Aleksey and to the law he then promulgated which specified that the sovereign should nominate his or her successor, a nomination not to be challenged on pain of death. Power, it would seem, was no longer to be considered a divinely bestowed prerogative but a matter of personal gift. So remote was this law from human realities, from Russian traditions and from the actual processes of transmission of power that in the rest of the 18th century—during which seven tsars and tsaritsas followed Peter—it operated properly only twice, and on both occasions in favor of shortlived and unsuitable successors. The first time was in 1740, when the Empress Anna bequeathed the throne to her newborn infant grandnephew (Ivan VI). This was not only a capricious legacy, but one disastrous for the recipient. The second such nominee was Peter III. Under Paul in 1797 Peter's law was discarded in favor of primogeniture, but even so another major succession crisis took place in 1825.

Peter's 18th-century successors, except for Catherine II, tend to be dismissed as mediocrities. It seems unfair to blame ordinary people, even if rulers, for not being exceptional; in any case a reign as exceptional as Peter's must have made most of his subjects yearn for a little ordinariness. The glee of various "little" people at the passing of Peter their great oppressor is memorably allegorized in the various popular woodcuts in circulation after Peter's death, illustrating "How the Mice Buried the Cat." The rulers in question were in fact very different from each other; some ruled only briefly. But it is not so much their personalities that are of interest as the way in which pressures and forces inherent in post-Petrine society manifested themselves as Russia settled down into a sort of normality after the long Petrine crisis. In fact a touchstone of Peter's individual reforms can be taken to be the degree to which they survived, were adapted or were quietly shelved in "mediocre" but calmer times.

Where autocracy relaxes its grip on the reins, various other hands will grab at them. The alternation of dominant interest groups, rising and falling rather abruptly, is a marked feature of the period. Catherine I's accession to the throne on her husband's death marked the apogee of Peter's senior servitors, notably Menshikov (whose unscrupulous greed had put him under a cloud in Peter's last years). Catherine, uninterested in policy-making, set up a "Supreme Privy Council" for the day-to-day running of the country: superior to the senate, it was an oligarchic "cabinet" containing both "new men" and representatives of the old aristocracy, but dominated by Menshikov. It grappled as

best it could with the complexities, obscurities and excessive exactions of the Petrine legacy.

Catherine, who was too fond of the bottle, lasted only two years. On her death only one male heir of the Romanov line remained, the unfortunate Aleksey's young—but tall, robust and intelligent—son Peter, now aged 11. Catherine supposedly made a detailed testament leaving him the throne, though it is a near certainty others were responsible; anyhow the succession was not challenged. The privy council acted as regent, and Menshikov made an immediate bid to take over the life of the boy tsar, as he had educated—and bullied—his father more than 20 years before: he even arranged a betrothal to his own daughter, Maria. Peter II, however, seems despite his tender years to have united his grandfather's decisiveness with his father's suspicion of the hangers-on of the "new age." In alliance with the old-aristocratic Dolgoruky family, Peter managed to engineer the arrest of Menshikov and sent him into exile where he died. Another specter from the past, Peter Tolstoy, betrayer of Peter's father Aleksey, already over 80, had already been similarly dealt with, and died in exile on an island in the White Sea. Grass grew in the streets of St Petersburg, and a formal shift of capital back to Moscow seemed imminent. Peter II, by now 14, was engaged to marry a Dolgoruky princess, but suddenly he was stricken with smallpox, and died in January 1730 on the day that had been fixed for his wedding. Some of the Dolgorukys claimed, unconvincingly, that he had left the throne to his fiancée. He was clearly already a ruler with a willful if untrained mind of his own, and it is interesting to speculate what direction Russia's destiny might have taken had he lived.

This popular woodcut (*lubok*) is one of several depicting a large cat being conveyed to burial by the mice it had tormented. They circulated widely after Peter the Great's death in 1725 as an allegory of the various groups in the population whom Peter had persecuted and who felt a sense of relief at his demise. The cheerful and expressive art form of the *lubok* (often carrying satirical messages) flourished from the 17th to the 19th century.

CATHARINA IMPERATRIX RUSSORUM

Catherine I (tsaritsa 1725–27), here depicted by Jean Marc Nattier, was humbly born in 1684 in Livonia as Marfa Skavronskaya. She became Peter the Great's companion in his military expeditions during the Northern War, then his second wife (1712). She was a soothing influence on Peter, being notably the only person who could quell the muscular spasms (probably mild epileptic seizures resulting from a severe fever) to which he was prone. He had her crowned empress in 1724, and when he died the following year without naming a successor, the Guards regiments, among whom she was a popular figure, put her on the throne, despite her lack of education and her humble birth.

Anna and the German ascendancy

In this sudden crisis the Supreme Privy Council, packed by now with Dolgorukys and Golitsyns, took upon itself the task of finding a successor. No male Romanovs in the royal line were left, and the council resorted to a bold gamble—one that, with its unintended consequences, marks an important if often underestimated turning point in Russian history. From Peter I's family the council turned to that of his senior co-tsar, Ivan V, who had left several daughters. The eldest was married to the Duke of Mecklenburg; the second, Anna, was the widowed Duchess of Courland (a small semi-independent principality in the southern part of modern Latvia). Led by Vasiliy Dolgoruky, a deputation from the council traveled in secrecy to Anna's capital, Mittau (in Russian Mitava), to put an unusual proposition: that she should ascend the Russian throne on acceptance of a series of conditions that would make her what we would now call a constitutional monarch—in effect, that all important policy decisions should be approved or instigated by the privy council.

The idea was a brilliant one. Though other women had ruled Russia before, they had all done so in the capacity of widows of tsars (Catherine I

and/or regents (Sophia, Natalya Naryshkina, Yelena Glinskaya, even the Kievan Olga). Anna, offered such a prize in her own right, could be expected to be suitably pliant, even grateful; yet she was not a novice at the task (having had Courland to run for many years) and was still, in her mid-thirties, young enough to marry again (at the privy council's discretion!) and produce an heir. All seemed to go to plan. Anna accepted without demur, signed the conditions and set off for Moscow, which she reached in late February. Earlier in the month, however, word of the conditions imposed by the privy council had leaked out. Hectic politicking among the lesser gentry, who formed the bulk of the Guards regiments, soldiers as well as officers, ensued: it seemed clear to most of them that an oligarchic clique of traditional aristocrats intended to remodel the Petrine system that gave at least chances of preferment to the low-born as well as to the mighty.

The showdown, in the great reception hall of the Kremlin palace, was dramatic. We have a detailed account of it from a foreign contemporary witness, General Manstein. Early in March the council, senate and a large number of gentry, watched closely by the Guards, assembled to clarify the situation. A deputy of the lesser nobility spoke, claiming that Russia had traditionally been governed by sovereign monarchs, not by council, and begging Anna to take the reins of government into her own hands. She affected surprise: "Was it not with the will of the whole nation that I signed the act presented to me at Mittau?" A shout went up "No!" This was repeated when each point of the conditions was read to the assembly by the unfortunately upstaged Vasiliy Dolgoruky. Anna then ceremoniously tore up the document she had signed with the words, "These writings then are not necessary," and claimed the prerogative of her ancestors by right of inheritance, not by the council's choice. So ended the one month of constitutional monarchy that Russia was to enjoy until 1906.

Who won, who lost in these events of 1730? The immediate losers, obviously, were the members of the privy council and the aristocrats it represented as the council was disbanded forthwith. Anna won, of course, insofar as she wished to exercise power untrammeled: indeed her reign became notorious for arbitrary acts and severe punishments. But despite the positive showing she made in the Kremlin she does not seem to have been much interested in the responsibilities of statecraft. The senate was not restored to its former eminence; instead, a small group—smaller even than the former privy council—wielded power. The key figure was a Baltic German baron, Johann-Ernst Bühren (Russified into "Biren" or "Biron"), Anna's favorite from Courland days. The whole oppressive period was given by Russians the name *Bironovshchina*, the "Biron regime."

In retrospect it, and the following short reign of Ivan VI, were thought of as a time of total ascendancy of the "German party." This is an exaggeration or oversimplification: the Germans in question were of varied origins and by no means in agreement with each other. They included Münnich (in Russian Minikh), a soldier and technical expert who eventually engineered Bühren's overthrow, and the wily, experienced politician Ostermann, completely Russified since he had entered Peter I's service at the age of 17 in 1703. In fact it has to be recognized that this "Germanization" of the aristocracy was a direct if unwelcome consequence of the Petrine heritage—and not only because he invited so many Germans and similar north Europeans into his service, particularly to staff his new ministries or "colleges." After Peter's own marriage to the lowborn Catherine I and his son's to a German princess, the Russian imperial family consistently found its brides and bridegrooms among the Western European (usually German) minor royalty, instead of the Orthodox Russian aristocracy as had been the Muscovite norm. More generally, it has been said that Russia in the first half or more of the 18th century had the cultural and political atmosphere of a minor provincial German principality.

Elizabeth

Anna did not in fact remarry and produce an heir as had been hoped, and she decided under the terms of Peter I's succession law to bequeath the throne to the two-month-old son of her niece Anna Leopoldovna, granddaughter of Ivan V, daughter of Charles Leopold of Mecklenburg and wife of the Prince of Brunswick. A document witnessed by Ostermann appointed Bühren as regent. This was taking Germanization too far. First Münnich and Manstein deposed Bühren and handed the regency to Ivan's frivolous and feather-headed mother, Anna Leopoldovna. Then, after some months' wavering, anti-German forces, including a couple of Frenchmen, grouped themselves decisively around the one figure at court who was truly Russian, authentically of the Romanov dynasty and not unwilling to be promoted for the throne: the 32-year-old surviving daughter of Peter the Great, Elizabeth. With the enthusiastic support of the older Guards regiments (Anna had instituted another) the coup d'etat was easily managed, and Elizabeth became empress late in 1741. Anna Leopoldovna, her husband and family were packed off into confinement at Kholmogory, near Archangel, where they languished for decades until released and sent back to the West by Catherine II, while the miserable deposed tsar Ivan was brought up on the fortress-island of Schlüsselberg in the Neva, his existence almost forgotten by all but his reluctant guards.

Elizabeth promised a new style of rule from that of Anna. Not only did she make a clean sweep of the "German party," she had a quite different and more attractive personality. She was good-looking, outgoing, shrewd and compassionate; she is famous for having abolished capital punishment, or rather for refusing to ratify death sentences. It is of interest that thereafter, throughout the 18th and 19th centuries, the death penalty was normally applied only in cases of treason or armed rebellion; however, sentences of, for example, 50 blows of the knout, normally sufficient to cause death, were sometimes passed. Her reputation for kindness is somewhat vitiated by the treatment of Ivan VI and his family; torture was not abolished, nor indeed were the secret police, which had been suspended by Peter II, but reintroduced under Anna. Favoritism was less capricious and blatant, but certainly

not done away with: new family names came to the fore, particularly the Razumovskys and Shuvalovs. Aleksey Razumovsky had a fairytale career: a simple Ukrainian farm boy, his fine voice brought him into the imperial choir where he attracted Elizabeth's attention; it is probable that they were secretly married. The statesman of the family was Aleksey's brother Kirill. Among the Shuvalovs the outstandingly capable and enlightened figure was Ivan, a prime mover in the foundation of the Petersburg Academy of Arts (1757) and Moscow University (1755).

Despite the differences of personality and of cultural atmosphere, Anna's and Elizabeth's reigns can be seen as something of a continuum. Russia's standing in the world of European politics, so painfully and uncertainly established by Peter I, steadily consolidated itself—thanks mainly to a now very efficient army (Russia's undefeated military genius Suvorov began his career at this time) and to intelligent diplomats. Russia faced renewed challenges from Sweden, which took advantage of the interregnum of 1741, and from Turkey (1736–39), gaining in consequence part of Finland and the elusive prize of Azov. By now Russia could not help but be entangled in the European system of alliances, the complexities of which need not be followed here. Its most reliable ally was Austria, its most permanent enemy France. Great Britain was on the whole a friend, not to mention a good trading partner. Prussia was generally hostile, and when Russia made its most significant European intervention of the period, in the Seven Years War, from 1756, its troops were so successful that it could have had East Prussia for the asking, and Frederick the Great was saved only by Elizabeth's death.

Both Anna and Elizabeth consciously tried to associate themselves with the achievements of Peter the Great, just as Catherine II, rather more plausibly, was to do later in the century. This had the practical consequence that St Petersburg was firmly re-established, after Peter II, as the seat of government, and indeed began to grow in this period into a great European city. As far as the more unbuttoned aspects of court life were

Schlüsselburg (its name meaning "Key Fort") occupies a small island in the River Neva, controlling the entrance to Lake Ladoga; it is seen here in a 19th-century print. Its capture from the Swedes was a vital final step before Peter I could found St Petersburg in 1703. It was the scene of most of the sad, short life of Ivan VI, who had been nominated by Anna as heir while still an infant, but deposed after 15 months by Elizabeth's supporters. He was brought up in secretive confinement in Schlüsselburg, and when an attempt was made in 1764 to rescue him and proclaim him emperor, he was killed here by his guards.

Elizabeth (tsaritsa 1741–62). Seen here in a baroque portrait by Grooth (1743), she cut a dashing figure in the early part of her reign—good-looking, benevolent and popular. The last surviving child of Peter the Great and Catherine I, she was brought to the throne (at the expense of the unfortunate child tsar Ivan VI, and of the whole "German party" of Anna's time) in a coup d'etat. Her connection with her formidable father was a deliberately fostered point of prestige, marking a new self-conscious Russianness in the cultural elite.

which point service would be deemed to have begun. The ground was prepared for the complete "liberation" of the service class in 1762. Such measures have led to the common description of the 18th century in Russia as the "Age of the Nobility." Certainly in that century the upper class—a small fraction of the population—received not just such material benefits as a growing, if primitively managed economy had to offer, but greater freedom of choice in life and a broadening of spiritual horizons that resulted from better educational opportunities, the possibility of foreign travel and immeasurably greater access to the printed word.

All this was to come to fruition in the last third of the century under Catherine II. Meanwhile, however, there is another aspect to the picture: aside from the tiny handful of really rich families, who were prone to squander their money in court circles, the state of the class commonly known as the "nobility" or "gentry" was neither very comfortable nor secure. For a start, who was in fact "noble"? In Western European countries with a landed aristocracy originating in feudal times the demarcations were reasonably evident. In Russia even before Peter the Great—with nobility dependent on service, a gift of the tsar rather than a right—the situation was far less clear. There were no titles in pre-Petrine Russia except for "prince," no orders of knighthood in a land that had known neither the crusades nor the traditions of chivalry. Even the books of precedence, *razryadnye knigi*, had been destroyed under Tsar Fyodor III. In the absence of primogeniture personal landholdings were subdivided from generation to generation, and to keep out of actual poverty most gentry families were dependent on service-linked land grants. Many "nobles" sank to peasant level: a whole class of such, the *odnodvortsy* ("freeholders"), particularly numerous in the south-central regions, struggled to little effect throughout the 18th century to maintain some vestiges of special status. At the same time commoners could, and at first frequently did, become ennobled through service, automatically so, once Peter's Table of Ranks was established. The 18th-century Russian hereditary nobleman could easily feel insecure, threatened by ambitious "new men" (especially sons of clergy) who might be mentally better equipped to rise in service, impoverished (despite Peter's salary scale for ranking servitors, pay was low and not always regularly received), remote from the country estate he was in no position to watch over and from the family he might seldom see, alienated by virtue of education and "foreign" ways from surrounding society and its age-old values.

concerned, Peter's satanic rowdyism repeated itself farcically in Anna's reign. Many tales of tasteless buffoonery are told; it is notorious that of her six court jesters four came from old aristocratic families. The more relaxed atmosphere of Elizabeth's reign encouraged frivolously conspicuous spending, notably by the tsaritsa herself, whose creditworthiness began to wear thin as the state finances became shakier. The one thing most people seem to know about Elizabeth is that at her death she left 15 000 dresses (though who bothered to count?).

More permanent and admirable were the results of a building spree that, beginning under Anna, took off spectacularly in Elizabeth's middle years. The sobriety of Petrine Baroque architecture was lightened through rococo detail, yet in Rastrelli's vast and intricate palaces the bones of a grand classicism show through. This age is known above all for the palace architecture that produced, most splendidly, Tsarskoye Selo and the Petersburg Winter Palace, but Elizabeth was in her own way pious, and her reign also witnessed a signal revival of Orthodox church building, marking incidentally the reinstatement of the dome as its culminating feature.

The 18th-century gentry

Both Anna's government and Elizabeth's understandably but fundamentally subverted the Petrine heritage in their tinkering with the balance inherent in Peter's severely just service state. A series of measures, none very decisive in itself, had the cumulative effect of making life considerably less onerous for the servitors and simultaneously harder for the peasants. Maybe Anna was repaying the gentry class for the support it had given her against the privy council. The unpopular Petrine law of undivided inheritance was abolished; the length of compulsory service was reduced; long leaves for landowners to live on their estates were awarded in rotation; one male member of a landowning family could avoid service altogether; it became possible to inscribe the children of the nobility in elite regiments from early childhood, at

The serfs

Changes in one part of the service state naturally affected its other elements. The good fortune, such as it was, of the 18th-century gentry class was matched and to some extent occasioned by a tightening-up of the conditions of serfdom. Some of this was simply the effect of greater efficiency: it became harder for serfs who wished to evade their lot simply to fade into the countryside. Those who took in such serfs and gave them work—there has always been a manpower shortage in many parts of Russia—would be prosecuted. Serfdom was also

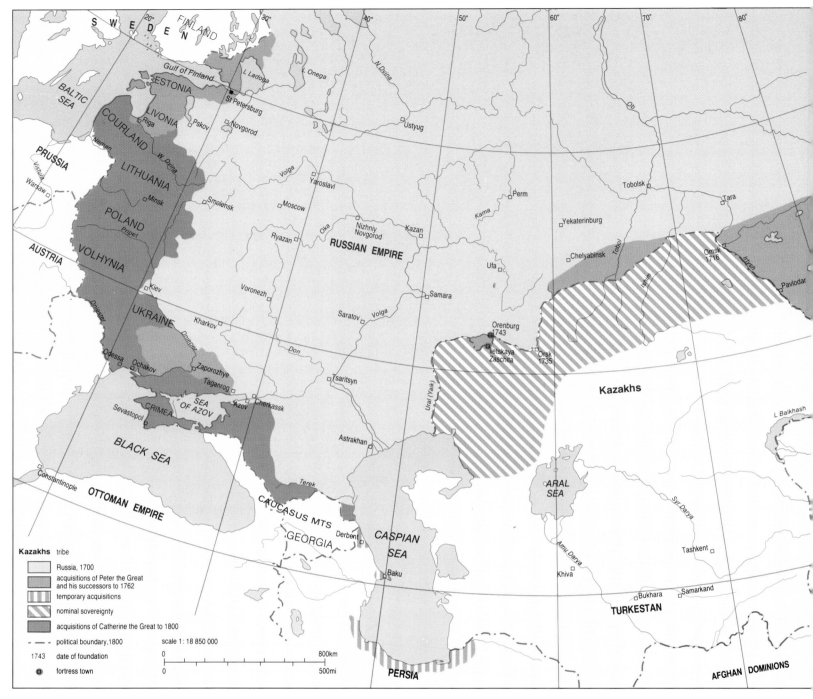

much extended in this period. Anna started the habit of handing out large areas of state land as rewards to servitors: the inhabitants, state peasants who had been bound to the soil but who otherwise, given that they paid their soul tax, were free to arrange their own lives, found themselves overnight turned into personal serfs, at the command of their landowner. Anna's successors enthusiastically continued the practice: it was a tempting resource in a country where cash, even at court, was in short supply, but where there was still much territorial expansion taking place, including, in the west, across well-populated and fertile lands. With the slackening of gentry service requirements, serfs everywhere had to face the likelihood of their landlord's considerably greater interference in their lives. The landlord would be physically present for much of his life, while under Peter his enforced absence led to a decline in productivity; the landlord might meddle with time-honored agricultural practices, causing the peasant

extra work and risk; he might with varying success institute quasi-military rules and routines.

More insidiously damaging to the old fabric of society in the 18th century was the uprooting of more and more serfs from the land. In the first place there was the enforced military recruitment instituted by Peter. Recruits admittedly became freemen after service, but at too high a price; they would already be old and probably alienated from their former lives. More generally there was the unwelcome uprooting of serfs for domestic service in the towns, for factory work and other non-agricultural employment. Life in the ancestral village might be monotonous and laborious, but at least one would be surrounded by one's own people, living in one's own house, to a large extent managing one's own life. In the 17th century, when serfdom first formally appeared in the law code, the government still regarded the serfs as people under its special care, even if bound to a location and its landlord. As the 18th century progressed the serfs

Expansion of the Russian empire in the 18th century. Once Peter the Great had secured the Baltic lands of Estonia and Livonia and had moved his capital to St Petersburg, the basis was laid for prosperity arising from increasing trade with the West. The greatest territorial and strategic gains however were achieved under Catherine the Great. Access to the Black Sea was finally secured for the first time since the 12th century. The Crimea was annexed in 1783 and quickly Russified under Potemkin's program for settling and incorporating newly acquired territories. When hostilities with the Ottoman empire ceased in 1791 the port of Odessa was founded as the southern complement to St Petersburg. The enormous expansion to the west resulted from the partition of Poland between Prussia, Austria and Russia.

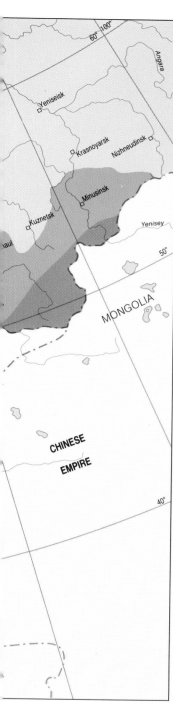

To the east the Kazakh tribes accepted nominal Russian sovereignty once its power was embodied in the visible might of the fortress towns along the River Yaik. It was not until the following century that firm control was established in this region.

were put more and more into the landlords' power. They could be, and were, bought and sold—in theory only with land and in families, in practice sometimes like chattels. Landlords could physically punish serfs for disobedience, though to kill them remained illegal. Late in Elizabeth's reign (1760) a decree permitted the exile to Siberia, with government assistance, of insolent or recalcitrant peasants. This has been described by Vernadsky as the nadir of the serf's legal status, even though it should be noted that rather little use was made of it.

Such a pattern of social relations had become, potentially if not actually, a corrupting force. Not only foreigners but Russians quite often referred to serfs as "slaves" around this time: agitation for the abolition of slavery in the Western world made the terminological point a delicate matter. Nevertheless there was always a dividing line between serfdom and slavery, tenuous as it might at times have seemed: it was not so evident in legal status, though serfs and slaves were never legally identical, as in the attitudes involved. The serf, as various Russian and foreign observers noted, had a dignity, humor and sense of self-worth that did not seem to suggest slavery. More to the point, perhaps, is the fact that serfs did not belong to an exclusive and identifiable caste: they were of the same race, language and religion as their masters, not to mention as clergy, tradesmen and indeed the free peasantry (peasants are called in Russian *krestyane*, a variant of the word for "Christians," and were regularly referred to as "souls"); there was movement, even if not much, into and out of the condition of serfdom. It would seem that the serfs considered that as well as their houses and movable possessions, in some fundamental sense they owned the land they worked, even while accepting that the landlord owned *them*: in both assumptions they were actually mistaken.

The most fundamental advantage of the serf over the slave, however, was that the former was able to dispose of the products of his work. The significance of this was to a considerable degree affected by the ways in which service obligations to the landlord could be discharged. These most often took one of two forms: *barshchina* (known in Western Europe as "corvée") and *obrok* ("quit-rent"). *Barshchina* involved obligatory labor on certain days each week in the landlords' fields; *obrok* commuted this obligation to a fixed payment. *Barshchina* predominated where the land was most fertile, particularly towards the south; this was "classic" serfdom, with the landlord able to exercise close control over the peasants, who would have little time or opportunity for further economic activity save for some basic cottage industries pursued largely in winter.

Obrok peasants, comprising three-quarters of the serf population in many northern regions, were in a very different situation. They could till the soil if they wanted, but because in the forest zone this was unlikely to be remunerative they would more often seek and gain permission to travel—while remaining "inscribed" in their native villages—in search of paid work, often in Moscow or Petersburg. They might join one or another *artel*, or cooperative guild of skilled workmen; they might sublet their land to other peasants, or employ serfs

themselves; considerable riches were sometimes thus amassed, and even serf millionaires were not unknown. Talented serfs might be sent by their landlords for professional training: among their number were several leading painters, musicians, actors and architects of the 18th and early 19th centuries. Those who achieved such fame might purchase or be granted their freedom, but if not would still remain at the arbitrary command of the master. Indeed it was the arbitrary nature of the serf system, rather than the exceptional cases of outright cruelty, that made it generally objectionable. In other respects the later 18th century seems to have been a time of comparative prosperity for Russian peasants, whether enserfed or not: their condition was often favorably compared by witnesses at the time with that of, for example, the Irish and Scottish rural poor or English factory workers.

The events of 1762

This remarkable year opened with the death of Elizabeth on Christmas Day 1761 (Old Style; 5 January 1762 New Style). She had been canny enough to choose her successor nearly 20 years before: it was a choice that looked good but turned out badly. Peter of Holstein-Gottorp was the son of her elder sister, yet another Anna, and more surprisingly the nephew of Charles XII of Sweden, the old antagonist of his grandfather Peter I. He might have had either throne, but was brought to Russia at the age of 14; nevertheless Germany kept its hold on his fairly limited mind, and Frederick the Great's Prussia fascinated him boundlessly.

In 1745 a wife was chosen for him, Sophie of Anhalt-Zerbst, another small German principality. At 15 she arrived in Russia, the match was arranged, and she was instructed in Orthodoxy and baptized under the new name of Catherine. At 16 she was married to Peter. The marriage brought no joy; Peter, marked physically and mentally by a near-fatal attack of smallpox, proved boorish and uninterested. Unlike him, Catherine made the effort to adapt herself to Russia, quickly attained a good colloquial knowledge of the language and gritted her teeth to endure her lonely, rather insignificant and even insecure position at Elizabeth's court. After years of childless-ness it was indicated to her that an heir should be produced, with or without Peter's assistance; in 1754 Paul was duly born, and to this day it remains uncertain, as presumably it was to Paul himself, whether he was actually Peter's son. A second son, certainly illegitimate, was in fact born to Catherine in 1762, and lived an uneventful life under the name of Aleksey Bobrinsky. (Reports of later children are unsubstantiated and improbable.) Both sons, to Catherine's sorrow, were immediately taken away from her to be brought up under court aegis. Meanwhile it was beginning to look likely that Peter would somehow contrive to repudiate Catherine and marry his own favorite, Elizabeth Vorontsova.

When Peter succeeded to the throne his enthusiasm for Prussia led him soon to pull the successful Russian forces out of the Seven Years' War without territorial or other compensation, so saving Frederick the Great from annihilation. Thereafter he embarked on an unnecessary war against Denmark in pursuance of his Holstein interests. His German, or at least Protestant, sympathies had an even more palpable impact on his subjects when he began to confiscate church property; his lack of respect for Orthodox ritual was evident, and it was rumored that he was about to burn almost all religious images and to force the clergy to shave and dress in the Western manner. Despite having alienated the army and the church, he does not seem to have been totally stupid—insensitive, rather—and two of the measures he promulgated in February 1762 have gone down in history as strikingly progressive. The more unambiguously liberal was the closing down of the "Secret Chancery," the much-feared office that had charge of all investigations into treason and related crimes. Its brief had been wide, its powers great and its methods depended usually on verbal denunciations and routinely involved torture. Security organs continued to exist but carried out their tasks in a better-regulated and more humane manner.

The other decree—one of the most famous in imperial Russian history, promulgated on 18 February, though anticipated in a speech in January—liberated the entire class of the gentry from obligatory service. The document is a curious one. Its preamble attempts to place gentry service in the historical context of the Petrine reforms, and sonorously bestows "on the whole Russian noble *dvoryanstvo* [gentry] freedom and liberty . . . for all time and for all generations," even to the extent (a strange throwback to Kievan Rus) of permitting its members to go into the service of foreign rulers. Then it starts to back-pedal: if "particular necessity demands" (probably war is envisaged) the sovereign can still decree compulsory service, and arrangements are made for the obligatory education of children. It ends with a curious appeal that members of the gentry out of gratitude should be inspired "not to absent or hide themselves from service": if they "spend all their time in sloth and idleness" they must be despised, scorned and excluded from court and public events.

It is impossible to know the extent to which either or both of these February decrees represent Peter III's personal initiatives or, as is likely, swift moves by the gentry-based bureaucracy to improve its lot. Certainly the liberation of the gentry, and the extent to which it should be economically privileged, were under high-level discussion towards the end of Elizabeth's reign; the decree as published looks like the result of uneasy compromises. But it probably took a new, not oversensitive ruler, much in need of gentry support, to gamble on gaining it with these measures.

Peter III personally lost this gamble, since he lasted less than half a year more, but in the longer term it paid off for Russia; the liberation decree achieved, more or less, its apparent objectives of increasing the gentry's sense of self-worth and expanded opportunity while preserving a lingering sense of moral obligation to do something useful for society and to educate its progeny. Though by and large the gentry continued to serve, it did so from a new position of strength and choice. Provincial life and agriculture gained, as more landowners put down roots in all parts of the countryside; so too did intellectual and artistic life, at least among those who could afford to devote themselves to it. Such people could now travel abroad at will and no longer be regarded as curiosities, or themselves regard all they saw with naive wonderment. New standards of comfort and international levels of aesthetic taste were to make the last third of the 18th century the golden age of the Russian country mansion and landscaped park.

There were other sides to the liberation decree, however. When it was promulgated it was thought of by some, including evidently Peter III's wife and successor Catherine, as a dangerously destabilizing measure. Destabilization indeed ensued, and on two separate fronts, though it only slowly made itself felt. The sudden dissolution of the tie between ruler and service class hastened the alienation of the latter from the former. The most fatal rift occurred however between state and peasantry. Not only the Russian intellectual class but equally and more immediately the huge class of serfs came to feel that Peter III's decree had gone only half way. Serfdom after all was in its origin and essence but another form of state service: equity demanded that the serfs be freed and given title to their land if the landlords' compulsory services were no longer required. When a complementary decree about the freeing of the serfs failed to materialize, rumor was rife: perhaps the powerful landowners had banded together to stop such a decree's publication. When Peter III was shortly afterwards first deposed, then killed, it seemed like confirmation of such a conspiracy. In the end, of course, the decree of full emancipation came—on 19 February 1861, 99 years and a day late. In the interim every Russian ruler and government had to face, solve or shelve the ever-growing problems that continuing serfdom entailed. Peter III himself lived an extraordinary consequent "after-life" as the most popular guise for Russian pretenders, and rallying point for their revolts, in the remainder of the 18th century: this totally Prussian-orientated, Lutheran-minded ruler of a land to which he never adapted became a symbolic figure for those who had not accepted Petrine Westernization. It was in the person of "Peter III" that Yemelyan Pugachov unleashed his peasant war in 1773–74.

Meanwhile the real Peter III's days were numbered as the summer of 1762 drew on. Despite his wooing of the gentry, he had antagonized too many people and interest groups, had threatened worse changes and had struck those who knew him as capricious, tactless and unstable. The return of the Germanization of Anna's days looked all too likely. Worse still, he had alienated and threatened the person whose support he most needed, his popular and strong-minded wife Catherine. It proved absurdly easy for Catherine's supporters in the Guards regiments, notably the Orlov brothers, to isolate him and force his abdication on his name-day, 29 June. Put under guard at a country estate of his choosing, he was killed a week later, apparently in a drunken brawl: a frantic scribbled note from Aleksey Orlov to Catherine, throwing himself on her mercy for the deed, survives, suggesting the new tsaritsa did not instigate it. Peter's death was publicly ascribed to "hemorrhoidal colic," but its violent nature was no great secret, and it cast a shadow over the start of Catherine II's reign both at home and abroad.

THE FLOWERING OF IMPERIAL RUSSIA

Catherine the Great

Between 1762 and 1825—the reigns of Catherine II "the Great" (1762–96), of Paul (1796–1801) and of Alexander I (1801–25)—the Russian empire reached almost its maximum territorial extent (a good deal more than the extent of the Soviet Union in the 20th century). It also attained the status of a great world power, playing a decisive part in the Napoleonic wars. Its prosperity and level of education rose dramatically and its artistic achievements were considerable. It remained however an overwhelmingly peasant, and largely illiterate, society; no systematic industrialization had yet taken place, and the economy was crudely managed; the more anachronistic and arbitrary features of the tsarist system were becoming steadily more evident; the growing intellectual class was asking more and more awkward questions; and nobody could work out a solution to the admitted problem of serfdom. But despite at times violent social discontent, it was an outward-looking and on the whole optimistic epoch, in which Russia culturally came of age.

Catherine II's sudden elevation to the throne with the coup d'etat against her husband Peter III is often described by historians as "usurpation." This seems unjust. Once the Guards officers had secured Peter III's abdication without a designated successor, the idiosyncratic Petrine succession law meant that no one had a foreordained right to the imperial title; Catherine was on past precedent the obvious choice. Her only serious rival was the child Paul, whose regent she would anyhow have been, but Peter III had refrained from nominating him while in power. As Paul grew up, however, there was much tension between mother and son on this score: it was clear that if Catherine were ever to be deposed Paul would be waiting to step forward as emperor. In fact theirs were very different personalities, and Catherine silently demonstrated her reservations about him by refraining in her turn from declaring him as her official successor. In her last days, indeed, it was to become clear that her choice was likely to fall on one of her already almost grown-up grandchildren, and Paul's eventual succession was secured only thanks to the fact that she ended her life in a coma after a stroke. A document expressing Catherine's wishes for the succession was probably destroyed by Paul or his supporters at this stage.

The reigns of both Catherine II and Alexander I can easily be seen to divide into a "good," liberal or at least reformist and modernizing first part and a "bad," reactionary or illiberal later period. In this the two monarchs would seem not only to be following a common human progression from radicalism to conservatism with age, but also a pattern particularly noticeable among some other strong-minded Russian rulers: Ivan IV and Boris Godunov before, Alexander II later. Such observations can be extended to moralizing conclusions about the Russian monarchs themselves: that their

"progressive" motivation was only superficial, that any real will to improve the system they inherited was lacking. The reputation of Catherine II has particularly suffered from such views. The truth is that these monarchs, in theory all-powerful, were themselves caught in a mesh of circumstances from which they could never wholly disentangle themselves and which hampered their every political movement.

Wars were an obvious external constraint upon their freedom of action: Ivan IV, Catherine II and Alexander I were all, though in varied circumstances, deflected from the restructuring of their society by one or more wars. But domestic constraints were more pervasively problematic. As Richard Pipes has neatly observed, these monarchs realized "as he or she accumulated experience that they simply lacked the capacity to lead their empire where they wanted and that the best they could hope for was to keep it from sliding into chaos." Any just assessment of the Russian political situation in the period under consideration will have to take account of such factors.

No Russian ruler, however, managed to keep national buoyancy and a sense of gradual social progress going longer than Catherine the Great: for nearly 30 years, until in her last half-dozen years things began to go sour. Most of the negative evaluations of Catherine's reign among her younger contemporaries and among later historians stem primarily from features of the years after 1790–91: the turn away from Enlightenment philosophy, the sanctions against free-thinking Russian intellectuals, the cynical, high-spending court dominated by unworthy favorites and hangers-on, the amoral foreign policy that led to the extinction of independent Poland, the general sense that the empress's flexible mind and ready sympathies were becoming rigidified. In this unsatisfactory coda to a generally successful reign, Catherine did not so much lose her grip or change her principles as face new situations to which there were no ready-made responses.

The lengthy main part of Catherine's reign perhaps also had a turning point within it, at the year 1774. The years before were years of promise; the years after were the time of achievement, though with sights set lower than had earlier been expected. The year itself was eventful in varied but important ways. One war ended, but the civil war against Pugachov reached its climax. Philosophy encountered practical politics when, with the arrival of Diderot in St Petersburg, Catherine finally met a major *philosophe* face to face over a period of several months. Most significantly for Catherine's private and indeed public life, she embarked on her liaison, probably marriage, with Grigoriy Potemkin (c.1739–91). This was immeasurably the most significant of her dozen or so love affairs over 30 years that have exercised the fantasies of romantic biographers to an absurd degree. It is no derogation of her achievement to say that Potemkin's complementary qualities of personality and statesmanship were as necessary for Russia's prosperity and future destiny as hers. He was a remarkable blend of man of action, intellectual and dreamer: his strange and moody temperament ensured they could not live together long, yet he remained her closest support and effective "prime minister." He died in 1791, and his death coincided with the passing of the best years of Catherine's reign and of the Russian 18th century.

Certain personal qualities helped set the tone for Catherine's reign. Her basic temperament was tough-minded but cheerful, notably kindly and optimistic (unusual enough qualities in rulers of any time or place). She was an instinctive learner, a role that stood her in good stead during her long and tedious years waiting in the wings during Elizabeth's reign, but did not desert her after her coronation: it shaded into her self-perceived function of teacher of her society. She was also a glutton for hard work, starting her day normally at 5 a.m. Lastly, and perhaps unexpectedly in view of her intellectuality, she was a natural politician. This implied a care for public relations that would nowadays be taken as the most normal political prudence, but in the past has led to the frequent charge of hypocrisy: more importantly, she developed a deep sense for politics (in Bismarck's famous phrase) as "the art of the possible." This meant she was by nature a gradualist, that her reforms were unspectacular, not aimed (as Peter the Great's were) at changing the appearance of things, but at transforming their essence. Although later reproached for halfheartedness, she ensured that what *was* done was done well, and with general consent. Only in her last years did her political skills turn sometimes to bossiness and intoler-

ance—years in which the French revolutionary crisis cast its shadow across all Europe.

Though there was goodwill towards Catherine in many quarters, the fact and the manner of her accession were not universally popular. Only one plot to unseat her had public consequences, however: a strange and reckless endeavor by a young Ukrainian officer, down on his luck, called Vasiliy Mirovich. Stationed at Schlüsselburg, he learned about the "nameless prisoner" held there—the sad former infant-Tsar Ivan VI, by now in his twenties. Catherine, who had interviewed him, hoped to persuade him into a monastery. Mirovich, apparently gambling on achieving personal glory, led a group of baffled soldiers to release Ivan and proclaim him ruler. But Ivan's jailers had orders, issued under Peter III, to kill their captive in such an eventuality—and immediately did so. Mirovich was executed; the whole episode, though in one sense strengthening Catherine's position, put another weapon in the hands of her detractors, particularly abroad.

Church and government under Catherine
In the first couple of years of her reign Catherine was learning how to rule, taking advice on institutional reform and setting up committees to examine recent measures such as the liberation of the gentry and the secularization of ecclesiastical land. The latter point was delicate. She needed the

The Razin rebellion.
The greatest Russian popular rebellion before Pugachov's in the 1770s was that of Stepan (known as "Stenka") Razin during the reign of Tsar Aleksey. Razin was a Don Cossack who with a band of followers engaged in daring exploits as pirate and freebooter on the lower Volga and along the Caspian to Persia. Early in 1670 his flotilla sailed up the Volga, stopping to slaughter officials and landowners and to proclaim liberation. His band grew hugely until government forces inflicted a heavy defeat on it at Simbirsk. His base at Astrakhan held out for a time, but then Razin was captured and subsequently executed at Moscow. His name, and that of his supposed "son," lived on in countless folk legends and songs as a deliverer who would bring freedom and justice.

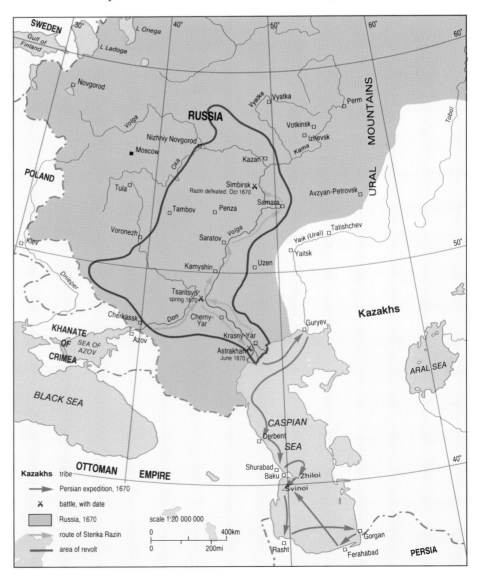

church's goodwill, which had already accrued to her as supplanter of the Lutheran-inclined Peter III; though she wore religion lightly, she seems to have been a sincere convert to Orthodoxy. Yet as a "Voltairean" she could hardly be an uncritical supporter of an organized religion that at the time was a byword for ignorance and sloth; moreover, it had a great deal of land without much in the way of educational activity or other socially useful results to show for it and on this land there was considerable peasant unrest. Many interests in Russia stood to gain from secularization. When, in 1763, it went ahead, only the bishop of Rostov denounced it, in terms altogether too thunderous for his or the church's good; he was unfrocked and, when he persisted, imprisoned. Catherine tried to soften the blow, but the fact remained that the loss of its land, following on Peter I's secularization of ecclesiastical administration, spelled the end of two-and-a-half centuries of the "Josephite" compact between church and state.

From the spiritual point of view this may have been no bad thing for Russian Orthodoxy, which underwent something of a renaissance in the later 18th century. Hesychast mysticism revived, producing the notable figure of Paisiy Velichkovsky, translator into Russian of the very influential *Philokalia*, and a little later St Serafim of Sarov. Intellectuals began to play a role in Russian Orthodoxy again: notably St Tikhon Zadonsky and the

Ukrainian Grigoriy Skovoroda. The latter, famous as teacher, philosopher and religious poet, took to the life of a wandering sage and ascetic, digging his own grave before dying (in 1794) and leaving his haunting epitaph on himself: "The world hunted but could not catch me" (*Mir lovil menya i ne poymal*). The sectarians began at the same time to recover from decades of persecution: in 1769 Catherine in effect restored their citizenship by permitting them to testify in court. A new mid-18th-century sect were the Dukhobors or "spirit-wrestlers," formed partly under the influence of Quakerism and similarly persecuted for disobedience to the state.

The main reforms of Catherine's early years were in the apparently humdrum but important area of local government. The vast country, 90 percent rural, with a low level of literacy and tenuous communications, was undergoverned and haphazardly policed: the central administration not only had little idea what was going on, but had no certainty, for example, that its decrees would even be promulgated throughout the land. With the liberation of the gentry in 1762 the government could no longer regard it as a conscripted class of its own agents in the countryside. Catherine had to secure its cooperation by persuasion and reward, culminating in a Charter of the Nobility in 1785 (the first ever to recognize outright title to land). Catherine upgraded and regularized local government administration; subsequently in her reign there would be a deliberate policy of instituting new regional urban centers and markets. The chief series of reforms, including the setting-up of judicial institutions independent of the administrators, came in the wake of the greatest explosion of rural discontent, the Pugachov rebellion, in 1775. But questions connected with serfdom proved intractable. Catherine herself preferred the prospect of a gradual ending of peasant bondage, perhaps by granting freedom when estates changed hands or by freeing all children born after a certain date. The general subject of peasant rights was publicly discussed—not least by the Free Economic Society, set up in 1765 and the first such autonomous society in Russia.

Late in 1766 Catherine made the most dramatic political announcement of her career. She summoned the various social estates in all parts of her realm, together with government offices, to send representatives to a huge gathering, over 500 strong, in Moscow. There they would explain the situation and needs of their communities and participate in the drafting of a new law code. This gathering is known as the "Legislative Commission," though it was really a great assembly (*zemskiy sobor*) in the spirit of 17th-century Muscovy, a curious political throwback, hinting that the whole style of Catherine's politics was a development more of the traditions of Aleksey Mikhaylovich than of Peter the Great.

In a sense nothing came of it. No law code emerged, nor did the assembly reach any conclusive point in its deliberations, since it was suspended *sine die* when Turkey declared war on Russia in the summer of 1768 and never reconvened (though subcommittees on various topics continued to meet). Some commentators have therefore considered the whole business a sham,

The Pugachov rebellion. Yemelyan Pugachov, a Don Cossack like Razin a century before, led the greatest of the Russian peasant rebellions. This time the source of the revolt was among the Yaik Cossacks who held specific grievances against the Russian authorities. Further strength was gathered among Old Believers and in the populous mining communities of the Urals, where there was a plentiful supply of firearms. As pretender to the throne of the tsar, Pugachov also won allegiance from non-Russian tribes in the east, notably the Bashkirs. By the summer of 1774 he was able at times to muster a huge force and seemed poised to attack Moscow. But the commitment of his followers was always uncertain and his fortunes waned. Before long he was forced to turn south towards his homeland, but was unable to drum up support among the better-off Don Cossacks. Almost alone now in his venture, he was eventually handed over to the authorities by his erstwhile adherents.

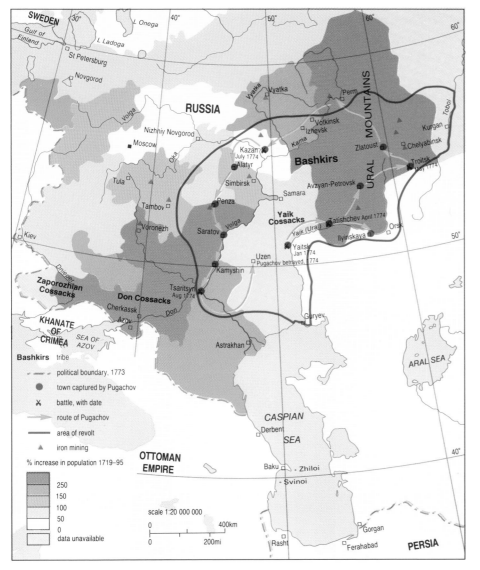

An allegorical engraving of Catherine the Great, made early in her reign, depicts her in triumphal progress across her empire. Above her are the figures of Peace, who offers to bestow garlands upon the empress, and Fame, who trumpets her virtues; prosperity is symbolized by the child dropping coins. Applauding peasants line the chariot's route, while from the clouds above Peter the Great, seated next to Jupiter, looks benevolently down.

completely extraneous to Russia's socio-political development. Certainly the assembly was never intended to be a step on the road to parliamentary democracy: the representatives, though chosen by ballot, were not elected delegates. As in Muscovite assemblies, there were representatives of the free peasantry but not of the serfs; non-Russian nationalities were well represented, the church scarcely at all.

What the members of the assembly (who were paid a salary and granted other privileges) did was talk. Three types of document resulted from the exercise. First, each representative came equipped with a *nakaz* or "instruction" from his place of origin, which could broach any topics save personal grievances (or might decline to do so: the town of Murom claimed it had no needs, suffered no oppression and needed no new laws). Then there were the records of the debates, often chaotic or inconclusive, yet a new and intriguing phenomenon in Russia. Most remarkably, the empress drew up her own *Nakaz*, the "Great Instruction," an immense document in 22 chapters and more than 500 articles, the fruit of over 20 years' reading and reflection on the main political philosophers of her day. Its aim was to set before Russians an ideal of what their society could or should be like. It was not the anticipated law code, still less a constitution; it was more an educational text, and was used as such for decades when it would be read out, passage by passage, on Saturday mornings to civil servants. Its libertarian sentiments seemed so subversive that it was banned in France, though it should be said that Catherine never pretended that Russia should be governed otherwise than autocratically (on account of its great size).

Civil and foreign wars

The whole exercise of the Legislative Commission was richly informative to the empress. What seemed to emerge was the lack of any general opposition to the way the country was ordered, but a good deal of class antagonism and many practical ideas for regularizing social relations, tax obligations and so on. Only half-a-dozen years later such antagonisms and grievances exploded with the Great Rebellion led by Yemelyan Pugachov. Like Razin a century before, Pugachov was a Don Cossack, but he found his focus of rebellion in the remotest of the Cossack hordes, that of the Yaik (north of the Caspian Sea—the Yaik River was renamed the Ural after the rebellion). Razin, the riverboat pirate, had kept to the Volga; Pugachov, a runaway soldier and general rolling stone, ranged more widely, as far as the factories and iron foundries scattered from Bashkiria to the Ural foothills, where he sought firearms. The Yaik Cossacks not only had specific grievances, but a generalized unease about their growing social marginalization and decline of privilege.

Unlike Razin, Pugachov was a pretender, who from the start gave himself out to be the miraculously saved Peter III. The phenomenon of the countless pretenders who emerged, and often met unpleasant ends, from the 16th to the 19th century in Russia has only recently begun to receive the anthropological attention it deserves. It accompanied the exalted Byzantine-derived concept of tsardom (there were no grand-princely pretenders!) as a God-bestowed condition, unrelated to personal worth. It was believed that a true tsar could be recognized by certain marks on his body—usually a cross or an eagle—and such, apparently, Pugachov had. Proclamations with strange seals and even stranger language were issued, and give an idea of the simple, archaic political ideology of the rebels.

None of the peasant rebellions, even Pugachov's, became true wars of liberation. It has often been observed that, of the two Russian words for "freedom," the peasantry had a strong attachment to *volya* ("existential freedom," unconstrained exercise of will), but little concept of *svoboda* (political freedom). Hugely successful Pugachov's rebellion may have been for almost a year, but its appeal to the common people is hard to judge: anyone who did not declare allegiance to him was liable to be put to death on the spot. The commitment of the Bashkir and other non-Russian peoples, where tribal leaders were involved, was probably deeper. Some intrepid government commanders managed to withstand sieges: eventually Pugachov withdrew southwards, failed to take Tsaritsyn and could not mobilize the better-off Don Cossacks. After exactly a year of rebellion he was handed over by erstwhile followers to a "just judge" at Yaitsk. He was subsequently executed in Moscow. The empress ensured that torture was not used, that he was beheaded rather than mutilated (to the surprise of the crowd) and that reprisals against his followers were kept to a minimum.

Among the factors that enabled the government to deploy effective forces against the Pugachov rebellion was the ending of the war with Turkey; the rebellion in turn helped to persuade Russia to bring that war to an end. Until then Russian successes, though not overwhelming, had been considerable. The Crimean khan was declared independent of Ottoman vassalage, and Russia established a toehold on the Black Sea for the first time since the 12th century. The Russian fleet (with two Scots among its admirals) sailed from the Baltic past Gibraltar to score a remarkable naval victory at Çeşme (1770) against the much larger Turkish navy. Though many Greek islanders swore allegiance to Catherine, it proved impossible to organize a general Greek uprising against the Turks, and the fleet did not try to force the Dardanelles to Constantinople. So passed the Russians' best chance of sponsoring a Balkan uprising that would bring down the Ottomans and recapture Constantinople for Orthodoxy. It was only later in the 1770s that Potemkin's vision would crystallize such ideas into the "Great Project," for a Russian revival of the Byzantine empire. As it was, he organized "New Russia" out of the vast, potentially rich lands, haunt of disorderly Cossacks, frontiersmen, nomads and pirates that Russia inherited from the Turkish war, becoming "Prince of Tauris."

Russia annexed the Crimea in 1783 and the Turks declared war again in 1787. Events assumed a worrying aspect for Catherine when Sweden, backed by Prussia and Great Britain, entered the hostilities. Diplomatic complications, deriving ultimately from the French revolutionary ferment, made all parties ready for peace in 1791, but not before Russia was menacing Constantinople after taking the key fortresses of Ochakov and Ismail, had confirmed possession of the Crimea and established protectorship over Georgia. This peace led immediately to the founding of the great international seaport of Odessa, southern complement to St Petersburg.

The Turkish question was, at least at the outset, entangled with the Polish question. Both countries contained large numbers of people whose religion and language differed from those of their rulers, and whom outside powers considered it their duty to protect. As Muscovite and Petrine Russia had strengthened central autocracy and homogenized society, so opposite processes were at work in the united state of Poland and Lithuania. There the landowning class (some 8 percent of the population) immensely strengthened its own autonomy, while central authority was weakened by the notorious right of "free veto," whereby a single dissenting voice could paralyze the business of the *sejm* or governing diet. The elected, often non-Polish kings could seldom act as more than military leaders. It is probable that the Polish example considerably affected the 17th- and 18th-century Russian rulers' attitude to their own exercise of power.

The first partition of Poland came in 1772. For Russia it merely meant reestablishing approximately the frontiers that had obtained under Tsar Aleksey; Prussia took the small but important "Danzig corridor" that had separated its two parts; Austria however took a rich and populous slice of the Polish heartland at the foot of the Carpathians. The shocked Poles, among whom there were sharp political divisions, notably into pro- and anti-

The social composition of Russia in the late 18th century.
Large-scale social upheaval through the 18th century brought a changing demographic pattern by the end of Catherine the Great's reign. Much migration resulted from the flight of serfs from central Russia, despite continual government attempts to halt this. Some joined the Cossacks of the Dnieper, Don, Volga, Kuban and Ural regions, whose control of the southern and eastern zones was rapidly growing; they prized their independence and often set themselves up as mercenaries. The German element in the population increased considerably as Catherine invited Germans to colonize the area north of the Black Sea, to which they brought social stability and efficient agriculture. Although urban communities were beginning to grow around factories and mines, 95 percent of the population was still rural.

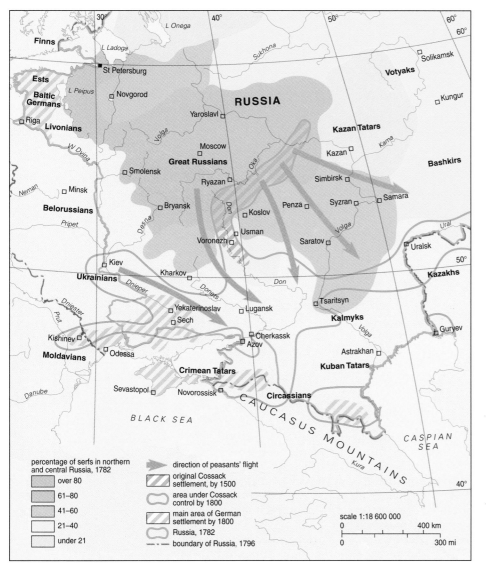

Russian parties, then made an effort to put their house in order. Reforms would have included a hereditary monarchy and a proper parliament with middle-class representation. Though its neighbors scarcely preferred a strong Poland to a weak one, all might have been well for Poland but for the disturbing factor of the spread throughout Europe of French revolutionary ideas. The Polish constitution, promulgated in May 1791, seemed altogether too Jacobin for Catherine's taste and even for some Poles, who formed the Confederation of Targowica to defend the old system. Russia, invited by the Confederation, occupied a great swathe of eastern and southern Poland (most of the former Russo-Lithuanian lands).

The second partition of Poland, in 1793, followed, with Prussia advancing almost to Warsaw. In 1794 the Polish national uprising led by Kosciuszko attempted to resist the annexations; its defeat led to the third partition, or end of independent Poland, in 1795. As a result of the final partition Russia obtained all Lithuania, Courland and the ancient Kievan province of Volhynia: "not a single Pole," as Catherine wrote in self-congratulation. Catherine undoubtedly saw her conquests partly in terms of restoring the Old Russian patrimony, though it meant the incorporation into the Russian empire of Lithuanians, Latvians and in particular a large Jewish population, mostly but not wholly urban. Catherine's successor, Paul, forbade any use of the term "Kingdom of Poland"; after the Napoleonic wars the rump Duchy of Warsaw, still with a few individual institutions, was given to the Russian crown, and in 1832 was incorporated into Russia.

Western public opinion was roused to the support of the Poles only after Kosciuszko's uprising; the general mood of the Enlightenment had been hostile to what was seen as the oppressive Catholicism and anarchy of the old Poland. Polish revolts in the 1830s and 1860s further mobilized European sympathies in favor of Poland and against the whole tsarist regime.

The empress and the Enlightenment

It has become commonplace to speak of Catherine's rule and that of other contemporary monarchs such as the Austrian Joseph II as "enlightened absolutism." Certainly Catherine saw herself throughout as autocrat—the proper type of ruler for Russia, as the *Nakaz* makes clear. Nevertheless she quickly grasped the fact that ultimately power rests on persuasion: "When I am already convinced in advance of general approval, then I issue my orders, and have the pleasure of observing what you call blind obedience. And that is the foundation of unlimited power . . .," as she once told a questioner. She also tried to train others in responsibility: often, when a problem was reported to her for decision, she would send it back with the comment that it should be decided according to the law. Obviously she was "enlightened," in the sense of trying at least to apply intelligence and flexibility to questions of government. But "the Enlightenment" is altogether too fluid a concept for use as some kind of yardstick by which to measure Catherine's Russia. Enlightenment thought in any case traveled far between a Montesquieu, Beccaria or Voltaire and a Diderot, Hume or

Rousseau: Catherine made her own synthesis of ideas. She carried on a copious correspondence with several *philosophes*: with Voltaire (who had a great interest in Russia as supposedly a "new civilization"), with Grimm (editor of the enlightened rulers' "house journal," *Correspondence Littéraire*) and with Diderot, whom she saved financially at a critical moment in his career by purchasing his library, lending it back to him and installing him as its permanent salaried curator.

Diderot was the one famous *philosophe* with whom she talked at length, when, after long hesitation, he went to Russia to signal his gratitude in the winter of 1773–74. The full story of this great encounter between intellect and politics is richly comic, sad and revealing. Their discussions ranged over every kind of social topic, without the philosopher ever being able to persuade the empress that his enlightened observations represented any kind of practical politics. Eventually, by Catherine's account, she pointed out to him that "You work only on paper, which can stand anything . . . whereas I, a poor empress, work upon human skin which is very different: irritable and quick to take offense." Diderot meanwhile, holed up in chilly St Petersburg, feeling ill and homesick, found it impossible to get straight answers when he wanted to find out statistical information about Russia, but was not blind to his surroundings: "It seems to me that your subjects err on the side of one extreme or the other, either in believing their nation too advanced or too backward . . ." Outside in the wide world the Pugachov revolt was reaching its climax, and St Petersburg jumpiness was heightened by a news blackout. Though the visit was hardly a success, Diderot and Catherine were both too good-natured not to part as friends; but it is likely that thereafter she decided to be her own philosopher.

"Enlightenment" in Russian implies also education, and Catherine, working with an exceptional minister, I. Betskoy, vastly increased educational levels and opportunities. Already under Elizabeth the Academy of Arts and Moscow University had rather uncertainly got under way, following Peter's Academy of Sciences, and Russia managed to produce its first great modern scholar, Mikhail Lomonosov (1711–65). His achievements as poet, literary theorist, physicist, chemist, mosaic-maker, geologist, astronomer and more besides made him a "one-man university," an emblematic figure of great significance—the more so since he was from a state-peasant family in the far north, who had to go by foot to study in the capital and pass himself off as a nobleman. Under Catherine a rather modern concept of education led to some forward-looking experiments, including in the education of women. One of the great female intellectuals of the time, Princess Dashkova, was appointed as director of the Academy of Sciences in 1782 and president of the new Academy of Letters the following year. Education also implied book publication, which increased dramatically, and the formation of public opinion. Catherine gave an energetic lead, promoting satirical journals and herself writing at least 30 plays (mostly comedies, mild satires and scenes from Russian history). She wrote her adopted language ungrammatically, but fluently and colloquially, as well as

Two remarkable self-made men from the Russian north came together in this fine portrait bust: its sculptor. F.I. Shubin (1740–1805) and his subject, Mikhail Lomonosov (1711–65), who incidentally was long dead when it was made (1792). Shubin grew up among peasant bone- and wood-carvers, to become the greatest neoclassic Russian sculptor. Lomonosov, from a fisherman's family, was an astonishing "Renaissance man," strong-willed and pugnacious: the outstanding baroque poet, he was also literary theorist, historian, economist, artist, geographer, but most notably a polymath scientist, far ahead of his time in physical chemistry. He was inspiration too for the considerable scientific, exploratory and scholarly activity of 18th-century Russia.

writing copiously in French.

As the reign progressed, the founders of modern Russian literature and public opinion began to emerge: the playwright Denis Fonvizin (1745–92), the novelist Fyodor Emin (c.1735–70), a poet of great rough-hewn genius Gavriil Derzhavin (1744–1816), the publicist and publisher Nikolai Novikov (1744–1818), a proto-Romantic poet and prose-writer, Nikolai Karamzin (1766–1826), who became also Russia's first great historian, and the most widely known of all, Aleksandr Radishchev (1749–1802). Radishchev's *Journey from St Petersburg to Moscow* is an unclassifiable work: its imaginary journey is punctuated by stops where the author observes, expatiates on and digresses from scenes of country life, which add up to a generally grim picture of serfdom. His appeal aims to touch the heart, in Rousseauesque manner; his journey ends rather unexpectedly with a paean of praise to Lomonosov, representing the genius of the people, and an "Ode to Freedom." The book is often naive and ill-coordinated—the fastidious Pushkin disliked it—yet powerful in its warnings of simmering popular rebelliousness. This aspect of it particularly riled Catherine when she read it in the tense summer of 1790: her copy with marginal notes has survived. The book was seized, its anonymous author identified, arrested, at first sentenced to death for treason, then exiled to Siberia. Five years later, under Paul, Radishchev returned to take some part in public life, then to commit suicide for what seem to have been ideological reasons.

Among intellectuals who crossed Catherine's path in those final years, Novikov too was arrested, in 1792. Here the trouble seems to have stemmed from his involvement in freemasonry, specifically with the secret Rosicrucian order, largely controlled from Prussia and excessively interested in the heir to the throne, Paul. The immense spread of freemasonry and fringe religion of various types in late 18th-century Russia was remote from Catherine's sympathies: the irritating hints of menace from her increasingly eccentric son's "small court" at Gatchina, outside St Petersburg, were probably worse. But it would be a pity to leave discussion of the intellectual atmosphere of Catherine's time on a sour note. There was in her reign an unprecedented explosion of the arts, particularly in the peaceful decade from the mid-1770s on, that make it one of Russia's best moments of cultural efflorescence. Catherine's tastes in personal life were relaxed and modest, if not spartan, but she liked a party, and court entertainments were splendidly done. The court theater was free and open to all who were respectably dressed, as were the palace parks. Music flourished under Potemkin's patronage, with a series of composers, from Galuppi to Paisiello, making their names in Russia. A native school of composers began cautiously to develop a national style, whether in church music, in keyboard folk-tune variations or in comic operas, long before Glinka.

Catherine herself claimed to have no ear for music, but her visual sense was acute. She founded the collection of paintings that forms the core of the great Hermitage collection in St Petersburg. Russia produced three major portraitists (Dimitriy Levitsky, F. Rokotov, V. Borovikovsky), catering for the newly built country houses and city mansions of the gentry rather than the grand aristocracy, who stand comparison with any in Europe. Sculptural portraiture flourished too, notably in the person of F.I. Shubin, who grew up among peasant

The Senate Square in St Petersburg, with the monument to Peter I (Falconet's *Bronze Horseman*, completed 1782). This great central square, just downstream from the Admiralty, is lined by the fine Senate and Synod buildings by K. Ross (1829) a late (Russian-born) neoclassicist. It fronts the Neva, with the Academy of Arts (1765) beyond. Here 3000 soldiers drew up in the failed "Decembrist" revolt of 1825. The *Bronze Horseman* has had—since Pushkin's narrative poem—a central role in the "myth of Petersburg." Its great granite plinth, mostly underground, suggests a breaking wave.

wood-carvers in the far north.

Buildings were the great visual expression of the age. The Petersburg Baroque of Rastrelli and his school ended rather suddenly at the beginning of the l760s, and Catherine's Russia developed an unusually clean-cut, proportionate and uncluttered version of international neoclassicism, equally adaptable to the grandeur of Pavlovsk or the Tauride Palace as to humbler porticoed provincial town houses or market rows. An early neoclassical practitioner was the Frenchman J.-B. Vallin de la Mothe, and other immigrant architects included the Scot Charles Cameron. There was a galaxy of native talent, among whom two demand mention: Matvey Kazakov (1738–1813) and Vasiliy Bazhenov (1737–99). The former worked only in and near Moscow, building copiously and setting his seal on the calm informality of Moscow classicism. Bazhenov, a leading freemason, became as famous for his unrealized projects as for his handful of standing buildings. The best-known plan was for a remodeling of the Moscow Kremlin (around the old cathedrals) featuring a colonnade as grand as that of Diocletian's palace at Split: work was started on its foundations. What he actually built includes the incomparable Pashkov House in Moscow, and St Michael's Palace in St Petersburg, commissioned by Paul in 1797—a strange manneristic interpretation in classical terms of a moated castle.

But perhaps the period's most worthy architectural memorial is St Petersburg itself, "one of the most consistently neoclassic cities in the world," as it has been called. Catherine gave it an aesthetic focus unmatched for its simplicity of concept combined with multiple symbolic resonances: the equestrian statue of Peter the Great, executed over 16 years (1766–82) under the supervision of E.-M. Falconet, who was recommended to Catherine by Diderot. The rearing horse crushes a snake— Peter's enemies—under its hooves; beneath is a 250-ton block of red granite, shipped in a huge operation from lower down the Gulf of Finland. Its top suggests a breaking wave. This is the statue known universally as the *Bronze Horseman*, from Pushkin's finest narrative poem.

The reign of Paul

When, after his long and sometimes tense wait, Paul came to the throne in 1796, it was made clear that the style of his reign was intended to differ from that of his mother's in every way he could think of. This was good news for dissident exiles such as Radishchev, Novikov and Kosciuszko, who were freed, but there was no great emptying of the prisons, since Paul himself was all too ready to mete out punishment on whim. He distrusted the gentry, whom his mother had made partners in running the country; conversely he was rather popular with the peasantry, though the nearest he got to mitigating serfdom was to lay down the principle that peasants should not do more than three days' *barshchina* work for landlords in a week. He was a well-read and cultivated man, who had worked out his own organic and authoritarian model of a proper society, but continually undermined anything positive in his vision by his capricious, irascible and neurotic temperament.

Foreign policy was dominated by the aftermath

of the French Revolution, and marked by Paul's abrupt changes of mind. First having proclaimed peace, he then joined the anti-French alliance: Russian forces under the great undefeated commander Suvorov (already nearly 70) had total success campaigning in Italy, then managed a remarkable crossing of the Alps. His fleet (in alliance with the Turks) seized the Ionian islands, and, as the 19th century dawned, Russia had an empire that stretched from the Adriatic Sea to the west coast of North America. What Paul really wanted, however, was Malta, where he had been elected Grand Master of the Knights of St John in 1798. Napoleon had occupied the island and, to Paul's disgust, his own allies the British then captured and held it. Paul, coming round to the idea of Napoleon as a bastion of strong rule and orderliness, abruptly changed sides in 1800, and sent off a Cossack army southeastwards—without maps or proper supplies—on a lunatic mission to conquer British-protected India. They were lucky not to all perish in the desert, but the adventure had a lasting side result in the annexation of the ancient kingdom of Georgia, which had been irregularly under Russian protection since the 16th century. British popular suspicions about Russia's Asiatic intentions (still going strong 180 years later when Brezhnev occupied Afghanistan) presumably date from this episode.

The disgruntled and scared aristocrats around the court had been plotting Paul's overthrow since 1799. Catherine had once told him that if he planned to counter ideas with gunfire his reign would be short, and short it was. One of Paul's first actions had been to commission Bazhenov to design the remarkable St Michael's Castle. At its gate he placed a baroque statue of Peter I (by C.-B. Rastrelli, father of the great architect) inscribed "To great-grandfather from great-grandson"—an "answer" to Catherine's *Bronze Horseman*. Anxious to shut himself away from his enemies, he moved into the castle before the walls had dried out: there, in the chilly damp, his enemies tracked him down a few weeks later and in a scene worthy of opera pulled him out from behind a screen, ceremonially deposed him and, in unclear but brutal circumstances, killed him. His eldest son Alexander, then in his early twenties, though warned by the governor of St Petersburg that Paul was to lose his throne, was unprepared for murder; he was peremptorily told "Enough childishness: now go and rule." Paul's end saved the bewildered Cossacks looking for India from a thirsty death, as they were promptly recalled.

Alexander I

Alexander, as soon as he had been persuaded actually to accept the throne which he had gained in so shocking a way, went out to reassure the Guards that the days of his grandmother would be restored. Certainly he then acted with suitable magnanimity, rehabilitating some 12 000 people punished by Paul and relaxing censorship, restrictions on travel and other circumscriptions of liberty that Paul had introduced.

The momentous war with Napoleonic France dominates the historical perspective of Alexander I's reign; however, it occupied quite short periods within it (1805–07 and 1812–14), and Alexander

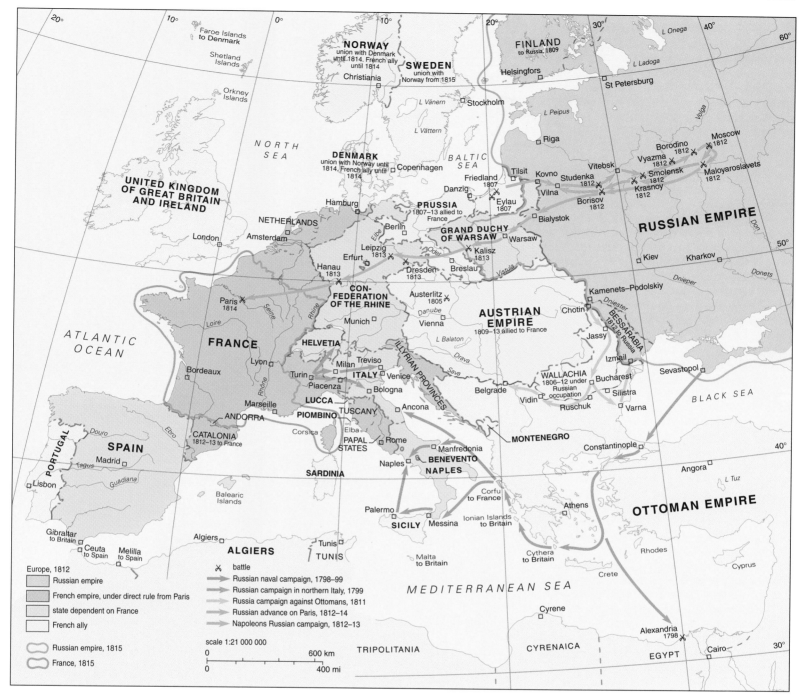

Europe, 1812
- Russian empire
- French empire, under direct rule from Paris
- state dependent on France
- French ally

- Russian empire, 1815
- France, 1815

✕ battle
➡ Russian naval campaign, 1798–99
➡ Russian campaign in northern Italy, 1799
➡ Russia campaign against Ottomans, 1811
➡ Russian advance on Paris, 1812–14
➡ Napoleons Russian campaign, 1812–13

scale 1:21 000 000

0 ——— 600 km

0 ——— 400 mi

had plenty of time to concentrate on domestic issues. At the start of his reign he made a methodical attempt to work out what needed to be done, in the company of an unofficial committee of reform-minded friends. No minutes were taken, but it is clear the ending of serfdom and even of the autocracy was discussed. Such momentous measures would have required a degree of statecraft and patient preparation that Alexander lacked: by 1805 he had lost interest. Measures to improve government were nevertheless undertaken, and the freeing of serfs by landlords was facilitated, though not widely practiced.

The war with France that Russia joined in 1805 was not the only one in Alexander's reign. Hostilities with Persia (1804–15) and with Turkey (1806–12) both resulted from the annexation of Georgia. In each, as in the two previous reigns, Russian military skill was able to deliver notable successes: from the Persians, much of the Caucasus area was gained (though it was to be decades before the wild

mountain valleys would yield their independence), from the Turks, Bessarabia and part of the eastern Black Sea littoral. Further successes against Sweden (1808–09) gained the whole of Finland. The first French war however went a lot less well either than these or the campaigns of Suvorov under Paul. After Austerlitz and Friedland, Alexander realized how great his losses threatened to be, and pulled out of the war. The legendary conference and treaty negotiated at Tilsit followed (July 1807). Napoleon and Alexander decided to confer personally and secretly on a raft in the middle of the River Neman, with a show of bonhomie that could scarcely cover their differences. At least they readily agreed on their dislike of England. Who outwitted the other? Alexander salvaged some concessions from the Napoleonic debacle, and gained time. Napoleon thought Alexander a "cunning Byzantine," and his devious charm seems generally to have been deployed to best effect in foreign policy.

The five-year breathing space after Tilsit allowed attention to be redirected to domestic concerns. Alexander followed and perhaps outdid his grandmother in his far-sighted investment in education, both at school and university level. Particularly famous is the elite Lycée at Tsarskoye Selo where Pushkin and other literary luminaries were excellently taught. But the most remarkable event of those years was the first coherent attempt to produce a constitution for Russia. This was worked out in 1809 by Mikhail Speransky (1772–1839). Speransky, of humble clergy origin, was a firm monarchist who believed equally firmly in the rule of law and participation of society in government. This would have been the chance for a reform-minded emperor to direct the gradual liberalization, or at least modernization, of the state: but Alexander hesitated, and meanwhile anti-Speransky forces built up. In 1812 Speransky, thought to be a Francophile, was dismissed. Later he was to come back to the political scene to some effect, but his grand scheme was never revived.

The story of 1812 is well known, not least to readers of *War and Peace*. Tensions between France and Russia had been building up in many different areas, and the renewal of war could only be a matter of time. Napoleon's "Great Army" numbered nearly half a million—more when reinforcements came—against a far smaller Russian force, at least at the outset. Over half Napoleon's men came not from France but from willing or reluctant allies: there was a large Polish contingent, hoping the war would lead to a reintegrated Polish state. Napoleon advanced, and later retreated, along the traditional highway into Russia, the great series of moraine ridges that lead through Smolensk towards Moscow, striking at the country's heart rather than at its administrative capital. Outside Moscow the indecisive battle of Borodino was fought in a mist, with huge losses (ultimately worse for the French) on both sides. Though Moscow could not be held, Alexander, his old and wily commander Kutuzov and the Russian people at large had no intention of suing for peace. Napoleon had left his entry into the deserted and soon incinerated city too late: he was undersupplied, and it was already September; no anti-tsarist peasant uprising had materialized; he could not live off the land, even though there was no systematic scorched earth policy. The retreat, starting in mid-October at the onset of the Russian winter was disastrous; disease was even more effective than Russian partisans at reducing the Great Army, of which scarcely a twentieth returned home. By the end of the year Russia had been cleared of the invaders. The Russian army continued in pursuit of Napoleon, and in 1814 occupied Paris where they left, supposedly, a linguistic memento behind in the word *bistro*, a drinking-place (from Russian *bystro!*, "quick!").

The saga of 1812 has remained high in the Russian historical consciousness; it was termed *otechestvennaya voyna*, "the Fatherland War" (often mistranslated "Patriotic War") from the fact that it unrolled on Russian soil. Hitler's invasion in 1941 was to be given the same appellation. As for Alexander, he was awarded the title *blazhenny*, "the Blessed," with the implication that he was a living saint. In the general euphoria of the conservative

1812

The events of 1812 and their consequences for Russia can only properly be appreciated in the context of a society whose educated class was intensely Francophile, irrespective of political inclination. Russia had vacillated in Paul's and Alexander I's reigns in its attitude to Napoleonic France. When Napoleon and Alexander concluded peace at Tilsit (1807), it is unlikely that either felt secure in the alliance; what each got was a breathing space. When Napoleon's assault eventually came he set out, disastrously, at midsummer, to be caught in autumnal Moscow. The retreat from the empty and incinerated city in early winter reduced the "Great Army" to a twentieth of its initial size.

Napoleon's war on Russia might have been a war of liberation. It was quite uncertain how the enserfed population would react to a self-proclaimed liberator, particularly in the extensive western areas reincorporated into Russia only a generation before. Polish irredentism was a strong political undercurrent of the Napoleonic venture, and Poles fought better than his other troops (under half were French). Some "Old Believer" schismatics became *Napoleonovtsy* ("Napoleonites"), on the basis that the man declared "Antichrist" by the Orthodox must be their salvation. But the bulk of the population held firm to the tsar. The psychological and political consequences for Russia of defeating Napoleon were great. It was Russia's most "European" moment: Alexander, convinced of divine approval, attempted to order Europe's destiny.

Bottom left Prince Mikhail Kutuzov, Russian military commander in 1812, already had (at 67) a distinguished career behind him. Napoleon continued from Vilnius not towards St Petersburg, the capital, but Moscow, Russia's heart. Russian public opinion was alarmed, and Kutuzov was put in command. One battle was fought, at Borodino (which Napoleon seems to have thought was for Moscow, though well over 100 kilometers away). It was indecisive, with great slaughter, though ultimately worse for the French with their extended supply-lines. The wily Kutuzov continued to retreat, luring the French into a trap. For the deterministic Tolstoy it was the down-to-earth Kutuzov, not Napoleon with all his pretensions, who understood the march of history.

Left Great artists were moved by the pathos of the retreat from Moscow: this is Géricault's drawing of wounded French soldiers. Napoleonic veterans, however, were few, even at the outset: the Great Army consisted largely of allies.

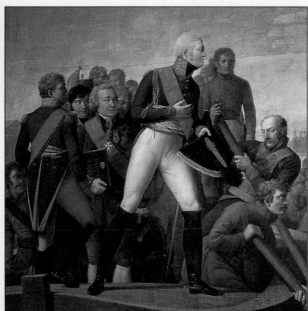

Above Tsar Alexander at Tilsit, by G. Serangeli (1810). For two years Russia had grimly resisted the Napoleonic military machine, despite Austerlitz and other allied reverses; finally the battle of Friedland forced the tsar to sue for peace. Russia avoided the humiliation meted out to Prussia: at the border town of Tilsit on the River Neman Alexander and Napoleon agreed in person to terms that, while committing Russia to the support of France, left it a free agent. Alexander, a charming, shrewd and devious diplomatist, must have known he was buying time. A dynastic marriage between his sister and Napoleon did not materialize, and a whole series of diplomatic irritations led inexorably towards 1812. Meanwhile the Russians were able successfully to take on a series of other enemies, from Sweden to Persia.

Left The retreat of the Great Army from the useless goal of Moscow, burnt out—probably deliberately—and empty of population, began on 19 October. The Russian forces harassed it more and more as the retreat became chaotic. Disasters such as that of the crossing of the Berezina River in Belarus reduced both numbers and morale, but in the end disease and hunger took the greatest toll. By the end of 1812 the entire remnants of the Great Army had left Russian soil. The retreat, with Napoleon at its head, is romantically portrayed in this later 19th-century painting by E. Meissonier.

Decembrists, Anarchists and Terrorists

Below The Decembrist rebels assembled in Senate Square, St Petersburg, by the statue of Peter the Great. There they were surrounded by loyal units, who fired upon them and dispersed them. The print shows the Decembrists fleeing to the left, with troops loyal to Nicholas I in formation around the square.

The all-encompassing pretensions of tsarist autocracy meant that opposition to it was often revolutionary in character—even when its proponents were liberals or mild socialists. Such were most of the 1825 Decembrists, who had great symbolic resonance for later Russian opposition.

Because of 1917, Marxism may well be seen as the main impulse behind Russian revolutionarism. During most of the preceding century however this was far from the case. The characteristic Russian trend was anarchism of various kinds. Its greatest proponent, Mikhail Bakunin (1814–76), was active throughout Europe, and managed to destroy Marx's First International; his successor, Peter Kropotkin (1842–1921), gave anarchism intellectual stuffing. Both, perhaps surprisingly, were revered more than a century later under the Soviet régime.

Russia's social peculiarities, notably the self-helping peasant commune, meant that anarchism blended easily with the populism dominant from the mid-19th century. Politics tended to polarize, and revolutionaries increasingly resorted to terrorism (see Dostoyevsky's hostile picture in *The Devils*). Late 19th-century revolutionism, marked by complexity and duplicity, achieved the assassination of Alexander II but little else: after a lull, leadership passed to the methodical Marxists.

Mikhail Bakunin (*far left*), greatest of anarchists, emigrated after imprisonment (1851–57) and achieved fame in the West. Originally (like many Russian thinkers) a Hegelian, he came to loathe all politics, religion and the slavery implicit in authority, upholding "the sacred instinct of revolt." He and similar theorists were lionized by the educated elite, whose tolerance of terrorism was sufficient to influence a jury's acquittal of Vera Zasulich (*left*), who shot and wounded the military governor of St Petersburg in 1878.

Bottom Sofya Perovskaya, from a family in the highest administrative class, was a leader of "People's Will," the terrorist group dedicated to assassinating government officials. Its ultimate target was Alexander II, but their repeated attempts at regicide failed.

Far left Alexander II was killed by a bomb thrown by an isolated terrorist. He was simultaneously stalked by the "People's Will" group, who had been responsible for unsuccessful earlier assassination attempts. The day he died, the emperor was due to finalize a proclamation of constitutional reform.

Left This photograph of women terrorists boarding a train for exile in Siberia illustrates the class divide confronting the revolutionaries of the late 19th century. The women are all conspicuously upper class; the railway workers are indifferent to them, and fascinated at being photographed.

forces in Europe after 1815 Alexander was on top of the world. Though still by inclination a constitutionalist, Alexander was a moving spirit behind the fantastical Holy Alliance (by which crowned heads of Europe pledged themselves to live in Christian brotherhood) and the more practical Congress System of political alliances intended to maintain the European order and crush revolution. He proposed an international law-enforcing army, coupled with disarmament, but his partners overruled him. The Greek rebellion against the Ottoman empire placed the Congress system in a quandary: should this be considered revolution, or a Christian war of liberation against the infidel? (Eventually, under Alexander's successor, the Russians were to come down decisively on the side of the Greeks.) Similar problems were to disturb the "Concert of Europe" up to World War I.

At home, movement towards reform came almost to a halt with Alexander's conviction of his special God-given destiny and absorption both in high international politics and in fringe religion. Another, decentralizing, constitution was drafted, this time by Count Nikolai Novosiltsov, but again Alexander vacillated. Little more was done towards alleviating serfdom, though in the Baltic provinces peasants were liberated, without land.

The Decembrists

On 1 December 1825 (O.S.) Alexander suddenly died of fever in the remote southern port of Taganrog. He was 48; he had confided not long before that he intended to abdicate at 50. Several odd factors combined to rouse later suspicions that the death was faked: a wandering hermit called Fyodor Kuzmich was subsequently thought to be the late emperor. News of the death took a week to reach St Petersburg. An extraordinary period of uncertainty began: Alexander had left no sons, and by Paul's succession law the throne should have passed to his brother Constantine. Some years before, Constantine, comfortably installed in Warsaw and married to a Polish lady, had renounced his rights; Alexander confirmed the succession must now pass to his youngest brother, Nicholas, but kept the change secret. Hasty correspondence passed betwen St Petersburg and Warsaw to establish Constantine's current intentions; Nicholas and his troops meanwhile swore public allegiance to him. But Constantine would not even accept power and then abdicate, so Nicholas's formal accession day was set for 26 December. These baffling and secretive goings-on alarmed educated opinion, while those who hoped for reforms were disconcerted at the prospect of rule by the stern Nicholas rather than the more amenable Constantine. If anyone could act swiftly enough the circumstances seemed right for a coup d'etat.

Those ready to hatch this have been named by posterity "Decembrists." They constituted a rather extensive network of mostly young army officers, organized in three main groupings, of which the most radical was the "Southern Society" led by Colonel Pavel Pestel; they were well organized but based at the southern army headquarters, far from the capital. Their plan was to assemble the troops under their command in the great Senate Square, by the Bronze Horseman, and with this show of force somehow to compel Nicholas to stand down

in favor of Constantine. About 3000 soldiers were drawn up in the late morning of a cold winter's day, shouting for "Constantine and Constitution." Legend has it that the men thought "Constitution" (*Konstitutsiya*) was Constantine's wife. But Nicholas, forewarned, had loyal troops surround the square. A messenger was killed; the rebels' proposed regent disappeared from the scene. Both sets of troops waited, watched and froze as hours ticked by. When darkness was approaching, Nicholas overcame his reluctance to baptize his reign in blood and ordered his artillery to fire. Some 50 men were killed, the rebellion collapsed and its leaders were arrested.

What the Decembrists all wanted was constitutional government and an end to serfdom: beyond that there was little agreement, and their schemes ranged from a mild liberalism to Pestel's rigorously centralized Jacobin republic. These plans had been maturing for some time, since the native roots of Decembrism stretch back at any rate for a decade, and maybe to Radishchev in the 18th century. Equally important was the example of similar political organizations in Western Europe (the Italian *Carbonari*, the German *Tugendbund*). The masonic lodges that proliferated in the late 18th and early 19th centuries in Russia proved a fertile breeding ground for unorthodox—often unworldly—political thinking. Historians often point to the fact that the large numbers of Russian soldiers who pursued Napoleon to Paris broadened their mental horizons by experiencing foreign ways at first hand. This may be so, but nevertheless most of the Decembrist officers were too young to have participated. What bound their disparate personalities together were certain behavioral modes and habits of everyday life: they believed in action, in blunt words, in a "Roman" straightforwardness. There is a splendid literary portrayal of the "Decembrist type" in the hero of Alexander Griboyedov's notable satirical verse play *Woe from Wit* (1824). Since they were recognizable in any gathering they were not very good conspirators: Alexander's government knew quite well what was afoot, but hardly bothered to respond, save by closing masonic lodges.

The Decembrists' revolt was essentially symbolic: some of its leaders assumed its failure before it had even taken place. Its symbolic nature made the image of the Decembrists, their frankness and courage, all the more powerful to later generations of revolutionaries, and indeed of liberals, in a society where indecision or cunning deviousness were notably pervasive among the progressive intellectuals. But what particularly impressed and alarmed the autocracy at the time was the fact that the Decembrists constituted a movement, and one that had spread widely among officers and intellectuals of the gentry, the most privileged class of the nation, the class on which its government depended. Even if they had little rapport with the mass of the people, the Decembrists nevertheless could not simply be dismissed as isolated dreamers or fanatics. They also had the intellectual power of a firmly Russian-based ideology, a view of history that centered on the ancient liberties of Kiev and Novgorod, on bold anti-tyrannical figures such as Prince Kurbsky, a vision, in fact, of an "alternative Russia."

THE LAST FOUR EMPERORS

Reaction and stagnation

Nicholas I came to the Russian throne in his thirtieth year, and reigned another 30: the period has entered the Russians' consciousness as an age of reaction, of political stagnation and social repression. It ended in the first war the Russians had lost since the ill-fated Crimean campaigns of the 1680s, with Nicholas aware at his death of the crumbling of all he had stood for. The black picture we get of the period is largely the work of the regime's eloquent opponents, notable among them the amiable émigré Alexander Herzen (Gertsen). From the point of view of Russian culture, however, there was much remarkable achievement: above all in literature, to some extent in the other arts and also in the sphere of socio-political thought.

Nicholas was a soldier and the chief engineer of his own army. Countering any threat to Russia's good order and discipline was his life's work. He had the "parade-ground" character that with startling regularity revealed itself in each alternate monarch from the mid-18th century to the end of the dynasty. Queen Victoria summed him up in 1844: "He is stern and severe with fixed principles of duty which nothing on earth will make him change . . . he is sincere even in his most despotic acts, from a sense that is the only way to govern." Nicholas was certainly not by nature brutal, but ruled in a way that encouraged a general brutalization. A notorious episode was the mock execution of the Petrashevsky Circle, an informal discussion group of vaguely utopian-socialist inclinations: 21 of them, including the young Fyodor Dostoyevsky, were sentenced to death in 1849. When the first batch had already been tied up to be shot, a stage-managed reprieve was granted; one victim was permanently deranged. Dostoyevsky remained in Siberia until 1856.

The beginning and end of Nicholas I's reign were marked by wars against Turkey: the first was successful, the second unsuccessful, though only after the British and French had joined in on the Ottoman side. The war of the 1820s, in continuation of Alexander's policies, eventually brought guaranteed independence to Greece and autonomy to other Balkan Christian provinces. In between came peace and good relations with the Ottomans, to the extent of Russia's helping to defend Constantinople against the Egyptian rebel Ibrahim Pasha in the 1830s. In 1848–49, the European "year of revolutions," Russia helped another foreign empire, Austria, to crush rebellion, this time the Hungarian national uprising led by Kossuth. The French revolution of 1848 and subsequently the accession of Napoleon III made a clash of some kind with France unavoidable; the Crimean war was the outcome.

In domestic policy, Nicholas's pursuit of good order had many negative results and one or two more positive. Speransky (who had been Alexander I's "prime minister" 20 years before) accomplished the task of codifying all the Russian laws since 1649. Order was brought to the chaotic state finances. There was growth in the economy, and grain exports (largely through Odessa) gained in significance, particularly after the repeal of the British corn laws. The lot of state peasants—nearly half the total—was improved; when they were given title to their land, they were effectively freed. Serfdom itself remained untouched, though in anticipation of its eventual end landlords quietly transferred over half a million serfs from the land into domestic service during the 1840s and 1850s, in the hope of minimizing the effect of any share-out of their own estates. Meanwhile Nicholas's personal commitment to the maintenance of social discipline, not to mention mistrust of the gentry class that had spawned the Decembrists, meant that he preferred to rule not through the established state organs, but less formally through special committees of a few like-minded assistants. "His Majesty's Own Chancery" grew in size and power: its Third Department (headed by Count Benckendorff) was effectively Nicholas's political police, existing in rivalry with the real police, highly intrusive in all areas of life, recipients of countless anonymous denunciations, yet at the same time ludicrously inefficient. Censorship of print and tight restrictions on foreign travel were characteristic.

Nicholas made it his personal concern to investigate the whole Decembrist revolt and its ramifications. Over a hundred participants were brought to trial, five were executed (including the considerable poet Kondratiy Ryleyev) and most of the rest sent to Siberia. The Decembrists, always ready to speak their minds, spelled out their hopes and beliefs in answer to long questioning under arrest, and in some cases in personal missives to the emperor. When Nicholas behaved mercifully there was sometimes a catch. Pushkin, friend of many of those arrested, told Nicholas personally that had he been in St Petersburg at the time of the revolt he would have been with his friends on Senate Square. Nicholas responded that he would pardon Pushkin and act as his personal censor: the poet was delighted at this show of magnanimity till he realized he would in fact have to take his works to Benckendorff, a more alarming prospect than the ordinary censorship. Later he was appointed humiliatingly to a minor court post, subject not just to boredom but to ultimately fatal intrigue.

The Decembrist uprising differed profoundly from previous Russian rebellions, elemental explosions of popular discontent, in having an ideological basis. Thus the authorities were greatly concerned to counter its ideas with ideas of their own: out of this immediate need, and out of the more general early 19th-century European effort to harness the new revolutionary forces of nationalism in the interests of established order, was hatched the doctrine of "Official Nationality." Its

despite the fact that each generation since the mid-18th century "Germanized" itself further, until by the 20th century scarcely a drop of Russian blood flowed through the imperial veins. In particular it tried to absorb the famous concept of "Holy Russia." This is first recorded in Kurbsky's letters to Ivan IV in the mid-16th century, becomes common from the Time of Troubles and seems to indicate a concept of the Russian land distinct from, and sometimes in opposition to, its sovereign rulers; it may have arisen from the phonetic similarity between *svyatoy*, holy," and *svetly*, "bright" (used, for example, in the 13th-century *Tale of the Ruin of the Russian Land*). The 18th-century "gentry culture" had no time for it, but after 1812, which was seen by many Russians as a war of Orthodoxy against the Antichrist, it was on everybody's lips. For tsarism to take up the concept indicated an attempt to bypass, or marginalize, not just the values of the Enlightenment, but the whole independent gentry class so feared and despised by Nicholas I.

It should not be thought that these and related ideas were propagated only by the creatures of the autocracy. The writer Nikolai Gogol (1809–52) in later years largely gave himself over to their exposition, in crazily extravagant form. Subsequently they would be powerfully voiced in Dostoyevsky's huge "polyphonic" novels and journalism. They infuse certain works by leading poets of the time, most notably Vasiliy Zhukovsky (1783–1852), who was chosen to tutor the future Alexander II, and Fyodor Tyutchev (1803–73). The quite false assumption is sometimes made that all significant 19th-century Russian writers were opponents of tsardom. In fact there was a diverse stream of articulate "conservative" thought in Russia dating at least as far back as Prince M. Shcherbatov, who was an effective speaker in the Legislative Commission of 1767, and later published polemical essays; it runs through figures such as the historian Karamzin and the "archaist" poet Alexander Shishkov (1754–1841).

The Slavophiles and mid-19th-century culture

The most notable debate to which the age gave birth was that between the Slavophiles and their various opponents, generally referred to as Westernizers (though unlike the Slavophiles they did not constitute any self-acknowledged group). What seems to have set the Slavophile enterprise in motion was the publication in 1836 of the first *Philosophical Letter* by Pyotr Chaadayev (1794–1856). He had Decembrist connections, an interest in the "Lovers of Wisdom" (*Lyubomudry*, a mystically minded discussion group disbanded after the Decembrist uprising) and a sympathy with European Romantic religious and historical thought. The burden of his letter was a rhetorical evocation of what he saw as Russian cultural aimlessness, lack of spirituality and absence of characteristic Western virtues such as a sense of duty, justice and logic. In such a country there could be no progress and no true history. Chaadayev's *Letter* caused an uproar, and he was declared mad.

The Slavophiles, in contrast, rallied to the defense of Russia's rich and ancient culture, which they saw as different in essence from that of the West (it has been a besetting sin of Russian

This French engraving shows Nicholas I (tsar 1825–55) reviewing his troops. Like Paul and Peter III before him, Nicholas was militarily minded, with a "parade-ground" attitude not just to his army but to the government of Russia; he was known as the "Gendarme of Europe." After the "year of the revolutions" (1848), his coercion of Russia was particularly stringent. Russian armies were successful throughout his reign until the major conflict in the Crimea (1853–56), which had begun as a Russo-Turkish war. The deficiencies that were shown up after the Anglo-French involvement darkened Nicholas's last days.

chief proponent, who had a long spell (1833–49) as Nicholas's minister of education, was Count Sergey Uvarov. Its principles were embodied in three concepts: Orthodoxy, Autocracy (the foundation of the whole structure) and the untranslatable *Narodnost*—usually rendered as "Nationality," but embodying certain presuppositions about the popular spirit and will as upholders of the idea of tsardom. *Narodnost* was to pop up unexpectedly again in the 1930s as one of the three principles of Soviet Socialist Realism. "Official Nationality" was forcibly propagated in schools and universities, yet was not an entirely artificial construct, since it seemed to many to articulate that characteristic 19th-century intellectual yearning for *Gemeinschaft*, "communality," the sense of the nation as an organic whole, held together by bonds deeper than merely laws or social conventions.

The particular Russian gloss was supplied by the attempt of the autocracy to take over popular myths about the relation between tsar and people,

Pushkin and Gogol

When foreigners speak of the classics of Russian literature, they are likely to have in mind Tolstoy and Dostoyevsky, perhaps Turgenev and Chekhov. Many Russians however consider their real classics to be two writers who were dead before the great age of the Russian novel had even begun: Alexander Pushkin (1799–1837) and Nikolai Gogol (1809–52). They knew each other: Pushkin welcomed Gogol's early stories; Gogol hero-worshiped the already famous Pushkin. Both came from the down-at-heel landowning class, but in all other respects they were utterly different.

Pushkin called himself a Romantic, by that meaning merely that he was a modern and admired Byron: his deeper instincts, like Byron's, were classical. He sensed responsibility to tradition and to society: Russia, he thought, needed "Shakespearean" drama, and *Boris Godunov* resulted. He also produced "the best novel Walter Scott never wrote," *The Captain's Daughter*. He turned his hand to all literary forms, investing each with balance, tact and wit. Wary of rhetoric and even metaphor, he can sound "flat" (as Flaubert complained) in translations where the linguistic precision, range and sparkle are missing.

Pushkin was the Mozart of literature; not just their art but their personalities and lives have uncanny resemblances. Pushkin sensed this, and anticipated Schaffer's *Amadeus* in his "little tragedy," *Mozart and Salieri*. Like many of his best works (*Queen of Spades, Bronze Horseman*), it is both a study in obsession and a "problem-piece" where readers have to formulate not only answers, but the questions themselves. Pushkin was much aware of the limits of literature, teasingly breaking off his great "novel in verse," *Yevgeny Onegin*, in mid-sentence at its climax.

Gogol, the country boy overwhelmed by St Petersburg, capitalized on his Ukrainian background in his early stories. Their knowing folkiness was considered hilarious; Pushkin spotted that Gogol's gaiety was "at once naive and cunning." Subsequent tales—*How the Two Ivans Quarreled*, the Petersburg stories—revealed alarming depths under a surface of comedy and pathos. A few years on either side of his 30th birthday, mostly spent abroad, witnessed his masterpieces: a play *The Inspector General, The Overcoat*, the first part of *Dead Souls*. In detail these works are uproariously funny: overall they terrify in their haunted soullessness. Critics took them as sociopolitical satire; Gogol objected violently, wishing them to be read in religious terms. But Gogol's idiosyncratic religion had little place for God, though the Devil was everywhere—operating above all through *poshlost*, pretentious vulgarity. Gogol's unruly genius deserted him, his projected "Divine Comedy," *Dead Souls*, remained a fragment and he died in pitiful dejection. Whereas the suave and fastidious Pushkin stimulated the whole Europeanized and intellectual vein in Russian writing, everything in it that is perverse, facetious, capricious, colloquial, in- or over-articulate, from Dostoyevsky to Zoshchenko, is Gogol's progeny.

Above A sketch drawn by Pushkin to illustrate a story in his *Tales of Belkin*.

Left An illustration of a Pushkin folk tale by I. Bilibin (1876–1942), associated with the Symbolist "world of Art" group and one of the best turn-of-the-century graphic artists. Pushkin's writings have had a remarkable "after-life" as material for many Russian operas, songs and ballets and also for artists.

Below left Portrait of Pushkin by O.A. Kiprensky (1782–1836). Kiprensky was one of the last in the unpretentious yet distinguished line of Russian 18th-century portraitists. This, one of the finest Russian portraits, invests the poet with a subdued Romantic tension and loneliness.

Below Mikhaylovskoye, in the Pskov region (much damaged in 1941 but restored) was the Pushkin family's estate and the poet's burial place. Here he was exiled for a couple of years in the mid-1820s (thus avoiding the Decembrist uprising in which

friends were involved), with little company save his old nurse Arina Rodionovina, from whom he acquired his lasting interest in folklore; like two or three other periods of isolation, it was a most productive period in his writing.

Above Pushkin was a compulsive doodler on his much-worked-over manuscripts, and beyond that a deft producer of album verses, sketches and caricatures, not averse to mordant or bawdy wit. His own face, often emphasizing the "African" features he inherited from one of his forebears, Peter the Great's Ethiopian servitor Hannibal, constantly recurs.

Left In contrast to the dashing Pushkin, Gogol, perhaps flatteringly portrayed here, was unprepossessing, gauche, scared of women, unself-confident yet manically egotistical. Unsure of his own superabundant but uncontrollable talent, he attributed to Pushkin the ideas for his best works.

thinkers from Chaadayev to Solzhenitsyn to talk sweepingly of "the West" as if it were a single entity). "Slavophile" does not necessarily imply an interest in fellow Slavs, or "Panslavism"—rather a concern with Russia's non-Western individuality and its deep religious and historical roots. The movement's leading writers, Ivan Kireyevsky (1806–56) and Aleksey Khomyakov (1804–60), developed a theory of history that saw the West's rationalism as having fatally "atomized" society, rendering social relationships sterile and legalistic. By contrast, the Russian people were and are in possession of "inner truth" and freedom, values inherent above all in the village commune (*mir* or *obshchina*) and the Orthodox Church. Khomyakov went on to develop his famous concept of *sobornost*, "communality"—an attempt to define the essence (rather than the mundane reality) of Orthodoxy, which stood for voluntary agreement and brotherhood, as opposed to papal authoritarianism. A practical consequence of Slavophilism was the methodical investigation of folk culture and creativity, manifested notably in the great collection of folksong made by Kireyevsky's brother Pyotr. After its "heroic period" in the 1840s and 1850s, during which it championed the cause of the emancipation of the serfs as essential to the revival of Russia's unique social and cultural heritage, Slavophilism was fragmented and to some extent passed into common currency; some of its survivors became establishment figures. Under Nicholas I, however, leading Slavophiles were often subject to censorship on account of an underlying note of anarchy and libertarianism in their ideology.

Censorship, not surprisingly, clamped down harder still on radical thinkers of the period, including several of those considered to be Westernizers. Even a work of an earlier generation, Griboyedov's *Woe from Wit* (1824), was unpublishable, though it circulated in thousands of manuscript copies and has become as quotable as Shakespeare. Alexander Herzen (1812–70), one of the great liberal thinkers of Europe, emigrated to England in 1847—not that he found "the West" wholly congenial—and issued a stream of uncensored writing, notably his vast discursive autobiography *My Past and Thoughts*. The first great Russian revolutionary anarchist, Mikhail Bakunin (1814–76), also emigrated. It was characteristic of the period that social thought and literature overlapped: partly because of the difficulty of expressing heterodox views directly in conditions of censorship, but also because of a general Russian sense of the indivisibility of culture.

Social determinists, however, might find difficulty in explaining how the period 1820–40, politically so unpromising, came to be considered the Golden Age of Russian literature. The phenomenon can be seen in two perspectives: either as the beginning of the modern flowering of Russian literature that continued after mid-century with the classic age of the novel, or as the culmination of a long time of preparation. The latter view has much to be said for it, since the leading genre of the period is lyric (and to some extent narrative) poetry, the end product of a tradition that had been developing from the 1750s onwards. The forging of the Russian literary language into a thoroughly modern, yet flexible and multivalent

СПАСИ ГОСПОДИ ЛЮДИ ТВОЯ

И БЛАГОСЛОВИ ДОСТОЯНІЕ ТВОЕ

ПОДВИГЪ ПРАПОРЩИКА
ЩЕГОЛЕВА.
при бомбардировании г. Одессы.
10 Апрѣля 1854 Года.

СРАЖЕНІЕ ПРИ БАШЪ-КАДЫКЛАРѢ.
19 Ноября 1853 Года.
взятіе Турецкаго лагеря.

СРАЖЕНІЕ НА ГРАНИЦѢ ГУРІИ.
4 Іюня 1854 Года.
и совершенное пораженіе.

Подвигъ канонира.

СИНОПСКОЕ СРАЖЕНІЕ.
18 Ноября 1853 Года.
истребленіе Турецкой
Эскадры.

Подвигъ Гончарова унт. Офицера.

СИМЪ ПОБѢЖДАЮ

Left This propaganda broadsheet—whose character is clearly akin to similar Greek politico-religious popular prints of the 19th and 20th centuries—invokes divine blessing on the Russian military endeavor in the war against the Turks. It commemorates a side of the so-called Crimean War little mentioned in Western textbooks: a series of Russian battle successes and acts of individual heroism in 1853–54, immediately before and after the Anglo-French entry into the war. The scenes are disposed on a Greek cross frame, as if on a St George medal (with the saint himself at the center). The lowest cross arm shows the action that most alarmed the Western allies: the destruction of the Turkish fleet at Sinope, on the north coast of Turkey. The cross arms show the relative geographic disposition of the actions (clockwise from Sinope: the Balkans; Odessa; Guria, i.e. Transcaucasia). The Crimea itself was not invaded until late in 1854.

growth of Russia

by 1739
1740–74
1775–1800
1801–28
1829–53
gained from Ottoman empire
political boundaries, 1853

campaigns 1853–55
Russian
Turkish
Anglo-French
Russian victory, with date
Allied victory, with date
Russian base
Allied base

AU
EM

SERBIA

MONTENEGRO

Sofia

OTTOMAN
EMPIRE

scale 1:8 000 000

200 km
150 mi

medium for poetry is above all the work of Alexander Pushkin (1799–1837), still considered the greatest of Russian poets. Yet in his day he was only the leading luminary of a whole Pleiad, of whom the greatest is probably Yevgeny Boratynsky (1800–44), a gritty, paradoxical pessimist. In his thirties Pushkin turned to prose, writing the first notable Russian short stories (*The Queen of Spades* being outstanding) and doing serious research into the history of the Pugachov rebellion. Gogol developed prose in a different and idiosyncratic way, but Pushkin both as poet and prosewriter had a successor of remarkable brilliance in Mikhail Lermontov (1814–41). Trying to avoid Pushkin's long shadow, and seeing himself as a Russian Byron, Lermontov substituted biting wit and rhetorical self-projection for Pushkin's cool ironies and delicacy of feeling. But his single mature prose work, *Hero of our Time* (1840), is his masterpiece, and one of the first great truly European works in Russian literature, a psychological novel that looks forward to the 20th century.

The visual arts in this period did not match the efflorescence of literature: the 18th-century tradition of portraiture continued to flourish, but the grander visions of Alexander Ivanov (1806–58) and Karl Bryullov (1799–1852) did not quite live up either to the foreign works from which they derive or to their own ambitions. The long-lived late neoclassicism of Russian architecture was still producing masterpieces of laconic grandeur in Alexander I's reign, such as the Admiralty in St Petersburg as remodeled by Andreyan Zakharov in 1806. It gradually faded out into the eclectic styles characteristic of all Europe in Nicholas I's time; a highly visible example is the Great Kremlin Palace in Moscow by Konstantin Ton, dated 1838. Music was splendidly represented in the person of Mikhail Glinka (1804–57); he was not, as is sometimes assumed, the first Russian composer but rather the summation of much that had been prepared during the 18th century. His two great operas, still very much in the repertory, use folksong imitation in an "international" musical context. However, it is the instrumental *Kamarinskaya*, which, in its approach to the transformation of folk-derived material, is the embryo from which the later 19th-century national school of Russian music grew.

The Crimean War and its consequences

The Crimean War served as catalyst for the most profound political and social changes introduced in Russia during the 19th century. Perhaps ironically, its causes, course and resolution were all peripheral to the internal condition of the empire. The background and general causes of the war were all bound up in the Eastern Question, the complex international power struggle between the major states of Europe in connection with the decline of the Ottoman empire. The chief participants were Austria, Britain, France and Russia; each was concerned to secure its influence over certain parts of the Ottoman domain in Europe in order to facilitate its wider imperial interests. For Russia these interests were the neutralization of a centuries-old enemy in the Turks and the dream of securing a passage from the Black Sea into the Mediterranean. The struggle began in the mid-1820s, was convoluted in the extreme and had by the early 1850s created a volatile atmosphere of mutual suspicion.

The immediate cause of the war was connected with events in the Holy Land. In 1852 the French persuaded the Turks to give the Roman Catholic Church custodianship of the Church of the Nativity in Bethlehem, a right traditionally held by the Greek Orthodox. Nicholas I, as the patron of the Orthodox population under Ottoman rule, demanded that the right be returned to the Orthodox. When the Turks refused, Nicholas ordered Russian troops into Moldavia and Wallachia. Britain and France suspected that Nicholas I might next launch an all-out war to destroy Turkey. When in 1853 Turkey declared war on Russia, Britain and France quickly came to the sultan's aid and dispatched a large expeditionary force to take the fighting to Russia.

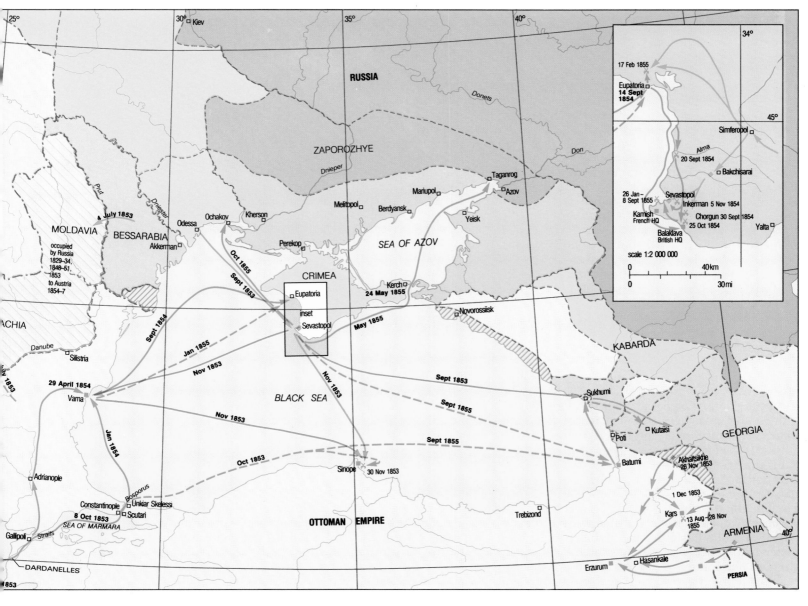

Signed on 3 March 1878, the Treaty of San Stefano concluded the Russo-Turkish war of 1877–78. Although a local conflict, the war was entangled in great-power diplomacy, and the settlement of San Stefano had to be redrafted at a subsequent European congress in Berlin. The Balkan territories of the Ottoman empire were emancipated, with Bulgaria gaining independence. and Bosnia and Herzegovina coming under Austrian suzerainty. The contemporary print shows the Russian negotiating contingent entering San Stefano, a small village near Istanbul.

The force sailed for Sevastopol in the Crimea, home base of the Russian Black Sea fleet, which had inflicted a major defeat on the Turkish fleet soon after hostilities began. The Russians scuttled their fleet and mounted a stubborn land resistance against the expeditionary force when it landed in 1854. The war that followed was essentially a stalemate, with terrible casualties on both sides.

In 1855 Nicholas I died and was succeeded by Alexander II. Almost simultaneously the Russians suffered new reversals in the Crimea and, despite initial determination to continue the war, the new tsar soon accepted that Russia at all costs needed peace. The Treaty of Paris, concluded in 1856, proved very unfavorable: Russia lost territories on the Balkan frontier, naval rights in the Black Sea, right of sea passage into the Mediterranean and protectorship over the Orthodox Christians in the Ottoman lands. The damaging loss of influence and prestige was greeted with public resentment in Russia. In reality, as Alexander II and his advisers recognized, it was necessary to end the war in order to ease the severe social and political strains it was generating.

The war had witnessed growing social unrest among the peasants of rural Russia. This was directed not against the war and the government, but against serfdom and the landowners. The condition of serfdom had grown especially oppressive in the decades before the Crimean War. One of the few ways out of serfdom was through long military service, upon completion of which a soldier serf was made a freeman. The war was therefore popular among the serfs, but at the same time fueled wild rumors to the effect that new forms of recruitment and civil guard duties would give more types of freedoms. These rumors caused popular meetings and even mass migrations, which had to be stopped by force. One rumor in particular spread like wildfire; this was that the new tsar, whose open-mindedness and goodwill had become widely known prior to his accession, had proclaimed an end to serfdom but that the news had been suppressed by the landowners. Popular uprisings against landowners ensued. When these were put down, the peasants were seized with rumors of a "promised land" without serfdom that existed somewhere in Russia; large spontaneous migrations in search of it disrupted the countryside.

The political strain brought on by the war affected the opposite end of Russia's social spectrum, the urban intelligentsia—journalists, educators, bureaucrats and the lesser nobility. Here the cause was two-fold: first, the intelligentsia's awareness of how badly the war was going and how badly Russia's prestige was suffering, and, second, the heavy wartime taxation imposed on the cities, with resulting economic disruption and price rises. The intelligentsia's disillusionment and anger erupted into popular demonstrations in Moscow. The liberals were having their first experience of shaping reasoned literary comment on pressing political matters. Much of this took the form of extended articles and letters which were circulated in *samizdat* form, and exercised a strong influence on the liberal wing of the press.

Alexander II was aware of these social and political strains and sensed that Russia's well-being depended on their being defused. The tsar's perceptivity was matched by resolution, and in his proclamation announcing the end of the Crimean War, he hinted clearly at his determination to abolish serfdom. This and other reforms which he initiated during the early 1860s were the most ambitious attempt to transform Russia's political and social structure undertaken before the revolutions of 1917.

Alexander II and the "Great Reforms"

Beginning in 1857, Alexander appointed a series of commissions to start preparatory work on reforms of serfdom, local government, the judiciary and the military. This work progressed with dispatch, despite complex consultative and drafting processes, but with the tsar's close personal involvement and encouragement. The result was a series of four reform acts promulgated from 1861.

The first reform dealt with the abolition of serfdom. Of immense complexity, the statute tried to give the peasants a measure of independence without simultaneously undermining the rural nobility and gentry. It provided for a gradual and partial emancipation of the serfs, together with indemnification of their former masters. Emancipation was to be gradual, going through a number of stages over 20 years. Whereas the peasants would get their personal freedom immediately, the question of dividing land between former master and serf was extremely complicated and entailed provisions for protracted handover. The peasants were entitled to an agreed proportion of the land they had worked as serfs, but the land had to be

The Eastern Question.
As the might of the Ottoman empire slowly declined, the European powers struggled to gain control of the Balkan peninsula and with it territorial access to the Near East. It was an arena in which Russia tried throughout the 19th century to exert its influence. Turkish atrocities against the Bulgarians in the 1870s provided Russia with a pretext for declaring war on the Turks. Russia's victory enabled it to compel Turkey, under the Treaty of San Stefano, to agree to the creation of a large independent state of Bulgaria (which Russia would naturally expect to be its ally in gratitude for liberation). However, Britain, Germany and Austria-Hungary together overruled this plan at the Congress of Berlin three months later and a much smaller Bulgaria was agreed, with adjacent territory being given to Romania, Serbia, Montenegro and Greece. In the 1913 Balkan War most of the remaining European territories under Turkish domination became independent, though with a large measure of Austrian influence. By 1914 Serbia was Russia's main ally in the Balkans, and it was on Serbia's behalf that Russia entered World War I.

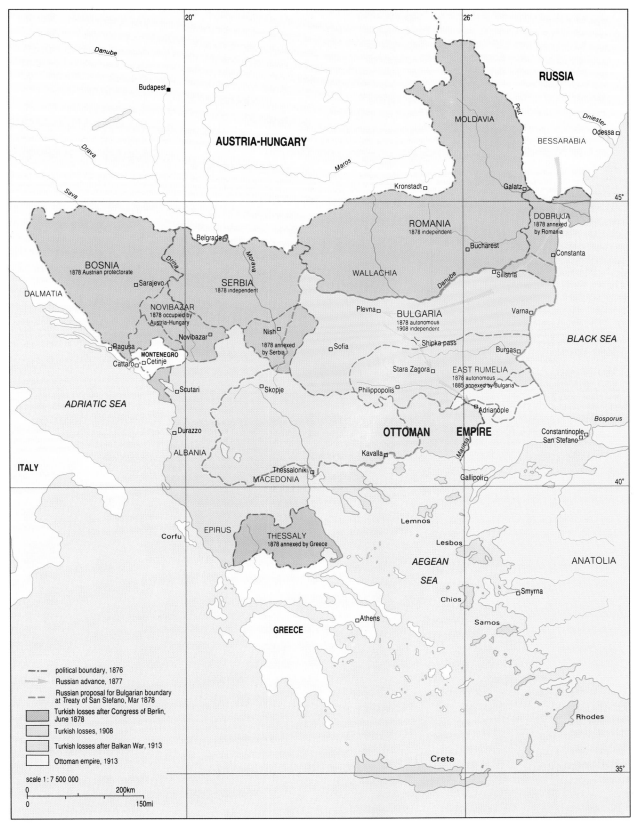

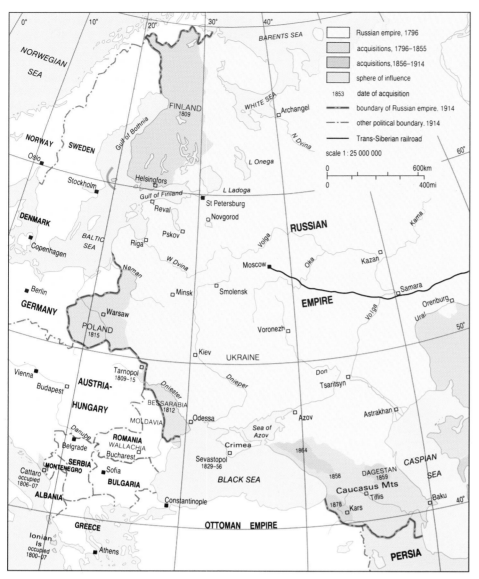

bought at prices effectively fixed by the existing owners. The freed peasants, having no capital of their own, had to accept unreasonable repayment conditions stretching over a 49-year period. Besides, the freed peasants were not permitted to own land individually: land was sold to peasant communes or villages, who took on collective responsibility for repayments and had the right to redistribute the land between their members. Thus the peasants were free in principle, but economically dependent in practice; also communal ownership deprived them of individual control over their land.

The high principle guiding the reform was thus obscured and, to a large extent, nullified by the provisions of its enactment. The peasants remained dependent and impoverished, obliged to seek transient work during the winter in order to meet the repayment debts which their agricultural work alone could not meet; this transient work took them to the cities, where they became politicized to a new degree. The emancipation of 1861 managed both to disappoint the Russian peasantry it was intended to benefit and to alienate the intelligentsia who had championed it.

The second reform (1864) instituted the first real system of local government in Russia since the Muscovite period. This rested on the *zemstvo*, an institution consisting of an assembly plus execu-

Right This Romanov family portrait shows Emperor Alexander II seated opposite his empress, Maria Alexandrovna of the ducal house of Hesse. Standing behind them is the Tsarevich and future Emperor Alexander III. His father's assassination made a powerful impression on Alexander III, whose reign was as a result deeply conservative, in contrast to his father's reformism.

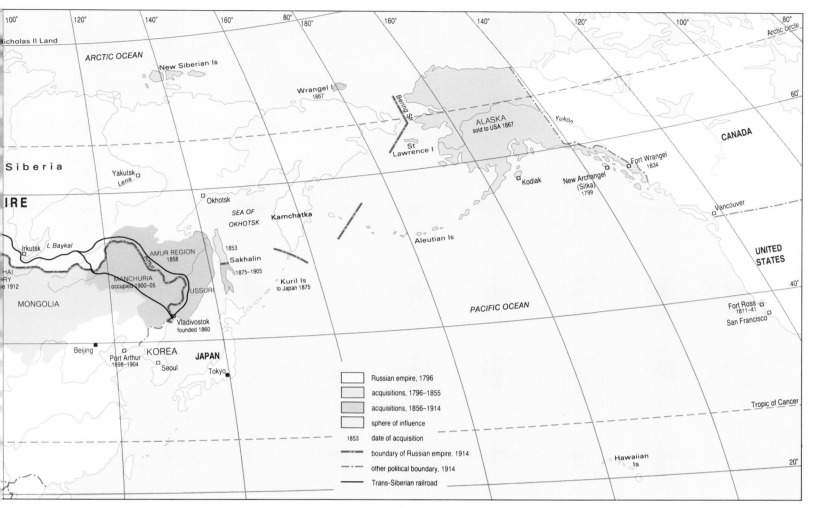

Russian empire, 1796
acquisitions, 1796–1855
acquisitions, 1856–1914
sphere of influence
1853 date of acquisition
boundary of Russian empire, 1914
other political boundary, 1914
Trans-Siberian railroad

The Russian empire at its greatest extent, mid-19th century.
By the mid-19th century the Russian empire extended round nearly half the world, occupying incidentally a considerably greater territory than its 20th century successor, the Soviet Union. Adding to the former Polish territories that it had acquired by the partitions of Poland in the 18th century, Russia was confirmed in possession of the Grand Duchy of Warsaw in 1815. The Grand Duchy of Finland was ceded by the Swedes to Russia in 1809; Bessarabia, Dagestan and some other parts of Transcaucasia and the Black Sea littoral were also gained from the Ottoman empire and Persia early in the century. A foothold on the Mediterranean Sea with protectorates over Montenegro and the Ionian Islands did not however survive the Treaty of Tilsit (1807).

Rather haphazard expansion in central Asia, generally filling power vacuums, brought Russia to the edge of Afghanistan, and in the later 19th century the khanates of Bukhara and Khiva became protectorates. In the east, Chinese weakness allowed Russia to establish the naval base of Port Arthur (lost in 1905 after the Russo-Japanese War). On the western fringes of America, Russian colonists temporarily established themselves as far south as Fort Ross in northern California. Alaska was eventually sold to the Americans for $7,200,000 in 1867.

tive board, elected at county level. Representatives were elected from the landowners, the peasant communes and the local town population, each group electing its representatives separately. The county representatives in turn constituted a provincial assembly, which elected its own board. The *zemstvos* had no executive power, but depended on the police and central government to enforce their decisions. The authority assigned to them was largely in local economic and civic administration: public works, communications, industry and commerce, agriculture, education, public health and welfare. The effectiveness of the *zemstvos* was further limited through severe underfunding and bureaucratic interference from central government. The local government reform was initially welcomed by liberal and radical public opinion, but this cooled to indifference when the new institution's limitations became apparent. Again, a reform intended to give more political participation at local government level managed to frustrate and alienate the intended beneficiaries.

The third reform, also in 1864, concerned the judiciary, and was more substantial and longer lasting than the preceding ones. The Russian legal system had for years been confused, arbitrary and corrupt, and the need to reform it had been recognized for some time. The reform passed in 1864 was based on the model of Western jurisprudence. Judicial procedures were systematized, the jury system and a formal bar instituted, judges of the lower courts became elected, defendants gained the right to representation and the duty of preliminary

examination was passed from the police to examining magistrates. A system of law courts based on competences was introduced, extending from the *zemstvo* assembly level to the Imperial Senate as the supreme court. There were, however, serious omissions in the equitable legal structure at which the reform aimed. Separate courts were created for the peasants. The reformed legal system also suffered from a certain measure of government interference and circumvention. Nevertheless, the juridical reform was on balance of much greater and more lasting impact than its predecessors. An indirect measure of the reform's success was the rising stature and influence of the legal profession.

The last reform, introduced progressively from 1863, concerned the army, whose performance in the Crimean War had clearly shown the need for reorganization and modernization. The army had in the past drawn on mass recruitment from the lower classes, especially the serfs; it also functioned as a penal service for criminals. The conditions of service were inhumane, brutal and long (although many peasants were still eager to endure them to escape from serfdom). The new reform was perhaps the most democratic of all those introduced by Alexander II. It provided for universal conscription with a much shorter term of service than before; draft priority classification geared to family obligations; shortened terms of service for those with elementary or higher education; a pervasive humanization of discipline; basic education for illiterate conscripts; and the elimination of class differences as a criterion for

Tolstoy the Revolutionary

No Russian of the 19th century became so colossally famous and revered, both outside his country and within, as Lev Nikolaevich Tolstoy. By the end of his long life (1828–1910) he was the "uncrowned tsar" of Yasnaya Polyana (his estate, south of Moscow), much as the elderly Voltaire had become "uncrowned king" of Paris on his final visit in 1778; in each case they were names that abroad were taken as emblematic of their country's culture, while each was a thorn in the flesh of a nervous government and established church at the threshold of revolution.

Tolstoy was one of the great subversives of the 19th century, rating in this respect with Darwin, Marx or Freud, yet unlike them (though like Nietzsche and his fellow countryman Dostoyevsky) in rejecting the pretensions of modern scientific progress. If he was a revolutionary, he was a strange one: loathing violence, socialism, even liberalism and bourgeois values with the contempt of the aristocrat he never ceased to be, yet denouncing the state, the established church and the whole artificial fabric of modern society in terms whose virulence few left-wing revolutionaries could match. His rhetoric was denunciatory rather than constructive, often sounding like anarchism; his vision of a just society patriarchal and populist; his terms of argument moral, his yardstick of evaluation the clear vision and simple values of a natural and uncorrupted life. Eventually he came to propagate what was in effect his own religion: a stripped-down Christianity, shorn of obscurantism, extracting from the Gospels a few essential precepts (notably "Judge not, that ye be not judged"; "Render to no man evil for evil"). There are "Tolstoyans" to this day.

Somewhat unusually, Tolstoy moved towards ever more extreme and in effect revolutionary views with advancing age. As a young man he had led the conventional and rather dissolute life of a young aristocrat and officer: brilliant, well traveled and well read, but never at home in intellectual, freethinking or artistic circles. Service in the Crimea and Caucasus not only roused his literary talent, but stirred moral repugnance towards war and curiosity about the fundamental values of human character. There followed marriage, the births of many children and settled life in the country: this was the period of *War and Peace* (1860s) and *Anna Karenina* (1870s), the vast novels on which his reputation was built, both largely concerned with family themes yet including much material that might seem incompatible with imaginative literature (a fully fledged theory of history, devaluing the pretensions of "great men," in the former; theorizing on rural topics in the latter). These pillars of the 19th-century European novel are themselves in literary terms subversive: pushing the form beyond its bounds, launching a deep and ultimately anti-novelistic investigation of causality.

Right Powerful and active still in his sixties, Tolstoy took his populism to an extreme conclusion, attempting to live by peasant values and emulate peasant labor. Clearly Ilya Repin, in this portrait of Tolstoy plowing in 1891 – the year he renounced his literary royalties – painted him as he wished to be seen. But Tolstoy's rural interests were no mere publicistic fad of his old age: he had plunged himself deeply in rural concerns, particularly educational efforts, from the 1850s.

Below Less familiar than the flowingly bearded patriarch is the dapper young man-of-the-world and army officer in his mid-twenties, immediately before the harrowing siege of Sevastopol.

Left By his last full year of life, when Repin painted a more sedentary Tolstoy, serenity seemed more elusive to the 80-year-old writer than ever. Never easily able to accommodate the idea of death into his view of the universe, he found its cheerless approach rendered yet more discomfiting by ineradicable family tensions and bitterness. His penetrating insight into life's problems, public and private, brought their solutions no nearer, serving to emphasize the unanswerability of questions he could not help raising. In the autumn of 1910 he left home secretively, intending to find monastic peace, but fell ill and died after 10 days in the stationmaster's house at Astapovo, on which the world's eyes were fixed.

Right Tolstoy and helpers organize famine relief in a village in Ryazan province in 1891. A consistent believer in personally putting his ideas into practice, Tolstoy immersed himself in direct charitable action on many occasions, from his organizing the village school at Yasnaya Polyana (1859) onwards.

advancement. The unexpected result was to make the Russian army into the most democratic institution in Russia.

The reforms of the 1860s were conceived on a grand scale, introduced in somewhat less promising form and implemented unevenly and haltingly. They served to raise hopes of change which were not fully satisfied. Flawed as they were, Alexander's reforms demonstrated that a vision of fundamental political and social change could be put into action.

Populism and the revolutionary movement

The emancipation of the serfs drastically altered the political thinking and sentiment of the Russian intelligentsia. The cause of the serf had in the 1840s and 1850s been championed by the Slavophiles, who had been a legitimist force for major social reform. The limitations of Alexander's legislation ensured that the claim to represent the peasantry, the preponderant mass of Russia's population, passed into the hands of the radical intelligentsia, which was intent on revolutionary change.

The new radicalism which emerged in Russia during the 1860s and 1870s was catalyzed by two forces from the West. One was the popularity of the major scientific achievements of the 1840s, which suggested that man and society could be understood and changed through application of scientific method. The other was the ideas of French utopian socialism, together with those of such individual Russian publicists as Pyotr Lavrov and Nikolai Mikhaylovsky. The main strand of new radicalism was *narodnichestvo*, a form of socialist revolutionary populism. This was based on the belief that a mass socialist revolution was needed to overthrow the existing order; that Russia's unique social structure would ensure an immediate introduction of socialism, bypassing capitalism; that the communal institutions common to Russia's peasantry were essentially socialist; and that peasants were therefore the natural revolutionary force ready to be activated. Beyond this, the *narodniki* ("populists") disagreed about what methods were appropriate for setting the revolution in motion. Some favored terrorist acts (Nechayev and Tkachov), others were for letting the revolution start organically (Lavrov), but the majority eventually decided on activating the peasants personally.

The attempt at personal contact came with the "To the People" movement of 1873–74. Large numbers of young *narodniki*, who were mainly urban students of comfortable background, donned peasant clothing and dispersed into the countryside in order to preach the revolution to the peasants, presuming the latter to be ready for their message. The result was total failure: the *narodniki* were ignorant of the realities of village life and of peasant mentality and motivation; the peasants in turn were baffled by and suspicious of young people of an entirely different class speaking in unfamiliar terms. The movement faltered, with many *narodniki* arrested and put on trial, and the peasantry left unmoved. A new "To the People" movement was launched in the late 1870s, but again without success.

The failure of populism in the 1870s had a twofold effect. Some of the participants retained a faith in peasantry as a revolutionary force: they would learn by their mistakes and become the progenitors of the Socialist Revolutionary Party. Others concluded that launching a revolution required more than just raising popular consciousness among the masses; these people turned partly to terrorism, and partly to the rationalized revolutionary politics of which Lenin was the prime practitioner.

The decline of populism was paralleled by the rise of terrorism. The underlying perception of revolutionary dynamics, however, remained the same; once the right method was found to stimulate mass rebellion, the established order would inevitably collapse. The method resorted to was public terror, and above all assassination.

The campaign of terror lasted during the late 1870s and into the early 1880s. It was organized by a small secret society called Land and Freedom (*Zemlya i Volya*), which was based in St Petersburg and consisted mostly of radical students from the privileged classes. The membership was tiny but fanatical, and could rely on sympathy and financial help from many in the elite which raised them. From 1878 onward Land and Freedom succeeded in assassinating numerous senior police and government officials throughout Russia. Their campaign culminated with the assassination of Alexander II in 1881, but the consequences spelled the end of terrorism. Land and Freedom was rooted out in a security clampdown, but, more significantly, its method was discredited: even the tsar's assassination did not lead to any uprising, the government remained stable and the imperial succession worked smoothly. The radicals began searching for other revolutionary methods.

The search took roughly two decades. The 1880s saw Marxism emerge as a new revolutionary theory in Russia. The founding father was Georgiy Plekhanov, an ex-populist who studied German Marxism in Switzerland and adapted its theory to Russian conditions. His principles were that Russia, like all countries, had to pass through a period of capitalist development before moving on to socialism; that the traditional peasant institutions had no socialist potential; that the urban proletariat was the social force for revolution in Russia; and that a disciplined and organized working-class party was needed to galvanize the proletariat into action. Plekhanov established the first Russian social democratic organization in 1883, and a network of affiliated groups spread through Russia soon afterwards. One of the young recruits joining the Marxists in the late 1880s was Vladimir Ulyanov, better known as Lenin.

Lenin was born into a civil servant's family in the Volga region in 1870. He became politicized in 1887, when his elder brother was executed for complicity in a plot to assassinate Tsar Alexander III. After some flirtation with *narodnichestvo*, he developed an interest in Marxism and became a follower of Plekhanov. In 1895 Lenin was put in charge of the first Marxist operational cell in St Petersburg: its objective was to propagandize the capital's workers, but the cell was discovered and Lenin arrested. He was sentenced to three years'

The assassination of Alexander in 1881 in St Petersburg stimulated a conservative revival in Russia. His funeral was made into a massive public occasion reaffirming the imperial principle and dynastic mystique. An ornate neo-medieval cathedral, the so-called "Church on the Blood," was built on the spot of the assassination. The contemporary photograph shows the funeral procession with imperial catafalque crossing the Neva River, with the Academy of Arts in the background. The far quayside is thronged with crowds, probably marking the previous route of the cortege.

Siberian exile (1896–99). The conditions of exile were very lenient, and Lenin spent the time writing his major political tracts and developing his own variant of Marxist theory. Immediately upon release, he was allowed to travel to Europe. The Russian social democrat emigration there was in discord, Plekhanov's position had weakened and Lenin succeeded in rising to a position of joint leadership with his former mentor. Significant differences were emerging between the two men about the nature and pace of revolutionary strategy. These differences led to a clash at the second convention of the Russian Social Democratic Party in 1903, with Plekhanov's camp being labeled the Mensheviks and Lenin's the Bolsheviks (from the words *menshe*, "less" and *bolshe*, "more").

While the Russian Marxist movement was developing abroad, other movements for political change were becoming active in Russia. Among the revolutionaries, remnants of the old *narodniki* metamorphosed into the new Socialist Revolutionary Party in 1900, and revived political terror operations in 1901. More importantly, it developed throughout rural Russia an extensive organization dedicated to propagandizing the idea of a socialist revolution among the peasantry. The Socialist Revolutionaries made an effort to convey their message in terms suited to the peasant, tailored it to the peasant's grievances and became the dominant revolutionary party in rural Russia.

The first years of the 20th century also saw the liberal opposition to the government organize into a political force. The prime movers were liberal politicians who dominated the *zemstvo* local government system, the authority and development of which were severely cut back in the early 1900s. These were joined by liberal landowners in the countryside and liberal academics in the cities, who had hoped that the *zemstvos* would lead to a gradual spread of parliamentary government in Russia. In 1903 the liberals formed a Union of Liberation, which formulated a program demanding full civil liberties; equality of all citizens before the law; democratization and expansion of the *zemstvos*; withdrawal of recently introduced restrictive legislation; full political amnesty; and the creation of a truly representative legislative assembly. Their aim was to convert Russia into a constitutional monarchy with a social order resting on the principles of a liberal democracy.

The government reacted to the revolutionaries with further repressive measures, and to the liberals with indifference. The latter response was largely due to the personality of Nicholas II, who ascended the throne in 1894; he saw little difference between the two challenges and particularly disliked representative government of any kind. Consequently, the revolutionaries were strengthened in pursuing the cause of violent revolution, while the liberals became increasingly hostile to the established order.

The arts in the later 19th century

The classic age of the Russian novel was short, in fact almost coincident with the reign of Alexander II. Since the literary Golden Age of the 1820s and 1830s, the reading public had become larger and better educated: in addition to the gentry, the *intelligentsiya* (a quasi-Latin word coined simply to indicate educated people) also included significant numbers of *raznochintsy*—those who were neither of gentry origin nor peasants, in other words a nascent middle class. Politics had become more polarized, with the radical thinkers impatient of the liberal compromises of their predecessors. The great wave of populism that powered the "To the People" movement in the 1870s variously affected many major figures in the arts, from Tolstoy to Musorgsky. The younger generation characteristically had, or affected, a no-nonsense attitude that dispensed with all metaphysical baggage, preconceived ideas and even ordinary politeness in a search for worthwhile secular and scientifically based values. The classic portrayal of this mentality is Ivan Turgenev's *Fathers and Children* (1862), which popularized the word "nihilist."

There were still excellent poets writing, including the veteran Fyodor Tyutchev (1803–73); the "civic poet" N. Nekrasov (1821–77); a rare proponent of "art for art's sake," Afanasy Fet (1820–92); and the interestingly versatile Aleksey Tolstoy (1817–75). But they formed no school and projected no sense of common purpose. The first truly professional Russian playwright, Alexander Ostrovsky (1823–86), wrote copiously throughout the period. Several fine storywriters—Vsevolod Garshin (1855–88), the satirist Mikhail Saltykov-Shchedrin (1826–89), and best of all Nikolai Leskov (1831–95)—also became known.

The novel emerged as the great Russian art form with peculiar suddenness at this time. Its senior practitioners were Ivan Goncharov (1812–91) and Ivan Turgenev (1818–83). The former, though he wrote three novels, is remembered for one masterpiece, *Oblomov* (1859). One of the great "plotless" works of European fiction, it explores the inner landscape of a hero whose retreat into apparent idleness and seediness assumes the character of a metaphysical crusade against the pain of activity. Was there anything specifically "Russian" in such a character? Certainly contemporaries thought so, and took up the term "Oblomovism." Turgenev came gradually to the novel, through early poetry and the *Sportsman's Sketches* (1845–52), a series of brief scenes from rural life that at their publication were seen to carry a strong message against serfdom. His relatively short, delicately crafted novels of human relationships, notoriously featuring strong-willed heroines and ineffectual men, were the first works of Russian literature widely read abroad (a seminal influence, for example, on Henry James).

Fyodor Dostoyevsky (1821–81) was a rather cantankerous and unstable personality, a compulsive gambler, the ideologist of a right-wing Slavophile tendency. He used certain personal experiences—his near-execution and subsequent exile in the Petrashevsky affair, his epilepsy, his father's violent death, a turbulent love affair—to great effect in his fiction, most extraordinarily in writing *The Gambler* (1867). To meet a publisher's deadline (in what was his own most colossal gamble with his present and future finances) he dictated the work in a month, then married his stenographer. He is chiefly remembered for his "big four" novels: *Crime and Punishment* (1866; the best known and most straightforward), *The Idiot* (1868–69), *The Devils* (1871; sometimes called *The Possessed*, a

EQO OXO (D) UK 13082 ATLAS OF RUSSIA (11/5/89)

fierce political satire) and *The Brothers Karamazov* (1880; the last, longest and richest). Religious, psychological and social threads are woven into an elaborate tapestry of ideas, where no one ideology has the last word—the "polyphony" of Dostoyevsky's novels, much explored by recent scholarship. To his great novels there is a briefer curtain raiser in the form of *Notes from Underground* (1864). Unlike Tolstoy, Dostoyevsky only slowly gained the reading public's affection: his time really came in the Symbolist period at the turn of the century, and soon afterwards he was being extravagantly hailed as a prophet throughout Europe.

During the first half of the 19th century the Academy had been exercising an ever more deadening effect on creativity in the visual arts. In 1863 a group of 14 students walked out of it in protest at the setting of "The Feast of the Gods in Valhalla" as the annual prize subject in history painting. The occasion may have been relatively trivial: the underlying dissatisfactions were profound, and led to the founding of the peripatetic exhibition society known as the Wanderers (*Peredvizhniki*). They wished to engage with the actualities, past and present, of their own culture, and to communicate with a wide, not merely metropolitan and moneyed public. They were fortunate in the support of the leading critic and aesthetic ideologist V. Stasov (1824–1900) and of a Moscow merchant collector, P.Tretyakov (1832–98), who was to found the greatest gallery of Russian art around the Wanderers' canvases. Their leader was Ivan Kramskoy (1837–87), their best-known (and longest-lived) representative was Ilya Repin (1844–1930). The outstanding artist and indeed harbinger of future developments among them was Vasiliy Surikov (1848–1916).

In music this period saw a burst of innovative creation. It is associated primarily with a group of friends known as "the Five," alternatively *Moguchaya kuchka*, "the Mighty Handful." In order of age they were Alexander Borodin (1834–87), César Cui (1835–1918; of French extraction), Mily Balakirev (1837–1910), Modest Musorgsky (1839–1881) and Nikolai Rimsky-Korsakov (1844–1908). Only Balakirev among them was a conventionally trained composer, and at first dominated the group. Borodin was a chemist, Cui a military engineer, Musorgsky a civil servant and Rimsky-Korsakov a naval officer, who became a Conservatory professor and simultaneously trained himself in the musical disciplines he had lacked. He composed far more than his friends, and after Borodin's and Musorgsky's untimely deaths he undertook to order and orchestrate their major uncompleted scores (not always to their advantage).

The "non-professionalism" of the Five contributed to their originality, as they were unconstrained by preconceptions of musical form and decorum. They followed Berlioz (much loved in Russia) in a rather belated Romanticism that was free-ranging, orchestrally colorful and strongly programmatic in impulse. From Glinka they inherited and developed a commitment to Russian folk music, sometimes spiced with a dash of orientalism. Alexander Dargomyzhsky (1813–69), a living link with the age of Glinka, through his friendship with Musorgsky inspired a rare intensity of seriousness in the best music of the Five. They and their suc-

cessors generally avoided abstract instrumental music and classical forms (Borodin's two string quartets are a splendid exception), cultivating instead song, programmatic tone poems and piano pieces, but above all opera. They chose their librettos with care, sometimes from Russia's history (Musorgsky's *Boris Godunov* and *Khovanshchina*, Borodin's *Prince Igor*), sometimes from its classic 19th-century literature; Pushkin is thus probably better known operatically than poetically outside Russia. Not only the Five, of course, are responsible for this: credit must particularly go to their great contemporary Pyotr Ilyich Tchaikovsky (1840–96), whose greatest operas derived from Pushkin's *Yevgeny Onegin* and *The Queen of Spades*. By some of his nationalist-minded contemporaries, Tchaikovsky was considered irredeemably Western and even frivolous: he was properly trained, wrote chamber music, concertos and symphonies, idolized Mozart and was appreciated by European audiences. Yet he was just as capable of employing folk inflections, intricate rhythms and instrumental color as his contemporaries.

Social and economic changes in the later 19th century

Russia's economic fabric altered profoundly between the 1860s and the beginning of the next century, with cities and factories as the centers of change. The cities of Russia nearly doubled in population over this period, and most of the industrial growth of the time occurred there. The pace of industrialization and urbanization mounted gradually, accelerating in the last quarter of the 19th century. This growth was initially hampered by the lack of a skilled working class, the lack of industrial and managerial expertise and the absence of a capital base and capital development skills. These resources were developed quite quickly, and with them an urban proletariat and an urban commercial class, destined to play differing roles in Russia's history.

The proletariat was rooted in the peasantry. The incomplete emancipation of 1861 coincided with the first wave of industrial modernization following the Crimean War, and many peasants were drawn to the cities in search of the new work. They initially came on fixed-term employment, returning to their villages and not integrating into city life. This soon changed, and the ex-peasant became a novice worker, resident in the city but still a peasant by habit and temperament. The working conditions were very hard, and the law stringently forbad trade union organizing of any kind. The protests which occurred were largely apolitical and concerned specifically with working conditions. By the 1880s the government introduced labor reforms, which eased working conditions somewhat. Further limited reforms followed in the 1890s, the first trade unions were legitimized in 1902 and accident compensation introduced in 1903. The condition of the proletariat improved gradually, though not dramatically, and the working class remained largely outside the interest of the revolutionary movement, except for the nascent Social Democrats.

The urban commercial class derived largely from the earlier merchants, who were highly accomplished traders with business methods and habits

Left The Rooks have Returned (1871), by A.K. Savrasov. Before the Wanderers, landscape had not been much developed in Russian art; Savrasov (1830–97) was one of the earliest exponents. The return from migration of rooks and starlings traditionally heralds spring in the Russian villages.

Below A group of porters and peasants relax over a game of cards in the outer aisle of a covered market in a provincial Russian town. The porters wear leather shoes, while the peasants are in bast slippers wih leggings.

more Levantine than European. Their talents, entrepreneurial but unsystematic, were the starting point of Russia's modern industrialization in the 1860s. By 1880 the new class had greatly expanded Russia's developmental base. Over 20 years, discount bills increased four-fold, short-term secured loans grew a staggering 25 times over and long-term loans rose by a third. At the same time, the total number of enterprises and workers employed rose by about a third. Productivity and profitability were, however, lower than in the West. Nevertheless, this start created a climate of confidence for foreign investment, and a succession of major Western companies diversified into Russian industry during the 1880s and 1890s.

The urban commercial class became involved in politics only in relation to their business interests. This involvement took the form of consulting and lobbying ministers responsible for the economy, particularly Ivan Vyshnegradsky (minister 1887–92) and Sergey Witte (1892–1903), who introduced extensive fiscal and administrative reforms aimed at stimulating further industrial and business development. The businessmen did not participate in political movements, nor were they very active in party politics when those emerged. Culture was a different matter. Many of the urban commercial class were sons of illiterate merchants, and therefore put a very high premium on education and the arts. Some became major patrons of the arts and theater, as well as collectors of Russian and European art: many of the major Soviet collections today, including the Tretyakov Gallery, were originally private collections of such men.

Symbolism and Russian arts

In the 1880s it became apparent that the artistic impetus that had led to such splendid results in the post-Crimean War period was slowing down. Dostoyevsky and Musorgsky died in the same year as Alexander II; Turgenev and Borodin soon followed; Tolstoy underwent an inner crisis at the end of the 1870s, producing thereafter only one more novel (*Resurrection*). Intellectual life under the tough regime of Alexander III (1881–94) gave little scope for intermediate positions between conservatives and revolutionaries. The 1890s brought a change of atmosphere, with a sense among the new intellectual generation that it was time for Russia to look to what was going on in the rest of Europe. The young poet Valeriy Bryusov (1873–1924) began publishing in 1894 a series of volumes called *Russian Symbolists*, containing translations from (and poems in the spirit of) the French Symbolist movement that had crystallized in the 1880s. Symbolism had enormous impact across the spectrum of the arts and intellectual life in Russia, leading not just to new, and divergent, artistic paths, but to a reassessment of Russian culture overall. Literary Symbolism in Russia is usually considered to have produced two generations. The younger Symbolists provided the most brilliant talents: Andrey Bely (1880–1934), whose fragmented, allusive and alarming novel *Petersburg* (1913) is the climax to nearly a century of evoca-

tion of that ambiguous city's spectral qualities; and Alexander Blok (1880–1921), who at 20 burst upon the literary world with his mystical *Verses about the Beautiful Lady*. Blok died prematurely, worn out and dispirited, but not before providing revolutionary Russia with its first two great poems, *The Scythians* and *The Twelve* (1918).

Musical life, however, was less inspired than in the 1860s and 1870s. Rimsky-Korsakov continued to develop, while remaining a master of colorful orchestration and spiky melody: his last opera, *The Golden Cockerel*, banned by the censor as political satire, is perhaps the best. The most notable new composer of the period was Alexander Scriabin (1872–1915). A post-Symbolist generation only slightly younger (Stravinsky, Prokofiev) would again put Russians among the foremost European composers, just before World War I. The strong development of Russian ballet gave great compositional opportunities (already exploited by Tchaikovsky), and performing standards were high; Russia produced one of the world's greatest singers, Fyodor Shalyapin (or "Chaliapine," 1873–1938).

The remarkable reinvigoration of the visual arts was signaled by the establishment in 1898 of *World of Art (Mir Iskusstva)*, the name both of a group of painters, led by Alexander Benua (or "Benois", 1870–1960), and of a luxuriously produced journal. The latter was the brainchild of Sergey Diaghi-

Right V. Kandinsky, *Sketch for Composition IV, Battle* (1910). Kandinsky (1866–1944) came late to art, after qualifying in law and taking part in ethnographic expeditions. A man of means, he settled in Munich where he studied and developed his own post-Impressionist, Symbolist style. His links with Russia remained strong; he returned in World War I and remained after the Revolution until it was clear that his pedagogical ideas were unacceptable.

After his *Blue Rider* almanac and his manifesto *On the Spiritual in Art* his figurative painting moved rather suddenly into abstraction; others were going in the same direction, but Kandinsky was trailblazer. Figurative elements from his intense, emotional, folkloristic world dissolve into writhing shapes, yet vestiges of them can still be detected here; lances, riders, a rainbow bridge, a city.

Left A photograph, taken in 1914, of Ilya Repin painting the celebrated singer Fyodor Shalyapin (1873–1938).

Below right Sergey Prokofiev (left), Dmitriy Shostakovich and Aram Khachaturyan together in a photograph of 1945. The three internationally known Soviet composers (Khachaturyan was Armenian), tuneful, popular and prolific, were far from immune from criticism. Prokofiev (1891–1953), known before the Revolution, had emigrated but returned when Stalin appeared to have reestablished order and prosperity in the 1930s. Shostakovich, 15 years younger, enjoyed a precocious triumph in the 1920s, but ran into Stalin's personal displeasure in the late 1930s with the 4th Symphony and *Lady Macbeth of Mtsensk* (an opera based on Leskov's grim tale). His 5th and 7th Symphonies, however, won public adulation. A general assault on "formalism" (roughly, any modernist techniques) in the music, as in literature, followed in the late 1940s.

lev (1872–1929), who before devoting himself to ballet was a remarkable artistic impresario, introducing recent Western art to Russia, Russian art to the West and also their own hidden artistic past to the Russians. Russian artistic Symbolism also had its own homebred precursor in Mikhail Vrubel (1856–1910). The *World of Art* journal closed in 1904: by that time a wealth of diverse talent of generally Symbolist orientation had emerged not only in the capital, but also in Moscow and various provincial centers. Two major painters, scarcely known outside Russia, were Viktor Borisov-Musatov (1870–1905), from Saratov, and P. Kuznetsov (1878–1968). Non-Russian subjects of the tsar began to make an equal contribution to modern art.

One of the colossi of modern world art emerged out of the artistic milieu of Russian Symbolism: Vasiliy Kandinsky (1866–1944). Kandinsky never forgot his Russian roots, and his progress to his epoch-making experiments in abstraction around 1910 came logically out of his preceding development. His essay *On the Spiritual in Art* (1912), one of the most influential books on art by an artist ever written, was first conceived as a lecture in Russia. Another notable artist who was a product of the ethos of Russian Symbolism, but who made his name in Paris, was Marc Chagall (1887–1985), whose origins, never forgotten, were in the Hasidic Jewish small-town life of Belorussia.

Peasant Life before the Revolution

Russia's population was always overwhelmingly rural: in 1914, 85 percent of the total was still in the countryside, though many northern peasants sought seasonal work in the cities. Around half the peasants (proportionately more in the central regions) were serfs, emancipated only in 1861. The terms of emancipation were restrictive: the peasants gained neither full ownership of land nor any real economic assistance. Agricultural production was difficult and inadequate to sustain the rural populace. Handicrafts were an important secondary industry, and temporary work in cities outside the farming seasons was necessary to make a living. Extensive self-government was granted to the peasantry, but this was kept separate from higher regional and central governments. Economic and political frustration led to widespread peasant destructiveness during the Revolution of 1905. Between 1906 and 1912, a series of fundamental reforms dramatically improved the peasants' condition. Agricultural productivity rose sharply, and many peasants rose from a state of marginal economic survival to rudimentary well-being.

Above Wood was a universal material for the Russian peasant. Three generations of the same family are seen carving wooden spoons for sale. Trunk sections like the one before the elder are worked into the finished spoons seen in the basket at the right. The family home is a large log cabin, made entirely of wood. The time is probably late autumn, after harvest, when peasants turned to handicrafts as a source of additional income.

Left Traditions of Christian charity were strong in pre-revolutionary Russia, and especially respected in rural areas. The peasants here have positioned themselves next to the entrance of a public building. The old man is seated, preserving a measure of dignity, with a single hand extended in traditional pose of supplication. The boy is a learner, perhaps the elder's guide. The woman giving alms is a member of the local gentry or urban middle class. Churchyards were the most common settings for almsgiving.

Right Many Russians of peasant background became first-generation industrial workers in factories such as this, here engaged in wartime production of shrapnel shells. Their personal and emotional ties to the village remained strong, and impressions and attitudes assimilated in the cities thus passed on to the rural world. Revolutionary ideas and moods were spread in this way as much as through the efforts of propagandists and agitators operating in the countryside.

Left This late 19th-century scene illustrates both the roots of peasant piety and the difficulties of land usage facing many Russian peasants. The chapel, placed over the spring that gives rise to the Volga, Russia's greatest river, probably echoes an ancient pagan cult at the site. Worship of water spirits was strong among early East Slavs, with specific cults associated with rivers, lakes, whirlpools and springs. These cults survived as similar Christian ones, dedicated to minor saints. Peasant culture was generally permeated with rituals, superstitions and traditions derived from pre-christian Slavic paganism. The landscape here is typical of much of central and northern Russia: forested and marshy, it provides proportionately little land that is easy to cultivate and harvest. Even land suited to cultivation gives low yields and is vulnerable to climatic fluctuation.

Below Peasant nutrition and hygiene were often poor, leading to much disease and frequent epidemics in bad years. The greatest harvest failure of the 19th century occurred in 1891, causing a massive famine that year and in 1892. The photograph shows the inside of an impoverished peasant house, with two victims of typhus (a disease often transmitted by body lice) lying on sleeping bunks. Such straw-covered bunks were normal sleeping places for adults and children; elders slept on similar bunks adjoining the single hearth stove in a house. The setting is near Nizhniy Novgorod where the famine was particularly severe.

139

1905

Below Terrorism continued through 1905, adopted particularly by the Socialist Revolutionary party. Their "Battle Organization" assassination unit, operational since 1902, succeeded in early 1905 in killing Grand Duke Sergey, the tsar's second cousin and brother-in-law, who was also commanding officer of the Moscow military region.

The turbulent events of 1905 set the political stage for the revolutions of 1917 and for Russia's subsequent 20th-century history. A year of extensive but disjointed civic disruption, 1905 ended with the introduction of a constitutional monarchy and an unsuccessful attempt at revolution in Moscow. Liberal and revolutionary movements had recently formed into political parties, with hostility between liberals and revolutionaries immediately apparent. Economic difficulties and the failures of the Russo-Japanese War combined with disruptive agitation by the revolutionaries to create great social volatility by late 1904. In January 1905 the bloody suppression of a loyalist protest demonstration in St Petersburg, known as "Bloody Sunday," ignited widespread protests.

The radical disruption was directed by Marxist parties, especially the Mensheviks and the Socialist Revolutionaries. The progressive opposition was directed by liberal parties, especially the Constitutional Democrats, whose objective was a constitutional monarchy with representative parliamentary government. The imperial administration eventually capitulated to the liberal demand, and issued the October Manifesto, which promulgated parliamentary government in the form of an elected national assembly (Duma). Popular support for the revolutionaries declined. Their call for national revolution resulted only in an armed uprising in Moscow in December, which lasted a week before being suppressed. The stage was set for the parliamentary experiment in Russia, with the revolutionary parties marginalized but waiting for other opportunities to seize power.

Left Many of the uprisings of 1905 saw rebels building barricades in their battles with the police and military detachments. The remains of a recently dismantled barricade are strewn in the foreground: it had been built of wagons and pushcarts, like those seen behind.

Right In 1905, Trotsky was a leader of the Menshevik wing of the Social Democratic party, as opposed to the Bolshevik one under Lenin, and he organized the first revolutionary Soviet council in St Petersburg. By 1917 he had joined the Bolsheviks, and his refined version of the Soviet enabled them to coordinate and manipulate the radical forces of revolution.

Far right Pyotr Stolypin, chief minister under the first Dumas, introduced far-reaching reforms aimed at stimulating Russian industry and improving the position of the peasantry. His measures to curb revolutionary terrorism made him a target for the extremists. After many failed attempts, like the one shown, he was assassinated in 1911.

Below left Nikolai Bukharin emerged as a Bolshevik activist during 1905. By the early 1920s he became a leading theoretician of the early Communist state and editor of the newspaper *Pravda*. Executed for alleged ideological treachery after a 1938 show trial, he was granted posthumous rehabilitation by President Gorbachev on 4 February 1988.

Below The insurrections of 1905 extended to the armed forces, and included the celebrated seizure of the *Potemkin* by its crew. The *Potemkin* was an old reserve battleship of the Black Sea fleet; under Menshevik leadership, its crew seized control of the ship and sailed it to Romania, where they surrendered it to the local authorities. The *Potemkin* became the object of a revolutionary cult as a result of Eisenstein's famous movie (1925). This work, intended to create a heroic myth, substantially distorts the facts.

REVOLUTION AND THE BUILDING OF THE COMMUNIST STATE

The Russo-Japanese War and Revolution of 1905

The underlying tensions in Russian society remained in check until 1904–05, when the combination of a foreign war and social crises at home set off Russia's first revolution. The Russo-Japanese War (1904–05) was a thorough failure for the Russians. Its causes lay in Russia's and Japan's conflicting aspirations to establish control over Manchuria and Korea after the collapse of Chinese authority following the Boxer Rebellion (1900–01). Hostilities began when Japan attacked Port Arthur, the new Russian naval base on the Liaodong Peninsula, in north China, without declaration of war. The war which followed was from the start unpopular in Russia, largely because Russia's strategic interests in the Far East did not fire the popular imagination.

The land campaign in Manchuria resulted in a string of Russian defeats, but after Mukden (February 1905) the Russian war machine succeeded in stopping further Japanese advances. The sea campaign, in contrast, was disastrous. The Russian fleet, blockaded at Port Arthur, tried to break out and was largely destroyed by the Japanese navy. The tsar ordered a quixotic and foolhardy expedition to relieve Port Arthur. This involved sending Russia's Baltic Sea fleet to Korea, via the Atlantic and Indian Oceans and the South China Sea. The fleet set sail in October 1904, reaching its destination in May the following year. Meanwhile, Port Arthur capitulated in December 1904, so when the Baltic fleet arrived, it had no refuge when confronted by the Japanese navy. The ensuing sea battle in the Straits of Tsushima ended with the entire Russian fleet sunk. The war ended in September 1905 with the Treaty of Portsmouth, where the tsar's chief negotiator, the redoubtable Count Sergey Witte, succeeded in extracting reasonable conditions. However, acute domestic disappointment with the war had before then helped set off the 1905 Revolution.

The capitulation of Port Arthur sent shock waves throughout Russia and coincided with a wave of industrial strikes in St Petersburg. These strikes were initially concerned with working conditions and related to social, rather than political, issues. In January 1905 a huge loyalist demonstration concerning the conditions of the proletariat massed at the Winter Palace with the intent of presenting a petition to the tsar. The troops cordoning the palace fired into the crowd, killing 130 and wounding many more, on a day that became known as "Bloody Sunday." The security disaster led to a national calamity.

A wave of revulsion swept all levels of Russian society, inflaming the simmering consternation over governmental slowness with reforms and the failures of the war. Political opposition of varying shades intensified its activity and found much greater public receptivity to its message. The

government's credibility declined further with the news of the Tsushima disaster. Discontent peaked in October 1905 with Russia's first general strike. The strikers' original demand was for a constituent assembly, the repeal of repressive emergency legislation, civil liberties and reduced working hours. However, the control of the strike soon passed to radicals, and the demands were changed to revolutionary ones. In St Petersburg leadership was taken by a newly created Soviet of Workers' Deputies, an extremist council claiming to be representative of the proletariat; it was dominated by the Mensheviks under Leon Trotsky.

In October, despite the tsar's stubborn opposition, the imperial government acceded to the main demand of the majority of the opposition by a proclamation transforming the autocracy into a constitutional monarchy. The work of the eminent statesman Sergey Witte, the October Manifesto provided for basic civil liberties (including those of the person, freedom of thought, assembly and organization), democratic franchise and legislative power vested in a new national assembly. The

Left An outstanding Russian statesman at the turn of the century, Count Sergey Witte (1849–1915) held different ministerial appointments and left his mark in many areas. His achievements ranged from economic reforms and the creation of the Duma at home, to successful negotiation of the Treaty of Portsmouth which concluded the Russo-Japanese War on reasonable terms for Russia.

Below Boris Kustodiev's painting, *The Bolshevik, 1905*, conveys the romantic image of the Bolshevik revolutionaries adopted by many Russian intellectuals and artists. Kustodiev is noted for his exotic treatment of provincial Russian scenes and peasant and merchant life, suffused with an underlying sense of life force and the dynamism of national character. The allegorical giant in the painting represents Bolshevism as a typical worker, striding with red banner and determined expression over a selectively assembled townscape of Moscow, whose streets are shown filled with swirling revolutionary masses.

assembly, to be called the Duma, was to be nationally elected on the basis of party political affiliation which extended to all parties, including the most radical revolutionary ones. This innovation gave Russia a representative democracy on a par with the best constitutional monarchies of contemporary Western Europe. The first elections were scheduled for spring 1906.

The majority of Russia's population responded with great excitement to the October Manifesto and to the prospect of the Duma. The general strike lost momentum and support, both because it had caused mass unemployment and hardship and because the Duma promised tangible change of a kind the revolutionaries had not formulated. Also, the mood of the country had calmed with news of the unexpectedly favorable terms of the Treaty of Portsmouth.

The revolutionary leadership decided, despite losing its hold over the proletariat, to intensify its activity. A new general strike called for November failed, as did forcible attempts at preventing workers from returning to work. The St Petersburg soviet led these disruptive measures, and in December was disbanded by the police. An attempted protest strike failed totally. The final, rearguard act of the revolutionaries was an armed workers' uprising in Moscow, which lasted for a week in December. The Revolution of 1905 failed because its revolutionary leadership was out of tune with the more liberal and gradualist political aspirations of the great majority of Russia's people.

Consequences of 1905

The collapse of the Revolution of 1905 was followed by a nine-year period of major evolutionary, rather than revolutionary, change within the political structure of the Russian empire, simultaneously with considerable diversification in most forms of culture. The reforms envisaged in the October Manifesto of 1905 were not easy to implement; the revolution was still in full swing, the imperial administration remained wary of sharing power with the Duma and the liberal politicians drawn into the new legislative institution had little experience of actual power. However, most people were essentially satisfied with what the manifesto promised, the revolutionary momentum declined and the government was able gradually to reestablish full authority.

The first Duma was elected in March 1906 and convened the following month. Over 40 political parties and groupings were represented, with dominant control held by the liberal Constitutional Democrats (*Kadets*). The Duma proved too liberal for the tsarist administration and for the right-wing parties which supported it. When the Duma proposed to pass fundamental land-law reforms, to the detriment of the conservative nobility, the tsar exercised his prerogative to dismiss the assembly.

The second Duma was elected and convened in March 1907. It proved even more hostile to the imperial government than the first; this was in part because Lenin and the Bolsheviks were present in this assembly. The second Duma was dissolved even more quickly than the first, after which the government, acting contrary to the provisions of the manifesto, changed the electoral system so as to give greater representation to the conservative

parts of the electorate.

The third Duma, as a result, was dominated by the parties of the right, and comfortably served out its full five-year term (1907–12). Despite its conservative bias, this Duma introduced many reforms, for example by extending full civil rights to the peasants, by improving local justice and by expanding the educational system. The fourth Duma (1912–17), still more conservative than the third, was occupied largely with wartime matters and the beginning of the 1917 revolutions.

Despite constant government interference, the idea of the Duma as a valuable participatory forum was widely accepted. The political participation remained broadly based, as evidenced by the large number of parties, spanning the full spectrum of political views and also some representing particular ethnic and regional groups. The results may have been patchy, but the commitment to parliamentary government was manifest. This evolutionary mood of the country was illustrated in another way by a dramatic decline in revolutionary activity and a sharp increase in economic productivity between 1905 and 1914.

The same years witnessed a considerable diversification in all forms of Russian culture. The unprecedented variety of choice available to the cultured Russian reader is illustrated by the existence in 1912 of 2167 periodicals, spanning virtually every shade of opinion. Censorship was lax, even towards those calling for revolution: the Bolsheviks and Mensheviks alone legally published 3300 titles between 1906 and 1914.

Literature was perhaps most affected by the failure of revolution, especially in poetry. The Symbolists, as exemplified by Alexander Blok and Andrey Bely, shifted from politicized messianism to mystical introspection and aestheticism. Symbolist prose-writers such as Dmitriy Merezhkovsky (1865–1941) and Leonid Andreyev (1871–1919) turned from current reality to historical novels and decadent fiction respectively. The realist movement grew in influence, with the novels of Maxim Gorky (1868–1936) building on his reputation as an acute social critic, and especially with the emergence of Ivan Bunin (1870–1954), whose short stories and novellas about the decline of the gentry combined realism with deep psychological insight. Other literary developments ranged from the growth of literary and political monthlies, comparable with the best in Western Europe, to the appearance of sensualist, even voluptuary, fiction, the most popular writer of the genre being Mikhail Artsybashev (1878–1927).

The most creative and diversified areas of culture in the period 1905–14 were the arts of the stage. Theater grew in influence and popularity, following the innovative lead of the Moscow Art Theater under Konstantin Stanislavsky (1863–1938) and the Imperial Alexandrovsky Theater in St Petersburg under Vsevolod Meyerhold (1874–1942). Ballet also grew in stature and inventiveness, inspired by the choreography of Mikhail Fokine (1880–1942) of the St Petersburg Ballet and epitomized by the Ballets Russes of Sergey Diaghilev. Both theater and ballet gave unprecedented attention to decor and stage sets, thus stimulating a flowering of the decorative arts. The painters drawn to stage art were largely connected with the

Chekhov and the Moscow Art Theater

Anton Chekhov (1860–1904), from remote Taganrog, grandson of a serf, studied medicine in Moscow and simultaneously earned money through brief comic journalistic sketches and playlets. He qualified and practiced as a doctor, but devoted ever more time to writing. His stories became longer and more serious, depending less on "point," more on character and atmosphere; in the 1880s he passed through a "Tolstoyan" period (Tolstoy however, though friendly, disliked his work). His full-length plays, ostentatiously "undramatic," met no initial success. Only when he was taken up by the new Moscow Art Theater (MAT) did he become, in his last years, a dramatist of international stature.

The MAT was hatched by Konstantin Stanislavsky (1863–1938) and Vladimir Nemirovich-Danchenko (1858–1943) at their famous meeting (1897) in the Slavonic Bazaar restaurant for a dinner and discussion that lasted over 12 hours. Dissatisfied with current theatrical life, they founded a company that was to be without "stars," avoiding cheap and melodramatic effects, demanding total dedication and inner truth. Looking for new talent to suit their approach, Stanislavsky and Nemirovich produced Chekhov's *Seagull* in 1898 and had instant success. Thereafter they encouraged Chekhov, though seriously ill with tuberculosis and forced to live in Yalta, to write his three masterpieces (*Uncle Vanya*, *Three Sisters*, *The Cherry Orchard*). Apparently inconsequential "slices of life," these plays are carefully structured tragicomedies.

Below A page of Stanislavsky's working copy of Chekhov's *Seagull* (end of Act 2), showing his intricately detailed notes on the production.

Right Though the MAT was to make its reputation with modern drama, its first season opened with the historical play *Tsar Fyodor Ivanovich* by the versatile mid-19th-century poet A.K. Tolstoy. Painstakingly accurate detail in costumes and properties became a hallmark of Stanislavsky's productions.

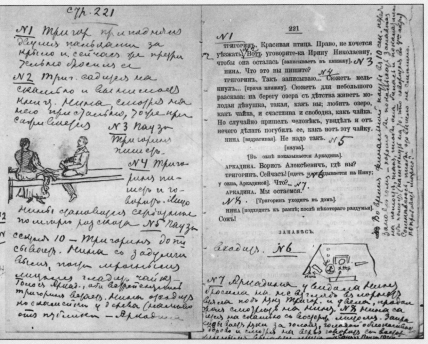

Below A page of Stanislavsky's working copy of Chekhov's *Seagull* (end of Act 2), showing his intricately detailed notes on the production.

Above Much depended on the final production of the 1898 season. Chekhov's *Seagull* had flopped in St Petersburg, but Nemirovich read the play and saw its potential. Its triumphant success in Moscow ensured the survival of MAT, which in gratitude adopted a stylized seagull as its emblem; to this day it adorns the safety curtain.

Right Chekhov reads through the text of *The Seagull* to the cast at the Moscow Art Theater. Stanislavsky peers over his right shoulder.

Left Chekhov (*left*) and Gorky in 1900. Chekhov, at 40, was already in poor health with the tuberculosis that was to kill him four years later. Maxim Gorky (born Aleksey Peshkov), eight years younger, was the "coming man" of Russian literature: the year before he had published his first novel *Foma Gordeyev*; in 1902 his "Chekhovianly" plotless play *Lower Depths* was to appear at MAT. In that year his election to the Academy was annulled because of his revolutionary sympathies, and Chekhov, though no revolutionary himself, resigned in protest.

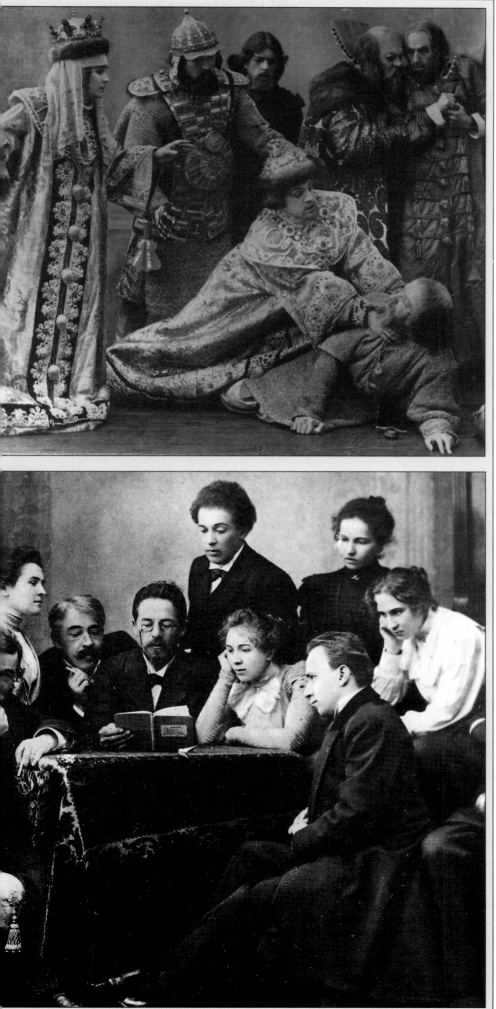

Mir Iskusstva group, the foremost among whom were all leading masters of new and experimental palette painting. The successful collaboration between imaginative producers, choreographers and painters gave the Russian public a stage art which was exciting and daring, and harmonized old elements of national culture with pure innovation.

The stage benefited greatly from the simultaneous enrichment of Russian music. An uncommonly varied group of composers came to prominence and a major part of 20th-century Russia's renowned musical repertoire was created then. Leading the innovators was Igor Stravinsky (1882–1971), whose *Firebird* was premiered in 1910, followed by *Petrushka* in 1911 and *Rite of Spring* in 1913. A symbolically innovative line of development was pursued by Scriabin. The classical tradition was developed above all by Sergey Rachmaninov (1873–1943).

The cultural scene, for all its richness, was at best indifferent, at worst hostile, to the evolution of a pluralistic political process in Russia. The hostility was strongest among poets, who mostly took an allegorical view of the reality about them, and longed for the revolution as the apocalyptic catalyst which would metamorphose Russia into a messianic new age. Prose-writers were prone to the same visionary fatalism. It was, to a real extent, the jaundiced view of Russia cultivated by the literary elite in the years 1905-14 that has fostered dismissive attitudes to the period. Political evolution and cultural diversification did not interact sufficiently to cultivate common civic values and aspirations within Russia's educated classes.

Imperial twilight

Political and cultural trends after 1905 left Nicholas II and the imperial court increasingly alienated from the mood of the time. The causes lay largely in Nicholas's own personality and in the eccentric life-style of the imperial family. The tsar was throughout his life a man of limited intellect and vision, strongly conservative by inclination and susceptible to like-minded influences and manipulation. He bowed to the inevitability of the 1905 October Manifesto without grace and without goodwill towards the institution of parliamentary monarchy. The ministers he appointed all shared his wariness of the Duma and were people of limited abilities who failed to deliver innovative or successful leadership on domestic or foreign policy. The single, striking exception to this rule was Pyotr Stolypin, prime minister from 1906 until his assassination in 1911, who introduced major land reform regulations not unrelated to changes advocated by the first Duma. Politically, the tsar became increasingly identified with extreme conservative forces. Public sentiment generally favored the constitutional experiment and set much hope in the Dumas, imperial hostility towards which only rebounded against the tsar and his administration. The tsar's image tarnished badly over this period, with indifference gradually giving way to contempt throughout most of Russia.

The waning of Nicholas II's popularity was exacerbated by the domestic circumstances of the imperial family, above all by the eccentric behavior of the tsaritsa. Alexandra, born a German

princess, was a woman of strong character and personality, who exercised a powerful influence over her weaker husband in all matters, including affairs of state. Her personal interest was not in politics, but in fashionable cultic mysticism, psychic phenomena and the occult. Through her, the royal household was suffused with seers, mediums and oracles. The tsaritsa's predilection for such charlatans became the subject of widespread gossip and ridicule even before her infamous discovery of Grigoriy Rasputin. Rasputin, a Siberian peasant supposedly possessing spiritual powers, became the dominant personality in the imperial household and at court from 1905 onward. His special position was due primarily to his ability to stop the internal bleedings of Aleksey, the hemophiliac tsarevich. The crude and salacious Rasputin enjoyed Alexandra's full confidence. His manipulative habit of commenting on matters of state meant that his views were indiscriminately imposed upon the tsar by Alexandra. Rasputin came to interfere directly with the running of the state when his personal favor or disfavor determined minsterial appointments. The Rasputin presence at court did untold damage to the Romanov image, already diminished by the dullness and weakness demonstrated by Nicholas II; among the people, however, he became something of a folk hero.

Russia and World War I

Russia's entry into World War I resulted from its complex involvement in Balkan affairs and its obligations within the Triple Entente alliance with France and Great Britain. Russia's foreign policy in the Balkans was guided by its determination to check the extension of Austro-Hungarian influence over the Balkan states, recently emerged from Ottoman domination. When Austria-Hungary threatened Serbia's independence, Russia felt compelled to come to its aid. A full mobilization of Russia's army was decreed, but without declaration of war.

Germany, as Austria-Hungary's stronger ally, chose this action as a pretext for declaring war on Russia, and immediately thereafter precipitated the full-scale world conflict by declaring war on France. Great Britain was consequently drawn in, and Russia's commitment to the conflict was finalized by its treaty obligations to the allies. The outbreak of war was greeted with a great wave of patriotism throughout Russia. Party differences were set aside (by all except revolutionary parties), social differences overlooked, strikes called off and even the tsar regained a measure of popularity.

War began in the first week of August, and over the rest of 1914 Russia experienced both defeats and victories. A major offensive against the Germans in East Prussia ended in a crushing defeat at the battle of Tannenberg, but the other big offensive against the Austro-Hungarians in Galicia was successful. In addition, a German offensive aimed at Warsaw was checked by the Russians. Fortune swung against Russia in 1915. The Germans heavily reinforced their armies in the east, and in the spring a massive offensive soon forced the Russians into general retreat: by the autumn they were driven out of Poland and the Baltic areas and had lost large parts of the Ukraine and Belorussia. Fortunately for the Russians, the Germans soon outran their supply lines, and their advance therefore came to a halt. The following year the Russians' counteroffensive against the Germans brought no results, but another against the Austro-Hungarians was successful. The latter was the famous summer offensive under Brusilov, which drove deep into Galicia.

The war put a great economic and social strain on Russia. The Russian armies suffered heavy losses and were chronically undersupplied in every way—weapons, munitions and food. The government's inability to anticipate the demands of war caused dissatisfaction in the ranks and also on the home front, whose well-being deteriorated

Right: Europe: alliances and frontiers in 1914.
There were two main power blocs in Europe in 1914: the Central Powers (Germany, Austria-Hungary) and the Triple Entente (Britain, France and Russia, soon to be joined by Italy). The foreign policies of both Russia and Austria at this time were directed towards the Balkan peninsula. The 1913 Balkan War saw the end of Turkish domination in the region, and Austria stepped into the resulting power vacuum, annexing Bosnia and Herzegovina. The independent South Slav Orthodox kingdoms, Serbia and Montenegro, were fearful of Austria and had Russian support. The assassination of the heir to the Austrian throne in Sarajevo, capital of Bosnia, by a South Slav nationalist thus precipitated Austro-Russian conflict and consequently, on account of the system of alliances, World War I.

Far left Russia's popular mood was generally stable and assured on the eve of World War I. High society events such as the Rose Ball, given by the Countess Shuvalov, brought together the Russian elite whose life would be disrupted by the war and then destroyed by revolution. The seated guests include military officers and civilians, probably both civil servants and industrialists. Younger officers like these would, after the world war, have joined the White movement to fight the Communist regime during the civil war.

Left The foreign view of Russia before the world war was at times skeptical. The French political cartoon shows Russia, in the person of Nicholas II, accepting financial aid from France, in the person of a caricatured governmental minister: their cozy exchange is observed by Germany, represented by the Prussian eagle.

sharply. Russia's economy was quickly distorted as it was put on a war footing. Manpower shortages resulting from the huge mobilization meant that military production could not deliver the combat equipment and supplies. Similarly, food supplies diverted to the front meant shortages in cities. Tax revenues declined as most men were at the front, state expenses increased while incomes fell and inflation accelerated as shortages intensified.

Social morale began breaking down in 1915, in part from economic difficulties and in part from political ones. The military failures of 1915 meant that the Duma began effectively to usurp the imperial administration's role in managing the war effort, and to make more insistent demands that the administration assemble a credible cabinet to head the government. Nicholas sought to sidestep the political crisis by assuming the mantle of commander-in-chief: his indecisiveness in this role diminished his image still further. A desperate loyalist attempt to purge the court was made with a plot to murder Rasputin; although successful as an assassination, it did not stimulate any new qualities

of leadership in the tsar; nor did it arrest what was by now the terminal decline of the Romanovs and the venerable concept of tsardom.

The internal state of Russia at the end of 1916 was dangerous. The tsar was politically isolated and the object of widespread disdain. The Duma was moving, without sufficient confidence and still within the framework of constitutional monarchy, toward the role of central government. In society at large, economic hardships and insecurity, disenchantment with the war and dismay over the confusion in the country's political leadership spelled a breakdown in national morale. Liberal and left-wing politicians could anticipate a fundamental political transformation; they planned for it, assuming that the change would be in the direction of pluralistic, parliamentary government. A smaller group of radical politicians, committed to violent revolution and including the Bolsheviks under Lenin's control, were cultivating the defeatist sentiment in public opinion and organizing the strike movement which reemerged and intensified in 1916.

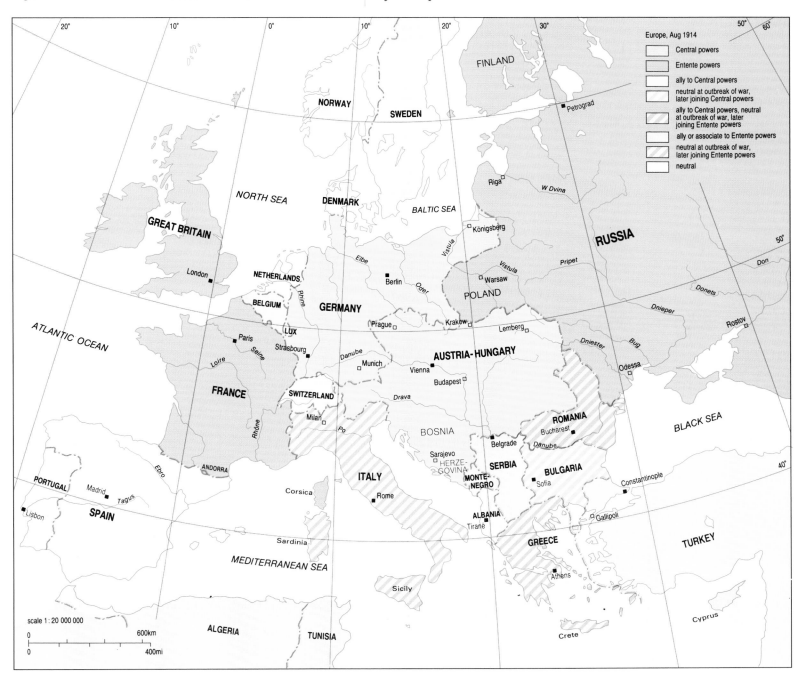

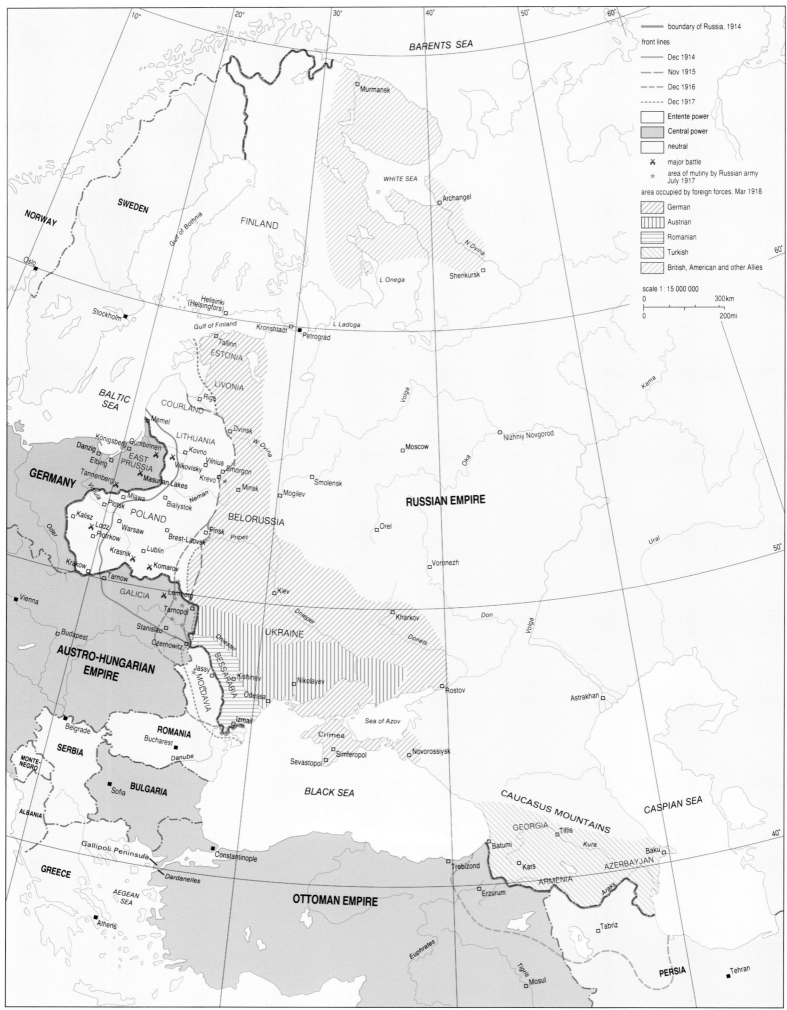

boundary of Russia, 1914

front lines
Dec 1914
Nov 1915
Dec 1916
Dec 1917

Entente power
Central power
neutral

✗ major battle
★ area of mutiny by Russian army July 1917

area occupied by foreign forces, Mar 1918
German
Austrian
Romanian
Turkish
British, American and other Allies

scale 1: 15 000 000
0   300km
0   200mi

BARENTS SEA

Murmansk

WHITE SEA

Archangel

SWEDEN

NORWAY

FINLAND

N Dvina

Oslo

L Onega

Shenkursk

Helsinki
(Helsingfors)

Stockholm

Gulf of Finland

Kronstadt
Petrograd

L Ladoga

Tallinn

ESTONIA

Volga

Kama

BALTIC
SEA

LIVONIA

Riga

COURLAND

Dvinsk

Memel

W Dvina

Moscow

Nizhniy Novgorod

LITHUANIA

Königsberg
Gumbinnen

Danzig
Elbing

EAST
PRUSSIA

Kovno

Vilkovisky

Vilnius

Smorgon

Tannenberg

Masurian Lakes

Krevo

Minsk

Smolensk

RUSSIAN EMPIRE

GERMANY

Mlawa

Neman

Mogilev

Vistula

Plotsk

Bialystok

POLAND

BELORUSSIA

Orel

Oka

Kalisz

Lodz
Piotrkow

Warsaw

Brest-Litovsk

Pinsk

Pripet

Ural

Oder

Krasnik

Lublin

Krakow

Komarov

Tarnow

Voronezh

GALICIA

Lemberg

Kiev

Dnieper

Tarnopol

Don

Volga

Vienna

Stanislau

UKRAINE

Kharkov

Czernowitz

Dniester

Donets

Budapest

BESSARABIA

AUSTRO-HUNGARIAN
EMPIRE

Jassy

Kishinev

Nikolayev

Rostov

Astrakhan

MOLDAVIA

Odessa

Izmail

Sea of Azov

Belgrade

ROMANIA

Crimea

SERBIA

Bucharest

Simferopol

Novorossiysk

MONTE-
NEGRO

Danube

Sevastopol

ALBANIA

Sofia

BULGARIA

BLACK SEA

CAUCASUS MOUNTAINS

CASPIAN SEA

GEORGIA

Tiflis

Kura

Baku

Batumi

Gallipoli Peninsula

Constantinople

Kars

AZERBAYJAN

GREECE

Dardanelles

Trebizond

ARMENIA

Araks

AEGEAN
SEA

Erzurum

Athens

OTTOMAN EMPIRE

Tabriz

Euphrates

Tigris

PERSIA

Tehran

Mosul

Right A Russian Orthodox priest blesses the wounded in a Russian field hospital on the German front during World War I. The conditions are primitive, with seriously and lightly wounded cases laid in rows on nothing more than scattered straw. Only a single nurse and few attendants are in sight. The priest is either giving individual blessings or performing last rites. Mortality was high in such conditions, and disaffection among survivors contributed to the breakdown of military morale on the eve of revolution.

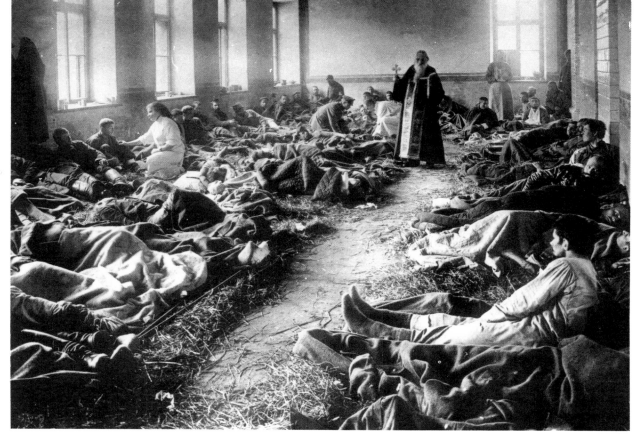

Left: World War I. Russia was drawn into the war under the obligation to support its allies, Great Britain and France. At first successes balanced defeats and sustained a morale that was temporarily boosted by the unifying effect of a patriotic war. But after Germany sent reinforcements to the eastern front and inflicted crushing defeats in 1915 the war brought enormous economic and social strain. By the autumn the Russians had been driven out of Poland and the Baltic areas and had lost parts of the Ukraine and Belorussia. In spite of some successful counteroffensives in the following year, notably under Brusilov into Galicia, heavy losses on the battlefield, coupled with severe food and ammunition shortages, demoralized the Russian army to the point of mutiny, a situation encouraged by Bolshevik propaganda, and there were massive desertions. Once the Bolsheviks came to power on a policy of ending the war, vast tracts of Russia were conceded to Germany by the Treaty of Brest-Litovsk (March 1918). The Ukrainian republic, which had been declared in July 1917, came under German and Austrian influence in its bid to defeat Bolshevism. With the same end in view, the British forces, originally sent to guard munitions dumps at Murmansk and Archangel against German attacks, stayed on in 1918 in a vain attempt to help the anti-Bolshevik Russian generals.

The February Revolution and the provisional government

Civil disorder increased sharply in the capital, Petrograd (St Petersburg Russified), during the winter of 1916–17. The Duma again demanded of Nicholas the formation of a new cabinet, acceptable to itself, which could aspire to popular confidence. The tsar issued a decree disbanding the Duma, but the latter refused to comply and on 27 February effectively assumed the role of government. Nicholas, isolated and powerless, abdicated on 2 March. The February Revolution was thus an essentially nonviolent resolution of the struggle for control between Duma and tsar which began in 1905, and which culminated in the triumph of parliamentary government over the monarchy. The Duma assumed for itself a caretaker's role, paving the way for a completely new and directly elected parliamentary government, and therefore reconstituted itself as the provisional government. But its ability to govern was severely hampered by the emergence of a parallel form of government, the network of councils called soviets.

The provisional government consisted mostly of the liberal and moderate conservative forces which had been dominant in the Dumas. Representatives of the socialist forces, especially the more radical type, looked for another base from which to exercise power. Such a base existed in the emerging Petrograd Soviet of Workers' and Soldiers' Deputies, a loosely structured and fluid popular council espousing a radical socialist form of government. The Petrograd Soviet became effectively an alternative government. The provisional government was supported largely by the educated and commercial classes, while the soviet depended on the marginally literate factory workers and soldiery.

The provisional government set about formulat-ing a series of fundamental reforms. The most important of these created the foundations for the convening of a constituent assembly, the freely elected and fully representative national parliament which would institute the structure of a new democratic government in Russia. The electoral reforms provided for a universal and equal voting franchise, together with a secret ballot. This contrasted with the election of the Dumas, which had been indirect and on the basis of a limited franchise. The system of local government, or *zemstvos*, was reorganized and charged with drawing up electoral registers for the elections to the constituent assembly, planned for the autumn of 1917. Throughout, the provisional government was concerned with strict observance of legality in the political process and exact observance of parliamentary procedures in the conduct of its business.

The soviet was an entirely different political institution, a haphazard assembly of representatives chosen by popular acclamation; its composition was highly fluid, it operated without any declared jurisdiction and it lacked any fixed rules or procedures. Sessions of the soviet tended to be chaotic, with the real control and the administration being concentrated in a small group of leaders. The political composition of the soviet was almost exclusively socialist, together with a few small radical groups that claimed to represent the real interests of labor. The soviet's aims were two-fold: first, the creation of an exclusively socialist order in Russia; second, the undermining of all non-socialist political forces, which were labeled "bourgeois" or "capitalist," and which included all those participating in the provisional government.

The largest group in the soviet were the Socialist Revolutionaries, a radical populist party strongly attached to the peasantry. Next in importance were

the Social Democrats, a party split into two groups, the majority Mensheviks and the minority Bolsheviks. In the spring of 1917 the Bolsheviks under Lenin's leadership broke away to form an independent party. The Bolsheviks were a small minority in the soviet, but, being better organized and more dynamic, they began exercising influence out of proportion to their numbers. They consistently took the extremist line that the soviet should seize all power immediately.

The soviet concept spread rapidly through Russia, with local soviets appearing in virtually every city, town and village, as well as within the ranks of the army. All these bodies acknowledged the ultimate national authority of the Petrograd Soviet. By mid-1917 the soviets effectively constituted a functioning prototype of national, regional and local government apparatus, spanning Russia in its entirety. By comparison, the provisional government rested on a much narrower base of support in Petrograd and exercised a far more tenuous authority over the established *zemstvo* local government in the country.

The soviet movement's potential as a national government was confirmed with the All-Russian Congress of Soviets in June. The Bolshevik Party accounted for only 16 percent of more than 650 delegates; their extremist positions were repeatedly rejected, and Lenin was unable to impose his views on the assembly. Indeed, it was not Lenin but another socialist politician, Alexander Kerensky, a vice-chairman of the Petrograd Soviet, who emerged as the leader in Russian government and politics until October 1917, and who brought about a temporary convergence between the soviets and the provisional government.

Late summer saw two major threats to the provisional government. The first was an attempt at a violent coup d'etat launched in Petrograd during July by the Bolsheviks under Lenin's leadership. He was able to mobilize only a group of sailors and soldiers from the Petrograd garrison, and this was defeated by a cavalry division from the front. Lenin and Trotsky, the co-organizers of the uprising, fled the country to await another opportunity of seizing power. The second crisis came with a revival within the disorganized Russian army under its new commander-in-chief, General Lavr Kornilov. Kornilov was a dynamic and successful front-line commander, with views that appealed to the conservative and moderate elements in the provisional government. Kerensky, who was made prime minister after the suppression of Lenin's uprising, was increasingly packing the provisional government with socialists, and Kornilov's rapidly growing popularity and political involvement threatened Kerensky's position. In September Kerensky tried to dismiss Kornilov, but the general refused to comply, appealed for public support and dispatched an armed force towards Petrograd. Kerensky turned for help to the socialist organizations, all of whom came to his aid; thanks especially to the transport workers, he was able to impede the movement of Kornilov's forces and therefore to survive as prime minister.

Kerensky's proved a pyrrhic victory. He had lost credibility with the moderate forces in the provisional government and by overreliance on the socialists had fatally undermined the government's independence. By rebuffing Kornilov he alienated the only force which could have defended his government. Meanwhile, the Soviets were gaining new momentum, popular opinion had swung massively in their favor and by September the Bolsheviks were dominant in the Petrograd Soviet.

The October Revolution and civil war

Lenin's plans for seizing power were timed in such a way as to undermine the constituent assembly, whose election and convocation were the

The revolutions of 1917 saw many popular assaults upon prisons, in order to release detainees. This prison in the imperial capital of Petrograd has been stormed and left a burnt-out shell. It was probably a minor transit prison: the location directly on a city street, without any surrounding compound, suggests it could not have been a high-security establishment. The collapse of municipal services during 1917 meant that large areas of Petrograd and Moscow were gutted in this way, leaving widespread urban dereliction.

The revolutions of 1917, especially the one in October, were accompanied by wide-ranging looting and wanton destruction. Middle- and upper-class homes were a main target of such attacks, and the fabric of their way of life was irretrievably shattered. Family possessions, heirlooms, collections, libraries, archives and records perished or were dispersed; the fragments that survive are now anonymous collectors' items, popular in Western antique markets. The photograph shows a ransacked room in the Winter Palace, not stripped bare of larger items but probably pilfered of smaller ones. Many finer items such as sculptures and paintings were systematically sold abroad by the Communist state during the 1920s to raise hard currency for its treasury.

security organization which relied on systematic terror to eliminate opposition, and the outlawing of the Constitutional Democratic Party, which presaged the extermination of all political parties except the Bolsheviks.

The constituent assembly convened in Petrograd on 5 January 1918. The non-Bolshevik majority faced pervasive intimidation from the Red Guards, but despite this and Lenin's declared hostility to the assembly, the delegates turned down by almost two to one a doctrinaire reform package proposed by the Bolsheviks. The Bolsheviks did not accept the majority decision and walked out. Later that night the delegates were forcibly evicted by the Red Guards, and the Bolshevik government formally dissolved the constituent assembly the following day. Thus, over 12 years' evolution towards a full parliamentary democracy in Russia was negated in one day. However, the ideal of the constituent assembly lived on, and was shared by virtually all of Bolshevism's opponents during the civil war.

The causes of the civil war lay in the repugnance to the Bolsheviks and their methods which grew during the October Revolution and spread widely in early 1918. This alienation was strongest in Petrograd and Moscow, where the Bolsheviks' refusal to cooperate with other parties and their strong-arm tactics in gaining power finally disgusted all other political forces, including effectively the entire socialist movement and the general urban population, who saw the Bolsheviks seize privileges, particularly in terms of food supplies. In the countryside it grew as the Bolsheviks incited class divisions in the peasantry and instituted a program of forcible food confiscation, in order to divert food supplies to their power base in the cities.

As it became clear that the Bolsheviks were determined to use any means to eliminate opponents, the opposition swung into action. It was too late to contest control of the capital cities, Petrograd and Moscow, where Bolshevik rule was established strongly and irreversibly. The history of the civil war was logistically a struggle between the Bolshevik central region and a wide periphery of disparate anti-Bolshevik governments. Being at the center, the Bolsheviks controlled Russia's war industry and communications network, giving them a military capability and logistical superiority which the opposition could never match.

All the main anti-Bolshevik governments emerged in early 1918. The most important area in this respect was the south of Russia, which was the base of the White (anti-Bolshevik) movement. This included the Volunteer Army, created around a core of non-socialist Russian army officers, under General Kornilov, and Constitutional Democrat politicians. The area was also the base for two newly emerged autonomous Cossack governments, one in the Don and the other in the Kuban area. After some time and effort, the Whites and Cossacks managed to combine their anti-Bolshevik operations; their common political objective was to reconvene the constituent assembly. Other governments emerged in eastern Russia and the Urals region. The Socialist Revolutionaries set up one in Samara, consisting of deputies from the disbanded constituent assembly. A Constitutional Democrat

provisional government's main objective. The elections were scheduled for early November, and the convocation for the first week of January 1918. Through early October Lenin, working closely with Trotsky and Stalin, finalized the plans and means for a coup d'etat, which took place on 24–25 October. The Red Guards, select detachments of Bolshevik workers and soldiers, seized all government buildings and communications centers in Petrograd. The provisional government, meeting in the Winter Palace and virtually undefended, was quickly dispersed and its leaders arrested. A second All-Russian Congress of Soviets was convened within hours: the program tabled by the Bolsheviks was approved, as was a cabinet headed by Lenin. Kerensky ignominiously fled Petrograd. The October Revolution was accomplished and the government was entirely in Lenin's hands.

The change in Petrograd could not, however, stop the elections to the constituent assembly. The turnout was high, particularly given the turmoil of the time: about 42 million out of an estimated 90 million electorate cast their votes. Out of the 703 known delegates, over 50 percent represented the Socialist Revolutionaries, 24 percent the Bolsheviks, 13 percent the Constitutional Democrats and 11 percent various nationalist parties. The Bolsheviks and their sympathizers controlled less than a third of the delegates. If the constituent assembly were allowed to function freely, Lenin's regime would have had little chance of survival. He was determined not to allow this threat to his power.

Under Lenin's direction, the new government immediately promulgated a number of radical reforms. Some were constructive and widely popular. These included the abolition of private ownership of land and the opening of negotiations for peace without annexations or indemnities. Others were ominous. These included the creation of the Cheka (from which the KGB derives), a state

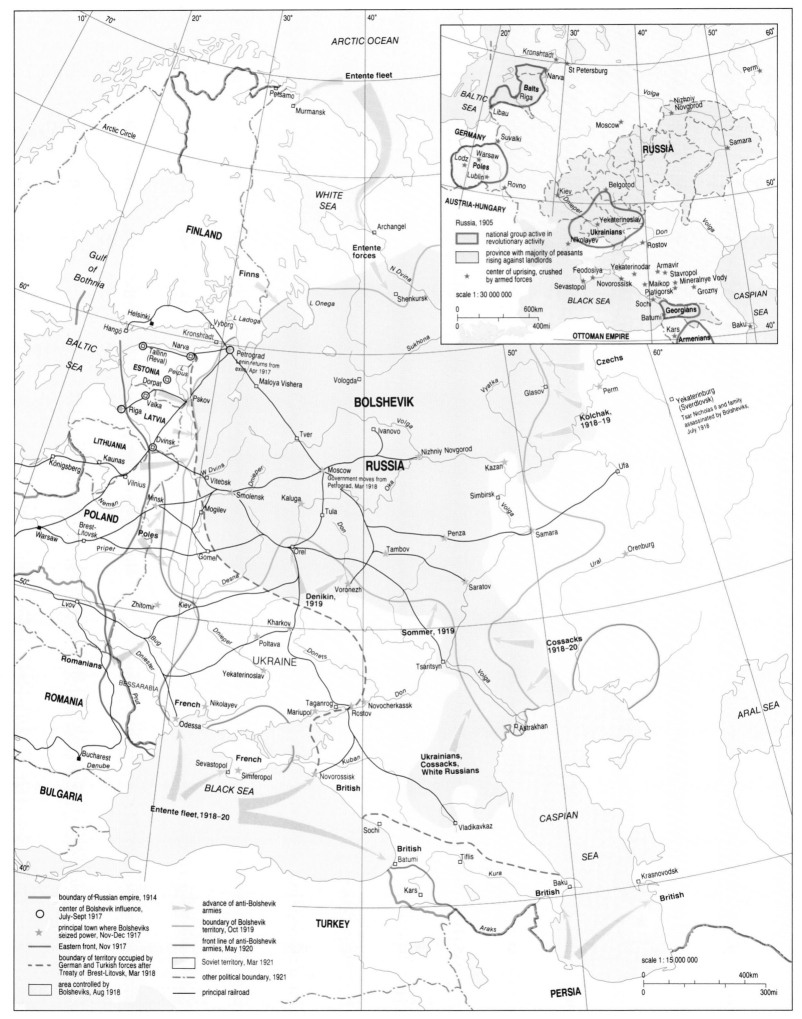

ARCTIC OCEAN

Entente fleet

Petsamo

Murmansk

Arctic Circle

WHITE
SEA

FINLAND

Archangel

Entente
forces

Gulf
of
Bothnia

N Dvina

Shenkursk

Finns

Helsinki

L Onega

Vyborg
L Ladoga

Hangö

Kronshtadt

Sukhona

BALTIC

Narva

Petrograd
Lenin returns from
exile, Apr 1917

Tallinn
(Reval)

Peipus

Maloya Vishera

Vologda

ESTONIA

Dorpat

Pskov

Valka

BOLSHEVIK

Riga
LATVIA

Vyatka

Glasov

Perm

LITHUANIA

Dvinsk

Tver

Ivanovo

Volga

Nizhniy Novgorod

Kolchak,
1918–19

Kaunas

W Dvina

Dnieper

Moscow
Government moves from
Petrograd, Mar 1918

RUSSIA

Königsberg

Vitebsk

Kazan

Yekaterinburg
(Sverdlovsk)

Vilnius

Minsk

Smolensk

Kaluga

Ufa

Tsar Nicholas II and family
assassinated by Bolsheviks,
July 1918

Neman

Mogilev

Tula

Simbirsk

Volga

POLAND

Don

Brest-
Litovsk

Warsaw

Poles

Pripet

Gomel

Orel

Tambov

Penza

Samara

Orenburg

Desna

Voronezh

Saratov

Ural

Denikin,
1919

Lvov

Zhitomir

Kiev

Kharkov

Sommer, 1919

Cossacks
1918–20

Romanians

Dnieper

Poltava

Dnieper

Bug

Donets

UKRAINE

Tsaritsyn

Volga

Dniester

Yekaterinoslav

ROMANIA

BESSARABIA

Prut

French

Nikolayev

Taganrog

Novocherkassk

Don

ARAL SEA

Mariupol

Rostov

Odessa

Kuban

Astrakhan

Bucharest

Danube

Sevastopol

French

Ukrainians,
Cossacks,
White Russians

Simferopol

Novorossisk

BULGARIA

BLACK SEA

British

CASPIAN

Entente fleet, 1918–20

Sochi

Vladikavkaz

SEA

British

Batumi

Tiflis

Krasnovodsk

Kars

Kura

Baku

British

TURKEY

British

Araks

PERSIA

Inset map (top right)

Kronshtadt

St Petersburg

Perm

BALTIC
SEA

Narva

Balts

Riga

Volga

Nizhniy
Novgorod

GERMANY

Libau

Suvalki

Moscow

RUSSIA

Samara

Lodz

Warsaw

Poles

Lublin

Rovno

Belgotod

AUSTRIA-HUNGARY

Kiev

Dnieper

Russia, 1905

☐ national group active in
revolutionary activity

☐ province with majority of peasants
rising against landlords

★ center of uprising, crushed
by armed forces

scale 1 : 30 000 000

0   600km
0   400mi

OTTOMAN EMPIRE

Yekaterinoslav

Nikolayev

Ukrainians

Rostov

Don

Volga

Feodosiya

Yekaterinodar

Armavir

Stavropol

Sevastopol

Novorossisk

Maikop

Mineralnye Vody

Sochi

Platigorsk

Grozny

BLACK SEA

Batumi

Georgians

CASPIAN

Kars

Baku

SEA

Armenians

Legend

— boundary of Russian empire, 1914

○ center of Bolshevik influence,
July–Sept 1917

★ principal town where Bolsheviks
seized power, Nov–Dec 1917

— Eastern front, Nov 1917

--- boundary of territory occupied by
German and Turkish forces after
Treaty of Brest-Litovsk, Mar 1918

☐ area controlled by
Bolsheviks, Aug 1918

➤ advance of anti-Bolshevik
armies

— boundary of Bolshevik
territory, Oct 1919

— front line of anti-Bolshevik
armies, May 1920

☐ Soviet territory, Mar 1921

–·– other political boundary, 1921

— principal railroad

scale 1 : 15 000 000

0   400km
0   300mi

Czechs

government emerged in Omsk, and a similar one in Yekaterinburg. The Samara and Omsk governments were eventually merged to form a single anti-Bolshevik authority under Admiral Kolchak.

The Caucasus also rejected Bolshevism, with socialist governments being established in Georgia, Armenia and Azerbaijan. All backed the reinstatement of the provisional government and recall of the constituent assembly. Eventually the three governments united into a single Transcaucasian Federal Republic, still dedicated to the ideal of federative affiliation with a democratic, non-Bolshevik Russia. Ukraine went a separate path, proclaiming an independent nationalist republic, but in fact heavily dependent on German support. Some local governments and movements tried to survive by flirting simultaneously with the Reds and the Whites. The most notable of these was the Green Army led by the charismatic Nestor Makhno. Makhno's territory spanned southern Russia and northern Ukraine, and his forces comprised Cossacks and peasants. Makhno, an anarchist leaning towards socialism, was dedicated primarily to the idea of local autonomy. Lenin made an unsuccessful personal attempt to convert him to Bolshevism in summer 1918.

The Bolsheviks in mid-1918 renamed themselves the Communist Party and moved the capital from Petrograd to Moscow. Through the first half of the year, fortune favored the Whites. Their forces, though much smaller than the Reds, were much more professional and better led, under the overall command of the experienced General Anton Denikin. The Communists, although experienced in urban combat, had difficulty adapting to the complexities of campaigning and warfare outside the cities. Finally, the Whites benefited from some equipment and assistance from the Allies, with the British, Americans, Japanese and French sending small expeditionary forces into Russia. The Communists were meanwhile deflected by the attempt to defuse the German offensive still under way on the Russian front. In mid-July the former tsar and his family, who had been interned for months, were murdered at Yekaterinburg by their Communist jailers.

By late 1918 the Communists were in the ascendant. Initial successes by the Whites had faltered, exposing their military and logistical limitations. For the Reds, an armistice with the Germans freed front-line troops under Communist influence, and Leon Trotsky succeeded in transforming the Red military into the highly organized and efficient Red Army. In September the Cheka, under Lenin's guidance, instituted the "Red Terror," a highly organized program of extermination of all political opposition, relying on systematic mass arrests, interrogation under torture, hostage taking of family and children and summary and mass executions.

The South Russian government, which had evolved out of the Volunteer Army, achieved some major advances against the Red Army during the winter of 1918–19, but this was a last success. Unable to sustain their effort, the Whites fell into retreat in southern Russia and collapsed in Siberia. The socialist opposition governments in Russia had perished by then and the Transcaucasian Republic was in peril. The South Russian government made a

sustained last stand under Wrangel's command in the Crimea, but was forced to evacuate to Istanbul in November 1920. With the opposition governments gone and the last White bastion abandoned, the Communist regime held undisputed authority in Russia.

The Communists still had to suppress popular resistance movements in the countryside. The peasants had suffered greatly from the forcible food expropriations, as well as from the extension of Red Terror into the countryside; the latter was especially severe because most peasants favored the Socialist Revolutionaries, whom the Communists were intent on exterminating. Numerous anti-Communist resistance movements emerged, culminating in massive revolts in Russia's central provinces, the Volga region and in Siberia during 1920–21. These were well organized and led, the biggest being in western Siberia and the Tambov area of central Russia. The full force of the Red Army and Red Terror was necessary to suppress and eradicate these popular uprisings. With this completed in 1921, the Communist government was finally in complete control.

Following the October Revolution and civil war, there was a wave of emigration from Russia. It consisted of the broad anti-Bolshevik sector of the population—the White military, liberal and conservative politicians, writers and journalists, lawyers and academics, scientists and engineers, officials and professionals, numbering probably over a million. The greatest concentration settled in Berlin up to the mid-1920s; the center later shifted to Paris.

A small part of the emigration, particularly the scientists and engineers, assimilated readily into the foreign environment. The intellectual majority created a Russian society and culture in diaspora. Émigré Russian literature developed with vitality, the leading authors being Ivan Bunin (who won the Nobel Prize for Literature in 1933), Boris Zaytsev, Ivan Shmelyov and the young Vladimir Nabokov. A few writers, including Ilya Ehrenburg, chose to return after a few years abroad.

Some émigrés remained staunchly anti-Communist, perceiving their mission as preserving pre-revolutionary Russian culture while it was being rooted out at home. The more ambitious formed organizations to infiltrate anti-Communist views into the Soviet Union. Of these, the most resilient was the NTS (National Labor Alliance), founded in Belgrade in 1930. Others came to believe that the Communist regime was mellowing into a benevolent successor to tsarist Russia, and some therefore chose to return; of these many were sent immediately or eventually to concentration camps.

The divided attitude towards modern Russia was epitomized in 1921 by a split in the émigré Russian Orthodox Church over whether to continue to accept the authority of the metropolitan of Moscow, who, in the face of brutal persecution, had made some accommodation with the Communists. One faction opted to continue accepting Moscow's primacy; this became the so-called Synodal Church, dominant in the European emigration. The other faction decided that Moscow had abrogated its religious mission and declared itself sole custodian of Russian Orthodoxy; this Church in Exile dominated the emigration in America.

The revolutions and civil war. The Revolution of 1905 (*inset*) brought a strong upsurge of nationalist feeling in several parts of Russia, as well as widespread revolts by the peasantry against their landlords. Ruthless suppression by the tsarist forces as well as the apparent promise of constitutional change held out by the Duma defused the situation. However, after years of conflict with the Duma and his disastrous leadership during World War I, Tsar Nicholas II was finally forced to abdicate by the February Revolution of 1917. The lack of strong central government allowed the new political phenomenon of local soviets to gain influence throughout the country. The well-organized, dynamic and uncompromising Bolsheviks won increasing power in spite of relatively small numbers. Crystallization of varied anti-Bolshevik forces (collectively termed "Whites") under leaders such as Denikin and Kolchak mainly took place in remoter areas, while the "Reds" held the central cities, where they controlled Russia's war industries and communications network. The Whites in some parts of the north and south of the country were aided by the British and their allies, fearful of the spread of Bolshevism, but this intervention was half-hearted. Even Polish intervention in Ukraine was insufficient to defeat the Reds.

Building the Communist state: first attempt

The first attempt to create a new Communist order in Russia spanned the years 1918–21, under a program called "War Communism." Its aims were to exterminate all vestiges of the old order, to introduce sweeping and radical institutional changes in accordance with an extreme vision of socialist utopianism, and to concentrate all power in the hands of the Communist Party. The old order was destroyed with the abolition of the existing governmental institutions, administrative organization, legal system, money and banking, commercial system, trade, educational system, all non-socialist political parties and family rights. People who served the old order in any way were identified as enemies of the new and subjected to wide-ranging persecutions, including regular summary executions. These, together with a large part of the peasantry, were officially classified as *lishentsy* (disfranchised people) and stripped of all civic and political rights.

Simultaneously, the new order was introduced. This brought a total nationalization of industry, a total communalization of property, a system of ration cards to replace money, political education and the creation of political agencies to perform intermediary and service functions. Economically, the overall aim was for the government to control all national production and all distribution of goods to the population, thereby introducing a socialist non-profit operation to replace the market mechanisms of capitalism. All organizations administering the new order were staffed by Communists chosen on the basis of their qualities as revolutionaries; it was assumed that the new order could not fail to succeed, and that the skills of government could easily be picked up. The Communist functionaries were accorded extensive special privileges, making them from the start into an elite class separate from the rest of the population.

The new order was intended to be highly centralized, under the administrative control of the Soviet government, which in turn was to be fully controlled by the Communist Party. The public structure of government consisted of the same soviet councils which had been the main catalyst of the revolutions. Even though controlled by Communists, these somewhat unpredictable assemblies included in their membership a residue of Mensheviks and Socialist Revolutionaries. The Communist Party and Lenin were intent that all real power should be held by them, and Lenin was equally determined that, within the Communist Party, full authority and power should be vested in a small elite. To achieve this, he created an institutional pyramid of ascending authority: an irregularly convened national Supreme Soviet assigned the function of national government to the Communist

Above The closeness between the two early Communist leaders is seen in this photograph, taken on Red Square in Moscow during 1919 festivities marking the second anniversary of the Bolshevik Revolution. Lenin strikes a Napoleonic pose, while Trotsky salutes, probably in acknowledgment of a passing contingent of the Red Army. The scene is posed, with the cleared opening in the crowd focusing on Lenin; the opening is lined with security men watching the photographer and token children are placed near the leaders to create an informal mood. The poster at the left reads "Radiant glory to those who died for Communism."

Party, immediately in the form of its permanent Central Committee, which was in turn supervised by the Party's permanent Politburo (Political Bureau). All ultimate power and decision-making rested with the Politburo, a tiny group of the top leaders: the first Politburo consisted of seven, headed by Lenin, Trotsky and Stalin.

Ideologically, the new order was justified by the concept of the "Dictatorship of the Proletariat." This posited that the Communists were acting in the name of the proletariat, which was still fluid in the post-revolutionary situation, and therefore needed dedicated revolutionary cadres to assist it along the predestined path towards workers' socialism. The Communist Party therefore assigned itself the role of the "Vanguard of the Proletariat."

Economically and socially, "War Communism" proved a disaster. The removal of market incentives spelled the death of work incentive and hence the effective collapse of industrial and agricultural production. This led to critical shortages, runaway inflation and social disruption, all intensifying just as the civil war drew to a close. The Communists safeguarded their privileged position in the cities by requisitioning the scant supplies and launched systematic requisitioning expeditions into the countryside in order to seize food from the peasants. These expeditions and droughts resulted in a massive rural famine in 1921, probably the greatest famine Russia had experienced until that time.

Hostility towards the government grew in both cities and countryside, meeting with increased repression and terror from the Communists. A wave of peasant uprisings swept the country in 1920–21, and in March 1921 the Communist regime faced its greatest threat in the Kronshtadt uprising. Kronshtadt was Petrograd's principal naval base,

and the sailors there were a major pro-Bolshevik force during the revolutions of 1917. By 1921 the same sailors were incensed at the Communists' abuse of power and disregard of their revolutionary pledges. The rebels' program called for new elections to the soviets, on the basis of a secret ballot; freedom of speech and press for all revolutionaries and radicals; release of all socialist political prisoners; a relaxation of trade restrictions to help feed Petrograd; and a lifting of restrictions on the peasantry. The program was essentially a broad socialist protest against the Communists' repressive monopoly on power. The latter responded by labeling the rebels as counter-revolutionaries, and the uprising was brutally suppressed by forces under Mikhail Tukhachevsky, later the Red Army's chief of staff.

The famine and the Kronshtadt incident spelled the end of "War Communism." Lenin decided that less doctrinaire and more practical means were needed in the short term to halt the slide into chaos and revive the nation's economy. In 1921 he proclaimed the abolition of "War Communism" and introduced instead the New Economic Policy, NEP for short, a series of economic and related institutional reforms which replaced the impracticalities of "War Communism" with more conventional measures. Economically, a modicum of private initiative was reintroduced into agriculture and manufacturing, while the government maintained a monopoly over heavy industry, foreign trade and finance. Peasants were given limited rights to sell produce privately, and small-scale private manufacturing concerns were permitted. Conventional trading practices were revived, banking reintroduced and normal financial instruments and transactions returned.

Private initiative was applied effectively to small-scale manufacture, retail trade and service industry. These sectors accounted for a minor proportion of the total economy, but their spectacular growth helped stabilize the national economy and generate some social tranquillity by meeting at least part of starved consumer demand. The small-scale entrepreneurs, nicknamed the "Nepmen," who catalyzed this growth, were essentially a final incarnation of the traditional Russian merchant, who had flourished particularly in the last decades before the October Revolution. The state monopoly sectors showed at best marginal improvements under NEP.

The flexibility introduced into economic matters under NEP was not matched by any similar political changes. The reverse was in fact true. Communist control and power were extended and severely tightened in 1921–22. The last remnants of non-Communist socialist parties, the Mensheviks and Socialist Revolutionaries, were abolished in 1921. Internal control became more rigid within the Communist Party, which had until then been relatively tolerant of internal debate. Members whose views differed significantly from Lenin's were accused of "factionalism," a charge tantamount to ideological treachery. The summer of 1921 saw the first systematic political purge of the Communist Party. The membership of the party at this time was less than 1 percent of the total Russian population; even the total proletariat, in whose name the Communists claimed to rule, accounted for only about 15 per-

Below The 1917 revolution left great destruction throughout Russia, and especially in its cities. Repairs and clearances were usually piecemeal, and in crucial places performed by units of Red Army out of security considerations. This Red Guard detachment is at work inside the Moscow Kremlin, the seat of the Communist government. The rampart wall in the distance overlooks Red Square; the domes of St Basil's cathedral loom beyond the smaller tower to the right. The small neo-Gothic chapel near the larger gate at the left, a famous sanctuary, was soon torn down.

cent. The Communist security police were strengthened to safeguard the party's minority position and internal discipline; in 1922 the Cheka was reorganized as the GPU, with much greater powers, a remit to operate outside the law and responsibility for security within the party, including the arrest and interrogation of party members. Thus, security policing was extended to thought policing.

It seems clear that Lenin saw increased flexibility in the economy and increased repression in politics as two sides of the same necessary coin: the former was a temporary, regressive measure to shore up the economy, while the latter would guarantee absolute power for the Communists. But Lenin did not clarify his thinking about what to do after NEP, and in May 1922 he suffered a stroke which left him partly paralyzed; in early 1923 another took away his speech and in January 1924 he died. This was effectively a period of interregnum in the Communist Party, with NEP continuing on borrowed time.

Among aspiring successors, Stalin and Trotsky were the leading figures. Stalin had risen to power through exceptional organizational ability and loyal obedience to Lenin, who had cultivated him as heir apparent. Trotsky had risen as a charismatic leader, especially of the military, and an ideologue whose views could complement and at times diverge from Lenin's. Stalin inclined towards concentrating on the development of a Communist order in Russia, while Trotsky was dedicated to the belief that Russia should catalyze worldwide Communist revolution. Both men were, however, equally committed to monopolistic Communist power, doctrinal unity and discipline within the party and intense security policing.

Stalin had the advantage from the start, due both to Lenin's favor and to his own control over all appointments within the Communist Party. Shortly before his death, Lenin rejected Stalin as his succesor, but without indicating who should be chosen instead. It is unclear whether this repudiation was the last flash of Lenin's insight or a sign of confusion in his terminal illness. In either case, it had no effect on the Communist Party. Stalin strengthened his position with a masterful orchestration of Lenin's funeral and a memorable oration in which he established himself as sole custodian of Leninism.

Building the Communist state: Stalin the creator

The actual content of Leninism was far from clear. Lenin had shown himself to be an authoritative theoretician, a successful revolutionary leader and an effective crisis manager during the civil war. However, he had proved an inept state builder. Stalin proved to have the vision and determination to shape the Soviet state and system as we know it, adapting Leninism to that image.

Stalin consolidated his position gradually between 1924 and 1927, while the Communist Party debated about what course it should take after Lenin. One group, headed by Stalin as leader and Bukharin as ideologue, favored continuing a program of pragmatic compromise, as exemplified in NEP. Another, led by Trotsky, favored a radically doctrinaire program, not unlike a return to "War Communism," together with increased centralization of the party organization and increased discipline within its ranks. The first group controlled the Central Committee and the Politburo of the party; the second was labeled the Left Opposition. Trotsky's Left Opposition tried to mobilize the Moscow proletariat, but this failed due to the workers' indifference. The failure proved that Trotsky was no longer a charismatic mass leader, even though he commanded strong influence within the party's ranks. Stalin succeeded in eroding that influence by launching a new recruiting drive, which nearly doubled party membership to over a million. By controlling the selection processes behind the recruitment drive, Stalin was able greatly to strengthen his power within the expanded party. In mid-1927 Stalin accused the Left Opposition of plotting to split the Communist Party and organized a purge of its adherents, including Trotsky, from the party's ranks. Trotsky was sent into internal exile and deported from the Soviet Union early in 1929. With this masterstroke, Stalin became the sole and undisputed leader of the Communist Party, and therefore of the Soviet Union.

At the end of 1927 Stalin proclaimed his design for the future economic development and social engineering of the Soviet Union. This was based on the concept of a planned economy: strategies and targets for national development were to be formulated by centralized planning bodies, with implementation and fulfillment of the plans being passed as orders to industry. The planned economy was to operate on the basis of successive five-year plans, which applied to every sector of Soviet industry and enterprise.

The First Five-Year Plan, authorized in early 1928, centered on two radical objectives: the introduction of an industrial revolution and the collectivization of agriculture. The industrial revolution was to include a total restructuring of the country's industrial base, an intensive expansion of heavy and manufacturing industry and a concentration of new industrial development in the Urals and western Siberia. The ultimate aim was two-fold. First, the Soviet Union was to become a modern and self-sufficient industrial state. Second, the accompanying growth of the proletariat would expand that class base in whose name the Communists claimed to rule. The latter consideration was especially important since Russia was still predominantly a peasant country.

The collectivization of agriculture was to reshape peasant Russia to conform with the Communist order. The peasants had not responded favorably to either Bolshevism or Communism and were treated with suspicion by all Communist ideologues. They had reacted with particular enthusiasm to NEP, and the increase of their private production under those conditions allowed normal food supply and provisioning to be reestablished. The five-year plan now did away with the private initiative permitted under NEP. All peasant communities and landholdings were to be merged into collective farms, which were to be run as industrial complexes under centralized Communist Party administration. All indigenous social and administrative institutions were to be abolished, and any slight differentiation of wealth that remained in peasant society was to be erased. The

Consolidation of the Soviet Union.
The seizure of power by the Bolsheviks in 1917 sparked off several similar attempts at revolution in other European countries: Hungary, Czechoslovakia, Bulgaria, even Germany, all looked at one time as though they might become ideological allies of Red Russia. But the most serious attempt to export revolution had ended disastrously: the Cossack Red Cavalry had moved from the civil war in the Ukraine straight into Poland, but had been repulsed near Warsaw. In the subsequent settlement Poland expanded far to the east. By 1922 the new state of the Soviet Union had lost a great sweep of pre-revolutionary Russia to the west. Not only Poland, but Finland and the Baltic states declared themselves independent; Bessarabia had been annexed by Romania. In the Caucasus an unsuccessful attempt was made to form an independent Transcaucasian Federation in 1917–18. After a brief period under independent socialist governments, Georgia, Armenia and Azerbayjan were incorporated piecemeal into the Soviet Union as autonomous republics.

ultimate aim was again two-fold. First, the new agricultural industrial complex was to increase production and rural food-supply potential. Second, the greatest passive resistance to Communism in Russia would be eradicated by destroying the established way of peasant life and replacing it with a quasi-industrial one under the party's full control. The foundation of a Communist order was ready for building on. The cost of doing this was horrific beyond any expectations.

The arts in the revolutionary period

Even before 1900 the Russian artistic avant-garde had vigorously taken up the idea of the "Modern Movement" in the arts. To the poets and painters in the quite capacious Symbolist category, to be part of this movement was to proclaim oneself internationally minded, anxious to ventilate a stuffy provincial culture with bracing foreign air. Marxists were internationalists almost by definition, but there were others, like the post-Symbolist writer Osip Mandelshtam, who in a haunting phrase described his poetry as "nostalgia for world culture." Many artists, writers and particularly musicians however saw modernism quite differently, in specifically Russian terms, as a way of exploring and extending their national heritage. In music the popular Sergey Rachmaninov (1873–1943) continued to compose through nearly half the 20th century as if Musorgsky and Rimsky-Korsakov had never existed. Similarly in painting followers of the Wanderers, notably Ilya Repin, were still going strong in Stalin's time, when they again came into their own.

The Russian Symbolist movement began to fall apart after 1905. The crisis was one of confidence: the revolution of 1905 jolted their somewhat rarefied and apolitical artistic milieu, forcing them to pay attention to social problems. One consequence was a conservative reaction that crystallized around the almanac *Landmarks* (*Vekhi*), whose contributors questioned the general previous adherence of the intelligentsia to revolutionary or at least liberal positions. A new generation, born mainly between the mid-1880s and 1900, superseded the Symbolists as leaders of modernism rather suddenly and comprehensively in the years around 1910. In all the arts the new post-Symbolist mood was marked by a down-to-earth approach, rejecting what seemed the over-refinement of Symbolism, its elitism and cosmic pretensions.

In Russian post-Symbolist modernism the visual arts made the running during the 1910s and 1920s. In particular they exported their methods and terminology to literature (a notable example is the concept of *faktura*, "facture" or surface texture). Even the music of the leading composer of the new generation, Igor Stravinsky, had the spectacular visual impetus of Diaghilev's ballet in his greatest innovative scores of the period; the painter Nikolai Roerich also had a great and specific influence. The greatest figure in the cinema of the period, Sergey Eisenstein (1898-1948), was a visual artist by training and instinct.

A great, perhaps surprising, event in the art scene was the rediscovery of the Old Russian heritage of icon and fresco painting. Both had been quite literally obscured—by overpainting, dirt or darkened varnish—to the point that their very existence was in doubt. The cleaning of Rublyov's Old Testament Trinity icon in 1903 signaled the start of this rediscovery: 1913 saw a remarkable exhibition of restored ancient icons. The effect was overwhelming. Russian artists, however they might feel about the Orthodox Church, understood that they possessed a rich and sophisticated painterly tradition that owed nothing to the post-Renaissance West. It was an art of transcendental spiritual purpose, yet also one of everyday use, not produced for commerce or for the enjoyment of connoisseurs. Above all it was Russian, a heritage to be built upon.

Together with the impact of icons, there came to Russian art in the years around 1910 an interest in neo-primitivism, in a range of uncanonical forms (children's and peasants' art, woodcuts, shop signs), a movement only partially inspired by Gauguin, Matisse and other Western artists. The younger generation, notably David Burlyuk (1882–1967) and Mikhail Larionov (1881–1964), enjoyed not just the direct expressivity but the considerable public shock value of "crude" primitivism. Burlyuk became one of the founders of Russian Futurism; Larionov went on in the 1910s to develop an abstract manner that he called "Rayism" (*Luchizm*).

The history of Russian avant-garde artistic movements becomes complicated after 1910 as the "left" (that is, experimental) artistic forces subdivided further, depending on how extreme or how anti-Western the artists in question saw themselves to be. Leading new talents were those of Kazimir Malevich (1878–1935), Pavel Filonov (1883–1941) and Vladimir Tatlin (1885–1953). All three went through a complex evolution in which French Cubism played a part. These artists and some of their contemporaries, such as the Burlyuk brothers, can all with some justice be termed "Futurists," at least in the early 1910s. But in a Russian context the name is more generally applied to the avant-garde writers associated with the painters, the best-known group of which called themselves "Cubo-Futurists." The extent to which Italian Futurism influenced them remains contentious, but the Russians could fairly claim that their leading poets, notably the ascetic and eccentric Velimir Khlebnikov (1885–1922), had developed an independent post-Symbolist manner by 1908.

Literary Futurism as a movement was hatched (by his own account) when a young art student, Vladimir Mayakovsky (1893–1930), walked out in disgust from a concert of Rachmaninov's *Isle of the Dead* and met David Burlyuk who had done the same. The cross-arts contacts were strong: the other major poet of the same tendency, Boris Pasternak (1890–1960), was the son of a leading painter, who studied philosophy and then became a composer under Scriabin's influence—switching suddenly to poetry chiefly because of Mayakovsky's example. Both were major figures in 20th-century European terms.

Poetry also flourished elsewhere. A school of "peasant poets," a specifically Russian phenomenon, had as its senior figure Nikolai Klyuyev (1887–1937): his work is complex, modern, yet rooted deeply in the countryside and in the folksongs and hymns of Old Believer sectarians. His

Communism

For much of the 20th century people spoke of "the Communist countries," and throughout the world there are "Communist parties," but from the 1920s to the 1980s neither the Soviet Union nor its allies claimed to live under Communism. Communism is a future order of society, postulated in the theories of Karl Marx, wherein means of production will be under communal control, social distinctions will have been obliterated and each will receive according to needs. Marx was understandably imprecise not only about details of this desired condition, but about how it would be attained, though believing that laws of history predicated its development. He thought Russia an unpromising location for revolution, though Russian followers later interested him in the traditional peasant commune. Lenin's Bolsheviks, suddenly attaining power, had to make theory practicable. Far from "withering away," the state was fortified into Stalinist totalitarianism: perhaps a logical outcome, perhaps a hideous aberration.

Right Karl Marx (1818–1883), with Friedrich Engels, worked out the historical, economic and political theory that implied Lenin's revolutionary action: "Philosophers have only interpreted the world; the point however is to change it." Out of their ideas Lenin developed his theory of "dialectical materialism.

Below "Long Live Worldwide Red October," a poster of 1920. The left panel shows Bolshevik triumph over domestic enemies; the right reflects a naive expectation that Red Guards would lead a workers' revolution across Europe.

Above "Prolitarians of the world unite!" The famous slogan from the communist Manifesto (1848) appears, perhaps unexpectedly, on a plate made in Leningrad (St Petersburg) in 1921. After 1917 it emerged that a vast stock of blank unglazed porcelain was held at the Imperial Factory: leading artists (even abstract Suprematists) produced new designs, often propagandistic.

Left Lenin addresses the Second Comintern Congress, 1920. Marx founded the Communist International, an assembly of workers' delegates: it disintegrated under anarchist pressure. The Second International crumbled in 1914 with the general resurgence of wartime patriotism. It was a priority of Lenin's to vindicate Marx's internationalist vision with the Third International (1919)—for which Tatlin's projected "Tower" (p.165) was to be both monument and headquarters.

Left Leon Trotsky (1879–1940) was a crucial Bolshevik leader in the civil war (1918–20), who forged the disciplined Red Army out of the unorganized, officerless Red Guards. Afterwards, though a political heavyweight, his influence waned. His belief in "exporting revolution" clashed with Stalin's "socialism in one country." His Left Opposition failed by 1926. There followed exile, the founding of a rival "International" and eventually murder in Mexico at Stalin's behest.

Right The Bolsheviks, fired both by theory and by Lenin's personal hostility, aimed to sweep away religion as part of the old order. Many substitute secular rituals were introduced, as happened during the French Revolution; some attempted to instill a quasi-religious reverence towards the Soviet motherland. This "Soviet baptism" involves a pledge of loyalty to the regime.

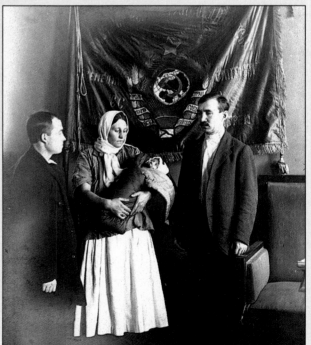

successor Sergey Yesenin (1895–1925), a village boy, became immensely popular for his delicate yet powerful lyric poems. He was notorious for an unruly life, including a stormy marriage to the great dancer Isadora Duncan, that ended in alcoholism and suicide.

The major non-Futurist group, however, were the cultivated and sophisticated poets dubbed "Acmeists." Their leader, Nikolai Gumilyov (1880–1921), shot for supposed involvement in an anti-Bolshevik plot, was a man of action, with a strong sense too of the ambiguities of history. His poem *Muzhik* memorably invokes, without naming him, the figure of Rasputin. Gumilyov's former wife, Anna Akhmatova (1889–1967), was supreme as a poet of love. The third great Acmeist, Osip Mandelshtam (1891–1939), was a difficult and subtle literary craftsman. His work and the hard circumstances of his life are evoked in two justly famous memoirs by his widow Nadezhda.

Prose and drama marked time somewhat after 1900. A founder poet of Symbolism, D. Merezhkovsky (1865–1941), turned to novels on historical themes, and won a European reputation. There were worthwhile storywriters, particularly Alexander Kuprin (1870–1938), Aleksey Remizov (1877–1957) and Ivan Bunin (1870–1953), the first Russian literary Nobel Prize winner (1933). The standard-bearer of the Russian novel was Maxim Gorky (1868–1936), a powerful, uneven writer of humble upbringing, imbued with an ambiguous

Far left The leading early Soviet movie-maker, Sergey Eisenstein (1898–1948) directing the shooting of *The Old and the New* (1926). Eisenstein left few completed masterpieces; his apparently spontaneous realism is the result of stylization and meticulously controlled directing.

Below Natalya Goncharova's scenery for Rimsky-Korsakov's last opera, *The Golden Cockerel*, based on a tale by Pushkin. Goncharova (1881–1962) was perhaps the most brilliant of the half-dozen major women artists in early 20th-century Russia.

sense of the Russian people's potential for both goodness and anarchic villainy. His revolutionary novel *The Mother* (1907) became a Soviet classic. His autobiographical trilogy (1913–23) was made into three of the most memorable early Soviet movies by Mark Donskoy. In music too there was something of a pause until two composers of world stature, Igor Stravinsky (1882–1971) and Sergey Prokofiev (1891–1953) burst precociously upon the scene.

World War I did not, as in some Western European countries, bring Russian artistic innovation to a halt, though some leading figures were called up for military service. These years saw the beginnings of a "proletarian movement" in literature, with A. Gastev's strange prose poems, exalting the toiling masses, published in 1917. The revolution of that year neither disconcerted nor surprised the Futurists; several figures from the Symbolist generation emigrated (but not Blok or Bely). Stravinsky was abroad during the war, and stayed; Prokofiev emigrated but returned in the 1930s; both Kandinsky and Chagall left in the 1920s. Other major artists to emigrate were Larionov and Natalya Goncharova.

The 1920s were a period of complexity and excitement in Soviet cultural life: the promise of a new order attracted many who were not necessarily Bolsheviks. The broad-ranging Constructivist movement partly took its cue from Tatlin's "culture of materials" (though Tatlin himself did not

like Constructivism), partly from Malevich's geometricity: it put its stylistic stamp on architecture, on stage, book and poster design, on objects of everyday use (including clothes), on photography (with the development of photomontage) and on sculpture. Constructivist architecture was of particular interest for its integrated plans in which factories, housing, clubs, shops, schools and transport were designed as a whole. Other tendencies were often strongly opposed to Constructivism's utilitarian aims: the spiritual concept of art realized in Malevich's Suprematism and the "Makovets" group; Filonov's "Analytic Art," which attracted many pupils in the late 1920s; the Realists; younger "Proletarian" groups. The hub of activity was the new artistic organization started in Moscow in 1920 under the acronym *Inkhuk*: there were other newly established or reorganized art schools in Petrograd and in Vitebsk, where the dominating spirit was L. (El) Lisitsky (1890–1941). There was considerable contact with the West, notably with the German *Bauhaus*.

Prose revived in the 1920s. One of the greatest 20th-century masters of the short story was Isaak Babel (1894–1941) who made his mark with the cycle known in English as *Red Cavalry* (1926); Babel's uncompromising objectivity in the face of the brutalities of war caused an uproar. Less known, but very subtle and strange, are the short stories of Andrey Platonov (1899–1951), the finest authentically proletarian writer to emerge. Yevgeniy Zamyatin (1884–1937), a naval engineer and committed revolutionary, had written his masterpiece, the anti-utopian fantasy *We*, by 1920. When late in the decade it appeared in the West, it was furiously denounced as anti-Soviet satire: Zamyatin, boldly appealing to Stalin, was able to emigrate. *We* clearly influenced George Orwell's *1984*. Zamyatin was earlier an organizer of the uncommitted group of excellent writers fancifully named the "Serapion Brotherhood." An important aspect of the literary scene was the development of a modern critical theory in the hands of the so-called Formalists, whose liveliest spirit was Viktor Shklovsky (1893–1985).

The Soviet government (with bigger worries to contend with) did not commit itself to any faction for over a decade. Censorship was mild, but at the end of the 1920s it became clear that the balance of approval was tilting against "left art" and towards the "proletarians" (RAPP). Experimentalism was still not dead: a new wave of Soviet-educated writers, notably the poet Nikolai Zabolotsky (1903–58), formed the witty and anarchic modernist circle *OBERIU* in Leningrad in 1928. Theater too was full of innovation, notably under the inspiration of Meyerhold. The first important Soviet playwright to emerge was a doctor turned writer Mikhail Bulgakov (1891–1940). His evenhanded drama of the civil war, *Days of the Turbins* (1926), somewhat surprisingly attracted Stalin (who saw it some 20 times), thus saving Bulgakov—whose sympathies were far from revolutionary—from a possibly unpleasant fate. The art form most encouraged by the Soviet government (because of Lenin's enthusiasm) was film: early Soviet directors, notably Sergey Eisenstein, developed the powerful "montage" techniques that influenced cinema throughout the world.

Left Sergey Rachmaninov (1873–1943) in a photograph of 1908. Almost all his major compositions predate the Revolution, after which he found fame in emigration as a virtuoso pianist.

Below As great a pioneer of modernism as Malevich or Tatlin, yet even less known, P. Filonov (1883–1941) lived in Leningrad as an ascetic visionary and teacher. In a series of paintings between about 1915 and 1920 he developed his principle of "universal flowering," discarding normal composition in the attempt to represent every atom of natural processes through minute brushstrokes.

Diaghilev and Stravinsky

Sergey Diaghilev (1872–1929) and Igor Stravinsky (1882–1971) were both forceful creative personalities who, had they never met, would each still have left an important legacy. Their fortuitous collaboration from 1909 however resulted in several hugely famous and innovative works.

Diaghilev irrupted dynamically into the Petersburg World of Art circle in the 1890s; he edited their journal, and arranged a string of exhibitions. In 1906 he organized a Russian art exhibition in Paris, and in succeeding seasons brought there Russian music (the Five), opera (*Boris Godunov*) and ballet. During his last 20 years, ballet became his definitive contribution: not only did he have great dancers but he paid the most stringent attention to the dramatic integration of decor and music. Caught by war and revolution, he and his company remained in the West. His genius was not of personal creativity, but of organization and appreciation. His questing temperament led him to a new generation of composers (Prokofiev, Poulenc) and artists (Larionov, Goncharova, Pevsner).

Stravinsky, a pupil of Rimsky-Korsakov, was professionalized as a composer by Diaghilev's commissions and enthusiasm. Stranded moneyless in Switzerland in 1914, he devised a contemporary version of Russian popular mobile entertainment (*Les Noces, The Soldier's Tale*). After the war he renewed collaboration with Diaghilev (*Pulcinella*), but the short Pushkinian opera *Mavra* (1922) was his last specifically Russian work. He lived long enough to revisit the USSR, to ecstatic acclaim, just before his death.

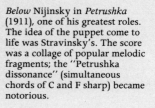

Below Nijinsky in *Petrushka* (1911), one of his greatest roles. The idea of the puppet come to life was Stravinsky's. The score was a collage of popular melodic fragments; the "Petrushka dissonance" (simultaneous chords of C and F sharp) became notorious.

Left Portrait of Sergey Diaghilev with his nanny (1903) by Leon (Lev) Bakst. Bakst (1866–1924), nowadays well known throughout the world for stage and costume designs, was, like several World of Art painters, initially an accomplished portraitist: he captures Diaghilev on canvas as half-barbarian, half-dandy. Part of World of Art's mission was to reinstate, within a "modernist" context, the artistic discipline and technique which had been somewhat dissipated in the heyday of the Wanderers.

Left Diaghilev and Stravinsky. No greater physical contrast could be imagined than between the stocky, dominating Diaghilev and the mercurial shrimp-like Stravinsky. Both escaped into art from tedious legal studies, and were full of a self-assured energy that bypassed several of their talented but languid colleagues.

Above The ugly, small, dynamic Stravinsky, with animated egglike face, disproportionate hands and natural aristocratism, was a gift for artists, and was sketched by both Picasso and Jean Cocteau. The latter shows him watching while the phenomenal dancer Nijinsky makes up for *Carnival*.

Below Costume sketches by Benois for the *Rite of Spring*. This ballet staged in Paris on 29 May 1913 marked the climax of Stravinsky's and Diaghilev's collaboration. This was the composer's most daring score, a landmark in modern music. Scraps of unrelated melody, often little more than rhythmic patterns, but including a Lithuanian folktune in an incredibly high bassoon register, weave in and out. The gruesome plot, of ritual and sacrifice in pagan Rus (seen *below* in a Bolshoy company production), was largely cooked up by the well-read artist N. Roerich (Rerikh, 1874–1947). Unfortunately Nijinsky as choreographer could not cope with the musical complexities.

Below Costume design by Bakst for *Firebird* (1910). With a mastery of line not inferior to (and probably influenced by) Beardsley, Bakst turned utilitarian theatrical design into high, if jovial, art: this costume sketch is an exquisite small study in gouache and gold paint. He and other World of Art painters were masters of eclectic stylization, with a liking, in Bakst's case, for oriental motifs. Golovin, Bakst's collaborator on *Firebird*, produced with Vrubel a remarkable narrative ceramic frieze that still adorns the Moscow Metropole Hotel.

The production of *Firebird* in Paris in June 1910 marked the emergence of Stravinsky as a major composer and of the Diaghilev Ballets Russes in its true originality. The score—intensely Russian, as befitted a folk tale, but also thoroughly modern, already leaving Borodin and Rimsky-Korsakov well behind—was hammered out over the preceding winter in close collaboration with the designers and with Diaghilev's greatest choreographer, Mikhail Fokine.

Two Paths to Modern Art: Malevich and Tatlin

Russian artists played a considerable part in the history of the European modern movement in the early 20th century. Vasiliy Kandinsky (1866–1944), working in Munich, simplified the forms of his apocalyptic late-Symbolist paintings to the point of abstraction before 1910, and was probably the first to do so. Several other Russians were almost as radical, but possibly the strangest and most spectacular painter of all was Kazimir Malevich (1878–1935). From folksy art-nouveau decorativeness he passed in rapid succession through coarse primitivism, Cubism and Futurism to what he called "alogism," a manner anticipating the Surrealists. In 1915 he developed a purely abstract, geometrical manner which he called "Suprematism." By about 1920 he was engrossed in constructing idealized "architectonic" models; before his death he returned to figurative painting with strong Suprematist overtones.

Vladimir Tatlin (1885–1953), Malevich's colleague and rival, developed under futurist and cubist influence; after visiting Picasso (1914) he launched into a series of abstract sculptural constructions of metal, wood and "found objects," developing his "culture of materials."

Above Malevich: *Girl with Rake*, 1930s. Malevich returned to figurative, but not anecdotal mode in the 1920s and 1930s. Peasant toil is a frequent theme. Suprematism has left its mark in the formal simplification of these works and in the frequent compositional element of the cross. Most characteristic is the uncompromising dualistic division of the human face and figure into light and dark halves.

Right Malevich: *The Knife-Grinder*, 1912. This dazzling work is doubtless the culmination of Malevich's early development, during which he underwent the very disparate influences of Matissean primitivism, Russian icons, Cubism and Futurism. Cubist dissection of the object into "metallic" segments (as with Léger) combines here with Futurist dynamism. But there is no cult of modernity or of the machine—as so often, Malevich is concerned with the age-old rhythms of peasant life. The painting's geometricity and clear patches of color look forward to Suprematism.

Below Malevich: *Suprematist Composition*, 1916. At the Zero-Ten exhibition of 1915 Malevich revealed his Suprematist works: free-floating geometric forms in white, black and unmodulated primary hues. High in a corner (the location for an icon) he hung a simple black square, the "zero of form" through which the new art had to pass.

Right Tatlin: *The Sailor*,
1911–12. This is a probable
self-portrait: Tatlin earned his
living at sea till nearly 30. The
sailing ship was perhaps his
ideal work of art (beautiful and
functional, dynamic, curvilinear,
in harmony with natural forces).
His paintings and drawings are
bold, simple, with iconic,
primitivistic and subsequently
cubist elements. At Zero-Ten he
broke violently with Malevich;
while Malevich's Suprematism
was ''dematerialized,'' Tatlin
was fascinated by the materiality
of objects, and exhibited
abstract three-dimensional reliefs
exploring the potentialities of
wood and metal.

Left Tatlin's project for the
monument to the Third
International (1919). It was to be
a gigantic double skew spiral,
open-ended (and angled on the
Pole Star) like a telescope,
supposedly bestriding the Neva.

Below Malevich: *An Englishman
in Moscow*, 1914. Characteristic
of Malevich in his ''urban''
period (c. 1913–14), this painting
seems an ''alogistic'' assemblage
of disparate objects, but a
private, suprarational order is at
work. The main lettering,
reassembled, reads ''PARTIAL
ECLIPSE.''

Religion in Russia and the Soviet Union

Russian religious culture is rooted in Eastern Orthodox Christianity, to which Russia converted in 988/9. The country's medieval culture was suffused with a unified Orthodoxy until the great schism of the 17th century. Since then, Russian Orthodoxy has followed two main currents, one of institutional church worship and the other of sectarian piety. But among peasants *dvoyeveriye*—coexistence of Christian observance with elements of pre-Christian belief system—never fully disappeared. After 1917 religion was repressed and persecuted in all its forms, from Orthodoxy and Catholicism to Judaism and Islam.

Among Christians, the most active denominations are the evangelical, especially Baptists and Pentecostals. The Orthodox Church preserves its millennial tradition, centered on the spiritual communality of liturgical worship and cultivation of reflective introspection. Its influence is strong throughout Russian culture, from medieval arts to the writings of Dostoyevsky and Tolstoy. In ecclesiastical art Orthodoxy has concentrated on icons and unaccompanied choral music, whose transcendent expressiveness is integral to Russian worship.

Left Archbishop Pitirim, who subsequently became a leading Orthodox Church figure: editor of the Journal of the Moscow Patriachure and a People's Deputy (1987).

Above The intense antireligious fervor cultivated by the Communist state during the 1920s is encapsulated by this cartoon entitled "The Holy Ghost descends upon the Apostles." Framed as an icon, it mocks the major faiths in the Soviet Union by depicting their spiritual leaders as grotesque and avaricious. The Holy Ghost, depicted as a flying purse under a capitalist top hat, showers coins upon a scrabbling mullah, Orthodox priest, Catholic priest and rabbi. Each is caricatured according to stereotypes used to stir loathing and hatred.

Right The Torah being read in one of the few synagogues allowed to function during the Soviet era. Jewish settlement was encouraged in Belarus and Ukraine under the late-medieval Polish-Lithuanian state, and large communities grew up. In imperial Russia Jews were restricted to specific areas of settlement, where they enjoyed relative religious freedom. In the Soviet Union, settlement restrictions were lifted, but Jewish worship and culture were repressed and teaching of the Hebrew language and religion was forbidden. Despite this, the Jewish tradition endured and revived somewhat during the 1970s and 1980s.

Below Buddhism was the least significant world faith in Russia and the Soviet Union, but under Communism it suffered persecution along with the rest. Buddhists in the Russian empire existed along the southern edge of eastern Siberia, adjoining Outer Mongolia. Their nearest holy city was Urga, with its great monastery and lamas, whose stature north of China was similar to that of the Tibetan lamas to the south. Urga was destroyed after the Communists seized power in Mongolia in the late 1920s. Buddhism survives among the Turkic and Mongol populations of Soviet Siberia, particularly Buryats.

Bottom Friday prayer in the Khajezud Murad mosque in Samarqand. Most of the worshipers are in traditional dress, but one man in the front row is in modern garb. In the post-Soviet era Islam remains very strong in Central Asia and in the eastern Caucasus. Communist attempts to suppress it were much less effective than in the case of other faiths. Central Asian Islam derives from the medieval culture of Transoxanian cities such as Samarqand, Bukhoro and Khiva. Recently Shiite influence has grown among Muslim groups, leading to a major revival of Islamic culture.

167

The Russian Orthodox Church

The Russian Orthodox Church was the main target of a militant atheist drive launched by the Communist state after the revolution and sustained during the 1920s and 1930s. By 1921 over half of Russia's monasteries were closed, countless churches destroyed or desecrated and converted to secular use, and nearly 30 bishops and over 1000 priests arrested or executed.

During World War II Stalin found it expedient to allow a revival of the church, as part of his plan to rekindle nationalist patriotism. This policy permitted the church to make a partial recovery from virtual annihilation, to expand the numbers of priests and to elect a patriarch. Repressions returned under Khrushchev, who was determined to eradicate the church while he loosened restrictions on secular culture. During the 1970s government hostility lessened, although restrictions on worship and proselytizing were left essentially unchanged until the mid-1980s. Simultaneously, the government allowed a new degree of care for religious art as a national heritage. Many churches were architecturally restored, but most were earmarked as historical monuments rather than returned as places of worship.

With the reforms of the late 1980s and the subsequent collapse of the Soviet regime, the Orthodox Church has once again become a powerful and cohesive force in Russian society, with many closed churches now being reopened to worship.

Left A work detail completes the demolition of a church during the 1920s, breaking up its frescoed vaulting. The power drill is operated by a Red Guard veteran of the civil war, wearing a cavalry cap of the period. Demolition of this kind was widespread, culminating with Moscow's Cathedral of Christ the Savior, which in the 1990s was rebuilt.

Bottom left Churches not destroyed were usually converted to secular uses, as social clubs, movie theaters and warehouses. This church is being converted into a grain store. A ladder and rough scaffolding to the right show that the building's ecclesiastical interior is being torn out.

Below Restoration of churches as works of art became widespread in the 1960s. Such work concentrated on exteriors, since most interiors were fully gutted. In a few cases, where interiors retained significant frescoes and mosaics, internal restoration was undertaken. This picture shows a rare case of restoration in the church of the Danilov Monastery in Moscow, returned to the Moscow patriarchate by the Soviet regime in 1983 to become the headquarters of the Russian Orthodox Church.

Below The vitality of contemporary Russian Orthodoxy is illustrated by large gatherings of the faithful for special services, such as this outdoor consecration of new priests. A consecrated priest stands on a rug before the officiating prelate. The clerics holding dome-like hats are bishops; those holding black hats are parish priests. Behind the former stand bareheaded monks in black; behind the latter veiled nuns in black habits. The surrounding congregation shows a wide range of age and social background. The photograph was probably taken from a church belfry.

Left Russian monasticism spanned cenobitic and anchoritic rules as well as the kenotic tradition, which stresses mutual humility and charity in relations within the community. Manual labor was important for all, less for material sustenance than as an aid to introspection and humility. Nunneries existed since the early Middle Ages and were numerous before the revolution, but suffered greatly during subsequent persecutions. These nuns are harvesting with traditional long scythes.

Above The choir of the great Pskov-Pechery Monastery, led by its choirmaster, sings in a service celebrating the community's 500th anniversary. The Pskov-Pechery Monastery, located west of Pskov and near the Estonian border, is a major center of monastic culture in Russia today. *Pechery* is old Russian for "caves," suggesting that the original community settled in local caves. The first and most revered monastery of Russia, the Kiev-Pechery, is known to have started in hill caves in Kiev.

The Art of Propaganda

Propaganda was a major priority for the Communist state from its inception till near its end. Organized as a state monopoly activity, propaganda was used to shape and direct mass consciousness in accordance with Communist objectives. Many genres of propaganda were developed as instruments of political indoctrination, closely linked to the expansion of mass education and literacy. The main objectives of Soviet propaganda were the glorification of revolutionary history, excitation of a socialist work ethic and vilification of all non-Communist forces and values.

The main genres of Soviet propaganda were always visual, favoring large-scale sculpture, posters and murals intended for mass viewing and accompanied by inspirational slogans. The established canon was modified and developed over time, but its basic themes remained constant. The most immediate, didactic one called for harder work and greater productivity. The more subliminal, inspirational one cultivated a cycle of myths about the early Bolshevik founders of the Communist state. The cult of Lenin was the single dominating heroic myth in Soviet propaganda. It included quasi-religious adoration of his embalmed corpse in a mausoleum designed for reverential viewing. A "totalitarian" architecture, similar to that developed under Hitler in Germany and Mussolini in Italy, characterized the Stalinist 1930s and 1940s.

Left An imperial poster, dating from World War I, announces the sale of war bonds. The caption reads, "If you are not repelling the enemy with your body, then buy war bonds at 5% interest." Early Soviet propaganda owed something to the simpler and less artistic propaganda of imperial Russia; both display a similar xenophobia and fanaticism. The obsessed faces of Russian soldiers going into attack anticipate similar images on Soviet propaganda posters during World War II. The level of artistry is incomparably inferior to Soviet posters, evidence of a low appreciation of propaganda's potential for influencing public sentiment.

Above "Away with muddlers and wreckers in the industrial supply sector." This early Soviet poster was part of a constant propaganda campaign against bureaucratic interference, either as the real or the imagined culprit responsible for industrial and consumer shortages. An obese bureaucrat, clutching a huge official file, guards supplies of fruit and vegetables for speculators, who are carrying off for personal gain crates of goods intended for the state supply system. A huge spade, guided by a worker's boot, is poised ready to uproot the bureaucrat. Posters like this were intended for display in public places and, especially, factories and warehouses.

Right "Let us meet fully the grain collection plan in specified time!" The positive call for industrious agricultural work which dominates this poster is set in the context of the collectivization of the early 1930s. The colossal toiler emptying a full sack is backed by a field crew of harvesters bringing in more grain for threshing.

Below Communist propaganda often adapted Russian folk art to immediate political themes, as in this civil war Bolshevik recruiting poster. The conventions of peasant lacquer decoration are used to show a charge of the Red Cavalry against the background of a burning town.

Far right top An appeal for increased metal production, this poster depicts a massive ironworks, with the slogan "More metal!" repeated three times in receding formation to convey the echoing of the call through the metal labyrinth of the plant. The poster was printed in 40 000 copies.

Far right center "Where's my money? What's for my family?" Soviet propaganda fought a never-ending campaign against alcoholism. The drunkard fumbles for money, having already spent on drink everything intended for his family. The huge bottle symbolizes the scale of the problem.

Bottom Porcelain commemorative plates were very popular propaganda items in the Soviet Union during the 1920s. The rim of this one is inscribed "Long live Soviet rule." The central motif combines the conventional hammer and sickle emblem with pliers, all set against a background of factories.

ПОПРЕЖНЕМУ ЗВУЧИТ НАШ РЕВОЛЮЦИОННЫЙ НАБАТ:
-РАБОЧИЕ, КРЕСТЬЯНЕ, ТРУДЯЩИЕСЯ
К НОВЫМ БИТВАМ И НОВЫМ
ПОБЕДАМ !

ПРОТИВ БЕЛОЙ КОННИЦЫ—ВЫДВИНЕМ КРАСНУЮ. СПЕШИТЕ В РЯДЫ КРАСНОЙ КОННИЦЫ!

ЗНАНИЕ
РАЗОРВЕТ ЦЕПИ РАБСТВА·

Left "Knowledge will break the chains of slavery." Encouragement of learning, according to communist precepts, was a vital theme in early Soviet propaganda. In this poster of 1920, an allegorical hand presses a stack of books, symbolizing learning, upon a restrictive chain, hung between two old-fashioned factories, stretching it to breaking point.

FROM STALIN TO YELTSIN

Collectivization, famine and terror

The collectivization program was launched in 1930. During the two preceding years the peasantry was deliberately weakened by increased taxation and direct levies. The program was announced as a campaign to exterminate the "rich" peasants (*kulaks*), who were at best marginally less poor than the rest but normally influential in the community. The term *kulak* extended to women, children and infants. These peasants were expropriated and forbidden to join collective farms, thus being instantly reduced to abject poverty. They were then deported to concentration camps in outlying parts of Russia. The conditions of transport ensured that many starved on the way. Simultaneously, expropriation was extended to all pea-

sants, as a precondition for enforced mass reorganization into collective farms. Even with the *kulaks* gone, many peasants resisted collectivization, both actively and passively, slaughtering their livestock rather than surrender it to collectives. Many simply fled their homes and went wandering.

The government adopted a new strategy, introducing a system of internal passports to fix the peasants to their place of residence and then deliberately starving them into submission. The Terror-Famine, run as a well-organized military campaign, began with total expropriation of all foodstuffs within peasant regions, which were then shut off from any external supplies. The campaign concentrated most strongly in the rich southern

Industrialization, urbanization and collectivization.
After the resource drain of World War I and the civil war, followed by famine in the early 1920s, the economy was stabilized under NEP. When NEP was ended (1928), Stalin embarked on the socio-economic transformation of the country under the first Five-Year Plan. A vast belt of farmland from the western border right across to south of the Urals was devoted to schemes of collectivization. New coalfields were exploited to fire new iron- and steelworks and electricity-generating stations. These in turn supplied the engineering sector, which provided for the farming,

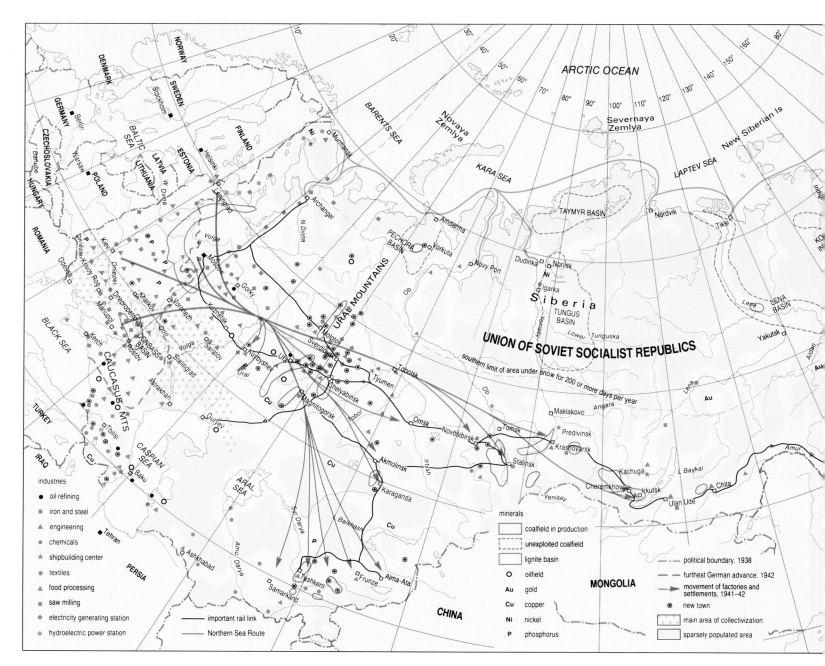

farmland region of European Russia. The result was a massive and unprecedented famine, deliberately sustained from 1930 to 1932. The areas most affected were the Volga, Don and Kuban regions of Russia proper, and also Ukraine, where the famine was used to exterminate Ukrainian nationalism as well as the traditional peasantry.

The human cost of collectivization and the Terror-Famine was immense. Recent estimates put the "excess" deaths of the period 1926–39 at 3·5 million, though some specialists go much higher. As a result numerous villages, towns and entire regions were left uninhabited. The economic cost was also enormous. Agricultural production collapsed both in terms of crops and livestock, cultivation contracted and food shortages intensified nationally. Despite this, the Communists were triumphant: the peasantry were subjugated, and rural desolation provided ideal building ground for new collective farms.

Systematic terror during the 1930s was applied with equally devastating effect in the realm of politics and government. The successive purges that culminated in the Great Terror of 1936–38 disrupted the entire fabric of Soviet society and the Communist Party itself. The first purge trials occurred in the autumn of 1930. Government officials, technicians and economists were accused of counterrevolutionary activity in league with nonexistent subversive organizations. The accused confessed to improbably fabricated charges and were executed. The purpose of these early trials was to create scapegoats for the inherent failures in the industrial development provisions of the First Five-Year Plan.

The major purges began in 1934 and reached their peak in 1936–38. The assassination in 1934 of Kirov, a prominent Politburo member, signaled the beginning of the Great Terror; the murder was probably instigated by Stalin, fearful of Kirov's popularity. There followed a wave of arrests in the upper levels of the party, including Kamenev and Zinovyev, two other Politburo members. They were brought to court in 1936, in the first of the great show trials. They were accused of sabotage and state treachery, on the basis of a fabricated charge of international conspiracy, supposedly designed to topple the Communist government and replace it with a semicapitalist order; the conspirators were allegedly supported by the German government and led from exile by Trotsky. Kamenev and Zinovyev were condemned on this charge and executed. Purges then spread through all levels of the government and party, from the Kremlin to the most provincial level. These always involved fabricated accusations of sabotage and treacherous conspiracy, arrest and interrogation under torture and sentences of either execution or long-term penal labor—with or without a staged trial. This mass terror was crowned with two further great show trials of leading Communists: of Pyatakov and Radek in 1937 and of Rykov and Bukharin in 1938. Another distinguished victim was Tukhachevsky, appointed one of the first five marshals of the Soviet Union in 1935 and shot three years later on charges of leading a military conspiracy. The purges cut a swathe through the upper ranks of the Red Army and the professions, ranging from industrial managers to academics, and

indeed every part of society.

Statistics originally prepared for Khrushchev and only recently published record that 3·75 million people were sentenced for counter-revolutionary crimes in 1930–53, of whom nearly 800,000 were shot; but these figures cannot be verified. Half the membership of the Communist Party, about 1·2 million individuals, were purged, and a large number of these died in the camps. With the fall of the police-chief Yezhov in the summer of 1938 the terror eased somewhat.

The dynamics and purpose of the Great Terror derived from Lenin's use of extensive political terror against all non-Communist opponents: the party had extended this in repeated internal purges during the 1920s. In this sense, the Great Terror and its purges were a logical extension of and sophisticated improvement on Leninist precedent. The party had deliberately cultivated political paranoia concerning domestic and foreign enemies, so public opinion accepted the fabricated charges of sabotage and conspiracy and willingly joined in wild denunciations rather than in protesting against the excesses. Stalin's own purpose in launching the Great Terror was to rid the Communist order of all potential opposition to his sole control of it. Mass destruction of the hostile peasantry and massive bloodletting in the infrastructure were means to ideologically correct state building. But whatever further extremes of state building Stalin may have envisaged, they were shelved with the advent of World War II.

Stalin and World War II

The Soviet prelude to World War II did not presage what followed. Stalin's foreign policy of the late 1930s centered on increasingly close relations with Nazi Germany, culminating in the Nazi-Soviet Pact of 1939. This was effectively an alliance, formulated as an agreement of nonaggression and neutrality, and linked with a trade treaty plus extensive exchange of raw materials and armaments. The pact also provided for the two powers to carve up Eastern Europe between them. Germany was thus free to overrun western Poland, while the Soviet Union simultaneously took control of eastern Poland and the Baltic states. Finland proved a failure for the Soviet Union. The tiny country fought the much larger Red Army to a virtual standstill during the Winter War of 1939–40, and the Soviets had to settle for limited territorial gains by way of a treaty. The Nazi-Soviet rapport was broken only by Hitler's personal decision to invade Russia.

The German invasion began on 22 June 1941. The attack was launched secretly, catching the Red Army unprepared; what resistance it could offer proved woefully inadequate. The Germans' advance was on a massive scale, and by November their troops had captured the entire Ukraine and were threatening Moscow and Leningrad. Only desperate rearguard action by the Red Army and the early onset of a severe winter checked the German steamroller. Three factors however ensured that the Germans would not regain full momentum. The first was the German policy towards conquered populations. The Russian and Ukrainian populations of occupied areas mostly greeted the Germans as liberators from Communist

food-processing and textile industries. New rail links were made, mainly running west–east, while the long south–north rivers could carry the exchange of raw materials and finished products between the mineral-rich Arctic and the newly developed manufacturing regions. The threat from Hitler in the early 1940s forced the pace of economic growth east of the Volga. Hundreds of factories and associated new towns were moved from western Russia to the Urals, central Asia and parts of Siberia, though most of Siberia remains sparsely inhabited.

173

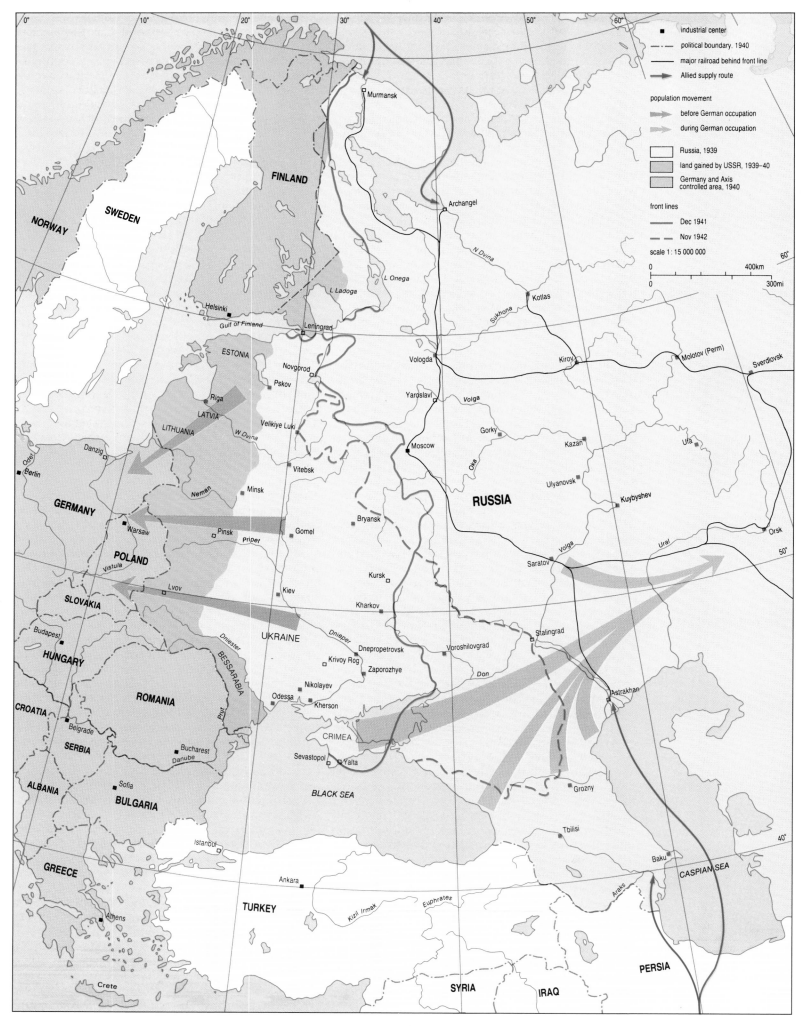

industrial center
political boundary, 1940
major railroad behind front line
Allied supply route

population movement
before German occupation
during German occupation

Russia, 1939
land gained by USSR, 1939–40
Germany and Axis controlled area, 1940

front lines
Dec 1941
Nov 1942

scale 1 : 15 000 000

0   400km
0   300mi

NORWAY

SWEDEN

FINLAND

Murmansk

Archangel

N Dvina

L Onega

Sukhona

Kotlas

L Ladoga

Helsinki

Gulf of Finland

Leningrad

Vologda

Kirov

Molotov (Perm)

Sverdlovsk

ESTONIA

Novgorod

Pskov

Yaroslavl

Riga

LATVIA

Volga

Gorky

Kazan

Ufa

LITHUANIA

W Dvina

Velikiye Luki

Moscow

Oka

Ulyanovsk

Danzig

Odel
Berlin

Neman

Minsk

RUSSIA

Kuybyshev

GERMANY

Warsaw

Pinsk

Pripet

Gomel

Bryansk

Volga

Orsk

POLAND

Vistula

Lvov

Kiev

Kursk

Saratov

Ural

SLOVAKIA

Kharkov

Stalingrad

Budapest

Dnieper

HUNGARY

Dniester

UKRAINE

Dnepropetrovsk

Voroshilovgrad

BESSARABIA

Krivoy Rog

Zaporozhye

Don

Astrakhan

CROATIA

ROMANIA

Nikolayev

Belgrade

Prut

Odessa

Kherson

SERBIA

Bucharest

Danube

CRIMEA

Grozny

ALBANIA

Sofia

Sevastopol

Yalta

BULGARIA

Tbilisi

Istanbul

BLACK SEA

Baku

CASPIAN SEA

GREECE

Ankara

Kizil Irmak

Euphrates

Araks

Athens

TURKEY

PERSIA

Crete

SYRIA

IRAQ

rule. Nazi policy, however, classified all Slavs as subhuman, and the local population was subjected to atrocities and forced labor conscription little different from that meted out by the Communists. Popular sentiment, in desperation, shifted back to its own kind and national patriotism was rekindled. The second factor was Allied lend-lease, which gave the Soviets massive supplies of military technology and munitions which the Red Army lacked and which the Soviet war industry could not at first manufacture sufficiently. This meant that the Red Army was fully resupplied soon after the initial debacle and the Soviet war industry given breathing space to gear up to full production. The third factor was Stalin's own leadership. He had not at all expected the German attack, and suffered a short nervous collapse when it happened. Recovering quickly, he assumed the posts of commander-in-chief and head of the war effort. In these roles, he proved a most able wartime leader, choosing good subordinates and delegating effectively, analyzing situations astutely and making decisions which subsequent events mostly proved right.

Stalin sensed that old-fashioned nationalistic patriotism, as opposed to Communist principles, would inspire the Russian people to a united defense of their homeland. Many traditional Russian institutions, previously suppressed, were now reintroduced; the Russian Orthodox Church, heavily repressed since the revolution, was permitted a partial revival. Stalin astutely dubbed the war as "the Second Great Fatherland War" (rather than World War II), invoking the precedent of Russia's resistance to the Napoleonic invasion of 1812. The result was a massive wave of popular patriotism.

The Soviet Union was revived and rearmed, presenting the Germans with severe opposition in the east at the same time as the Allies were registering their first successes in the west. The need to fight a multifront war sapped German capacity in Russia, which was also handicapped by Hitler's inept decisions. The farthest German thrust reached Stalingrad on the Volga in mid-1942, with disastrous consequences. Thereafter the German armies were in steady, if slow, retreat before the Red Army, whose capture of Berlin in May 1945 brought the war to a close. Its cost to the Soviet Union was huge. About seven million Russians were killed in battle, while the total mortality may have reached 20 million. Industrial and agricultural destruction was also catastrophic. In two important respects, however, the benefits of victory outweighed the costs.

First, the Soviet Union acquired a really modern industrial base in the form of German industry seized as assets and war reparations. A great many German industrial plants, especially in Silesia, were dismantled and shipped to Russia for reassembly. A large number of German engineers, technicians and industrial managers were taken as prisoners to Russia to man the booty industry. Thus, the destruction of war cleared out much of the Soviet Union's ineffective industry, while the spoils of war gave substantial, piecemeal modernization.

Second, the Soviet Union succeeded in extending its control over the countries of Eastern and Central Europe. The Tehran and Yalta conferences agreed to an effective partition of Europe between the Allies, with the Soviets given administrative control over the eastern parts, on the understanding that they would supervise free elections allowing each country to determine its destiny. In fact, the Soviets used local Communist parties either to manipulate elections or to seize power when election results went against them. By 1948 almost all Eastern Europe (except Greece and Finland) was under Communist governments loyal to Moscow, and the Soviet Union had extended its domain over half of Europe. World War II thus left the Soviet Union more powerful than before, with a better industrial base, and with Stalin enjoying an unprecedented popularity and total power.

Immediately the war ended, Stalin reimposed upon the Soviet Union a rule as rigid and coercive as any during the 1930s, but with major new innovations geared to the conditions of the time. Under the repatriation policy agreed by the Allies, Soviet prisoners of war and civilian forced labor held in Germany were all repatriated, all declared traitors and mostly shipped directly to distant concentration camps. Large numbers of Russians and Ukrainians, who had either fought against the Communists during the war or had resided as émigrés in Europe since the revolution, were forcibly repatriated by the Americans and British into Soviet hands. Many of these were either executed or incarcerated in concentration camps. Well over two million people were repatriated in this way. For Stalin, this was a great security coup, cauterizing the nation of Western impressions and exterminating many representatives of the non-Communist Russian tradition surviving in the emigration.

Another concern was to check the modest measure of initiative and independence which the Russians, and especially the educated elite, had developed in wartime conditions. To this end, Stalin authorized a new campaign of purges, placing this under the direction of Andrey Zhdanov. Launched in 1946, these purges targeted the world of the arts, the theater, academics and the creative professions. The aim was to root out "cosmopolitanism," seen as any hint of disposition towards contemporary European culture. Zhdanov died in 1948, but the campaign continued, extending deeper into academe to include such specialized disciplines as linguistics, archaeology and theoretical natural sciences. Simultaneously, Stalin built on the rekindled Russian patriotism to create a fabricated history of scientific achievement that would fire nationalist sentiment into chauvinistic pride. The fabricated history presented Russia as a nation of great inventors during the 18th and 19th centuries, whose discoveries predated Western European ones; only the backwardness of pre-revolutionary Russia prevented exploitation of those inventions. The conclusion was that the Russians were brilliant enough to do without Western Europe, and under Communist leadership their brilliance would be fully realized.

The nationalistic bunker mentality was well suited to the expanding membership of the Communist Party. The party, decimated by the purges of the 1930s, had expanded its intake during the war in order to broaden its base of support.

World War II.
In June 1941 Hitler reneged on the Nazi-Soviet Pact of 1939 and invaded Russia. The Red Army, still recovering from Stalin's purges and from a costly war with Finland, was underequipped to offer any effective resistance. The German forces advanced relentlessly: by December they had marched through the territories of eastern Poland and the Baltic states, assigned to Russia under the 1939 pact, had captured the entire Ukraine and were on the outskirts of Moscow and Leningrad. Many Russians and Ukrainians greeted the Germans as liberators from Communism until they were pressed into hard labor to service the German war effort. Many others fled or were moved en masse eastwards. Late in 1941 the German advance slowed, and blitzkrieg became a war of attrition: Leningrad was besieged for two-and-a-half years.

Military aid from the Allies was channeled via the Arctic and the Persian Gulf, and slowly the tide began to turn. The German thrust eastwards was resisted, then repelled, at Stalingrad in late 1942. The last major German assault, around Kursk, was defeated the following summer. Thereafter an inexorable German retreat was enforced until the Russians captured Berlin itself in 1945. The war was won at enormous cost to Russia: up to 20 million lives were lost and huge industrial and agricultural resources destroyed.

Between 1940 and 1947 membership doubled, but the quality of newcomers, particularly in terms of education, was significantly lower than before. This was both bad and good: bad in the sense that they needed training, good in the sense they were malleable. The Stalinist precedent seemed safe with such people.

The Soviet Union's postwar economic problems were severe. Heavy industry was in relatively good shape and growing, owing to the acquisition of German plant and expertise and the development of Soviet capacity in war-related production. Agriculture, however, was in a parlous state, both because much of the war was fought in the farming areas and because the peasantry was demographically crippled due to government policies of the 1930s. All other sectors of the economy were also precarious. Stalin addressed these problems by reimposing the planned economy with a degree of severity as great as during the 1930s. The first postwar five-year plan was launched in 1946: it set unachievably high industrial production targets, coupled with severe restrictions and penalties upon the work force, and aimed to reform agriculture by merging collective farms into much greater agro-industrial complexes. Results were to show that the plan was unrealistic.

A second wave of emigration followed World War II, and consisted of Russians and many other Soviet nationalities variously determined to escape the Soviet Union. In general, these were people of lower education and standing than the first wave, but with few romantic delusions about the realities of Communism. Many had been victims of repressions and terror during the 1930s, had welcomed the Germans as liberators in 1941 and ended up as forced or menial labor in Nazi Germany. At the war's end, they chose to flee westward in hope of finding freedom. Those who chose to go home, or were forcibly repatriated by the Western Allies, were shipped directly to concentration camps. In the West, the second wave first publicized the terror of Stalin's rule and brought first news of the Gulag. This news shocked the Western Allies, whose image of the Soviet Union until then was shaped by official Soviet propaganda and distorted reportage by Western socialist sympathizers, such as Sidney and Beatrice Webb. While the first wave of emigration was based largely in Western Europe, the second went mostly to America.

The Gulag: concentration camps and forced labor

The Soviet system, as devised by Lenin and developed by Stalin, was dependent on concentration camps and forced labor. The first concentration camps were legalized by Lenin in 1918. Their purpose was to isolate and often to exterminate the civil war opponents of the Communist regime. The first true death camp, intended for extermination only, was established in 1921. The number of camps and inmates grew as the government eliminated all socialist opposition, as internal party purges grew and as the practice of arresting all relations and associates of detainees accelerated.

The Khrushchev figures (see page 173) give the numbers in camps at 179,000 in 1930, 510,307 in 1934, 1,296,494 in 1936, and 1,881,570 in 1938. The maximum (2,561,351) was reached in 1950—earlier western estimates of the numbers in camps were considerably higher. These numbers covered the full sweep of society: *kulaks*, intellectuals, engineers, technicians, scientists, professionals, scholars, officials, Communist Party members. The mortality rate in camps was high; many consider that the average lifespan was about two years. Few prisoners were actually released at the legal end of their sentences.

Until 1930 the camp system was administered directly by the NKVD (which succeeded the GPU and indirectly preceded the KGB). In that year a Special Administration of Camps (Gulag for short) was established to control what was effectively a separate administrative region. The camps were located primarily in the north of European Russia, Siberia, Central Asia and the Far East. Living conditions were deliberately kept primitive and brutal, prisoners were treated inhumanely and deprived of all rights and food rations were fixed at starvation levels. Most people were quickly broken, in body or spirit or both, and reduced to subhuman level before perishing.

Politically, the camps served to break whatever real or imagined opposition the Soviet government could perceive and to isolate opponents from the rest of society. Economically, the camps proved of great value as a large and constantly replenished supply of slave labor. The heavy industry in the Urals and the major transportation systems in the Russian north created during the 1930s were all built with work forces from the camps. The camp population was assigned primarily to heavy construction work—underground and surface mining, lumbering, excavation, building—which was done manually, without technological aids. The cost of such work was almost nil, being no more than the sustenance supposedly provided for the workers, and the labor supply was inexhaustible, given that high mortality among the prisoners was more than outweighed by their increasing numbers.

During World War II the camp population was put to work at the war effort. Many of the country's leading designers were by now in camps, so specialist design teams were founded. The leading Soviet aircraft of the war were designed by Tupolev, who headed a prisoner design team in a camp. The T34 tanks which proved superior to German armor were manufactured by slave labor in the Urals.

The camps swelled still further after the war. Foreign captives (including German prisoners of war, repatriated Russians and Ukrainians, citizens and politicians from Central and East European countries) and Soviet citizens swept up in the new purges added to the numbers. By 1950 the number of prisoners in the Gulag had reached a maximum. The late 1940s and early 1950s saw a succession of camp uprisings, all of which were brutally suppressed, with mass punitive executions following. Controlling this burgeoning population was becoming a problem; one solution tried by Gulag in 1950 was a blanket execution of 5 percent of the camp population.

With Stalin's death, the camp population stopped growing, but the Soviet leadership realized that the subject was highly damaging to their country's image abroad. Until recently, the Soviet Union claimed that Western images and estimates

Above A relaxed, informal meeting between Stalin and Churchill at Yalta reveals the human side of Stalin's personality. Quick and astute mentally, he could be humorous and charming at will. His smile at such moments was famous, and was repeatedly depicted by both official portraiture and Western cartoonists. The latter saw behind its immediate beneficence a sharp cunning, which can be detected in Stalin's bonhomie on this occasion.

Right: the Soviet bloc. c.1950. At the end of World War II the Soviet Union was given by the Allies administrative control over Eastern Europe, having agreed to oversee the establishment of freely elected governments. In practice, local Communist parties either manipulated elections or seized power. By 1948 Bulgaria, Poland, Hungary, Romania, Albania, Yugoslavia and finally Czechoslovakia were under Communist governments loyal to Moscow, and the Soviet Union had extended its effective dominion over half of Europe. The independent Baltic states which the Soviet Union had annexed between 1939 and 1940 but had subsequently lost to Germany were now reincorporated. Germany, Austria and Berlin had each been divided into zones between the four victorious powers: the Soviet zone of Germany became the GDR. An attempt to deny Western access to Berlin was thwarted by the Berlin airlift of 1948. Finland became a neutral independent state, and in 1955 a

The Khrushchev era and the "Thaw"

Stalin's death was announced unexpectedly in March 1953. The shock was profound: he had kept so tight a grip on the Soviet regime for a quarter century that a future without him was scarcely imaginable. His funeral was an awe-inspiring occasion, with an ominous portent: clumsy police crowd control meant that dozens of Muscovites were trampled to death. His corpse was laid beside Lenin's in the Mausoleum on Red Square.

Shortly before his death Stalin was seemingly planning a new purge of the leadership. There was a brief but intense struggle between the contenders for power: Stalin's Georgian compatriot, the ineffably sinister police chief Lavrentiy Beria, was apparently shot dead by apprehensive rivals at a Central Committee meeting. Others of his entourage disappeared. A small but important sign of changing times was the dropping of charges against those, mainly Jews, arrested in the "Doctors' Plot" during a final paranoid episode (worthy of the court of Ivan IV) of the late leader's life.

The nominal new leader, Georgiy Malenkov, was a rather colorless figure who less than two years later publicly admitted to failures in economic management and resigned, being eventually dispatched to manage a power station. Nikita Khrushchev, who had been strengthening his at first peripheral position in the leadership, now took the crucial role of Party general secretary; Marshal Nikolai Bulganin, an amiable, less dynamic figure, became head of state. The two became well known abroad, improving the image of the Soviet Union in their frequent travels. Khrushchev himself, of southern peasant background, known chiefly as an agriculture manager, struck observers as quick-witted, frank, rather voluble and mercurial.

In 1956 rumors of a remarkable speech delivered by Khrushchev to a closed session of the Twentieth Party Congress began to circulate. The "secret speech" (soon an open secret) comprehensively denounced aberrations of Stalin's rule, his purges, wartime mistakes and "cult of personality." The trickle, then flood, of prisoners released under "amnesty" brought firsthand testimony of the vast concentration-camp realm that the press still ignored. Awkward questions were raised in Party circles and beyond about the new leader's own complicity in the Stalinist regime and the overall legitimacy of the Party's rule. Meanwhile a noticeable loosening-up of the political and intellectual climate began to be apparent: the period known (from Ilya Ehrenburg's novel of 1954) as the "Thaw." Genuine debate on a variety of issues emerged, censorship became less stringent, literary and artistic life (moribund in the early 1950s) revived. Foreign tourists began to arrive in considerable numbers from 1957. Khrushchev's rather unpredictable diplomatic initiatives gave other nations the feeling that Soviet leaders were prepared to discuss matters of world concern.

Khrushchev's political life was marked by crises. Within a few months of the "secret speech" the Hungarians rose up in what the Soviet Union considered to be counterrevolution; Soviet troops withdrew, then returned to overthrow Imre Nagy and install the longlived Kadar government. By summer 1957 Khrushchev was facing a massive

similar arrangement was reached for Austria when the four powers agreed to end their occupation.

In southeastern Europe the situation was volatile: the Yugoslav Communist leaders broke with Stalin in 1948; Albania subsequently allied itself with China, in isolation from the rest of Europe; the Greek government, with British aid, defeated a prolonged Communist challenge in a bitter civil war in the 1940s.

of the Gulag were wildly exaggerated. However, the writings of Solzhenitsyn and investigations of Academician Sakharov have shown that the system was even more developed and less humane than even pessimistic observers had assumed. The taboo on these topics was only lifted in the Soviet Union in 1985; since then the media have been allowed to investigate the subject critically and the Russian people are beginning to come to grips with the heritage of camps and forced labor. How and when the system began to contract remains far from clear.

challenge to his power in the Politburo; he just saved himself by appealing to the 300-strong Central Committee. For a few years the domestic omens seemed good: industrial productivity rose, the desperate housing shortage began to improve, consumer goods (but not yet automobiles) became available at reasonable prices. Food production was temporarily improved by extending cultivated steppeland, and the miserable lot of the collective farmers under Stalin was eased. National morale rode high in the wake of the astonishing launch in 1957 of an artificial satellite (*sputnik*, "companion") and of the first manned space flight by Yury Gagarin (1961). "De-Stalinization" was resumed and intensified.

Abroad things went less well. Hungary put the West on its guard. "De-Stalinization" led to an acrimonious break with China in the early 1960s. Soviet adventurism led to the Cuban missile crisis late in 1962; from this confrontation with the Americans Khrushchev only just managed to extricate himself. Despite his boasted economic successes, agricultural realities forced him humiliatingly to buy Canadian wheat. These factors contributed to the sudden vote for his removal in October 1964. Completely stripped of power, Khrushchev lived on for more than a decade; he read, educated himself, apologized to writers he had criticized ("but I made sure not a hair of your head was touched") and produced a volume of remarkable memoirs. His period of dominance left a curiously ambiguous heritage, raising expectations without fulfilling them. Khrushchev's rule remained authoritarian, and there were some extremely illiberal phenomena, such as a tough antireligious policy that closed down nearly half the operational Orthodox churches. But the period saw the demise of totalitarianism—at least in the strict, Stalinist sense—an event whose psychological jolt to the Soviet system cannot be overestimated.

Politics and society in the Brezhnev years

Leonid Brezhnev came to power as the leader of a conservative reaction against Khrushchev's policy of de-Stalinization and his attempts to weaken the official bureaucracy. The bureaucracy was politically strongly pro-Stalin and socially hostile to Khrushchev's populist attempts to create social homogeneity. Brezhnev himself believed that an iron discipline needed to be reimposed on the country and viewed social critics as political deviants and renegades. Khrushchev's liberalization policies were replaced by a sustained and systematic persecution of the people of the "Thaw," beginning with the arrest in 1965 of Andrey Sinyavsky and Yuly Daniel, two writers who had published pseudonymously in the West. In 1966 the authorities staged a show trial, the first since Stalin's time, where the authors were convicted of "anti-Soviet propaganda." This charge, taken from the criminal code and previously not used against intellectuals, was thereafter used frequently against dissidents. The criminal code was extended, also in 1966, to cover "violations of public order," a clause also to be used extensively against the dissidents—as they came to be called. In 1966–67 a wave of show trials swept the country, with major ones in Moscow, Leningrad (St

Above An early attempt at detente diplomacy has Khrushchev addressing Richard Nixon, then the American vice-president. Khrushchev was well known for the blinkered forcefulness with which he argued his case, and the impact is clear upon Nixon, who is left with no choice but to listen mutely. The entourage includes the youngish Leonid Brezhnev, second from the right. In the early 1970s he and Nixon, both by then presidents, were to pursue a more substantial attempt at detente.

Petersburg), Kiev (Kyyiv), Lvov (L'viv), Gorky (Nizhniy Novgorod), Riga, Tashkent and Omsk.

The dissidents set up monitoring of such trials and associated legal abuse; the results were reported in underground (*samizdat*) publications, most notably in the periodical *Chronicle of Current Events*, which appeared from 1968 onwards. Also in 1968, the dissidents initiated regular contact with Western journalists in Moscow. In so doing, the dissidents exposed themselves to another severe provision of the criminal code, which defined as subversion any link with the Western media which was detrimental to the officially projected image of the Soviet Union.

The dissident movement was formed of many strands, chief of which were: a Leninist revivalism, which argued for a return to the supposedly pure form of Communism that had existed in Lenin's time; a humanistic liberalism predicated on non-ideological politics; and a Russian nationalism linked to pre-revolutionary Russian culture and the Orthodox Church. In addition, strongly nationalist dissident movements existed in most republics, with the strongest in Ukraine; there were also fundamentalist religious movements, such as Baptists and Pentecostalists. The Jews formed a distinctive movement, concerned primarily with the right of Soviet Jews to emigrate to Israel. There was close cooperation and liaison between the various groups, creating an integrated if varied movement of opposition.

Intense Western interest in the dissidents frustrated Soviet attempts to solve the problem with traditional Stalinist methods. Indirectly, it also seems to have defused a movement within the Soviet bureaucracy towards a full rehabilitation of Stalin. However, the crushing of dissent remained a top priority, and in 1972 the government launched a new and more effective campaign of repression, based on different methods for breaking up the dissident movement, whose success until then relied on good internal organization and communication. The campaign was planned by the KGB chief Yury Andropov, who was elected to full Politburo membership in 1972 and in due course followed Brezhnev as head of state. Dissidents were subject to intense and overt personal surveillance by the KGB, whose methods included intimidation and physical violence directed against individuals, their families and associates. Simultaneously, they were encouraged to emigrate, often after the completion of a jail term resulting from a staged trial. One method of separating and isolating dissidents was internal exile to provincial towns, where detainees lived under blanket surveillance. Another was to expel people from their jobs while ensuring that they would be unable to find another; then they could be accused of "parasitism," a jailable offense. Finally, dissidents were subjected to the old practice of long sentences to hard labor in the camps of Gulag.

An ominous new method of repression was pioneered by the KGB in the early 1970s: the use of mental hospitals to imprison dissidents. Fabricated diagnoses were used to certify dissidents as insane: the victims were then isolated in mental hospitals and treated with mind-altering or physically debilitating drugs. This method bypassed the legal system: no term of sentence was imposed and the prisoner could be detained indefinitely. Soviet psychiatry was internationally ostracized for complicity in such repression and in 1983 was forced to withdraw from the World Psychiatric Association.

By the end of the 1970s the dissident movement was reduced and fragmented; its members either isolated in internal exile, or terrorized into passivity or public recantation. By far the greatest number, however, were incarcerated in prisons and camps or assigned to penal labor elsewhere; the former numbered at least three million and the latter two million. These especially included nationalist and religious dissidents, such as Valentin Moroz among the Ukrainians and Anatoly Sharansky among the Jews. The dissident movement and the government's reaction illustrated two salient points. First, it showed the resilience and variety of opposition to doctrinaire Communism that survived in the Soviet Union through decades of Stalinist repression and extermination, and which had manifested itself quickly under Khrushchev's "Thaw." Second, it showed that the Communist practice of governing continued to rely on repression, ingenious new methods of which could be invented in changing times.

The forces that deposed Khrushchev were guided by three main concerns: to reestablish the preeminence of the entrenched bureaucracy in government and within the Communist Party; to pursue administrative efficiency within the framework of administrative stability; to rationalize and make permanent the responsibilities of officialdom. The domestic policies pursued by Brezhnev were formulated primarily to ensure stability by appeasing the vested interests of the bureaucracy and other entrenched interest groups such as the military, and to justify this conservatism, Brezhnev developed the ideological doctrine of "developed socialism" to describe the time and to guide policy. In practice, it meant a conservative deference to the

entrenched bureaucracy, combined with reformist momentum aimed at industrial modernization to be achieved with only logistical administrative changes.

The political stability of the Brezhnev era was achieved at the cost of social stratification and stagnation. The upper elite within the bureaucracy attained a position of unprecedented influence and privilege. Known as the *nomenklatura* (the list of nominees), it remained effectively a political and social oligarchy, living separate from the rest of the population and enjoying luxuries and privileges unavailable to others. Their total number in 1970 was slightly over 400 000, or 0.35 percent of the total population. The other social groups favored under "developed socialism" were the military and the technical intelligentsia, the latter only so long as its political loyalty was absolute and actively demonstrated. The rest of the population was in contrast restricted.

The Brezhnev years saw an intensification of existing restrictions on social and geographic mobility. The system of internal passports and living permits, introduced by Stalin during the 1930s, was made more rigid. People were more tied than before to their original place of residence or to their work, so that moving to major urban areas, above all to Moscow, Leningrad (St Petersburg) and Kiev (Kyyiv), became increasingly difficult. The major centers were always magnets to the population, primarily because they were much better supplied with food than elsewhere, but also because they provided the few opportunities for job mobility available. The severest restrictions were imposed on the agricultural workers on collective farms, who were deprived of all right of unsupervised movement.

The leaders of the Soviet economy knew already in 1965 that development prospects were ominous. Agriculture was the major problem area. Organizational and administrative innovations were introduced by Aleksey Kosygin, Brezhnev's virtual co-ruler in the late 1960s; these failed to produce results, due in part to their limited scope, in part to bureaucratic opposition. The Kosygin approach was abandoned in the wake of the Prague Spring of 1968; the government never attempted any innovative reform, however mild, thereafter. Food production and agricultural development declined sharply in the late 1960s.

In contrast, sustained heavy investment in military production allowed the Soviet Union to expand and modernize its armed forces on a massive scale, achieving superpower parity with the United States by the early 1970s. The military simultaneously gained much higher influence than before within the government and the Communist Party. The increased military might of the Soviet Union became a major factor in Soviet foreign policy, with important domestic implications too. Within the Soviet sphere of influence, the practice of military intervention was revived along lines followed during the 1950s. Dubbed the "Brezhnev doctrine," it began with the Warsaw Pact invasion of Czechoslovakia in 1968. The object was to crush the social and economic experiments launched by Dubcek's innovative brand of Communism. The lesson, both for the East European Communist states and for the Khrushchev liberals and dissi-

Above This poster illustrates the new replacing the old in Moscow during the Stalinist period. The building being erected is one of the ornate skyscrapers scattered around the periphery of central Moscow to create a grandiose, thrusting horizon for the city. The skyscrapers were surmounted with pinnacles in a style partly classical and partly 17th-century Russian.

179

dents at home, was that any deviation from conservative doctrinaire Communism would be suppressed. The "Brezhnev doctrine" was also used to justify the intervention in Afghanistan in 1980.

On the international scene, Soviet military might was put to diplomatic rather than operational use in the detente process of the early 1970s. Detente was devised by Brezhnev to encourage economic cooperation with the West, in order to accelerate internal Soviet modernization by the acquisition of Western technology and expertise. The diplomatic incentive offered was arms limitation talks. Western willingness to pursue detente on this basis brought the Soviet Union considerable technological benefits at small military cost. Conservative Soviet instincts, however, undermined detente. The process ended in 1975 when the Americans insisted on linking further economic cooperation with human rights in the form of freer emigration for Soviet Jews.

A third wave of emigration occurred in the 1970s, largely in connection with the process of detente. These were mainly urban members of the educated and professional elite, born and raised in the Communist system. The majority were Soviet Jews who settled either in Israel or America. The Russians included leading dissidents, such as Alexander Solzhenitsyn and Iosif Brodsky—both of whom settled in the United States—Andrei Almarik, Vladimir Maksimov and Vladimir Bukovsky. The third wave has been extremely productive in literary terms, with political and polemical writings being the favored genres. Their in-depth personal accounts and first-hand analyses of conditions in the Soviet Union gained much greater circulation in the Western press than the writings of the preceding waves. The full-scale and pervasive habit of Soviet human rights violations, from the Gulag of the 1940s to psychiatric abuse of the 1970s, became widely known in the West from their writings.

At home the civilian economy was catered for in a new five-year plan launched in 1971. Its main objective was to achieve faster growth in production of consumer goods than in industrial production. The plan failed in all its objectives, with the greatest shortfall in food production and consumer goods supply. The advent and conclusion of the plan were marked with mass food riots against bad working conditions and poor housing in nearly a dozen major Soviet cities. These were forcibly broken up, and attempts to establish independent trade unions in 1977 and 1978 were extinguished by the KGB. The Soviet Union was reduced to importing grain from the United States.

Towards the end of Brezhnev's reign it looked as if "developed socialism" had succeeded politically, by instilling continuity and stability in the apparatus of government, but economically it had proved a total failure. Disregarding the evidence, Brezhnev continued to declare success after spectral success in the Soviet economy. The bureaucracy, comfortable in its power and privilege, provided him with bedrock support. This support was, however, aging with its leader. The average age of Politburo members rose from 55 to 68 during Brezhnev's time, and nearly half the members of the 1966 Politburo were still there in 1981.

Shortly before Brezhnev's death, sharp criticism of his leadership began appearing among younger Soviet economists. Their general view was that the traditional, centralized mechanisms of planned economy were too rigid to generate the required results and were beyond hope of improvement. By implication, they hinted that the bureaucratic stability cultivated by Brezhnev was antithetical to the country's need of economic development. In a few years, with Gorbachev in power, such critics were to be drawn into the state's attempt to reform fundamentally its ailing economy.

The 1980s: from conservatism to change

Brezhnev's two immediate successors were in a similar mold, old men dedicated to the perpetuation of the established order, suppression of dissent and cautious experiment aimed at improving the efficiency of the system. The first was Yury Andropov, who masterminded the crushing of the 1956 Hungarian uprising. Andropov intensified state repression of dissidents and religion, while at the same time cultivating an appearance of personal liberalism designed largely for the Western media. With its ex-chief as the country's leader, the KGB attained higher status and influence than ever before. Economic and agricultural production continued to decline. There was half-hearted talk of economic reform, and while Andropov himself was probably the first Soviet leader to recognize the depth of the economic crisis and the need for change, he was already ill and lacked the authority to carry his ideas through. He died in early 1984, only 14 months after assuming power.

Andropov's protégé for the leadership was Mikhail Gorbachev, a youngish senior bureaucrat whose background was in provincial administration. But the Communist Party leadership chose instead Konstantin Chernenko, a frail and anonymous leader who had been deputy both to Brezhnev and Andropov. His year in office was marked by conflict within the leadership and all thought of reform was frozen. When he died in March 1985, there was again conflict over who should become general secretary. This time, Gorbachev emerged victorious, but only by the slimmest of margins. His elevation appears to have been assisted by Andrey Gromyko, the Soviet Union's veteran foreign minister, who was subsequently rewarded with the post of state president (until 1989).

Gromyko's removal from the foreign ministry also freed Gorbachev to start reformulating Soviet foreign policy and correcting some of the political errors of the Brezhnev era which had been so costly to the Soviet Union's reputation abroad. In particular, he announced Moscow's intention of withdrawing troops from Afghanistan if a satisfactory agreement could be achieved. This was reached in April 1988, and the troop withdrawal was completed on schedule in February 1989.

Gorbachev also embarked on restoring relations with the United States. Under Andropov the relationship had reached its coolest point since the cold war over the question of NATO's plans to deploy new medium-range nuclear missiles in Western Europe. The superpower thaw led to a series of summit meetings inaugurated in Geneva in November 1985. Gorbachev also showed that his

Massive orchestrated ceremonies marked every anniversary of the revolution, which was the Soviet Union's most important national holiday. The 70th anniversary in 1987 was especially important. The scene shows massed contingents with banners lined up at the end of Moscow's Red Square, ready for a march-past before the government leaders' review tribunal atop Lenin's mausoleum. The photo is taken from near the foot of the mausoleum. March-pasts of this kind included civilian contingents and military units, often displaying up-to-date weaponry.

interests went beyond the establishment of an equal relationship with the United States. While negotiating with President Reagan, he also speeded up the Soviet rapprochement with China, attempting to bridge the political and ideological schism which nearly led to war in the early 1960s. The resumption of full party-to-party relations was sealed in May 1989 when Gorbachev traveled to Beijing for the first Sino-Soviet summit for 30 years (involuntarily instigating student antigovernment demonstrations there).

In domestic policy, Gorbachev began cautiously. His first two big set-piece occasions, the 26th Communist Party Congress in February 1986 and the 70th anniversary of the Bolshevik Revolution in November 1987, disappointed those who believed that he was a radical reformer in that they produced no radical blueprint for change. Only at the Central Committee plenum of June 1987 did he give a glimpse of the changes to come, announcing a comprehensive program of decentralization for industry and removing from the leadership the more outspoken members of the old guard. Thereafter he more than made up for his initial caution and introduced into the Soviet and Western vocabulary two Russian words which were to become shorthand for his policies: *perestroika* and *glasnost*. *Perestroika* referred to his program to reform the Soviet economy, increase efficiency and improve Soviet living standards. *Glasnost* referred to the opening up of Soviet cultural life and the media, to his plans to limit censorship and encourage freer discussion of political and cultural questions. He also argued for the introduction of greater democracy into Soviet society, including the principle that more than one candidate should contest each party and government election.

The reasons for Gorbachev's apparent change of heart are uncertain: it may have been the accident at Chornobyl' nuclear power station in April 1986, which opened the eyes of the leadership to the dangers of secrecy and dishonesty. It may have reflected the leadership's gradual realization of how far the Soviet Union lagged behind not only the developed world, but even some of the developing countries of Asia, and the scale of its economic stagnation. Or it may have reflected Gorbachev's steady gain in authority over opponents.

Whatever the explanation, late 1987 and 1988 saw Gorbachev embrace the need for political reform in parallel with economic reform and mount a swingeing attack on the Brezhnev era as the "period of stagnation." At a special Communist Party conference in June 1988, he introduced new constitutional mechanisms providing for elections to a new Congress of People's Deputies and a new-style Supreme Soviet, or parliament, designed to give more people an interest in government and stem widespread disaffection. The hallmarks of Gorbachev's economic reform program included self-financing for factories, permission for individuals to start cooperative enterprises in production and service sectors and permission for peasants and collective farmers to lease their land. There was also a drive to improve long-neglected welfare and medical provisions.

While economic reform was impeded by widespread bureaucratic and ideological opposition, Gorbachev's advocacy of *glasnost*—widely seen as

a means of winning intellectual opinion over to his side—enjoyed greater success. In Moscow, Leningrad (St Petersburg) and other Soviet cities informal groups sprang up representing diverse interests, including those of different ethnic groups and environmentalists. Stalinism was bitterly attacked and many prominent purge victims, including the Bolshevik theorist Bukharin, were rehabilitated by the Party leadership.

In human rights, too, Gorbachev showed a more liberal face than his predecessors. The numbers of Jews and ethnic Germans permitted to emigrate rose sharply; individuals who had become symbols of the 1970s dissident movement, such as the Jewish campaigner Anatoly Shcharansky and the nuclear physicist Andrey Sakharov, were released, as were many of those imprisoned for political and religious offenses. Regulations were introduced to attempt to outlaw psychiatric abuse.

In a reversal of previous Soviet policy, the Gorbachev leadership also made overtures to prominent members of the emigration, especially those cultural figures who had left the country during the Brezhnev years. As a result, a number—including the ballet dancers Rudolf Nureyev and Natalya Makarova, the stage director Yury Lyubimov and the writer Andrey Sinyavsky—were permitted to return on visits. It also became easier for artists, musicians and indeed ordinary citizens to travel and work abroad.

One consequence of greater freedom of expression was the resurgence of nationalist sentiment across the Soviet Union. The dismissal of the Kazakh party leader in 1986 led to rioting in the Kazakh capital, Alma-Ata (Almaty). In 1988 old hostilities revived in violence in the Caucasian republics of Armenia and Azerbaijan; in the Baltic states of Estonia, Latvia and Lithuania, popular front organizations, which had been encouraged by the authorities as a controlled outlet for nationalist feeling, called for independence from Moscow. Simmering nationalism also gave rise to nationalist and anti-Soviet demonstrations in Belarus, Moldova, Ukraine and Georgia, with people demanding the right to use their native language and preserve their culture.

These pressures were to be among the most powerful ingredients in the complex of forces that would eventually cause Gorbachev's downfall—particularly since they were matched by a new spirit of self-assertive independence in the former "satellite" countries of Eastern Europe. With startling suddenness (and little social upheaval) Communist governments were forced from, or simply withdrew from, office during the latter part of 1989 in Hungary, Poland, Czechoslovakia, East Germany, Bulgaria, Romania and a little later Albania. The Soviet Union did nothing to help them survive, and in consequence the Warsaw Pact ceased to exist.

Meanwhile parliamentary processes began in Moscow and were avidly followed on television and radio by the mass of the population, who seemed to find little difficulty in adapting to a spirit of democracy. In the early stages there was complete freedom of debate but no effective new political parties. Public figures called more and more insistently for a radical rethinking of the economic policy (e.g. through the shock therapy of the

Left A Moscow commuter studies Mikhail Gorbachev's *Perestroika: New Thinking for Our Country and the World.* Gorbachev showed himself willing to gamble with his popularity; one of his first measures in 1985–86 was to restrict the availability of alcohol and to launch a campaign against corruption.

so-called "Shatalin plan") rather than a mere tinkering with discredited Soviet methods: proposals that put in question the entire Party and bureaucratic *nomenklatura* systems.

Gorbachev himself, evidently in sympathy with the spirit of freedom he had so dramatically conjured up, but alarmed by the possibilities of chaos, seemed for several months in 1990–91 to be looking for a lead—while events overtook him. In the summer of 1990 the first price rises for a generation began a period that led within a year to galloping inflation. At the same time, a "hard currency" economy was operating beside, and eclipsing, the rouble economy. Stories of both an organized and an opportunistic crime-wave alarmed the inhabitants of the big cities. The conservative forces that dreaded the breakup of the Soviet Union—most eloquently represented in parliament by the Latvian Colonel Viktor Alksnis—evidently gained some sway over policy early in 1991. Half-hearted repressive measures in Lithuania and Georgia were (as usual in such cases) counter-productive. Before the year was out both—together with the other Union Republics—were to be independent: in Lithuania, against the wishes of its Polish minority; in Georgia, with civil strife in Abkhazia, Ossetia and in the streets of Tbilisi itself.

In Russia, the tough populist Boris Yeltsin, a reformer more ready than Gorbachev to move against the Party, was elected President after a close ballot. The conservative forces realized that time was running out. In August 1991 a motley alliance of old guard politicians (including the deputy president, Aleksandr Yakovlev) took advantage of Gorbachev's summer absence in the Crimea to mount a coup d'état. The plotters appeared to have little positive policy and made no attempt to appeal to Communist principles. Their precautionary measures were so defective that Yeltsin was able to voice his defiance, and that of the Russian parliament, to the world's assembled media in the heart of Moscow—while the bulk of the population looked on to see what would happen. The putsch collapsed ignominiously within three days, and Gorbachev returned to office: it was soon clear however that central power was ebbing away to the Republics. In December 1991 Russia, Ukraine and Belarus simply sidestepped the Soviet Union by setting up a loose "Commonwealth of Independent States"—soon joined by all the Republics save the Baltic states and Georgia; by the end of the month Gorbachev had resigned, central institutions—even the Communist Party—were dismantled and the Soviet Union came to a quiet end.

For Russians it was curiously hard to draw up a balance-sheet of these dramatic events. On the one hand they could congratulate themselves on the political maturity and good sense that had enabled them to wind up the 70-year Soviet experiment almost without bloodshed or social disruption, on their strengthening the prospects for world peace by voluntarily renouncing "superpower" confrontationalism, on their magnanimity in letting subject peoples go their own way. But the other side was grim: the acceptance of national humiliation (particularly for the once-proud army); economic turmoil and, for many, impoverishment; the realization that the market economy was no "quick fix" and that the West would help out only grudgingly; the eruption of ethnic tensions in many parts of the old USSR. In the aftermath, the "stagnation" under Brezhnev began to seem a "golden age" of stability and rising middle-class living standards.

The arts from Socialist Realism to the 1990s

The ending of NEP, the inauguration of the five-year plans and the growing ascendancy of Stalin marked a change in mood in Soviet cultural life. In 1929 Anatoly Lunacharsky, the first commissar for enlightenment (that is, minister of education and the arts) resigned; a cultivated and benign figure, he had been appointed by Lenin to gain the confidence of the intellectuals and had himself been a Symbolist playwright. The 1930s began with the undisputed dominance of the "proletarian" organizations, RAPP in literature and AKHRR in art. In 1932 however the Central Committee unexpectedly issued a decree banning all literary and artistic groupings, including the proletarians. To those who wanted simply to get on with their work, without propagandist commitment, this seemed to offer welcome relief.

It soon became clear that the arts were to exist under a much tougher regime, with continual scrutiny and far-reaching censorship. From 1934 a single artistic method was promulgated, known as Socialist Realism. Three abstract, scarcely translatable principles underpinned it: *ideynost* (presence of identifiable ideas), *partiynost* (agreement with Communist Party principles) and *narodnost* (popular spirit). What Socialist Realism meant in practice is not always easy to see; it has been cynically defined as "praise of the leaders in terms they can understand."

Real talents continued to flourish, even to emerge. The novel revived, with Mikhail Sholokhov (1905–84) undoubtedly its best exponent: *The Quiet Don* (1928–40) represents an authentically epic treatment (from a Cossack viewpoint) of the civil war period. In poetry, Pasternak for a few years became almost the Soviet poet laureate. Music saw the brilliant rise of Dmitriy Shostakovich (1906–75). The most abstract of the arts, music was naturally the hardest to define in Socialist Realist terms (though it was clear that melodiousness was required); it suffered considerably in the late 1940s, when virtually every composer of originality underwent harsh criticism. In the visual arts the revival of figuration delayed the impact of the new doctrine, with several artists, veterans as well as newer talents, doing inventive, sometimes exciting work. Theater and cinema retreated gradually into conventionality, without ever becoming wholly uninteresting, but Meyerhold, bold and outspoken, was arrested and shot.

In the traumas of 1937–38 the best thing writers or artists could do was to keep their heads down. Literary victims included Mandelshtam, Babel and the novelist Pilnyak; Zabolotsky was almost the only established writer to experience a prison-camp sentence and live to tell the tale. The 1941–45 war brought a slackening of controls, with real instead of imaginary enemies; some good poetry was written. But further attacks on writers (notably Akhmatova and the satirical storywriter Mikhail Zoshchenko) in 1946–48 "froze" the situation until after Stalin's death. Aesopian language or fantasy could sometimes be successfully

Right Russians queue patiently in the snow to taste the delights of McDonald's hamburgers and french fries. The American fast-food chain was one of the first Western companies, along with Pizza Hut, to set up outlets in the former Soviet Union after the collapse of communism, with the first branch being opened in Moscow. The American hamburger, whilst being a far cry from the traditonal Russian fare, has been a huge success with those who can afford to splash out on such luxuries. For the average Russian, one trip to McDonalds is equivalent to a week's wages; for the bemused Russians who first found jobs there, it was an introduction to a whole new, American-style work ethic.

employed: Yevgeny Shvarts (1898–1958) wrote attractive plays for children, loosely derived from Hans Andersen's tales, which carry adult sub-texts. Few writers wanted even to write "for the desk drawer" in the hermetically isolated atmosphere of the Soviet Union. Two remarkable exceptions, published much later, are the novels *Master and Margarita* by Bulgakov and *Doctor Zhivago* by Pasternak.

Although the novel called *The Thaw* by veteran survivor Ilya Ehrenburg gave its name to the period that began in the mid-1950s, and lasted around a decade, his memoirs published in the 1960s are actually a more significant "Thaw" document. The optimism of the cultural atmosphere stemmed partly from a feeling that there was a world of experience waiting to be explored, a public anxious to explore it and that the Soviet Union could be part of the cultural world again. It was often assumed abroad that Soviet writers or artists could be categorized as "official" or "unofficial," but the situation was never quite like that. Khrushchev blew hot and cold by turns, but took care not to instigate fullscale repression.

The "Thaw" encouraged new talent, reinvigorated those who had lived through the Stalin years and led to rediscoveries. The new writers were led by poets: a remarkable phenomenon was the growth of mass poetry readings by such as Yevgeny Yevtushenko (b. 1933) and Andrey Voznesensky (b. 1933). New prose followed soon, notably short stories by Yury Kazakov; other writers included V. Soloukhin, V. Aksyonov and V. Shukshin (also a fine movie-maker). In art, rediscoveries were singularly important, particularly of the great modern French collections in Moscow and Leningrad (St Petersburg), but Russian modernists such as Malevich remained in the storerooms. Shostakovich, battered throughout his career by public adulation followed by denunciation, was "reborn" for the new age: by his death he had completed an impressive corpus of 15 symphonies and the same number of string quartets.

The stagnation under Brezhnev set in gradually

in the later 1960s. Among the gloomier symptoms were the trial and imprisonment (1966) of Andrey Sinyavsky and Yury Daniel and the expulsion (1974) of Alexander Solzhenitsyn (b. 1918), who had sprung to fame when his story *One Day in the Life of Ivan Denisovich*, breaking the taboo on prison-camp literature, was published in 1962 in the important "liberal" monthly *Novy Mir*. A series of long works, located at the intersection of fiction with recent history, had already won him the Nobel Prize (1970). Under Brezhnev all forms of "dissidence" (a new term of the period) began to be treated with harassment and, increasingly frequently, with deportation and deprivation of citizenship. Sometimes those forcibly expelled flourished abroad, as did the Nobel prize-winning poet Iosif Brodsky (1940–96); sometimes they sank without trace, but the result was if nothing else a public relations disaster for the Soviet regime. Among the notable talents lost were the movie-maker Andrey Tarkovsky (1932–87) and the notable director of the Moscow Taganka Theater, Yury Lyubimov. However, the Brezhnev government was never remotely as oppressive as Stalin's, and a thriving "underground" culture, in all the arts, could exist—so long as it did not become too prominent. Ballad-singing was one of the activities that continued to flourish, while the "official" press nurtured the school of "village prose," deeply concerned with both old and new problems of the countryside.

Intellectual life witnessed a growth of disinterested scholarship even before Brezhnev's death. Soviet ideology had long ceased to have positive meaning, and became little more than a set of irritating but circumventable obstacles to art and thought. From 1985 a "thaw" far more comprehensive than Khrushchev's set in, and by 1990 there was effectively no more censorship. "Taboo" works, by literary figures such as Zamyatin and Solzhenitsyn, or painters such as Malevich and Filonov, entered public consciousness, while a lively artistic avant-garde emerged. Important figures who emigrated or were exiled under Brezhnev could come and go freely, while travel abroad became possible for ordinary citizens. Splendid as the prospects for Russian cultural life looked, however, they were clouded by the realization that most activities had been heavily subsidised by the Soviet system. Institutions and individuals alike now faced a risky if exhilarating future in the market-place.

Politics and Society since 1991

In the half dozen years between the dissolution of the Soviet Union and the time of writing there has been greater stability in the territories of the former USSR than most commentators could have dared expect, or hope. Boris Yeltsin survived fears for his health and considerable unpopularity to win the Russian Presidential election of 1996. The old constituent Republics of the Union managed, by and large, an effective transition to independent nationhood—with civil strife erupting only in Georgia, Tajikistan and to a small degree in Moldova. The most serious inter-republic border dispute, between Armenia and Azerbaijan over Nagorno-Karabakh, settled down into a *de facto* ceasefire (advantageous to the Armenian claims). The dispute between Russians, Ukrainians and Tatars over Crimea did not descend into violence. Apocalyptic Western European visions of the mass invasion of its frontiers by millions of hunger-crazed Eastern refugees have not yet materialized.

It has nevertheless not been an easy time for ordinary Russians and other former Soviet citizens. The rouble was made convertible and the state monopoly on economic power and land-ownership slackened—but all this proved to be at the cost of nightmarish inflation and the unaccustomed spectacle of widespread unemployment. Both industrial productivity and the overall standard of living swiftly declined. The flimsiness, undercapitalization and inflexibility of the Soviet industrial achievement became apparent; so did serious ecological problems, notably concerning water supplies and the shrinking of the Aral Sea in Central Asia. "Rustbelt" and single-industry cities were especially vulnerable to the new circumstances, while the possibility of major disasters involving nuclear power had been apparent ever since the notorious accident at Chornobyl' (1986), which itself had played a part in precipitating the Gorbachov reforms. Public employees, from teachers to miners, were particularly hard hit not only by inflation but by the tardy and irregular payment of state salaries. Protection-rackets and similar organized criminal activities (loosely attributed to the "Mafia"—an imprecise term) moved in to take advantage of a general weakening in law enforcement and indeed of legal uncertainties. Privatization (masterminded most notably by Yeltsin's deputy premier Anatoly Chubais) made bumpy, in some respects over-hasty, progress; much privatized industry remained in the hands of the old *nomenklatura*.

On the political front the most extended and traumatic crisis concerned Russia's relations with one of its own autonomous regions, Chechnya. A small nation (under a million) on the northern flank of the Caucasus, the Chechens have loomed disproportionately large in the Russian imagination, if not demonology, over the last 200 years or so: they were famously fierce fighters, hindering Russian imperial expansion in the Caucasian area. Their present territory straddles the main road, railway and oil pipeline from Russia to the Caspian region. At the dissolution of the Soviet Union the Chechen leader, the wily ex-Soviet General Dudayev, claimed full independence. Protracted negotiations, clumsily handled, got nowhere, and led eventually to a fullscale Russian military assault on Grozny, the capital. Dudayev was killed, but the insurgents could not be defeated, and eventually the tough General Lebed settled for terms that left Russia with no more than nominal sovereignty. The Chechen war was deeply unpopular in Russia itself, and demonstrated the demorilization of its largely conscript army. The Russian authorities had feared a knock-on effect from Chechnya among its many other national groupings, but this did not fully materialize: important autonomous areas such as Tatarstan and Yakutia (Sakha) settled for a large degree of self-government and economic control.

The Russian parliament (*duma*), suspicious of the precipitate reforms, quickly became alienated from the president. Yeltsin responded in spectacular fashion, increasing his powers, demanding compliance and in the autumn of 1993 (in a strange reversal of the events of two years before) actually bombarding the "White House" in Moscow (seat of the *duma*) to get his way. Despite this monstrous *démarche*, political culture in Russia made steady progress. The 1996 election was conducted with remarkable efficiency and fairness, with evident public appreciation of the issues as well as personalities. For the reformed communists, whose presidential candidate was Gennady Zyuganov, this was clearly a crucial moment: he was defeated through the solidity of Moscow and St Petersburg for Yeltsin. General Lebed did well in the old north-central heartland (e.g. Yaroslavl); the extreme nationist Vladimir Zhirinovsky made little impact. Despite governmental attempts to influence the media, a vigorous and uninhibitedly free press remains characteristic of 1990s Russia. The other former Union Republics have generally adhered to democratic processes (sometimes freely electing former communists)—but some, in particular Belarus (Belorussia) and Turkmenistan, have entrusted their destiny to dictatorial strongmen. The CIS (Commonwealth of Independent States; *S N G* in Russian) proved rather inert as a political entity, though the continuing economic and cultural interdependence of the Soviet Union's successor states provides a rationale for its existence.

In the second half of the 1990s Moscow, and to a lesser extent St Peterburg, were clearly recovering from post-Soviet chaos and impoverishment. Both had vigorous elected mayors intent on giving them a face-lift. The gap between capital and provinces widened, however (though even remote places had their share of "new Russians", grown suddenly rich in the wake of the economic reforms). Even as the vast bulk of the Cathedral of Christ the Saviour (a replica of that demolished in the 1930s) was being rushed up for the 850th anniversary of Moscow's foundation (1997), provincial restoration work had almost come to a halt. Smallscale artistic, theatrical and publishing enterprise continued to flourish throughout Russia, nevertheless—a pledge of its apparently unconquerable vitality.

PART THREE
REGIONS AND COUNTRIES OF THE FORMER SOVIET UNION

Latvia
pp192

Estonia
pp192

Lithuania
pp192

to Russia

Belarus
pp186–187

Moscow and
St Petersburg
pp206–207

Moldova
pp186–187

Ukraine
pp186–187

Georgia
pp198–199

Russia
pp204–205

Armenia
pp198–199

Azerbaijan
pp198–199

Kazakhstan
pp216–217

Uzbekistan
pp216–217

Turkmenistan
pp216–217

Kyrgyzstan
pp216–217

Tajikistan
pp216–217

The final section of this atlas turns from the specifically Russian concerns that have occupied most of the volume to examine the republics that until recently constituted the Soviet Union, and can still be regarded as a geographical unit, whose economic interdependence is unlikely to disappear in the foreseeable future. Russian remains the *lingua franca* throughout this region, in which well over 100 languages are spoken.

The Soviet Union inherited most of the territory of the former Russian Empire (less Poland and Finland). But unlike the Empire it was constitutionally a federation of—eventually—fifteen separate republics, each with its own governmental structures and theoretically able to secede from the Union. To most Western eyes this arrangement looked merely like a typical bit of Stalinist window-dressing, and it came as a surprise when political developments in the late

1980s brought the republics' legal status into sharp focus. The Gorbachev government struggled unavailingly to keep some sort of union together, and in 1991 the Soviet Union simply dissolved into its constituent republics—most of which came together again in the much looser "Commonwealth of Independent States". The national situation the republics inherited, however, was complex and full of potential for strife, both between republics and within them: the many "autonomous republics" (ASSRs) and "autonomous regions" (AOs) of the former Soviet Union had helped to preserve or foster a sense of national identity among ethnic groups too small to have a union republic.

Special considerations apply to the transliterations used in maps and text of this section of our volume: see last paragraph on p. 229 for full descriptive notes on this subject.

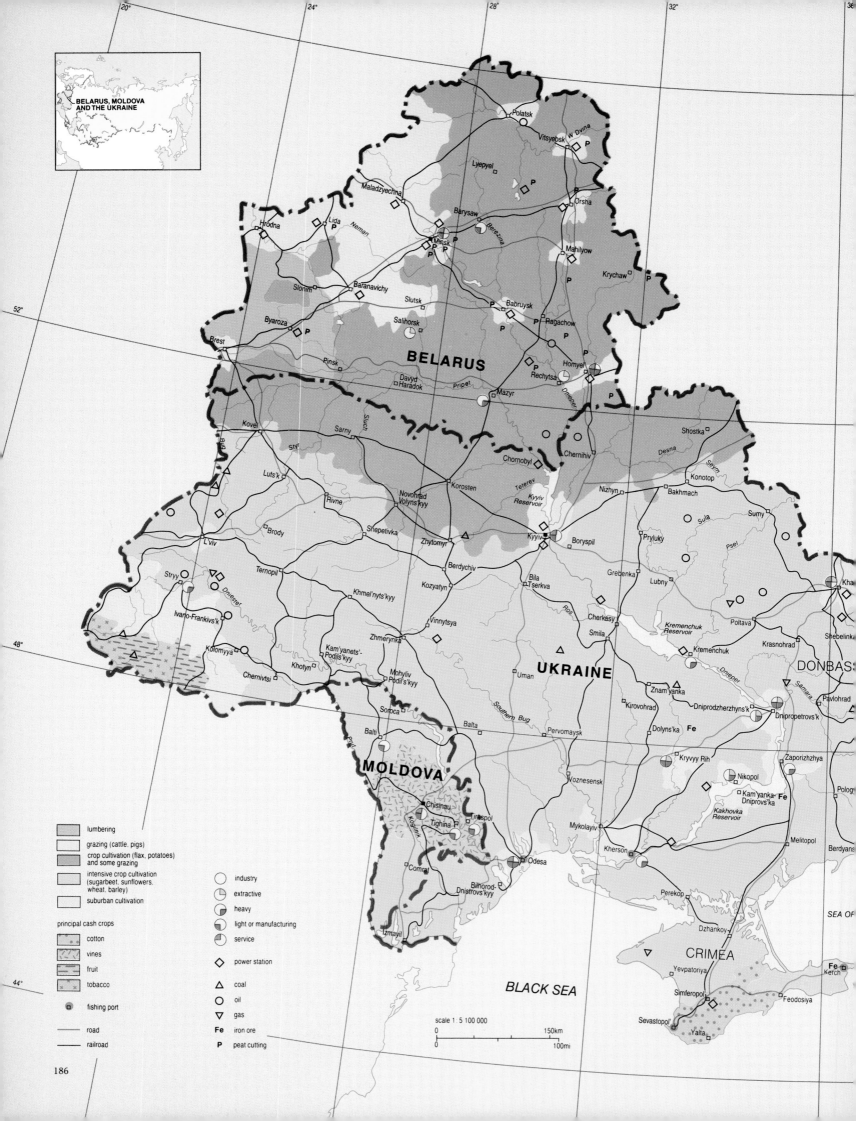

BELARUS, MOLDOVA AND THE UKRAINE

20°　24°　28°　32°　36°

Polatsk
Vitsyebsk
W Dvina P
Lyepyel
P
Maladzyechna
Orsha
Barysaw
P
Minsk
P
Mahilyow
Hrodna
Lida
P
Krychaw
P
Neman
Slonim
Baranavichy
Slutsk
Babruysk
Byaroza
P
Salihorsk
Ragachow
P
Brest
Pinsk
BELARUS
Homyel
P
Davyd
Haradok
Pripet
Mazyr
Rechytsa
P
Dnieper
Kovel
Sarny
Sluch
Chornobyl
Chernihiv
Shostka
Desna
Styr
Bug
Luts'k
Novohrad
Volyns'kyy
Korosten
Teterev
Kyyiv
Reservoir
Konotop
Seym
Nizhyn
Bakhmach
Rivne
Brody
Shepetivka
Zhytomyr
Kyyiv
Borpyspil
Pryluky
Sumy
L'viv
Stryy
Ternopil
Berdychiv
Bila
Tserkva
Grebenka
Lubny
Psel
Dniester
Ivano-Frankivs'k
Khmel'nyts'kyy
Kozyatyn
Ros
Cherkasy
Kremenchuk
Reservoir
Poltava
Krasnohrad
Shebelinka
Kolomyya
Vinnytsya
Zhmerynka
Kam'yanets'-
Podils'kyy
Smila
Kremenchuk
Khotyn
Chernivtsi
Mohyliv
Podil's'kyy
Uman
UKRAINE
Dnieper
Samara
Pavlohrad
DONBASS
Soroca
Balta
Southern Bug
Pervomaysk
Znam'yanka
Dniprodzherzhyns'k
Dnipropetrovs'k
Balti
Kirovohrad
Dolyns'ka Fe
MOLDOVA
Voznesensk
Kryvyy Rih
Nikopol
Zaporizhzhya
Chisinau
Kam'yanka-
Dniprovs'ka Fe
Pology
Tighina
Tiraspol
Mykolayiv
Kakhovka
Reservoir
Melitopol
Comrat
Kherson
Berdyans
Bilhorod-
Dnistrovs'kyy
Odesa
Perekop
SEA OF
Izmayil
Dzhankoy
CRIMEA
Yevpatoriya
Fe
Kerch
BLACK SEA
Simferopol
Feodosiya
Sevastopol'
Yalta

lumbering

grazing (cattle. pigs)

crop cultivation (flax, potatoes)
and some grazing

intensive crop cultivation
(sugarbeet. sunflowers.
wheat. barley)

suburban cultivation

principal cash crops

cotton

vines

fruit

tobacco

fishing port

road

railroad

Fe　iron ore

P　peat cutting

○　industry

◑　extractive

◑　heavy

◑　light or manufacturing

◑　service

◇　power station

△　coal

○　oil

▽　gas

186

BELARUS, MOLDOVA AND UKRAINE

Republic	Belarus	Moldova	Ukraine
AREA	207 600 sq km	33 700 sq km	603 700 sq km
POPULATION	10·4m (est 1997)	4·4m (est 1997)	51·4m (est 1997)
CAPITAL	Minsk	Chişinău (Kishinev)	Kyyiv (Kiev)
POPULATION OF CAPITAL	1 671 000 (1997)	753 500 (1991)	1 895 000 (1996)
LANGUAGE	Belarusian; also many Russian speakers	Moldovan, i.e. Romanian; Russian around R. Dnester	Ukrainian; Russian dominant in Crimea, Odessa and east of R. Dnieper

These three republics, formerly the western borderlands of the Soviet Union, are agriculturally fortunate, with a less extreme continental climate and a better pattern of rainfall: much of Ukraine and Moldova also has the benefit of fertile chernozem, "black earth." In Belarus steppe gives way to the poorer soils of the mixed forest. Where Ukraine and Belarus meet is a huge area of lakes, rivers, woodlands and swamps, known as the *Polesye* or Pripet marshes which, since the disaster at the nuclear power stations of Chornobyl' (Chernobyl) in 1986, have sadly become severely polluted.

The Ukrainians and Belarusians are East Slavs, who differentiated themselves from the Muscovite Russians only from the later Middle Ages; they share with the latter the heritage of Kievan Rus, of which all three were integral parts. They shared too the legacy of Orthodoxy: after the Tatar invasion, however, they passed for several centuries under the control of Lithuania and subsequently Poland, and their upper classes became largely Catholic. Moldova, by contrast, lived through centuries of Ottoman Turkish rule and remained Orthodox; its inhabitants are not Slavs, but Romanians in language. It was liberated from the Ottomans and incorporated into the Russian empire as "Bessarabia" in the early 19th century, but it was made part of Romania between the two world wars. In the same period the newly independent Polish state took back large parts of western Ukraine and Belarus (all these territories were thus spared the worst excesses of Stalinist terror in the 1930s). After World War II the Soviet Union moved its frontier westward again to include all historic Ukrainian and Belarusian lands.

The upland scenery of the Carpathian region (*right*), typical of the mountain zone of much of Central Europe, contrasts with the more open, rolling countryside of Ukraine, farther east (*below right*) Trans-Carpathian "Ruthenia" was incorporated into Ukraine by the Soviet Government in 1945.

Belarus

Belarus (or "White Russia"—the significance of the name is uncertain) is a country of rolling plains and forests. To the south it is closed off by the dense forests and waterways of the Pripet marshes: to the north a series of glacial moraines give higher elevation and drier soil, while the Western Dvina provides a historic waterway to the Baltic. On the Polish frontier lies the remarkable Belovezha primeval forest and nature reserve, the last home of the great European bison.

Historically Belarus is heir to the important and effectively independent Kievan principality of Polotsk. After the Tatar invasion of 1240 it passed into the hands of the grand princes of Lithuania. After the union of the Lithuanian and Polish crowns in 1386 Belarus participated in the Renaissance culture of Poland in the 16th and 17th centuries; perhaps a quarter of the population became Catholic, although the peasantry remained predominantly Orthodox. Only with the late 18th-century partitions of Poland was most of Belarus incorporated into the Russian empire.

Lying on the direct route between Berlin and Moscow Belarus suffered greater loss than any other area of the Soviet Union at the hands of the invading Nazis. During their occupation (1941–44) 1·5 million Belarusians were evacuated east of the Volga River, a large section of the Jewish population fled or was murdered and over three-quarters of the towns and cities were destroyed. But perhaps the tenacity of the people played a part in the revival of this devastated nation which grew rapidly in the post-war years, only to suffer the ill effects of the devastating pollution of 25 percent of its territory after the Chornobyl' (Chernobyl) disaster.

The traditional occupations of lumbering and potato-growing are still important. Damp summers and sandy soils make ideal conditions in which to grow potatoes, mainly used for animal fodder and the potato-alcohol industry, although these crops are now exposed to contamination. One-third of the territory is forested and the numerous lakes and waterways are used to float timber to factories for the manufacture of furniture and building materials. Sand is used to make silica bricks and glass. With the pollution of much agricultural land, Belarus now concentrates on the manufacture and export of agricultural machinery, such as tractors and trucks produced at a major motor works at Minsk.

Moldova

The undulating steppe country of Bessarabia, between the rivers Prut and Dniester, passed from the Ottoman to the Russian empire in the early 19th century. Its indigenous people, the Moldovans, are linguistically and culturally indistinguishable from Romanians. They have had a separate state only since 1940, when Bessarabia was parted from Romania, under the German-Russian pact, and joined with the

Moldavian ASSR of the Ukrainian SSR. This considerably increased the proportion of ethnic Moldovans within the state to 66·5 percent. Since then, immigrating Ukrainians and Russians have furthered this heterogeneous trend, so today more than one-third of all families living in towns are ethnically mixed.

Moldova became the most densely populated, though the smallest, of all the former Soviet republics. The lack of mineral resources puts great pressure on the land to sustain the economy, with the majority engaged in highly intensive agriculture. Fortunately, the fertile black earth covering gently rolling lowlands combines with probably the best climate for cultivation, making Moldova now a major international producer and exporter of wine. The benefits of long warm summers, mild winters and moderate rainfall are supplemented by irrigation systems channeled from the Prut and Dniester rivers. Other typical produce is fruit, vegetables, nuts, maize, winter wheat and sunflowers. Industry tends to follow agriculture: food-canning, meat-packing, textile manufacture, sugar-refining, fertilizer production and woodworking (timber comes from the wooded steppe of the northern region). Despite a perceptible transition from a traditional agricultural economy towards light industry in recent years, economic progress has been interrupted by continuing unrest and conflict between Moldova's various ethnic communities.

Above Wine-production, here seen in Kishinev, is a major growth industry in the small, land-locked republic of Moldova, where the country's temperate climate is ideal for the cultivation of grapevines. Grapes, along with grain and sugar beet are now the country's most important source of revenue.

Left Springtime at Tsybulyovka, in the Dubossarsky region of Moldova. Fertile soil and a kindly climate encourage Moldovans to produce a wide range of crops.

Below Tradtional methods of farming are still prevalent in many of the former republics of the Soviet Union. In the struggle to adapt to a market economy, and more efficient methods of farming, many in the villages still use the traditional methods of threshing corn, as seen here in Moldova.

Ukraine

The name "Ukraine" implies "borderland" and was first applied to the territories to the east of the Dnieper, the wild and largely unpeopled steppe that was only slowly subdued for settled habitation. In this, and in the formation of a specific Ukrainian consciousness, a key role was played by the Cossacks, frontiersmen who lived on the lower reaches of the Dnieper and Don. Only from the 1780s was the steppe fully secured by Russia to the Black Sea, and thereafter exploited properly for agriculture. For a time Odesa became a great grain-exporting port. Stalin's collectivization of agriculture, virtually a war on the peasants, had a devastating effect in Ukraine, leading to famine and millions of deaths and deportations. From these and the depredations of World War II, it has slowly recovered. Kyyiv (Kiev) has again become one of the great cities of Europe.

Ukraine, with over 51 million inhabitants, is by far the most populous republic of the former Soviet Union after Russia. Out of more than a hundred nationalities present in Ukraine, the great majority count themselves ethnic Ukrainians, and most of the others speak closely related Slavonic languages such as Russian and Polish. Ukraine is now a major industrializing nation, where the traditional pattern of mining coal for use in the local steel furnaces has broadened to involve other industries associated with the republic's vast agricultural resources, such as flour-milling, sugar-refining and sunflower oil extraction. The rolling lowlands of wheat, barley and other cereal crops, sugarbeet and sunflowers support a largely indigenous and settled rural population. By contrast, the Donets-Dnieper basin in the east is heavily urbanized and is now struggling to maintain

Right The 18th-century exterior of St Sophia, Kyyiv (Kiev), with its onion-shaped domes and baroque detailing, conceals the cathedral's 11th-century Byzantinesque structure.

its industrial primacy in the face of competition from cheaper and higher-grade resources in Siberia. The industrial heartland of the Donets-Dnieper basin with its 400 or so coal mines and its huge deposits of iron ore, manganese, salt and oil, is now one of the largest industrial complexes in the world, but towards the end of the twentieth century was suffering from the effects of severe pollution. The steel plants, of which Kryvyy Rih is the main one, though no longer able to produce the quality necessary for precision engineering have now put Ukraine on a par with China, as the world's fourth largest producer of steel, for the making of combine harvesters and in canning processes. Natural gas from vast deposits at Shebelinka and Yefremovka supplies many cities in Ukraine and Russia.

Nuclear power was also a major industry in Ukraine, until the accident at Chornobyl' (Chernobyl) in 1986 brought a halt to development. The cost of cleaning up over 30,000 square miles of contaminated farmland severely damaged Ukraine's economy. In 1997 Western nations committed $3 billion worth of aid to close the plant by the year 2000.

Left House decorating at Odesa. Built in the neoclassical style of St Petersburg, Odesa enjoyed its heyday as a free port in the first half of the 19th century. It suffered much damage after 1918 during the civil war and was captured by the Germans in World War II, but many older buildings and quarters survive as reminders of its cosmopolitan past.

Below Holidaymakers pack the beach at the Black Sea resort of Yalta in the Crimea. The dry Mediterranean climate of this strip of coast, sheltered from the north wind by the limestone Yayla mountains, has long been a magnet for visitors; Chekhov is among the famous invalids who have sought health here. Numerous large holiday complexes belonging to trade unions and institutes are a feature of the coast; earlier palaces with their magnificent gardens are kept up as museums.

The indigenous Crimean Tatars of the interior were deported by Stalin during World War II, and most of the peninsula's permanent residents are now of Russian stock. In 1954 Krushchev made the Crimea part of the Ukraine. Since the collapse of Communism some Russians have campaigned to see it restored to Russia, while many Tatars have returned.

Above Cabbages piled high in a Ukrainian field. The period of harvest in September brings fevered activity, since crops like cabbages cannot stand out in the fields to overwinter as they can in more temperate climates.

Ukraine owes much of its prosperity to its exceptionally fertile chernozem (black earth). The enormous extent of fields in Ukraine arose out of Stalin's policy of turning agricultural land into huge collective farms (*kolkhozy*). These farms were actually owned by the members of the collective and their fortunes depended upon the productivity of their land. Under perestroika in the 1980s Ukrainian agriculture was slowly restructured and the *kolkhozy* were broken up into smaller, independent farming units. Continuing privatization of the old state collective system is part of the drive towards establishing a market economy.

Left This road sign on the outskirts of the now deserted town of Pripyat, in Ukraine is a stark reminder of the aftermath of Chornobyl', the world's worst nuclear power accident. Here motorists are warned of the risks they take by entering a radioactive zone. The fallout from the accident at Chornobyl' in 1986 was so severe that the whole of nearby Pripyat's population had to be evacuated.

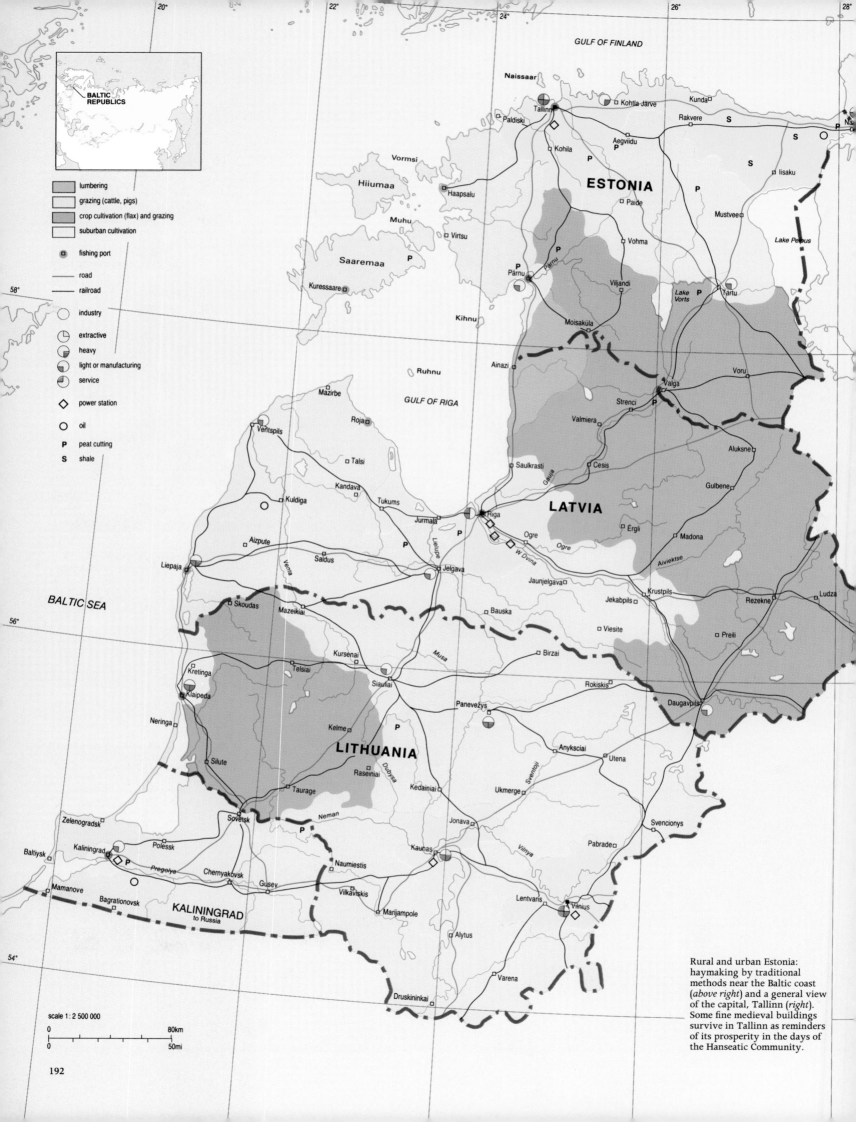

GULF OF FINLAND

BALTIC REPUBLICS

lumbering
grazing (cattle, pigs)
crop cultivation (flax) and grazing
suburban cultivation

fishing port

road
railroad

industry
extractive
heavy
light or manufacturing
service

power station

oil

P peat cutting

S shale

58°

ESTONIA

Naissaar
Tallinn
Paldiski
Kohila
Kohtla-Jarve
Kunda
Rakvere
Aegviidu
Iisaku
Haapsalu
Paide
Mustvee
Vohma
Vormsi
Hiiumaa
Muhu
Virtsu
Saaremaa
Parnu
Parnu
Viljandi
Lake Peipus
Kuressaare
Kihnu
Moisakula
Lake Vorts
Tartu
Ruhnu
Ainazi
Voru
Mazirbe
GULF OF RIGA
Valga
Strenci
Roja
Valmiera
Aluksne
Ventspils
Talsi
Saulkrasti
Cesis
Gulbene
Kandava
Gauja
LATVIA
Kuldiga
Tukums
Riga
Ergli
Madona
Aizpute
Jurmala
Ogre
Aiviekste
Saldus
Lielupe
Ogre
W Dvina
Liepaja
Jelgava
Jaunjelgava
Krustpils
Rezekne
Ludza
Venta
Jekabpils
BALTIC SEA
Skoudas
Mazeikiai
Bauska
Viesite
Preili
56°
Kursenai
Birzai
Kretinga
Telsiai
Musa
Rokiskis
Klaipeda
Siauliai
Daugavpils
Neringa
Kelme
Panevezys
Naumiestis
LITHUANIA
Anyksciai
Utena
Silute
Raseiniai
Dubysa
Kedainiai
Sventoji
Taurage
Ukmerge
Svencionys
Sovetsk
Neman
Vilnya
Pabrade
Zelenogradsk
Polessk
Jonava
Kaunas
Kaliningrad
Baltiysk
Pregolya
Chernyakovsk
Gusev
Vilkaviskis
Lentvaris
Vilnius
Mamanovo
Bagrationovsk
KALININGRAD
to Russia
Naumiestis
Marijampole
Alytus
Varena
Druskininkai

Rural and urban Estonia:
haymaking by traditional
methods near the Baltic coast
(*above right*) and a general view
of the capital, Tallinn (*right*).
Some fine medieval buildings
survive in Tallinn as reminders
of its prosperity in the days of
the Hanseatic Community.

scale 1 : 2 500 000

0 80km
0 50mi

192

THE BALTIC REPUBLICS

Republic	Estonia	Latvia	Lithuania
AREA	45 100 sq km	64 600 sq km	65 300 sq km
POPULATION	1·5m (est 1997)	2·5m (est 1997)	3·7m (est 1997)
CAPITAL	Tallinn	Rīga (Riga)	Vilnius
POPULATION OF CAPITAL	499 000 (1994)	917 000 (1996)	593 000 (1995)
LANGUAGE	Estonian; also many Russian speakers	Latvian; also many Russian speakers	Lithuanian; also a Polish minority

Since the early Middle Ages the east Baltic littoral has attracted successive conquerors and adventurers, whilst the interior continued to support the indigenous inhabitants—Lithuanians, Letts and Estonians—whose distinctive languages and way of life survive to the present. All three employ Roman rather than Cyrillic script. The Swedes eventually incorporated most of the area into their east Baltic empire in the 17th century. The Russian Tsar Ivan IV struggled in vain for a permanent Baltic foothold; Peter the Great was finally successful. Lithuania and Courland (southern Latvia), allied to the Polish crown, became Russian in 1795. Between the two world wars all three countries were independent states; the Soviet Union annexed them in 1940, was driven out by Hitler's invasion in 1941 and reabsorbed them at the end of the war. But the nationalist instinct here was always strong and they were the first republics to press for independence from the Soviet Union in the late 1980s.

Though the elevation of the region reaches no great heights, the underlying rocks are older and harder than in central Russia. The shelving sandy beaches of the Baltic give way to many cliffs, inlets and rocky islands bordering the Gulf of Finland. Timber from the extensive forests is important, as are shipbuilding, precision engineering and the fishing industry in the coastal cities. Importantly, modern icebreakers can normally keep the Baltic ports open in winter. There are peat deposits and oil shale in the north. An ancient source of wealth is amber, in which the eastern Baltic coast is rich.

Estonia

Estonia's capital is Tallinn (meaning "Danes' Town"), a 13th-century Danish foundation and one of the best-preserved cities of the Hanseatic Community in the Baltic region. After perhaps a third of the population had been lost during the German occupation and the Stalinist purges, the farming community was collectivized and a rigorous development plan set in progress. Today Estonia is a highly industrialized economy. Despite the fact that it had to grapple with high inflation rates in the early 1990s it is now the richest of all the former republics of the Soviet Union.

The high standard of living attracted many ethnic Russians to the region after World War II, and nationalistic feelings have been fierce. Estonians constituted only 60 percent of the population by the 1990s, and they have one of the lowest birthrates in the country. Their determination to preserve their cultural heritage was reflected in the reduction in numbers using the Russian language during the 1970's and the country preserved a strong ethnic tradition in its music and literature. Playwrights dared to be more outspoken than those in Moscow or Leningrad (St Petersburg). Modernist painters and musicians were attracted from other areas, and the ballet and symphony orchestra established a strong reputation. Fashion design, always enhanced by access to Western media via Finland, feeds off a sophisticated textile industry with its center at Narva.

Ethnically, Estonians share a common descent with the Finns. Due to their past links with the Germans, who controlled a great deal of the territory up to 1917, most are Lutheran (a characteristic which they share with the Letts from neighboring Latvia) with a strong commitment to work and the family. In spite of a land that is stony and damp—though the climate is less extreme than that of its neighbors further east—farm production is high. The predominant dairy industry exports 90 percent of its output to neighboring republics. The other main sources of wealth are centered in the north around the oil-shale deposits, which are put to a variety of uses: the generation of thermal electric power, conversion into gas for factory and home consumption and the manufacture of petrochemical and chemical products. Textiles, shipbuilding and precision engineering have all prospered as a result.

Shops are well stocked, the people smartly dressed and cosmopolitan, and cafés, restaurants and hotels are learning to cater to the developing tourist industry. Educational levels are high; Tartu (formerly Dorpat) has one of the great universities of Europe, originating in a college founded by the Swedes in the 17th century; since World War II, this has made a unique contribution to Russian as well as Baltic intellectual life.

Below Sunbathers on a sandy beach near Tallinn. The Gulf of Finland is a popular summer holiday destination which, since the collapse of Communism, is now being opened up to foreign tourists.

Left This phosphate mine at Maardu in Estonia is a symbol of Estonia's industrial growth since the collapse of Communism. The country is now the richest of all the former republics and it extensive deposits of high-quality phosphorites are contributing to this wealth.

Below Folk dancing at a students' Gaudeamus festival at Tallinn. The word "gaudeamus" is Latin for "let us rejoice." Estonians are particularly attached to their rich heritage of folksong and to other traditional aspects of their culture which they zealously maintain in the face of what they see as alien Slav influences. Culturally and linguistically, their affinities are with their northern neighbors, the Finns.

Below right The freedom monument in Rīga, capital of Latvia, dates from 1935. Latvia was independent in the period between the two world wars, and Rīga played an important part in the Baltic independence movement of the 1980s.

Latvia

Latvia, like Estonia, has come under the domination of successive external powers: of the German knights in the 13th century, the Swedes in the 17th, then the Poles, until the Russians annexed the country at the end of the 18th century. At this time large numbers of Germans settled in the region; many came at the invitation of Catherine the Great, and have left their mark on Latvian society through the predomination of the Lutheran church. At the turn of the century Germans made up nearly half the population, with only 23 percent Latvian (i.e. Letts).

Latvia remained part of the Russian empire up to 1919, after which it enjoyed, with the other Baltic republics, a period of independence until 1940. During the Nazi occupation half a million Latvians lost their lives and almost the entire Jewish community was wiped out.

Wholesale rebuilding of the economy was required after World War II, and an influx of labor from the Russian Federation, Ukraine and Belarus gradually altered the ethnic composition of the population to the extent that nearly a third were non-Latvian. Of the present population 32 percent are ethnic Russians and the question of their continuing citizenship of Latvia has become a contentious one since the demise of the Soviet Union. The Latvian language,

Left A street flower market at Tallinn. Prosperous and sophisticated, Tallinn retains a distinctly northern European— as opposed to Russian— appearance and atmosphere. The old city walls with their numerous surviving towers add to its charm.

which together with Lithuanian and the extinct Old Prussian forms a separate Baltic group within the Indo-European family, is now assuming precedence over Russian in all aspects of Latvian life and culture.

Industrial expansion has been rapid but overconcentrated around Rīga, which has long been far the largest and most international of the Baltic cities. It has a long tradition of trade, both seaborne and internal, via the Western Dvina (Daugava) river, which flows to Latvia from Russia and Belarus. Timber and furniture, dairy products and flax are all exported, while sugar, industrial equipment, fertilizers, coal and other raw materials needed for local industries are imported. As a Baltic port, Rīga is an important center for shipbuilding and fish processing, but it now has an advanced engineering industry producing tractors, buses, railroad rolling stock and electrical and radio equipment. Electricity is either generated from local peat supplies or cabled from the oil-shale plants in Estonia. Tourism is now growing in importance: the beaches along the Baltic coast attract tourists from many parts of Europe and ensure good seasonal trade.

Left A Latvian wooden windmill. Much of Latvia's terrain is marked by glaciation and the soils are cold and waterlogged; damp springs and summer rainfall militate against crop growing, and mixed forest, with a high percentage of conifers, covers large areas of the land. Timber is therefore an important resource, both for local building and for export.

Right A legacy of the Soviet era, Juknaichai village housed 1800 people on a state farm in Lithuania, called after the 25th CPSU Congress. The director of the farm and the architect involved were awarded a Lenin Prize in 1988 for their imaginative design. The dourly rectangular and functional accommodation blocks in the foreground give way to a more irregular arrangement of dwellings constructed in a local idiom, mimicking the organic growth of a real village.

Lithuania

The Lithuanian language, part of the Baltic group in the Indo-European family, is the most archaic Indo-European language still spoken. The Grand Duchy of Lithuania began to extend its power over west Russia from the 13th century and survived as a separate entity until 1569, when it was linked in a binational state with Poland; this lasted until the end of the 18th century. Although a long period to 1918 was spent under Russian suzerainty, ties with Poland and other European states were maintained through trade and through the Roman Catholic Church. The Lithuanians were the last pagan nation in Europe, accepting Catholicism in 1385, though most of their subjects were Orthodox Russians, and pagan survivals have remained strong in the countryside. Today, 80 percent of Lithuanians are Roman Catholics and the religion is a strong part of their national identity.

A whole religious heritage is evoked through the arts—in music, painting and architecture. Up to 1940, when Lithuania was reannexed to Russia after 22 years of independence, much of daily life, including schooling, involved the church. In league with the Popular National Front, formed out of a number of human rights movements in 1974, the church became the foremost institution for national self-assertion during the, at times violent, dissident movement which campaigned for independence.

Under the Soviet regime a relatively larger number of interfarm cooperative enterprises was set up here than in the other two Baltic republics; this had the effect of depopulating rural areas and flooding the previously insignificant urban ones, whose growth became very rapid. Until 1961, when a gas pipeline was laid to the region, industry was dependent on either its peat supplies or coal imports for electricity generation. A new period of growth began in which a range of gas-based chemical plants opened up, and marshlands were cultivated more effectively. Conditions are best suited to dairying and livestock rearing, and modern intensive farming methods maximize fodder crop yields producing grazing meadows to support these enterprises. After struggling with hyperinflation in the early 1990s, the economy has begun to grow again and Lithuania is now an important machine-tool producer. Two-thirds of the world's amber can also be found here.

Left The docks at Rīga, situated near where the Western Dvina (Dangava) River flows out into the southeastern end of the Gulf of Rīga. The major port on the eastern Baltic, Rīga is linked via the Dvina and canals with the basins of the Dnieper and Volga rivers.

Below left Rīga has for centuries been the metropolis of the eastern Baltic. It suffered heavily in both world wars but retains much of its medieval heart.

Below House building in the 1980s on a collective farm in the Kapsuksky region of Lithuania. Housing shortages were endemic in many parts of the Soviet Union; here an effort is being made to improve both the quantity and quality of available accommodation.

Above Lithuania's Baltic Sea trade has always been an important component of the nations economy. Commercial traffic and the transportation of freight has increased dramatically in the last fifty years. Here at the major port of Klaipeda fish-processing is still an important industry.

Left A political rally in Gediminas Square, Vilnius, capital of Lithuania, in November 1988. It was organized by the Lithuanian movement Sajudis to demonstrate support for the principles of *perestroika*. Nationalist sentiment and unrest in Lithuania and Estonia grew throughout the late 1980s. All three Baltic States achieved independence in 1991 and were admitted into the U N.

Left The Transcaucasian region has for centuries enjoyed a reputation for its fine saddle horses. Particularly prized among the local breeds was the Karabakh, which had a characteristic golden color; the Cossacks of the Don and Volga regions formerly bought large numbers of Karabakhs to improve the quality, speed and stamina of their own horses. In the hilly Transcaucasian terrain horses have still a useful role to play in a pastoral economy.

TRANSCAUCASIA

Republic	Armenia	Georgia	Azerbaijan
AREA	29 800 sq km	69 700 sq km	86 600 sq km
POPULATION	3·6m (est 1997)	5·4m (est 1997)	7·6m (est 1997)
CAPITAL	Yerevan	T'bilisi (formerly Tiflis)	Baku (Baki)
POPULATION OF CAPITAL	1 283 000 (1991)	1 253 000 (1994)	1 700 000 (1993)
MAJOR LANGUAGE	Armenian	Georgian	Azeri (a Turkic language); also many Russian speakers in Baku

The geophysical tension between the Russian shelf to the north and the Arabic shelf to the south has produced the mountainous landscape of Transcaucasia and reflects the historical conflicts that have dominated the peoples of the three republics: Armenia, Georgia and Azerbaijan. Successive empires—Hellenistic, Roman, Byzantine, Khazar, Arab, Mongol, Ottoman, Persian and Russian—have all coveted the region for its wealth and strategic location. A neck of land between the Caspian and Black seas, on the old spice and silk routes, Transcaucasia links the Mediterranean with Central Asia, the steppe country with the Near East. This comparatively small region has a cultural and artistic diversity reflecting both exposure to numerous outside influences and the tenacity of native traditions; within the three main republics there are enclaves of other nationalities, several of which are clamoring for autonomy.

The rich valleys and plains of Armenia and Georgia are intensively cultivated. Their wines are now becoming famous around the world. An ancient and patriarchal way of life characterizes particularly the high valleys of the Caucasus, where to this day there is an amazing profusion of languages. To the west the river systems drain down to the humid, subtropical lowlands of ancient Colchis at the eastern tip of the Black Sea; eastwards they flow through the arid plains of Azerbaijan, with its far greater extremes of climate and its need for extensive irrigation.

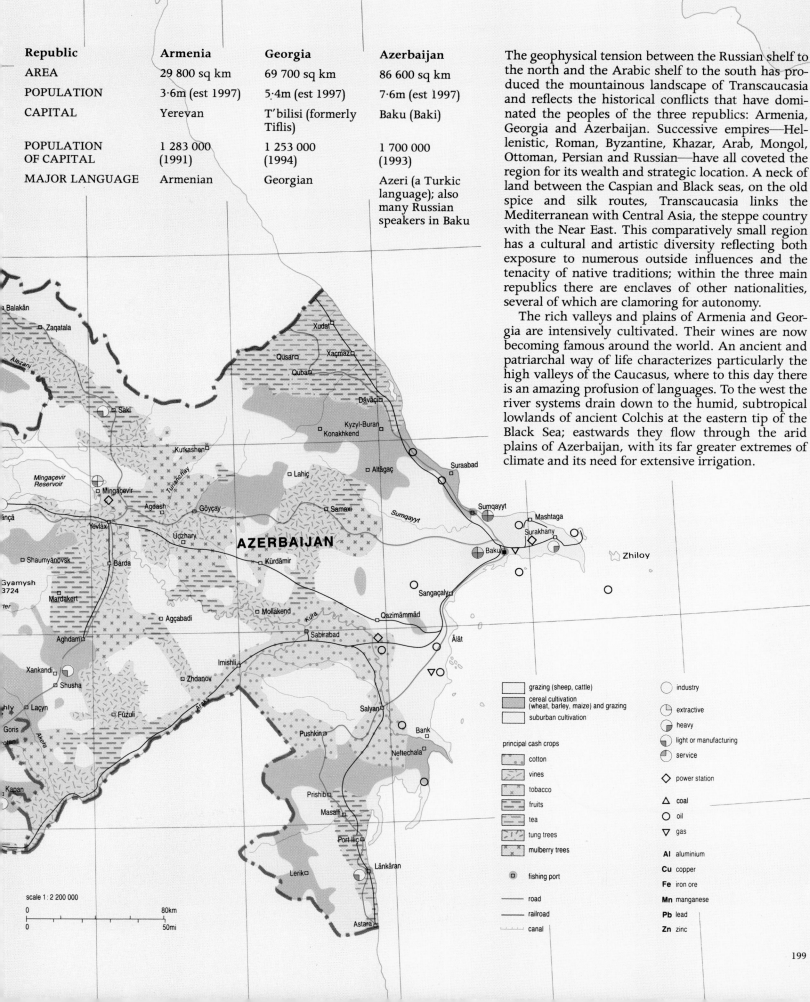

	grazing (sheep, cattle)
	cereal cultivation (wheat, barley, maize) and grazing
	suburban cultivation

principal cash crops

	cotton
	vines
	tobacco
	fruits
	tea
	tung trees
	mulberry trees

fishing port

— road
— railroad
···· canal

○ industry
◔ extractive
◑ heavy
◕ light or manufacturing
◓ service

◇ power station

△ coal
○ oil
▽ gas

Al aluminium
Cu copper
Fe iron ore
Mn manganese
Pb lead
Zn zinc

scale 1 : 2 200 000

Armenia

Armenia is a land of ancient civilization, as the striking remains of Urartu culture (7th–8th centuries BC) at Arinberd, Karmir-Blur and elsewhere testify. "Urartu" is a name cognate with "Ararat," the great mountain that dominates the plain of Yerevan and is the heart of historic Armenia. Tantalizingly for Armenians, it, like the ruins of their great medieval capital Ani, is just on the far side of the Turkish frontier. Armenia has waxed and waned frequently over its long history, at some periods (notably 1st century BC) extending over parts of the former Soviet Union, Turkey, Iran, Iraq and Syria. Armenia claims to be the first state officially to have accepted Christianity, at the beginning of the 4th century: its distinctive alphabet may date from the same period. Its national church, the Armenian Apostolic Church, which has doctrinal differences with other churches of the Orthodox communion, is vigorous, with the seat of its catholicos (primate) at Yejmiadzin (Echmiadzin).

The fragment of ancient Armenian territory that constitutes the modern republic of Armenia is the smallest in the former Soviet Union, though not in population. Almost as many Armenians live elsewhere—notably in the enclave of Nagorno-Karabakh in Azerbaijan which saw bitter fighting between Armenians and Azerbaijanis in the early 1990s. Armenians—famous as merchants and traders—are indeed today scattered throughout the Near and Middle East, Europe and the Americas.

The republic is ethnically extremely homogeneous, with over 93 percent Armenians. Their language is Indo-European, without close relatives. Their vibrant culture is rich in folk and liturgical music, in stone carving and in illuminated medieval manuscripts. Their architecture is notable, among other things, for employing the pointed ("Gothic") arch as early as the 11th century. The tradition of viticulture in the Armenian highlands is ancient and the area may even be its original homeland.

Although the average altitude of the terrain is 1800 meters above sea level, it can bear a great variety of produce. A mainly equable climate, combined with a southerly latitude, allows large quantities of fruits, such as figs, pomegranates and almonds, to grow on the terraced hillsides, as well as nurturing extensive industry of wines and brandies. Wheat, barley and maize are grown on the lower plains, and cattle and sheep can graze on the higher plateaux. Armenia's major agricultural district in the Araks valley, produces high-quality, Egyptian-strain cotton, grown under intensive irrigation.

The whole farming system is now served by hydroelectric generating stations, especially the Sevan-Razdan project. Hydroelectric power was instrumental in rapid economic development; enormous financial investment under the Soviets diversified industry and developed the infrastructure, exploiting the rich mineral resources. Armenia is now a major producer of chemicals, machine equipment, precision instruments, textiles and canned food. The development of pipelines to carry oil from Azerbaijan's oil fields on the Caspian across to Turkey also promises economic renewal after several years of political upheaval and hostilities with Azerbaijan.

Below Two young men enjoy a drink of *kvass*, bought from a sidewalk vendor in Yerevan, capital of Armenia. This low-alcohol drink is immensely popular in the region. It is made from a fermentation of cereals and ryebread, sometimes with the addition of fruit as flavoring.

Bottom A demonstration in Yerevan. Conscious pride in Armenia's long, if troubled, history and the ethnic homogeneity of the republic's population made Armenian nationalism a force to be reckoned with under the Soviet regime.

Below Geotectonic activity makes Armenia vulnerable to devastating earthquakes. In December 1988 an earthquake devastated much of northern Armenia, killing 25 000 people. At Spitak, its epicenter, it measured over force 10 and it virtually wiped out the town.

Armenia's economy will take a long time to recover from the severe damage to its infrastructure.

Azerbaijan

Much of Azerbaijan, the largest of the Transcaucasian republics, is scenically closer to Central Asia than to Georgia or Armenia. Culturally, too, there are similarities, since its people are Islamic and it has for much of the last millennium been an arena where Turkic and Persian influences have struggled for supremacy. Since ancient times it has been strategically important, controlling the passage between the end of the Caucasus and the Caspian Sea. The present Azerbaijanis are a Turkic people, hence relative newcomers to the Caucasian scene: nonetheless their culture crystallized (in the upland regions, including Karabakh) well before the Mongol invasions, with notable poets and singers. A little later the modern capital of Baku on the Caspian began to flourish under the khans of Shirvan, who built the surviving palace and citadel there (14th–15th centuries).

Though Persian influence, sometimes control, was strong—with a preponderance of Shiite over Sunni Muslims—the population remained aware of their distinctive Azeri culture. Several local khanates came under Russian protection. The country was fully incorporated into the Russian empire in the late

1820s after a successful war against Persia. The Russians soon realized the economic importance of the Baku area, where the naturally occurring naphtha had been known since ancient times; by the beginning of the 20th century it had become the largest oilfield in the world. Since the collapse of Communism Western investment in Azerbaijan's oil has resulted in its export through two major pipelines from Baku.

Industry in the environs of Baku—a great Russian as well as Azeri city—built up around its oil production during the Soviet era and attention has now turned to exploitation of offshore reserves in the Caspian Sea, which is now the largest oil field in the world after the Middle East. Azerbaijan's major commodity is cotton. Extensive irrigation schemes in the Kura lowlands provide a splash of green in an otherwise largely semiarid environment. Breeding of sheep, cattle, pigs and riding horses can be supported on unirrigated steppes in winter; transhumance takes the animals to the adjoining high-altitude pastures in summer. The cultivation of fruit, tobacco, tea and vines that is common to Transcaucasia is also practiced, Azerbaijan's once renowned fisheries, along the Caspian coast, from which top-quality caviar is obtained and exported are under threat from pollution and uncontrolled exploitation.

Right Civic building in Baku, capital of Azerbaijan, with a statue of Lenin in front. Baku suffered severe damage in the period following the October Revolution when it was briefly (1918–21) the capital of an anti-Bolshevik republic.

Below Row upon row of nodding donkeys and oil platforms have now become a familiar feature along the coast of the Caspian Sea in Azerbaijan. The rich oil reserves of Transcaucasia will provide new-found wealth for the till now impoverished former Soviet republics of this region.

Georgia

Georgia, between the Greater and Lesser Caucasus, is 80 percent mountainous. Fast-flowing mountain rivers provide huge energy resources for an economy which is now recovering after the hyperinflation of the early 1990s. In T'bilisi, the capital, hot hydrogen sulfide waters are tapped for their medicinal properties. The population has a reputation for longevity.

The Georgian language is non-Indo-European and apparently unique, providing a focus for national cultural identity; it is written in a distinctive and ancient script. Like the Armenians, the Georgians accepted Christianity as their state religion in the 4th century; their tradition of fine architecture in stone has left churches and fortresses from almost all subsequent periods. There is a comparably ancient literature, including the notable medieval epic *The Man in a Tiger's Skin* by Shota Rustaveli. To the Georgians their land is "Kartveli" (in Russian "Gruziya").

Contacts with Russia go back to Kievan times. In the 1780s Georgia voluntarily came under Russian protection and was fully annexed under the Emperor Paul. From 1918 to 1921 it was independent, under a Menshevik government; it was then incorporated into the Transcaucasian SFSR, becoming a union republic in 1936. Stalin was Georgia's most famous son. The beautiful city of T'bilisi which grew into a great multinational city and cultural center, with large populations of Russians, Armenians and others, sadly became the location of bitter fighting, along with the breakaway regions of South Ossetia, Mingrelia and Abkhazia, in the three years of civil war which followed the collapse of the Soviet Union.

The landscape is varied and beautiful, from permanently snow-capped mountains to the reclaimed farmlands of the swampy delta of the Rioni, with dense forests and fertile valleys. Although only 16 percent of the land is arable, there are intensive irrigated cultivation schemes, and Georgia supplies tobacco, tea and citrus fruits to many neighboring republics. The central lowlands, watered by the rivers Rioni and Kura, produce fine grapes, one of Georgia's oldest crops, particularly around K'ut'aisi, where silkworm culture also still flourishes. Among unusual crops are the groves of tung trees, whose oil is used in hardening steel. At the end of the Soviet era, Georgia's economic growth, above all in the engineering, machine building and chemical industries was interrupted by the instability of civil war.

Georgia has a cultural richness and continuity of which its people are justly proud. Traditions of metalworking in bronze, gold and silver are of particular note: icons often took the form of metal plaques. Textiles are still embroidered in gold and silver thread. Much medieval fresco painting and stone carving survive, and Georgia has produced good modern painters.

Right Mtskheta, situated at the confluence of the Aragvi and Kura rivers, north of the modern Georgian capital T'bilisi. Its location at the intersection of the east-west route from the Caspian to the Black Sea and the northward route through the Aragvi valley contributed to Mtskheta's former eminence; it was the capital of the ancient kingdom of Georgia between the 2nd and 5th centuries AD. Its fine 11th-century cathedral was formerly the seat of the primates of Georgia.

Left Mountain scenery in Svanetia, northwestern Georgia. The distant towers, doubling as dwellings and defensive strongpoints, characterize many older villages in Georgia's uplands. The alluvial gold of Svanetia may have given rise to the legend of the Golden Fleece.

Below Football is now enjoying the attraction of many new and talented national teams on the international scene. With the former republics now free to field their own national sides, the game, always a focal point for fierce national pride even under the Soviets, is undergoing a major resurgence.

Left Young dancers in T'bilisi show off their skills in traditional dress. Georgian folk dance is renowned throughout the world for its richness and variety, and the Georgians are also very proud of their ancient and distinctive musical tradition.

Right A cobbled street in an old quarter of T'bilisi, overlooked by the ruins of the former citadel on the summit of the hill. The balconies with their intricately carved patterns and stylized animals reflect a venerable tradition of Georgian wood carving.

RUSSIA

Russia is the world's largest country in area, covering 10 percent of the total land mass of the Earth. It includes not only Russia in Europe but the whole of Siberia and some smaller non-Russian regions such as Finno-Karelia, part of former East Prussia, Tuva in the Altay, and others—in total almost 160 minority groups. For 74 years the vast bureaucratic machinery of the Soviet state, administered from the political heartland of Russia, provided a secure, if rigid, "cradle to the grave" existence for its citizens. With the demise of Communism and the loss of many of its old, secure trading ties with the rest of the Soviet Union, Russia now finds itself with lower levels of economic prosperity than many of its neighbors, who are now reaping the benefits of their vast, untapped oil and natural gas reserves.

Russia's extent is interestingly similar to that of Muscovy just before its transformation into the Russian empire in the first decade of the 18th century. The Russians' main direction of expansion since the

Republic	Russia
AREA	17 075 400 sq km
POPULATION	147·7m (est 1997)
CAPITAL	Moscow
POPULATION OF CAPITAL	8 717 000 (1996)
MAJOR LANGUAGE	Russian; also a large number of other languages

ARCTIC OCEAN

RUSSIA

LAPTEV SEA

EAST SIBERIAN SEA

BERING SEA

SEA OF OKHOTSK

SEA OF JAPAN

Nordvik
Khatanga
Tiksi
Kazach'ye
Cherskiy
Pevek
Anadyr'

Ust' Nera
Indigirka
Kolyma

Lena
Yakutsk
Okhotsk
Magadan
Ust' Kamchatsk

Mirnyy
Olekminsk
Lena
Aldan
Meya

Aldan
Petropavlovsk-Kamchatskiy

Angara
Au
Bodaybo
Nagornyy
Au

Bratsk
Fe
Skovorodino
Magdagachi
Ogodzha
Au
Nikolayevsk
Amur

Mogocha
Au
Belogorsk
Amur
Sn
Komsomolsk

Irkutsk
Lake Baykal
Chita
Au
Au
Pb Zn
Sn
Fe
Khabarovsk

Ulan Ude
Au
Sn
Pb Zn
Yuzhno Sakhalinsk

Petrovsk
Sn
Au

Sn
Pb
Au Zn
Vladivostok
Sn
Pb Zn
Pb Zn

△ coal
○ oil
▽ gas
Al aluminum
Au gold
Cu copper
Fe iron ore
Ni nickel
Pb lead
Sn tin
Su sulfur
Zn zinc

rough grazing, reindeer breeding and trapping
lumbering with pockets of subsistence farming
grazing
crop cultivation (flax, potatoes, sugarbeet)
cereal cultivation (wheat, millet) with sunflowers, sugarbeet and some grazing
suburban cultivation

— road
— railroad
⊥⊤⊥ canal
◐ industry
◑ extractive
◐ heavy
◓ light or manufacturing
◒ service
◇ power station
P peat cutting
S shale
◆ diamond field

principal cash crops
vines
fruits
tobacco
fishing port

scale 1: 18 200 000

0   600km
0   400mi

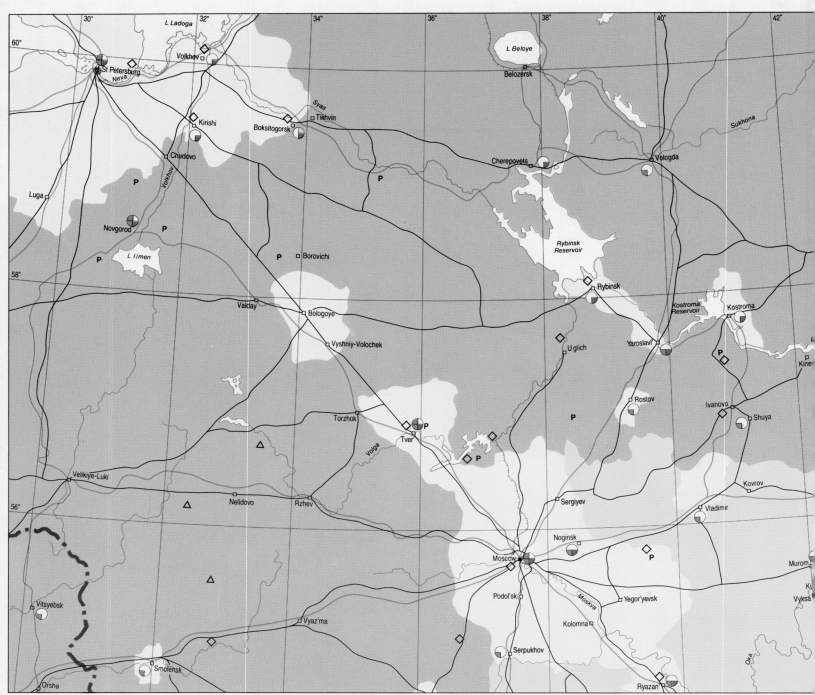

Above: The Moscow region.

Right The roofline and domes of the Cathedral of the Nativity of the Virgin at Suzdal have been somewhat altered but its fabric is basically pre-Tatar (1222–25). In total stylistic contrast is the reerected wooden Nikolskaya church, dating from 1766. Between the two churches is the 17th-century episcopal palace, now a museum. The three buildings represent major, but very different traditions of architecture in Russia.

Far right Decorative window surrounds (*nalichniki*) attain the status of folk art; they are a feature of many older wooden houses, especially in eastern Russia and Siberia. Woodcarving was a traditional peasant skill, particularly practiced in the winter when the harsh climate prevented work outside.

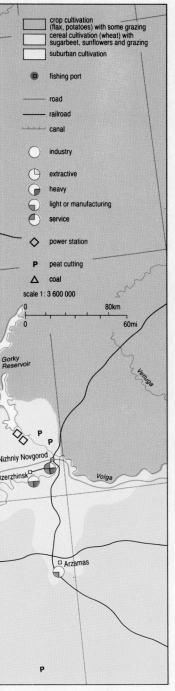

crop cultivation
(flax, potatoes) with some grazing
cereal cultivation (wheat) with
sugarbeet, sunflowers and grazing
suburban cultivation

fishing port

road
railroad
canal

industry
extractive
heavy
light or manufacturing
service
power station

P   peat cutting
△   coal

scale 1 : 3 600 000

0   80km
0   60mi

mid-16th century has been eastwards: in the process they have become thoroughly ethnically mixed, with physical characteristics ranging from the Scandinavian to the Asiatic. The basic distinction made was traditionally not between races but, medieval-fashion, between Orthodox and non-Orthodox. Russia's non-Russian and non-Orthodox peoples include numerous relict populations of Finnic and Turko-Tatar origin scattered across north-central and eastern Russia—such as the Bashkirs—the Buryat Buddhists of southern Siberia, a far north-eastern unexpected Turkic "island" of Yakuts and a kaleidoscope of peoples in the northern Caucasus. Some, like the Chechen and Ingush Muslims have a tradition of fiercely resisting Russian and Soviet Rule, a resentment which boiled over into bloody civil war in the 1990s.

Geographically Russia has three great regions: the undulating plain of European Russia, the tangled mountainous eastern part of Siberia from the Lena River to the Pacific, and west-central Siberia, most of it very flat and lowlying. Additionally there are the mountain barriers that close off Siberia to the south, and the less prominent but economically important range of the Urals separating Siberia from Europe. But the real contrast is between the coniferous forest—the vast taiga—and everything else. It is so empty of habitation that the "Tunguska event" of 1908—probably the result of a meteorite, destroying

hundreds of square kilometers of forest—passed unreported at the time. Much taiga is doubly unexploitable through having large patches of permafrost in its subsoil. Along the great rivers there are meadows and some pockets of fertile land, notably around the middle Lena, in Yakutia. For the sparse population the age-old occupations of fur-hunting, reindeer-herding and the growth industries of lumbering and wood pulping offer employment.

These remote regions also have areas of great gas, oil and mineral wealth which are now attracting western investment. Under Stalin huge complexes of prison camps around such places as Vorkuta and Magadan attempted to exploit these resources, though inefficiently in economic terms as well as at vast human cost. The use of Siberia as a place of exile goes back to the 17th century, but became a major phenomenon only in the 19th. It was opened up to full-scale settlement and industry with the construction of the Trans-Siberian Railroad (1893–1903).

The metals and precious stones of the Urals, by contrast, have been known and exploited for centuries, although the main industrial development of the southern Ural area did not take place until after 1917. Communications under the Soviet government were improved so that iron from the vast industrial complex at Magnitogorsk could be smelted with coal from the Kuzbass (Kuznetsk basin) in middle Siberia and Karaganda in Central Asia. The tendency

Right Winter festival at Kolomenskoye, on the banks of the Moskva River.

Below Wooden house at Suzdal, which is virtually a small "museum town" of various types of Russian architecture.

Below right The oval hall at Arkhangelskoye, a former estate of the Golitsyn family. The palace—used for receptions and visits, not permanent residence —dates from the early 19th century and was largely the work of local serfs. The wealthy collector Prince N. B. Yusupov, who bought the estate in 1810, completed the buildings in their present form; part of his art collection is still housed there.

Right In the north the sun scarcely appears above the horizon during the midwinter months. House roofs are steeply sloped to prevent the accumulation of snow. Rural depopulation has been a problem in much of Russia proper, but rising automobile-ownership has made parts of the countryside reasonably accessible from the towns and may assist revitalization.

of Russia's industrial heartland to move eastwards became a matter of strategical urgency in World War II. The primacy of the Volga-Urals oilfield has since the 1920s yielded to Siberian reserves of oil and natural gas, concentrated in Tyumen province.

Since the dissolution of the Soviet Union in 1991, Siberia has witnessed extensive exploration for oil, natural gas, diamonds and gold, bringing with it much damage to the environment. The Tyumen fields, for example, sited far to the north, are difficult and expensive to exploit and long-distance pipelines have had to be laid. The extreme conditions associated with the tundra make life very hard for the labor force who have now settled there. Another remote site is Norilsk at the mouth of the Yenisey where a nonferrous metal mining and smelting complex processing copper, nickel, cobalt and platinum is a major contributor to Russia's mineral production and source of potential economic prosperity. Yet its only link with the country is via the northern sea route which requires nuclear icebreakers to keep up operations all the year round. The 3000-kilometer-long Baykal-Amur Main-line (BAM) railroad, which was planned to open up export through Pacific ports, is not yet fully viable and is unlikely ever to justify its great cost (Stalin's political prisoners began it in the 1930s). In the central "black earth" region a high proportion of the land is arable. Good soils in the Amur valley support mixed farming of wheat, sugarbeet, sunflowers, meat and dairy products. The north Caucasus is also predominantly agricultural, the warmer climate allowing semitropical produce, such as vines, fruit and tobacco.

In recent years international pressure has mounted over the need to decommission Russia's aging and dangerous RBMK nuclear reactors. Meanwhile, eastern Siberia remains the major power base for the country: the immense hydroelectric power resources of the Angara and Yenisey rivers attract industries needing high levels of power, such as aluminum smelting. The Angara has a hydroelectric store equivalent to the combined output of the three largest rivers in European Russia: the Volga, Don and Kama. The Far East is now being opened up; extensive diamond mining in the Vilyuy valley around Mirny is now rivalling South Africa's industry and the gold of the Lena valley and Barguzin river is attracting settlement in the areas.

Like all the neighboring former Soviet republics, Russia had to grapple with hyperinflation and falling standards of living in the years after the dissolution of the Soviet Union. It has to deal with the pressing issues of heavy industrial pollution in its urban areas, where the drinking water is frequently unsafe to consume and the air has become dangerous to breathe. Social needs are also pressing, with a plummeting birth rate and lower levels of life expectancy than in Soviet times. A mushrooming black market economy, much of it controlled by organized crime, is also hampering the transition to a Western-style market economy.

Left Inhabitants of a taiga settlement pose in their home. Although electricity has reached this particular village, conditions in the remote settlements in this vast northern forest can still be harsh and isolated for much of the year, and domestic life depends heavily upon the pickled or preserved produce of the short summer season.

Below Conventional wheeled vehicles have their limitations in the trackless and marshy northern wastes, and dog power, in this case harnessed to a light buggy rather than a sled, still has its uses.

Left A hunting party on Sakhalin Island in the Sea of Okhotsk, in the far east of Russia. Ethnically the population is mixed and includes Russians (some of them descendants of convicts sent to the penal settlements on Sakhalin in the 19th century), Japanese, Koreans, Ainus and others.

Right Hundreds of skiers take part in a winter event at Murmansk. Cross-country skiing is enormously popular.

Far right Rafts of timber are floated downstream from a Siberian forest. The great rivers like the Yenisey and Lena provide the easiest access to the remote interior; in winter many rivers freeze so solidly that they can be used as roads. The taiga is not entirely undifferentiated: the height and closeness of its trees vary, as does its composition (to the west firs, to the east larches, predominate).

Moscow

Since the 1960s, Moscow's boundary has been a 150-kilometer beltway—though a forest still penetrates to the inner suburbs. The Ordynka and other highways with ancient names converge on the Kremlin. This area, with the adjoining Red Square, may monopolize a visitor's attention, but Moscow has a rich collection of buildings identified as pre-1700, including the leafy, rather rustic neoclassical quarters, rebuilt after the fire of 1812. In the Soviet period Moscow underwent much reconstruction in the attempt to turn it into an ideal Soviet city. The center was opened out for parades, and several churches and other monuments were demolished—among them the Cathedral of Christ the Savior, built to commemorate victory over Napoleon. In the late 1990s this cathedral was rebuilt, and Moscow was given a face-lift in honor of its 850th anniversary in 1997.

Above The grandiose GUM emporium in Moscow, for long the preserve of the rich and privileged apparatchiks of the Soviet bureaucracy and foreign tourists, whilst now opening its doors to swish fashion outlets from the West and offering a wider range of luxury goods in its shops, is still very much the domain of those with money.

Right A celebratory anniversary procession in Red Square, with slogans extolling the Communist Party.

Far right Produce vendors in Moscow's central market offer fish, fruit, vegetables and dairy products from the provinces.

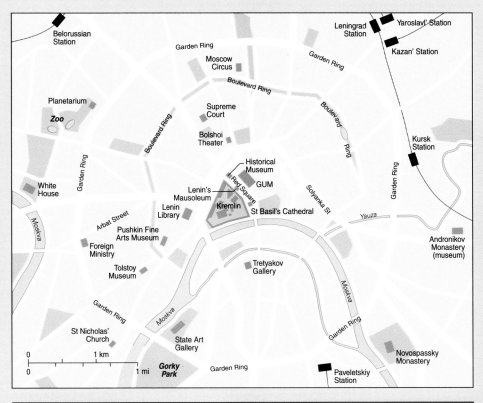

Below The Church of Intercession on the Moat, known as St Basil's Cathedral from its association with the "Holy Fool" Basil the Blessed, was commissioned by Ivan IV to commemorate his capture of Kazan (1552). Nine churches in one, it remains unique of its kind.

Overleaf The Kremlin, viewed from the northeast by night. The fantastic onion domes of St Basil's Cathedral form a striking foreground focus. Among the floodlit buildings are (*left to right*) the Archangel Cathedral, the belltower Ivan Velikiy, the Dormition Cathedral and the Spassky Tower.

Above The Moscow skyline in a winter twilight is dominated by the huge bulk of the government offices on Smolensk Square, 26 stories or 171 meters high. Such skyscrapers, erected during the late Stalinist period on the periphery of central Moscow, are often facetiously called "Stalinist Gothic."

Above right A Russian woman struggles to squeeze a brand new Sony TV set into the back of her Lada. The end of Communism opened the floodgates to the import of much-desired and unobtainable luxury electrical goods from the West.

Right Russian women, many of them elderly, frequently undertake clearing operations after snowfalls. This woman, in a tram-lined city street, wears characteristic village footwear: bulky felt boots called *valenki*.

St Petersburg

St Petersburg ("Petrograd" 1914–24; "Leningrad" 1924–91; colloquially, "Piter") is uncompromisingly spectacular. From the Winter Palace bridge endless 18th- and 19th-century facades, baroque and neo-classical, stretch into the distance. But the breadth of the River Neva and the speed of its dark waters are a reminder of the forces of nature which so much arti-fice challenges; like Venice, St Petersburg rests on countless wooden piles to prevent its subsiding into its marshes and it was built at the cost of many thousands of human lives. A trio of golden spires (on the Peter-Paul Cathedral, the Admiralty and St Michael's Castle) punctuate the skyline, together with the golden dome of St Isaac's; the absence of any loftier buildings preserves the visual integrity.

St Petersburg was founded as part of Peter the Great's drive to modernize Russia and to rival old, traditional Moscow. In the 1800s it overhauled Moscow in population and became a great 19th-century industrial metropolis. It is no less remarkable for its cultural life and its great art collections, notably the Hermitage, attract many Western tourists. Despite Westernizing encroachments in the 1990s, it remains strangely muted, over-spacious, haunted. Its high latitude (60°) gives strange "white nights" in June and early July. Intended as a "window into Europe," it feels neither quite Western nor quite Russian.

Above The Peter-Paul Fortress, St Petersburg, built on Hare Island in the River Neva by order of Peter the Great, shortly after he had captured the site from the Swedes in 1703. Over it rises the slender gilded spire of the cathedral, the burial place of Peter and of most subsequent emperors and empresses. The bastions of the fortress are named after Peter and his chief commanders.

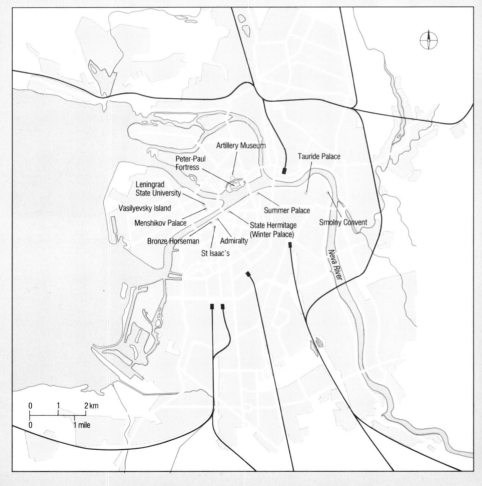

Left The "Church on the Blood" (1882–1907), built on the site of the assassination of Tsar Alexander II. Designed by A.A. Parland, this is a lone ecclesiastical representative of the so-called neonationalist style, which drew upon specifically Russian motifs and architectural elements in deliberate reaction against the Western European neoclassical canons that had dominated post-Petrine architecture.

Below The present Winter Palace, the fourth on the site, was begun in 1754 on the orders of the Empress Elizabeth; it is one of the last and finest palaces by the architect B.F. Rastrelli. The Hermitage and subsequent buildings were added to the complex later, beginning with Catherine the Great's Small Hermitage (l764–67). The buildings house one of the world's greatest art collections, started by Catherine.

Above A great St Petersburg landmark: the gilded spire of the Admiralty building, seen from Palace Square. Although a building existed on the Admiralty site from 1704, the spire was not put up until 1732. The work of I. Korobov, it is topped by a weather vane in the form of a sailing ship. When the Admiralty was remodeled by A. Zakharov in 1806, the spire of the earlier building was preserved.

Left Fountains and cascade at Petrodvorets (Peterhof), Peter the Great's palace overlooking the Gulf of Finland. The core of the complex with its elaborate grounds was designed to Peter's specifications in emulation of Versailles, which he visited in 1717. When Peter's daughter Elizabeth became empress, she commissioned B.F. Rastrelli to enlarge and improve the palace. Among the sculptors who contributed statuary to the cascade and gravity-fed fountains were Shubin and Martos.

48° 52° 56° 60° 64° 68°

Petropavl

Komsomolets

Ubagan

Ishim

Qostanay Uritskiy Köshetau

Fe Ruzayevka Shchuch'insk

Kushmurun Makinsk **Au**

Oral Djetygara **Au**

Aksay Atbasar Aqmo

Ural **Al** **Cu**

Dzhambeyty Tengiz

Novaya Kazanka Turgay

Aqtöbe Arqalyq

Inderborskiy Uil Uil Shubarkuduk Oktyabr'sk Torghay

Temir Irgiz Irgiz

Embi **KAZAKHSTAN**

Ganyushkino Shalqar Sarysu

Makat Emba Bayqongyr Sarysu

Atyrau **Su** Zhezqazghan

Kulsary Aral

Koschagyl **Cu**

Kultay Zhangaqataly

Fort Shevchenko **Mangyshlak** Kazarlinsk Qyzylorda

Dzhusaly

ARAL SEA Chiili

Aqtau **Pb Zn** Ashchysay

CASPIAN Muynoq **Pb Zn**

SEA Turkistan

Qünghirot Borisovka

Fetisovo **Su** Nukus Syr Darya

Su Kodzheyli Shymkent

Kara-Bogaz-Gol Kara-Bogaz-Gol Dashhowuz Arys

Kara-Bogaz-Gol Urganch **UZBEKISTAN** Chardara Chirchik

Cheleken Khiva Türtkul Tashkent

Nebitdag **U**

Gizhduvan **Cu Zn**

Zeravshan Guliston

TURKMENISTAN Bukhoro **Pb Zn** Qugor

Gyzylarbat Kagan Ursatyevskaya Khujand Kambarata

Samarqand Jizzakh

Esenguly Airek Kagan Urateppa Sülüktä

Bakharden Chärjew Qarshi Urgut **Sb TAJIKISTAN**

Ashgabat Sakar Dushanbe

Mary Kerki Norak

Tejen Bäyramaly Qurghonteppa Kulob

Mulghab Karakum canal

Saragt Termez

Gushgy

scale 1:800 000

0 ———— 200km
0 ——— 150mi

216

CENTRAL ASIA

Central Asia is a vast territory, covering nearly 3.9 million square kilometers. Its five constituent, predominantly Muslim republics share many features, and are separated by desert, semidesert or the Caspian Sea from the rest of the former Soviet Union. Some of the world's highest mountains also isolate them from the rest of Asia; despite this, considerable populations are closely related to ethnic groups in Iran, Afghanistan and China. In four of the republics the languages are Turkic and similar enough to be largely intercomprehensible; in Tajikistan an Iranian (hence Indo-European) tongue is spoken.

Central Asia's history is characterized by the continual interaction of settled agriculturalists, nomads and passing conquerors, including Alexander the Great and Timur (Tamerlane). It straddled the traditional caravan routes between China and Europe known as the Silk Road. Arab invaders of the 8th century brought Islam. Turks formed a settled population from the early Middle Ages—hence the name "Turkestan" applied until 1924, when the Soviets redistributed the area into five republics. As a result, the boundaries of the modern republics are rather artificial, interlocking curiously to give each a share of productive land. Oases and well-watered river valleys, benefiting from the long, hot summers, are extremely fertile. But irrigation schemes have had deleterious side-effects, leading to salination of agricultural land and the shrinking of the freshwater Aral Sea. The major agricultural development of the *tselina* ("Virgin Lands") during the 1950s took place in the feather-grass steppe of northern Kazakhstan where the climate is more humid.

Republic	Kazakhstan	Uzbekistan	Turkmenistan
AREA	2 717 300 sq km	447 400 sq km	488 100 sq km
POPULATION	16·8m (est 1997)	23·6m (est 1997)	4·2m (est 1997)
CAPITAL	Aqmola (Astana)	Tashkent	Ashgabat
POPULATION OF CAPITAL	1 172 000 (1995)	2 121 000 (1993)	416 000 (1991)
MAJOR LANGUAGE	Kazakh, Russian	Uzbek (a Turkic language)	Turkmen (a Turkic language)

	Tajikistan	Kyrgyzstan
	143 100 sq km	198 500 sq km
	6·0m (est 1997)	4·4m (est 1997)
	Dushanbe	Bishkek
	592 000 (1991)	641 400 (1991)
	Tajik (an Iranian language)	Kyrgyz (a Turkic language)

Legend:

- grazing (cattle, sheep)
- semiarid land with some grazing (cattle, Astrakhan sheep)
- cereal cultivation (millet, maize) and grazing
- intensive crop cultivation (wheat, barley, rice, sugarbeet)
- suburban cultivation
- land unsuitable for cultivation

- road
- railroad
- canal

principal cash crops
- cotton
- vines
- fruit
- mulberry trees
- tobacco

- fishing port

- △ coal
- ○ oil
- ▽ gas
- Au gold
- Cu copper
- Fe iron ore
- Hg mercury
- Pb lead
- Sb antimony
- Su sulfur
- U uranium
- Zn zinc

- ○ industry
- extractive
- heavy
- light or manufacturing
- service
- ◇ power station

Kazakhstan

Kazakhstan guards the western end of the pass known as the "Dzhungarian (or Jade) Gates," the high road into China, and its people are culturally and linguistically close to the Uighurs of Xinjiang. The bulk of the land is desert or semidesert, with an extreme continental climate. Thus, the Kazakhs were traditionally nomads (the name means "rider" in Turkish) who herded sheep and horses from one small rural settlement to another. Grouped into three hordes, they dominated a vast tract of Central Asia. In the 18th century they passed first under Russian protection and then rule. The Russians set up forts in this sparsely populated land and in the mid-19th century established the capital of Verny, now called Almaty ("Father of Apples"), notable for its earthquake-proof wooden architecture. Between 1959 and 1970 the population increased by 40 percent with the immigration of large numbers of Russians, Ukrainians and Belarusians (many other ethnic groups are also represented); despite some subsequent emigration, Kazakhs still make up scarcely half of the population. In 1997 govenment offices were transferred from Almaty, the main centre of culture and population, to Aqmola (formerly Akmolinsk, Tselinograd) in the northern "Hungry Steppe".

During the Soviet era huge tracts of steppe in northern Kazakhstan were brought into cultivation of wheat under Khrushchev's "Virgin Lands" project. Strips of land along the southern Syr Darya and Chu rivers are irrigated for rice, tobacco, sugarbeet, grapes and cereals. Further east, where the land begins to rise, vegetables are grown and dairying, sheep-rearing and horse-breeding are important.

Large reserves of coal have been found, and exploited at the opencast mines of the Ekibastuz basin in the northeast. The Tengiz oilfield is one of the largest in the world. But the country is now paying the costly legacy of ill-considered initiatives of Soviet technology and industry. The Aral Sea shrank disastrously with the diversion of the water of its main inflowing river, Syr Darya, from the 1970s; it is being stabilized, but with a smaller area, and its surrounding land has been badly affected by salinity. Kazakhstan also contains the former Soviet Union's major nuclear weapons testing site and the famous Baykonyr space centre. Despite their effects on the environment, however, Kazakhstan remains an exceptionally rich and interesting land ecologically.

Above Beehives in the mountainous region on the southern fringes of Kazakhstan.

Below left These children at Kaskelen represent the second generation of communities that grew up in the 1950s and 1960s with the "Virgin Lands" project. Under this scheme, 35 million hectares of wild steppe, largely in Kazakhstan, were turned over to the cultivation of wheat, with mixed success. With the departure of many European Russians in the 1990s, there has been a distinct shift over to the study of Kazakh history, literature and culture in the schools, where instruction is now given in Kazakh and not Russian.

Right Tashkent originated as an oasis on the Chirchik River, conveniently sited on a major trade route. Under the Russian empire it was developed as the strongpoint of Turkestan. Elements of its ancient past remain in the bazaars, but much of the city is thoroughly modern, with Western-style buildings like this "House of the Press." Following the catastrophic earthquake of 1966, measures have been taken to design new buildings to withstand seismic stress.

Below The Zeravshan mountains in the southeast of Uzbekistan are the source of the Zeravshan River which flows westwards to irrigate the Samarkand area until it loses itself in the desert near the Amu Darya.

Above A citizen of Samarqand. The Turkic inhabitants of Central Asia still wear the time-honored dress of the Middle Eastern peasant, which has been banned in Turkey itself since Ataturk's Westernizing reforms.

Below Cotton is the major crop in irrigated areas of Uzbekistan; as a "monoculture", however, it is harmful ecologically and economically. Pickers here gather to celebrate the harvest according to ancient traditions.

Uzbekistan

Between the Fergana basin and the Amu Darya (Oxus) River lie most of the richest oases and ancient cities of Central Asia. Here the western end of the Tien Shan range reaches out towards the fiercest of the region's deserts, the Kyzyl Kum. Beyond, saltpans and stony wastes stretch eventually to the Caspian.

Uzbekistan was the homeland of some of the early tribes that migrated to the fringes of Kievan Rus: the Pechenegs, Kipchak and Oghuz. When the Mongols overran Central Asia in the 13th century, the White Horde established a powerful base at Bukhoro (Bukhara), which became one of the main trading links between Russia and Central Asia and, farther afield, Europe and the Orient. The Mongols destroyed Central Asia's greatest city, Afrosiab, and in the late 14th century Timur (Tamerlane) founded Samarqand beside the huge empty hill that marks the site of the earlier metropolis. Since the late Middle Ages, when Samarqand (Samarkand) was one of the great intellectual and artistic centers of the world, the area has been the heartland of the Uzbek clan. They have multiplied to the point at which Uzbekistan is now the third most populous of the former Soviet republics, and their rise has been paralleled by the relative decline of their erstwhile dominant neighbors, the Kazakhs. Today the Uzbeks remain the least Russified of all the Turkic peoples of the region, with 98 percent having Uzbek as their primary language. Uzbekistan is also a region of considerable historical interest, with three magnificent medieval cities in Samarqand, Bukhoro and Khiva, all of which are now being opened up to the tourist trade, with large programs of restoration from the 1970s on.

Tashkent was taken by the Russians in 1865 and became a major administrative, commercial and industrial center. Large numbers of Russians settled there, but relations were soured by dreams of "Pan-Turkism" on the part of the indigenous peoples: nationalist disturbances continued beyond the Revolution. The Uzbek SSR was the first republic in Central Asia to declare its sovereignty as the Soviet Union disintegrated in 1990.

Tashkent is also a great Islamic center. Mullahs go there for their training, and the spiritual directorate also oversees most Islamic publications. The resurgence of Islam in the post-Soviet era has seen a return of religious instruction in schools and the changeover to instruction in Uzbek.

Although much of Uzbekistan is desert, it is rich in reserves of natural gas and oil such as the oilfield at Kokdumalak. The rivers in the more mountainous southeast provide hydroelectric power; this supplies energy for large-scale irrigation of cotton, of which Uzbekistan is the world's third largest producer. However the country's desperate water shortages have led to serious depletion of the rivers feeding into the Aral Sea, which has lost 60 percent of its water and 40 percent of its area since 1961, creating huge environmental and economic problems.

Left A minaret dominates the skyline of Khiva in Uzbekistan. From the early 16th century Khiva was the capital of a khanate of the same name; it became a Russian protectorate in 1873. Although much of Khiva was rebuilt in the 19th century, it remained traditionally Islamic in style. The minaret and some of the domes are decorated with the brilliantly colored ceramic tiles which are characteristic of Central Asian Islamic architecture.

Right A gigantic bank of mirrors at a helio station at Tashkent generates power by focusing sunlight onto an array of photovoltaic cells. In recent years—and in particular since the Chornobyl' (Chernobyl) nuclear accident—safety and environmental factors have increasingly influenced the choice of energy sources. Solar power, being safe, renewable and non-polluting, is an attractive option in suitable localities.

Left An imam and his assistant kneel in prayer at the Central Mosque in Margilan, Uzbekistan. There has been a huge resurgence in Islam across Central Asia since the demise of the Soviet Union. In Uzbekistan, where 88 per cent of the population are Sunni Muslims, religious practice which was suppressed under the Soviets is now becoming a focal point of everyday life again and the educational system is being restructured to take in observance of Islamic tradition and religion.

Turkmenistan

Turkmenistan was occupied by Parthians and Sasanids, Huns, Arabs and Ghaznavids; it contains Mary (Merv), one of the oldest city-sites in the world, of great arachaeological importance. The Oghuz from Mongolia in the 11th century gave the region its Turkic character, which it has retained to the present day. Despite Persian incursions, the Oghuz coalesced into a single people, albeit with clan distinctions. The southern section of the region fell under Persian Safavid rule between the 15th and 17th centuries, but it was reunited by the Russians with the north in 1881. The struggle for power at the time of the Revolution involved the British army, concerned about Russia's southward advance towards India.

As 90 percent of Turkmenistan is occupied by desert, irrigation is essential for cultivating the land, but great problems of insufficient supply and of salination remain. Cotton is the main crop, but varieties of grain (wheat, barley, maize, sorghum and millet) are also important. Carpet-making remains a major industry, with its famous Karakul sheep being reared to supply the wool; equally famous are its horses, and the Turkmenis remain great riders. The Caspian Sea, bordering on the west of the republic, supports a certain amount of fishing. More important in this vicinity are the sulfur and sodium sulfate deposits, which are the largest in the world. The republic also has huge resources of lead, zinc, copper, mercury and gold. Oil extraction is a growth industry in the western Caucasus and on the Cheleken peninsula of the Caspian Sea, with Turkmenistan now being dubbed the "Kuwait of the Caspian." Turkmen has now been designated as the country's official language.

Above right This arid featureless expanse of salt flats at the Karakum Canal zone in Turkmenistan is typical of this, the most underpopulated region of Central Asia. Much of the republic is uninhabitable desert and the Karakum Canal was constructed to bring irrigation across to the barren deserts in the east of the country from the more fertile river areas to the south and west.

Right A Turkmen patriarch poses with his unveiled womenfolk and other members of his extended family. A large family is the norm in Central Asia, and in Turkmenistan the population increase is such that the authorities are hard pressed to provide enough housing, schools and jobs. Turkmenis have always had a reputation for a fierce, unorthodox piety. Women do not wear the veil, but work—and have sometimes fought—alongside the men.

Tajikistan

Tajikistan is 90 percent mountainous and is one of the poorest and most rural of the republics in the region. Until recently many villages had no piped water or electricity and communications were difficult. One of the earliest Soviet water-management projects was the Great Fergana Canal, which, together with the enormous hydroelectric potential of the republic's rivers, provides irrigation for the cultivation of the characteristic terraced hillsides.

The history of Tajikistan in the last century is an extension to that of Uzbekistan; it was ruled first by the Bukhara emirate and then by the Russian tsar. The Tajiks are however ethnically distinct and speak an Iranian language rather than the prevailing Turkic, having strong ties with northern Afghanistan. Having established a national entity before the arrival of the Turks, they represent one of the earlier layers of Central Asian civilization. Their prolonged resistance to the Russians between 1921 and 1925 was comparable to resistance in Afghanistan; in the 1990s the country witnessed a violent power struggle after the collapse of Communism, with many calling for the establishment of an Islamic State.

The mountainous geography tends to dictate the character of economic life. Pastures support livestock reared for wool and meat, rather than dairying. Hydroelectric power provides energy to manufacture machinery adapted to hillside cultivation. Fine-fiber cotton, silk and carpets make up a developed light industry, and schemes for extracting brown coal, petroleum and natural gas, together with nonferrous metallurgy, are the important heavy industries. There are also steam power plants in Dushanbe.

Above left Carpet-making was established in Tajikistan as the result of contact with Persia. Some still follows traditional lines, involving entire families in a cottage industry in which specialized skills are passed down through the generations. When the region was annexed by Russia in the 19th century a huge market opened up in the West, and nowadays many Central Asian carpets are mass-produced in factories.

Left This textile factory in Khudjand in Tajikistan represents the republic's most important, growth industry - cotton. Under Communism, Takikistan was a major producer of seed cotton for the rest of the Soviet Union, but now no longer shackled to a state monopoly, it is seeking a place in the open, competitive market with its high quality cotton and textiles. These, together with the traditional craft of carpet weaving are all crucial to the economic survival of a country which is largely mountainous and has little productive terrain.

Kyrgyzstan

The history of Kyrgyzstan explains a certain wariness towards outsiders that persists to the present, the result of interference, often violent, in the affairs of the area by outside forces. Ruthless rule by the khanate of Kokand (in Uzbekistan), massacres by the Russians in 1916 that forced 150 000 Kyrgyz to flee to China and the purges of the 1930s have forged a cast of mind that is distrustful of powerful neighbors.

Its scenery is spectacular, with the mountain lake Issyk and the Tien-Shan range, containing the highest peaks of the former Soviet Union. But its complex geography leads to a certain lack of unity. The south is a fervent center of Islam; the southern capital, Osh, is called "the second Mecca," and the rural population is 90 percent Muslim. Sufism exerts a strong hold on the people; it probably has more holy places there than anywhere else in Central Asia, the throne of Suleyman (Solomon), near Osh, being a popular pilgrimage center. The northern areas, by contrast, were not Islamized until the 18th century, and then only superficially, leaving a minority even today with shamanistic and totemistic beliefs. It is here that the majority of Soviet immigrants, especially Russians, settled. The indigenous Kyrgyz remained a minority in their own country until the 1990s.

By the 1970s Kyrgyzstan had become the Soviet Union's main producer of antimony and mercury. Its other resources, such as uranium, coal, oil, natural gas, lead, zinc, copper and gold are now being more heavily exploited to fund the changeover to a market economy. Expanded production of building materials, and prefabricated buildings has become important. Stock-breeding, especially of fine-fleeced sheep and pigs, and agriculture are all practiced within the limitations of the terrain, but economic hardship is reflected in the republic having the lowest standard of living in the region.

Below Kyrgyz men queue with their fleeces; once collected, the fleeces will be graded, with the inferior wool being used for felt and the better quality for woven items. The strongly Mongoloid features of the men are a reminder of the proximity of China. The hardy horses of the region were always important to the Kyrgyz in their nomadic past and feature prominently in their folklore; on a more practical level they are still used in the tending of sheep and cattle and even for meat.

BIBLIOGRAPHY

A bibliography of Russian history and culture could itself fill many volumes. Within this vast territory it will perhaps be of most use to the student or other interested reader to provide a highly selective annotated list, particularly of background works (with a few more detailed studies), concentrating on those that for a variety of reasons have proved useful in writing this book and are (with a few exceptions) available in English. The selection is arranged thematically.

General histories

The foundations of modern Russian historiography are the great 19th-century Russian-language multivolume works by N.M. Karamzin (*History of the Russian State*, uncompleted at his death in 1826; note also his *Memoir on Ancient and Modern Russia*, trans. and ed. R. Pipes, Cambridge, Mass. 1959); V.O. Klyuchevsky (*Course of Russian History*); and S.M. Solovyov, *History of Russia from the Earliest Times*). To these can be added the many individual works on 16th- to 18th-century history, and *History of Russia* (London, 1925) by S.F. Platonov. These works constitute the basic "reference points" against which other analyses or interpretations measure themselves, and are themselves landmarks in Russian cultural history. The only equivalent multivolume study in English was undertaken by G. Vernadsky in association with M. Karpovich: unfortunately the deaths of both interrupted the project at the end of the Muscovite period. The five extant vols. remain indispensable.

There are many useful single-volume histories of Russia in English. Among them B.H. Sumner, *A Survey of Russian History* (London, 1944), unusually arranged, remains stimulating after over half a century; G. Vernadsky's single-volume *A History of Russia* (5th edn., New Haven, 1961) is sound and readable; L. Kochan and R. Abraham, *The Making of Modern Russia* (Harmondsworth, 1983), is strongest on recent history; P. Dukes, *A History of Russia* (3rd edn., London, 1998), usefully compares many variant interpretations; the *Cambridge Companion to Russian Studies*, vol. 1 (Cambridge, 1976), eds. R. Auty and D. Obolensky, by a variety of authors, strikes a good balance between early and modern history, with separate studies of geography, the Church, politics and economics. The fullest and probably best such history is N. Riasanovsky, *A History of Russia* (3rd edn., New York, 1977), incidentally with a useful annotated list of Russian historians.

G. Vernadsky et al. (ed.), *A Source-book for Russian History* (3 vols., New Haven and London, 1972), is an outstandingly rich collection of documents relating to political and cultural history up to 1917 in English translation. D. Kaiser and G. Marker (eds.), *Reinterpreting Russian History: Readings 860–1860s* (Oxford, 1994) has source-materials and interpretative articles. Note also P. Dukes, *Russia under Catherine the Great: Select Documents* (2 vols., 1977–78), including a translation of Catherine II's *Nakaz*.

The most ambitious interpretative cultural history of Russia is J. Billington, *The Icon and the Axe* (London, 1966), with much curious and detailed information in its notes. The *Cambridge Encyclopedia of Russia*, ed. A. Brown et al. (new edn. Cambridge, 1994), is very full, particularly on modern subjects, though, with its many contributors, rather fragmented. R. Milner-Gulland, *The Russians* (Oxford, 1997) is a study of the traditions of Russian culture.

The outstanding socio-political history of Russia up to the late 19th century, pungent and opinionated, is R. Pipes, *Russia under the Old Regime* (London, 1974). It has a good opening chapter on the geographical setting, as also does the Cambridge *Companion to Russian Studies* (see above; by D.J. Hooson); see also Hooson's *The Soviet Union: Peoples and Regions* (London, 1966). A fundamental work among the many textbooks on Russian geography is W.H. Parker, *An Historical Geography of Russia* (London, 1968). On some other broad topics: J. Blum, *Lord and Peasant in Russia* (Princeton, 1961); R.E.F. Smith and D. Christian, *Bread and Salt* (Cambridge, 1984)—food in social history; A.G Cross (ed.), *Russia under Western Eyes* (London, 1971), the best anthology of travelers' accounts of Russia.

Historical topics and periods

On Old Russia's civilizational "location": D. Obolensky, *The Byzantine Commonwealth* (London, 1971); see too his important article "Russia's Byzantine Heritage" (in *Oxford Slavonic Papers*, vol. 1, 1950). On the early Slavonic world: F. Dvornik, *The Slavs, Their Early History and Civilization* (London, 1959) and *The Making of Central and Eastern Europe* (London, 1949); A. Vlasto, *The Entry of the Slavs into Christendom* (Cambridge. 1970). M. Gimbutas, *The Slavs* (London, 1971); P. Dolukhanov, *The Early Slavs* (London, 1996).

On the history and status of the Russian language: G. Vinokur, *The Russian Language—a Brief History* (Cambridge, 1971); W.K. Matthews, *The Structure and Development of Russian* (Cambridge, 1953); B. Unbegaun, *Selected Papers on Russian and Slavonic Philology* (Oxford, 1969); D. Ward, *The Russian Language Today* (London, 1965). G. Corbett (ed.), *The Slavonic Languages* (London, 1993).

On pre-Tatar Russia: G. Vernadsky, *Ancient Russia* (New Haven, 1943) and *Kievan Russia* (New Haven, 1948) are fundamental (however his *Origins of Russia* (Oxford, 1959) is highly speculative). S. Franklin and J. Shepard, *The Emergence of Rus 750–1200* (London, 1996), wide-ranging and up-to-date. J. Martin, *Medieval Russia 980–1584* (Cambridge, 1995) concentrates on political history. A very detailed account of society, trade, international relations etc. is given in B. Grekov, *Kievan Rus* (Moscow, 1959—unfortunately in an inadequate translation); note too M. Tikhomirov, *The Towns of Ancient Rus* (Moscow, 1959); R.E.F. Smith, *The Origins of Farming in Russia* (Paris, 1959). Original sources may be found in Vernadsky (ed.), *Source-book* (see above), and in S. Zenkovsky, *Medieval Russian's Epics., Chronicles and Tales* (London and New York, 1963). *The Russian Primary Chronicle*, trans. and ed. S.H. Cross (rev. edn., Cambridge, Mass. 1953), is scarcely up-to-date but has a serviceable commentary; the classic commentary by D.S. Likhachov (Moscow and Leningrad, 1950) is unfortunately available only in Russian. Constantine Parphyrogenitus, *De Administrando Imperii*, trans. and ed. G. Moravcsik and R. Jenkins (London, 1962–66), has detailed commentary concerning Rus by D. Obolensky.

On Russia under the Tatars: G. Vernadsky, *The Mongols and Russia* (New Haven, 1953). C. Halperin stimulatingly reinterprets the psychological impact of Tatar conquest in *Russia and the Golden Horde* (London, 1987). Several important studies of the political history of the time by J.L.I. Fennell include *The Emergence of Moscow 1304–1359* (London, 1968) and *The Crisis of Medieval Russia 1200–1304* (London, 1983).

On post-Tatar Muscovy: G. Vernadsky, *Russia at the Dawn of the Modern Age* (New Haven, 1959) and *The Tsardom of Muscovy* (2 vols., New Haven, 1969); R.H. Crummey, *The Formation of Muscovy 1304–1613* (London, 1987). Apart from J.L.I. Fennell, *Ivan the Great of Moscow* (London, 1961), there is a dearth of good specialized studies in English of individual Muscovite reigns and rulers until we reach P. Longworth's concise and readable *Alexis* (London, 1984). S.F. Platonov's works on *The Time of Troubles* and *Boris Godunov* are now however available in English (Gulf Breeze, 1970, 1972). A remarkable original source for Ivan IV's reign is the tsar's correspondence with Prince Kurbsky, which has been translated and edited with notes by J.L.I. Fennell (Cambridge, 1955). See too Martin (above); note P. Bushkovich, *Religion and Society in Russia (16th–17th cc.)* (Oxford 1992).

On the Petrine period, much literature is available in English, but probably the best modern study of Peter, by R. Wittram, is in German. There are good concise biographies by M.S. Anderson, *Peter the Great* (London, 1976), and A. de Jonge, *Fire and Water* (London, 1979); a comprehensive biography by L.A. J. Hughes is in the press. The long account by R. Massie, *Peter the Great: His Life and World* (London, 1981), is best on the Petrine wars. Diverse views on the "Petrine revolution" are collated in M. Raeff (ed.), *Peter the Great: Reformer or Revolutionary?* (London and New York, 1963). The remarkable short study of Peter's self-image by B. Uspensky, *Historia sub specie semioticae*, has been translated in D. Lucid (ed.), *Soviet Semiotics* (Baltimore, 1977).

On the 18th century after Peter, most English-language literature concentrates on the reign of Catherine II. Here all other general studies have been superseded by the only full-scale modern biography: I. de Madariaga, *Russia in the Age of Catherine the Great* (London, 1981), which disposes of many myths. Several important aspects of Catherine's reign—education, enlightenment, Diderot's visit, freemasonry, town-planning—are the subjects of essays by various hands in J. Garrard (ed.), *The Eighteenth Century in Russia* (Oxford, 1973). The book's scope is wider than just Catherine's reign, as is P. Dukes, *The Making of Russian Absolutism 1613–1801* (London, 1982); P. Longworth, *Three Empresses: Catherine I, Anne and Elizabeth of Russia* (London, 1972), covers the 1725–62 period; note also his *The Cossacks* (London, 1969); J. Brennan, *Enlightened Despotism in Russia* (New York, 1987), concentrates on Elizabeth's reign. M. Raeff, *Origins of the Russian Intelligentsia* (London, 1966), despite its title, is a remarkable "psychohistorical" study of the 18th-century gentry. H. Rogger, *National Consciousness in 18th-century Russia* (Cambridge, Mass. 1960).

On 19th-century Russia there is a vast literature in English. Riasanovsky and most general historians already mentioned have much detailed information. Among other works: M. Raeff (ed.), *The Decembrist Movement* (Englewood Cliffs, 1966) and *Michael Speransky* (The Hague, 1957). N. Riasanovsky, *Nicholas I and Official Nationality in Russia* (Berkeley, 1959). S. Monas, *The Third Section* (Cambridge, Mass. 1961). The memoirs of the Marquis de Custine, *The Empire of the Czar* (London, 1843 and subsequent edns.), sharp-witted but disingenuous, are a much-quoted source on Nicholas's Russia. On Alexander's reforms: W.E. Mosse, *Alexander II and the Modernization of Russia* (London, 1958); T. Emmons (ed.), *Emancipation of the Russian Serfs* (London and New York, 1970). C.L. Black (ed.), *The Transformation of Russian Society: Aspects of Social Change since 1861* (Cambridge, Mass. 1960). Some broader studies: H. Seton-Watton, *The Russian Empire 1801–1917* (Oxford, 1967); G.T. Robinson, *Rural Russia under the Old Regime* (New York, 1932): R. Charques, *The Twilight of Imperial Russia* (London, 1968): G. Katkov et al. (eds.), *Russia enters the Twentieth Century* (London, 1971); also M. Raeff, *Plans for Political Reforms in Imperial Russia 1730–1905* (Englewood Cliffs, 1966). G. Hosking, *Russia: Empire and Nation 1552–1917* (London, 1997) opens up important themes.

On the revolutionary and Soviet periods, the field is even broader. M.T. Florinsky, *The End of the Russian Empire* (new edn., New York, 1961); L. Kochan, *Russia in Revolution, 1900–18* (London, 1966); W.H. Chamberlain, *The Russian Revolution* (2 vols., New York, 1935); S. Harcave, *First Blood: The Russian Retolution of 1905* (London, 1970); B.J. Williams, *The Russian Revolution 1917–21* (Oxord, 1987) a concise introduction. G.A. Hosking, *The Russian Constitutional Experiment: Government and the Duma 1907–14* (Cambridge, 1975) and *A History of the Soviet Union* (London, 1961); D. Footman, *The Civil War in Russia* (London, 1961); A. Ulam, *Lenin and the Bolsheviks* (London, 1969); B. Woolfe, *Three who Made a Revolution* (New York, 1960); M. Levin, *The Making of the Soviet System* (London, 1985); M. Heller, *Cogs in the Soviet Wheel: the Making of Soviet Man* (New York and London, 1987); M. Fainsod, *How Russia is Ruled* (Cambridge, Mass. 1953); L. Schapiro, *The Communist Party of the Soviet Union* (London, 1970); R. Conquest, *The Great Terror* (London, 1968) and *Kolyma* (London, 1978). S. Fitzpatrick, *The Commissariat of Enlightenment* (Cambridge, 1970), on early Soviet education and culture. M. McCauley, *Politics in the Soviet Union* (Harmondsworth, 1977); D. Dyker, *Soviet Economics* (London, 1976). E.H. Carr, *History of Soviet Russia* (14 vols., London, 1952–78), is a magisterial investigation of the early Soviet period. On later developments, H. Arendt, *The Origins of Totalitarianism* (New York, 1951), is a classic text. T.H. Righy (ed.), *Stalin* (Englewood Cliffs, 1966); R. Medvedev, *Let History Judge: The Origins and Consequences of Stalinism* (New York, 1971); A. Dallin and T.B. Larson (eds.), *Soviet Politics since Khrushchev* (Washington, 1958); M. McCauley, *The Soviet Union under Gorbachov* (London, 1987); M. Gorbachov, *Perestroika* (London, 1987). There have been many memoirs by eyewitnesses and participants: by foreigners such as John Reid, B. Pares, M. Djilas; by Russians including Trotsky and Khrushchev.

History of ideas

On religion: there is not yet a comprehensive history of the Russian Church in any language. Valuable substitutes include G. Fedotov, *The Russian Religious Mind* (2 vols., Cambridge, Mass., 1966) and *A Treasury of Russian Spirituality* (New York, 1961); also J. Fennell, *A History of the Russian Church to 1448* (London, 1995). Convenient introductions to Orthodoxy are provided in T. Ware, *The Ortho-*

dox Church (Harmondsworth, 1964), and J. Meyendorff, *The Orthodox Church* (New York, 1965); note too V. Lossky. *The Mystical Theology of the Eastern Church* (London, 1957). On some specific topics: W.K. Medlin, *Moscow and East Rome* (London, 1952); F.C. Conybeare, *Russian Dissenters* (London, 1921); D. Stremoukhoff, *Moscow the Third Rome—Sources of the Doctrine* in *Speculum,* 1953:1; A.V. Soloviev, *Holy Russia: The History of a Religious-Social Idea* (The Hague, 1954). On folk belief, M. Balzer (ed.), *Russian Traditional Culture* (New York, 1992) has several important recent Russian studies in translation.

On general thought many books already mentioned (e.g. Billington, Cherniavsky, Pipes) are very useful. A. Walicki, *History of Russian Thought* (Oxford, 1980), characterizes significant ideas and their proponents from the late 18th century to the Revolution. M. Raeff, *Russian Intellectual History—An Anthology* (London, 1966), reaches further back. Note V. Zenkovsky. *A History of Russian Philosophy* (2 vols., London, 1953). On political thought: F. Venturi, *The Roots of Revolution* (London, 1960); E. Lampert, *Sons against Fathers* (Oxford, 1965); S. Utechin, *Russian Political Thought* (London, 1963); E.C. Thaden, *Conservative Nationalism in 19th-century Russia* (Seattle, 1964). Particularly impressive are the essays on 19th-century themes and figures (e.g. Belinsky, Herzen, the Populists) brought together in I. Berlin, *Russian Thinkers* (London, 1977). For the early period, note *The Problem of Old Russian Culture*, a symposium to which N. Andreyev, J. Billington, G. Florovsky and D. Likhachov contributed in *Slavic Review* 21–22 (1962–63). M. Cherniavsky, *Tsar and People* (New Haven, 1981), is a seminal work. Two vols. titled *Medieval Russian Culture* (vol. I, Berkeley, 1984, ed. H. Birnbaum and M. Flier; vol. II, Berkeley, 1994, ed. M. Flier and D. Rowland) contain a rich medley of scholarly articles, above all on religion, literature and art.

Some most valuable contributions to Russian "psychohistory" and cultural semiotics have been made since the 1960s by the "Tartu school," notably Yu. Lotman and B. Uspensky. Selections of their studies (on such topics as 17th- and 18th-century pretenders, Peter the Great, the Decembrists in everyday life) have been translated in A. and D. Niakhimovsky (ed.), *The Semiotics of Russian Cultural History* (New York, 1985), and A. Shukman (ed.), *Semiotics of Russian Culture* (Ann Arbor, 1984). On the great cultural theoretician Bakhtin, K. Clark and M. Holquist, *Mikhail Bakhtin* (Cambridge Mass. 1985).

Literature

There is a lack in English of a comprehensive unified history of Russian literature (the older volumes by D.S. Mirsky and M. Slonim are outdated). Encyclopedic and collective volumes help to fill the gap. A.K. Thorlby (ed.), *The Penguin Companion to Literature: Europe* (Harmondsworth, 1969), includes nearly 200 Russian entries. H.S. Weber (ed.), *The Modern Encyclopedia of Russian and Soviet Literatures* (many volumes, in progress), has more detailed essays. *Companion to Russian Studies,* vol. 2, ed. R. Auty and D. Obolensky (Cambridge, 1976), is strong on pre-Petrine literature and in its sections on language, writing and printing. Better still are V. Terras (ed.), *Handbook of Russian Literature* (New Haven, 1985) and N. Cornwell (ed.), *Reference Guide to Russian Literature* (London, 1998).

On early literature the most stimulating and detailed work remains D. Cizevskiy, *History of Russian Literature from the 11th Century to the End of the Baroque* (The Hague, 1960); note also J.L.I. Fennell and A. Stokes, *Early Russian Literature* (London, 1974). The only varied and comprehensive collection of early texts in translation is by S. Zenkovsky (see above). It is even harder to track down translations of 18th-century literature, save in H. Segal's anthology, *The Literature of 18th-century Russia* (New York, 1964), though *Russian Literature Triquarterly* devoted a recent number (20) to it. Some of the chief works of e.g. Fonvizin, Radishchev and Karamzin have been published individually. Note the critical essays in A.G. Cross (ed.), *Russian Literature in the Age of Catherine the Great* (Oxford, 1976).

From Pushkin's time things are different: there is a range of translations of nearly all important writers. and monographs in English on most of them; poets however are less well served in both respects than prose-writers.

Pushkin: many translations exist; W. Arndt, *Pushkin Threefold* (New York, 1972), has both literal and verse translations of the poems. V. Nabokov, *Eugene Onegin, a Novel in Verse* (London, 1964), has a plain translation and remarkable commentary. Charles Johnston's poetic translation of *Eugene Onegin* (London, 1977) has superseded previous attempts. T. Wolff (ed.), *Pushkin on Literature* (London, 1972), is an anthology of texts with continuous commentary. J. Bayley, *Pushkin* (Cambridge, 1971), is a detailed and authoritative study; A.D.P. Briggs, *Alexander Pushkin* (London, 1983), is shorter and more accessible.

Gogol: few if any translations can be unreservedly recommended. There is much critical literature from a bewildering variety of viewpoints: R. Maguire (ed.), *Gogol from the Twentieth Century* (Princeton, 1974), gives a good sample of these. V. Nabokov, *Nikolay Gogol* (London, 1944), is one of the most idiosyncratic and fascinating literary studies ever written.

Lermontov: the translation of *Hero of Our Time* by I.P. Foote (Harmondsworth, 1966) is highly readable; there is also one by V. Nabokov. The best close study is C.J.G. Turner, *Pechorin* (Birmingham, 1978); J. Garrard, *M. Lermontov* (Boston, 1982), is a serviceable general introduction.

Dostoyevsky: as hard as Gogol to translate, for somewhat similar reasons. There is a vast literature on him, including the multivolume biography by J. Frank (1977–). An anthology of 20th-century views (1962) has been edited by R. Wellek; note too V. Seduro, *Dostoyevsky in Russian Literary Criticism* (New York, 1957). M. Bakhtin, *Problems of Dostoyevsky's Poetics* (Ann Arbor, 1975), twice translated, is a seminal work opening up cultural-historical perspectives going far beyond its title.

Tolstoy: again, much critical literature in English (more on his literary than his publicistic role). A. Maude, his English disciple, not only made translations checked by the author (thus "canonical") but wrote a *Life of Tolstoy* (2 vols., London, 1929–30). On his view of history, I. Berlin, *The Hedgehog and the Fox* (London, 1953); of art, T.J. Diffey, *Tolstoy's What is Art?* (London, 1985). On his imaginative writing R.F. Christian, *Tolstoy: A Critical Introduction* (Cambridge, 1969); J. Bayley, *Tolstoy and the Novel* (London, 1966). V. Shklovsky's unusual discursive biography (Moscow, 1967) has been translated.

Chekhov: some widely available translations are unsatisfactory. Outstanding is the near-complete collection of stories and plays in the multivolume *Oxford Chekhov* (1964–), trans. R. Hingley; note also his critical biography (London, 1950, 1974); there is very full new *Life* by D. Rayfield (London, 1997). Recent versions of individual plays by M. Frayn are also commendable.

A selection of other individual monographs and translations worthy of note follows. A.G. Cross, *N.M. Karamzin: a Study of his Literary Career* (Cambridge, 1971). V. Setchkerev, *Ivan Goncharov: a Study of his Life and Works* (Würzburg, 1974). R. Freeborn, *Turgenev* (Westport, 1960). N. Leskov, *The Enchanted Pilgrim,* stories translated by D. Magarshak (London, 1946). R. Gregg, *F. Tyutchev: the Evolution of a Poet* (New York, 1965); *Versions from F. Tyutchev,* translated by C. Tomlinson (Oxford, 1960). R. Gustafton, *The Imagination of Spring* (New Haven, 1966) on Fet; translations from him in *I Have Come to You to Greet You*, trans, J. Greene (London, 1982). A. Bely, *Petersburg,* new (full) translation by R. Maguire and J. Malmstead (Hassocks, 1978). J. Elsworth, *Andrey Bely* (Letchworth, 1972). A. Blok, *The Twelve and Other Poems,* trans. P. France and J. Stallworthy (London, 1970); A. Pyman, *The Life of A. Blok* (Oxford, 1979–80). A. Akhmatova, *Selected Poems,* trans. R. McKane (Oxford, 1969). O. Mandelshtam, *Selected Poems,* trans. C. Brown and W. Merwin (London, 1973); *The Prose of Osip Mandelstam,* trans. and ed. C. Brown (Princeton, 1965); C. Brown, *Mandelstam* (Cambridge, 1973); N. Mandelstam, *Hope against Hope* (London, 1971) and *Hope Abandoned* (London, 1974), both trans. M. Hayward, V. Khlebnikov, *The King of Time,* trans, P. Schmidt (a selection from various areas of his work, Cambridge, Mass. 1985); R. Cooke, *Velimir Khlebnikov: a Critical Study* (Cambridge, 1987). V. Shklovsky, *Zoo, or Letters not about Love* (novel, trans. New York, 1971), *A Sentimental Journey* (memoirs, New York, 1970), *Third Factory* (criticism, Ann Arbor, 1977), all trans. R. Sheldon, W. Woroszylsky, *The Life of Mayakovsky* (told through documents; Eng. edn. London, 1972); L. Stahlberger, *The Symbolic System of Mayakovsky* (The Hague, 1964); V. Mayakovsky, *The Bedbug and Selected Poetry,* trans. M. Hayward, G. Reaves and P. Blake (London, 1962)—most English translations of Mayakovsky's poetry are totally inadequate, though the Scots versions by Edwin Morgan are good. J. Falen, *Isaak Babel: Master of the Short Story* (Knoxville, 1974); Babel's *Collected Stories* in new trsln. by D. McDuff (Penguin, 1994). A. Platonov, *The Fierce and Beautiful World,* stories trans. J. Barnes (Lon-don, 1971) and *The Foundation Pit* (transl. R. Chandler, London, 1996). C. Bearne, *Sholokhov* (London, 1969). D. Richards, *Zamyatin* (New York, 1962). G. McVay, *Esenin: a Life* (London, 1970). Pasternak: the poems have been translated by many hands, often inadequately, but with some success by P. France and J. Stallworthy, *Selected Poems* (London, 1983). The translation of *Doctor Zhivago* by M. Hayward and M. Harari (London, 1958) needs to be supplemented by D. Davie, *The Poems of Doctor Zhivago* (London, 1965). Note Pasternak's important *Essay in Autobiography* (London, 1959). There is a remarkable memoir of Pasternak (and Akhmatova) in I. Berlin, *Personal Impressions* (London, 1980). The fullest biography will be that by C. Barnes, of which one volume has so far appeared (Cambridge, 1989). E. Proffer, *Bulgakov* (Ann Arbor, 1984). Solzhenitsyn's *One Day of Ivan Denisovich* reads better in the translation by M. Hayward and R. Hingley (New York, 1963) than that by R. Parker; M. Scammell, *Solzhenitsyn* (London, 1985), is a detailed account. N. Zabolotsky, *Scrolls,* trans. D. Weissbort (London, 1971); note too N. Zabolotsky *The Life of Zabolotsky* (Cardiff, 1994). D. Kharms *Incidences* (London, 1993). A. Voznesensky, *Antiworlds* (Oxford, 1967)— outstanding translations by M. Hayward with several poets, including W.H. Auden.

Important modern literary autobiographies and memoirs include those of I. Ehrenburg, V. Katayev, K. Paustovsky (see also Shklovsky, Pasternak above). Highly unusual is M. Zoshchenko's autobiographical fragment "Before Sunrise" (in *Dissonant Voices in Soviet Literature,* see below). Prison memoirs by literary figures include N. Zabolotsky, "The Story of my Imprisonment," trans. R. Milner-Gulland (*Times Literary Supplement,* 9 Oct. 1981), E. Ginzburg, *Into the Whirlwind* (London, 1967) and *Within the Whirlwind,* trans. I. Boland (London, 1981); and Solzhenitsyn's lightly fictionalized novels.

Some studies of broader areas in 19th- and 20th-century literature: H. Gifford, *The Novel in Russia* (London, 1964)—a concise critical account, R. Poggioli, *Poets of Russia* (Cambridge, Mass. 1960). J. West, *Russian Symbolism* (London, 1970). V. Markov, *Russian Futurism* (London, 1969). P. Steiner, *Russian Formalism* (London, 1985). R. Hingley, *Nightingale Fever* (London, 1982), on the poets Akhmatova, Mandelshtam, Tsvetayeva and Pasternak, C.V. James, *Soviet Socialist Realism* (London, 1973). V. Dunham, *In Stalin's Time* (Cambridge, 1976)—a witty account of "official" literature, D. Brown, *Soviet Literature since Stalin* (Oxford, 1973). G. Hosking, *Beyond Socialist Realism* (London, 1980)—particularly strong on "village" prose. On contemporary literature: R. Porter, *Russia's Alternative Prose* (Oxford, 1994).

Anthologies are often useful for getting to know modern literature: P. Blake and M. Hayward (eds.), *Dissonant Voices in Soviet Literature* (London, 1961), reaches from c. 1930 to 1960. G. Gibian, *Russia's Lost Literature of the Absurd* (New York, 1971) on the OBERIU Leningrad writers, R. Milner-Gulland and M. Dewhirst (eds.), *Russian Writing Today* (Harmondsworth, 1977), prose and poetry c. 1945–75. D. Weissbort (ed.), *Post-War Russian Poetry* (Harmondsworth, 1974). S. Massie (ed.), *The Living Mirror* (London, 1980), good translations by various hands of modern St Petersburg poets. P. Blake and M. Hayward (eds.), *Halfway to the Moon* (London, 1974)—excellent selection of "Thaw" writers, C. and E. Proffer, *Contemporary Russian Prose* (Ann Arbor, 1982)—"long short" stories, E.J. Brown (ed.), *Major Soviet Writers* (Oxford, 1973), is an anthology of criticism, particularly notable for Roman Jakobson's articles on Khlebnikov and Mayakovsky. On social background: J. Andrew, *Writers and Society during the Rise of Russian Realism* (London, 1980).

The Arts

The most detailed history of Russian art in English is still G.H. Hamilton, *Art and Architecture of Russia* (2nd edn.,

Harmondsworth, 1975), though it gives little coverage to the 20th century and is in some respects out-of-date. R. Milner-Gulland and J.E. Bowlt, *An Introduction to Russian Art and Architecture* (*Companion to Russian Studies*, vol, 3, ed. R. Auty and D. Obolensky, Cambridge, 1980), is shorter and more recent. W. Brumfield, *A History of Russian Architecture* (Cambridge, 1993). T. Talbot Rice, *A Concise History of Russian Art* (London, 1963), has copious small-format illustrations but is factually unreliable. A work to be used with caution (a product of the Stalin age) but valuable in its integrated approach to the visual and other arts is M. Alpatov, *The Russian Impact on Art* (2nd edn., New York, 1969). A. Bird, *Russian Painting* (Oxford, 1987), is strongest on the 19th century. A good critical guide to extant monuments and museums exists in German: E. Behrens, *Kunst in Russland* (Cologne, 1969). A. & V. Opolovnikov, *The Wooden Architecture of Russia* (London, 1989), with much information on rural life generally.

On Old Russian art: H. Faensen and V. Ivanov, *Early Russian Architecture* (London, 1975), a scholarly, copiously illustrated and detailed, though not exhaustive, account, V. Lazarev, *Old Russian Murals and Mosaics* (London, 1966) and *Novgorodian Icon Painting* (Moscow, 1969); K. Onasch, *Icons* (London, 1963); B. Uspensky, *The Semiotics of the Russian Icon* (Lisse, 1976)— a concise and subtle study. The Byzantine artistic background can be studied in many works, e.g. A. Grabar, *Byzantium* (London, 1966), and G. Mathew, *Byzantine Aesthetics* (London, 1963). W. Brumfield and M. Velimirovic (eds.), *Christianity and the Arts in Russia* (Cambridge, 1991) links high art, folk art and music with religion. See too *Medieval Russian Culture* I and II ("History of Ideas," above) and Milner-Gulland, *The Russians* ("General Histories," above).

Art of the Petersburg era: J. Cracraft, *The Petrine Revolution in Russian Architecture* (London, 1988). T. Talbot Rice, "The Conflux of Influences in 18-century Russian Art and Architecture," in J. Garrard (ed.), *The 18th*

Century in Russia (see above); A. Kaganovich, *Arts of Russia*, vol. II (Geneva, 1964). Many recent Russian albums of 18th- and 19th-century artists have English or French as well as Russian-language text: e.g. K. Mikhaylova, *Rokotov* (Leningrad, 1971). On the "Wanderers" and their age: E. Valkenier, *Russian Realist Art* (Ann Arbor, 1977); B.W. Kean, *All the Empty Palaces* (London, 1985), on patronage. See too P. Roosevelt, *Life on the Russian Country Estate* (Yale, 1995).

On 20th-century art: C. Gray, *The Russian Experiment in Art 1863–1922* (only the 3rd edn. with additional notes can be recommended, London, 1988); J.E. Bowit, *Russian Art of the Avant Garde: Theory and Criticism 1902–34* (New York, 1976); V. Marcade, *Le Renouveau de l'art pictural russe* (Lausanne, 1971)—an important study. There are too many works in English on individual artists and architects to list more than a sample. Kandinsky studies are an industry in themselves; the most useful edn. of his *On the Spiritual in Art* is that by J.E. Bowlt and R.C. Washton Long (Oxford, 1980). P. Weiss, *Kandinsky and Old Russia* (London, 1994) is a highly original study of him in the light of (largely) pagan imagery. On Malevich: W. Simmons, *Malevich's Black Square* (New York, 1981); *Malevich*, essays, some important, by various hands in English and German (Cologne, 1978); K. Malevich, *Essays on Art*, trans. T. Andersen (Copenhagen, 1968). J. Milner, *Vladimir Tatlin and the Russian Avant-Garde* (London, 1983); L. Zhadova (ed.), *Tatlin* (London, 1988) copiously documented. J.E. Bowlt and N. Misler, *Pavel Filonov: a Hero and His Fate* (Austin, 1983)—Filonov's own writings, with detailed biographical commentary. A. Parson, *Larionov* (Princeton, 1993). A. Kopp, *Town and Revolution: Soviet Architecture and City Planning 1917–33* (New York, 1970). V. Shvidkovsky, *Building in the USSR 1917–32* (London, 1971). C. Lodder, *Russian Constructivism* (London, 1983). S. Bojko, *New Graphic Design in Revolutionary Russia* (New York, 1972). M. C. Brown, *Socialist Realist Painting* (Yale U.P., 1998).

Miscellaneous artistic topics: R.C. Williams, *Artists in Revolution: Portraits of the Russian Avant-Garde* (Bloomington, 1977), brings together studies of writers, politicians, artists and movie-makers in an uneven but interesting synthesis. J.E. Bowlt and S. Bann (eds.), *Russian Formalism* (Edinburgh, 1973), includes studies and original documents relating to literature, cinema and the visual arts. K. Berton, *Moscow: an Architectural History* (London, 1976). N. Gosling, *Leningrad* (London, 1963). A. Voyce, *The Moscow Kremlin* (Norman, 1954). E. Ivanova, *Russian Applied Art* (Leningrad, 1976). Yu. Ovsyannikov, *The Lubok* (Moscow, 1963) and *Russian Folk Arts and Crafts* (Moscow, 1975). A. Hilton, *Russian Folk Art* (Bloomington, 1995). On cinema: L. and J. Schnitzer (eds.), *Cinema in Revolution* (London, 1973); Y. Barna, *Eisenstein* (Bloomington, 1973). On ballet: A. Haskell, *Diaghileff* (New York, 1935) and *The Russian Genius in Ballet* (Oxford, 1963), a very concise introduction; R. Buckle, *Nijinsky* (London, 1971). On modern theater: K. Stanislavsky, *My Life in Art* (New York, 1924); A. Ripellino, *Maiakovski et le théâtre russe d'avant-garde* (Paris, 1965)—an important study, also in Italian; E. Braun (ed.), *Meyerhold on Theatre* (London, 1969)—translations and excellent commentary.

On music: a good many memoirs (e.g. by Glinka, Rimsky-Korsakov, Stravinsky) are available in English, and there are individual monographs on the main composers. Note too A.J. Swan, *Russian Music and its Origins in Chant and Folk Song* (London, 1973); G.R. Seaman, *History of Russian Music*, vol. I (Oxford, 1967)—up to Dargomyzhsky; interesting articles by A. and J. Swan and J. Spiegeiman in J. Garrard (ed.), *The Eighteenth Century in Russia* (see above); G. Abraham, *Slavonic and Romantic Music* (London, 1968). But the outstanding source for up-to-date information is S. Sadie (ed.), *The New Grove Dictionary of Music and Musicians*, 20 vols. (London, 1980), with detailed articles on all significant and many insignificant composers and selected musical topics.

GLOSSARY

The purpose of this glossary is to give informal explanations of some important words and concepts that, though frequently encountered, may cause difficulty to readers unfamiliar with their social, historical or linguistic context. Less common Russian terms that are adequately explained where they occur in the text are not included. Bold type in the text indicates a cross-reference.

Boyar In broad terms, a male member of the higher aristocracy (*boyarstvo*) in medieval Russia. The female equivalent is *boyarinya*. More specifically, a boyar was a member of the boyar council (*Boyarskaya duma*), the tsar's permanent advisory committee until the time of Peter I, chosen by the tsar usually (but by no means always) from the highest aristocratic families.

Byzantine empire The modern name for the eastern division of the Roman empire, whose capital was established by Constantine the Great in 330 at the ancient Greek colony of Byzantium, renamed by him "New Rome" and generally known as Constantinople. It provided early Russia with a focus for trade, an object of envy, subsequently a religion, an art, a literature and a cultural example.

Cossack A distinct group of Russian frontiersmen in the hazardous, underpopulated southern steppe. The name (*Kazak*) comes from a Turkic term for "rider" or "freebooter," as, confusingly, does the name of the modern Turkic Kazakhs. Known from the 15th century, they formed militarized, democratic colonies chiefly around the Dnieper (the Zaporozhian host), Don and Yaik (or Ural) Rivers; at their most powerful (in the 17th century) they played off Muscovy, Poland and Turkey and intervened significantly in the Time of Troubles. The attractions of settled life gradually weakened their institutions, but they retained their role as a cavalry elite until the Russo-Polish War of 1920.

"Cross-in-square" The standard Byzantine church plan after the 9th century, adopted throughout the Orthodox world and universal in Russia until the 16th century. Three bays intersect three naves, all barrel-vaulted, with apses at the east end. The central nave and transept may be vaulted at a higher level, forming the "cross element; there is a narthex (porch) at the west.

druzhina The immediate retinue of the princes in Kievan times, constituting both bodyguard and advisory committee, zealous of its independence.

dvoryanstvo The landowning class of tsarist and imperial Russia, variously translated "gentry" or "nobility," but not quite corresponding to Western models (there was no landed aristocracy and no developed feudalism in Russia). The *dvoryanin* might hold land hereditarily (*votchina*) or conditionally (*pomestye*), but in practice the Muscovite system made all privilege dependent on state service. From 1762 service ceased to be obligatory (though remained the norm): the *dvoryanin* could reside on his estate, to which in 1785 he gained full title. The *dvoryanstvo* played a vital role in maintaining authority and collecting taxes in the provinces.

dvoyeveriye "Double belief," the persistence of pagan customs and habits of thought alongside Christianity in the Russian countryside until recent times.

Gulag A Soviet Russian acronym for "State Directorate of Camps," controlling the widespread network of prison camps of various kinds characteristic of the 1930s to 1950s; its quasi-autonomous status and geographical spread led Solzhenitsyn to refer to it as an "archipelago" in the title of his work (1974–75) that brought the word to public attention.

Horde Originally denoting a Turko-Tatar clan encampment (*orda*), the term used by medieval Russians to designate the vast Western territorial division of the Mongol empire (the "Golden" Horde on account of its wealth), their immediate overlord.

icon The representation of sacred personages or events, in whatever medium, from the Greek word for "image." It has come to have the narrower connotation of a wooden panel-painting, executed in tempera on a plaster ground according to traditional models. Icons were fundamental to worship throughout the Orthodox world from the 9th century, and were ubiquitous in churches, homes and shrines. Stylistically they underwent rich development on Russian soil, with its climax marked by much local variety in the 15th century.

iconoclasm Literally, "image-breaking." A lengthy episode in 8th-9th-century Byzantine history during which the imperial authorities forbade the display and veneration of representational sacred art, following the Second Commandment against "graven images." Popular and monastic resistance by the venerators of icons ("iconodules") eventually triumphed, and with the restoration of images came their systematic integration into Orthodox theology (as symbolizing the Incarnation) and into the adornment of churches.

iconostasis An icon-screen. Early-medieval Eastern churches had a low balustrade separating nave from altar sanctuary. On this icons were placed. In the later Middle Ages it became a multitiered wooden framework, the finest examples of which survive at Zagorsk and in the Moscow Annunciation Cathedral. Normally the lowest tier of the iconostasis displays locally venerated icons, the next the Virgin, the Baptist, Evangelists and others interceding with Christ on behalf of the worshipers, the next the feastday icons and the highest the Prophets.

intelligentsia The "thinking," self-aware and educated class as a whole (with no necessary implication of intellectual brilliance). It soon acquired overtones of a critical attitude to the established order; thus those who served the state, however intelligent, would not normally be considered *intelligenty*. A loose coinage from Latin that arose in the mid-19th century, the word was popularized, like other catchwords of the time (e.g. "superfluous man," "nihilist"), by Ivan Turgenev.

kremlin The fortified citadel at the heart of most medieval Russian cities (Russian *kreml*, related to the modern word for "flint" ("*kremen*"). From the early 16th century kremlins were usually built of brick. There are notable examples at Smolensk, Tula and Serpukhov, generally linked with the 16th-century system of fortifications south of Moscow intended to prevent incursions from the steppe.

kulak A rich peasant (literally, "fist"). The term had derogative connotations and is associated particularly with the "dekulakization," forcible repression of the wealthier (often only marginally wealthier) peasantry accompanying Stalin's collectivization.

mestnichestvo The Muscovite system of appointments by precedence: boyars would serve only in posts equal or superior to those of their forebears, and posts had to be distributed hierarchically within families. The system was complex and inefficient, leading to constant squabbling, and had to be suspended in wartime; it represented nevertheless a constraint on the ruler. In 1682 Fyodor III's government abolished it, and the *razryadnye knigi*, books recording details of precedence, were burnt.

mir Traditionally, the village commune (sometimes termed *obshchina*), an institution significant in imperial Russia as the basic organizing unit of society at peasant level. In modern Russian *mir* means either "peace" or "world." The mir was responsible for the allocation of agricultural tasks, recruitment, the repartitioning of communal land and payment of taxes. As an expression of, apparently, spontaneous grass-roots cooperation, it was of great interest to Russian populists (even to Marxists).

narodnichestvo Russian populism (deriving from *narod*, "people"): the dominant oppositional ideology after the 1860s, with many ramifications from the conservative to the violently revolutionary, having in common

admiration for the peasantry, their innate wisdom and communal institutions, A populist is a *narodnik*.

narodnost Literally, "popular quality," though often loosely rendered "nationality" (the word is hard to translate precisely). With "autocracy" and "orthodoxy," it formed the trinity of principles that supported the doctrine of "Official Nationality" propagated under Nicholas I, and it carried ideological overtones of supposed popular support for the tsarist system. It was perhaps surprisingly invoked again as one of the principles of Socialist Realism in the 1930s.

NEP "New Economic Policy," introduced by Lenin's government in the summer of 1921 to replace the rigorous regime of "War Communism," which had brought the country to the point of collapse. The government, while controlling the "commanding heights" of the economy, permitted small-scale industry, private trade and retailing and encouraged peasant food production: public accountability and taxation returned. NEP quickly proved a success, though it caused ideologically committed Communists much disquiet as so-called "Nepmen" and **kulaks** flourished. Stalin ended NEP, introducing the first Five-Year Plan (*Pyatilerka*) and agricultural collectivization late in 1928.

odnodvortsy "Single-homesteaders," a diverse social group, fairly numerous in the southern provinces, at the lower margin of the landowning class. Generally too poor to hold serfs, they differed little from state peasants, but expended much effort in the 18th century in trying to maintain their separate status. They originated in the military settlement of the southern frontier.

Old Believers
See **starovery**.

Orthodox Church The church of Eastern Europe and the Near East, deriving from Byzantium, nowadays with adherents worldwide. In its own eyes it represents the direct continuation of the early apostolic church, from which other branches of Christendom diverged. Differences of ritual and problems of authority led to schism between Constantinople and Rome from 1054, but this had little general impact until the 4th Crusade sacked Constantinople (1204). After the mid-15th century Muscovite Russia identified itself ever more directly as the true defender of Orthodoxy.

Orthodoxy in Byzantium and Old Russia was characterized by the ideal of close symbiosis (*symphonia*, "harmony") between ruler and church. In imperial Russia the church was treated as an arm of state (which tarnished its reputation among the 19th-century **intelligentsia**). Liturgically and theologically, Orthodoxy has much in common with Roman Catholicism; both accept the first seven councils of the church. They differ over the wording of the Creed ("*filioque*") and some other doctrinal points, but more importantly over what Orthodoxy sees as the authoritarianism and scholastic nature of Catholicism.

The Orthodox priesthood, traditionally living close to the peasantry and often scarcely literate, was obliged to marry; bishops, being celibate, came from the monasteries: there are no separate monastic orders. An Orthodox heritage much valued in the 19th and 20th centuries is that of "communality" (*sobornost*). A tradition of hermits, holy men (*startsy*), fools in Christ (yurodivye), mendicants, uncanonized and locally venerated saints is more characteristic of Orthodoxy than formal theology, yet mystical Hesychasm provided a specifically Orthodox impulse to believers from the 14th century onwards.

parsuna An iconic portrait (deriving from the Latin *persona*, via Polish). Examples of the **parsuna** probably go back to the late 16th century, and become common in the 17th: they often commemorated recently dead people of distinction. Using the techniques of icon painting, the *parsuna* aims at recognizable depiction, though without great individuation or "realistic" modeling; it nevertheless played a transitional role between Old Russian and Western art.

patriarch Head of one of the five areas of jurisdiction in the early church (Rome, Antioch, Alexandria, Jerusalem, Constantinople). The Pope (patriarch of Rome) was traditionally regarded as "first among equals," but came to claim larger authority. Russia, the head of whose church until then had been a metropolitan, negotiated the establishment of a patriarchate in 1589; it was suspended by Peter I and reestablished in 1918.

samizdat "Self-publication": a parody acronym on the model of *Gosizdat,* "State Publishing House." The term became well known from the 1960s, but the activity of deliberately circulating writings that have been, or might be, banned by censorship is much older and was particularly widespread under Nicholas I.

serfs Peasants "bound" to the land they worked (as is implied by the Russian term, *krepostnye*). Serfdom in Russia developed gradually in the Muscovite period (as it waned in the rest of Europe) and was not fully institutionalized until the law code of 1649. Until the late 15th century peasant workers could change landlords at will around St George's Day (in November): this right was abrogated in years of famine or war, and in the 16th century it ceased to exist. The Muscovite government thereby ensured that the estates with which it rewarded **dvoryanstvo** were viable. Serfs worked part of the week for the landowner (*barshchina*) or paid quitrent (*obrok*), or both, but were technically serving the government, like the landowners themselves. Serfdom was not slavery, though at times the practical distinction was slight. Serfs never constituted more than half the Russian population (contrary to received opinion), as there were substantial numbers of "state peasants," tied to place of residence but otherwise free to arrange their lives; serfdom never took root in remoter parts such as Siberia, the Cossack lands, the far north.

service state The social system fully developed in Muscovy under Ivan IV whereby all classes were regarded as the tsar's servitors (cf. **dvoryanstvo, serfs**). The tsar also exercised general control over the church and the merchants, holding several trade monopolies. Tax-gathering was farmed out (*kormleniye,* literally "feeding"). Peter I, in modernizing and in some ways "Westernizing" the service state, actually made it more efficient and oppressive.

Slavophilism An ideology that developed from the 1840s, as an idiosyncratic Russian version of European romantic nationalism. In various transformations it has continued to affect Russian sociopolitical thought ever since (most clearly in such writers as Dostoyevsky and Solzhenitsyn). Slavophiles perceived a special and precious historical destiny in Russian native institutions and religion (particularly in *sobornost* ("communality"), a term they popularized). They are usually contrasted with "Westernizers," their more diverse opponents.

Socialist Realism Neither a "style" nor a "theory," but defined by its proponents as the creative "method" for the arts in the Soviet Union, implying also a critical approach to art in general. The term seems to have been devised in 1932, if not by Gorky then with his approval, and was officially promulgated, at first in literature, from 1934. Its fundamental precepts were **narodnost,** *partiynost* (agreement with Party principles) and *ideynost* (intellectual quality, i.e. identifiable ideas). Since Stalin's time Socialist Realism, though retaining official approval, came to be tacitly ignored.

starovery (or **staroobryadtsy**) "Old Believers": those who would not accept the Orthodox Church reforms of Patriarch Nikon and Tsar Aleksey of the 1650s, confirmed after Nikon's downfall in 1666. The reforms split the country: there are no reliable statistics, but perhaps half of all Russians adhered to the Old (in their eyes, True) Belief. A major division soon arose between those who retained clergy and those wh0—because their clergy could not be consecrated—did not (*bezpopovtsy*).

tsar The autocratic ruler of Russia. The term, an early import into the Slavonic languages, derives from "Caesar." In the early Middle Ages it referred to the Byzantine emperor, subsequently also to the Tatar khan. Russian rulers were from the 12th century styled "grand prince" (*veliky knyaz*). They were informally sometimes called "tsar" (perhaps under Serbian influence) from the late 14th century; the first to be so crowned was Ivan IV (1547). Peter I upgraded the royal title to "emperor" (accepted only reluctantly in other European countries), though "tsar" remained in popular use.

veche The popular assembly, consisting of all heads of households, in the towns of Kievan Rut. This quintessentially democratic, if rather ill-organized, institution was probably of prehistoric origin; it varied in its power, but seems to have often played a significant role in deciding large issues, even of peace and war.

zemskiy sobor An "assembly of the lands" or estates, a Muscovite institution summoned irregularly for special and important purposes. The Russian word *zemlya* means "land," and historically also denoted the territorial units or principalities into which Old Russia was divided. The first known assembly was in 1549; the most famous marked the end of the Time of Troubles by choosing Michael Romanov as tsar in 1613. Little is known about the proceedings of these assemblies, but they certainly included representatives of various elements of the population (even on occasion state peasants).

Note on dating

Until the end of January 1918 Russia adhered to the Julian calendar—11 days behind the Western (Gregorian) calendar in the 18th century, 12 days in the 19th, 13 days in the 20th. The date given is that which applied in Russia at the time referred to, though in some cases, where it it necessary to be more specific, the abbreviations O.S. (Old Style, i.e. Julian) and N.S. (New Style) are used. The Russian Orthodox Church continues to use O.S. dating for liturgical purposes.

Note on transliteration and names

No single system of transliteration from the Cyrillic alphabet has been generally agreed in the English-speaking countries, partly because of the vagaries of English spelling and pronunciation, partly because of the varied purposes transliteration has had to serve.

We have chosen the system used in the three-volume Cambridge *Companion to Russian Studies,* with slight modifications for the ease of the non-specialist reader. It provides a good idea of how Russian words should be pronounced. Note that *zh* (χ) represents the -s- sound in "pleasure," *kh* (**X**) the -ch sound in "loch." The letter *y* has three functions: (1) at a consonant similar to the y- in "yes," it is heard in Russian as the first component of ye, yo, ya, yu-, each indicated by a single Cyrillic letter, and when -i- follows the palatalizing "soft sign" (e.g. in *Ilyich*); (2) at an independent vowel it represents the Russian sound, not found in standard English, but approximating to the -i- in Scots pronunciation of "little"; (3) after a vowel (e.g. -ay-, -oy- etc.) it forms a diphthong (Russian **X**) The common adjectival case-ending that should be represented -yy has for simplicity been rendered as -y in this volume (similarly names in -kiy become -ky). After *zh, sh, ch,* "ye" and "yo" have been rendered "e" and "o" in accordance with pronunciation; following English convention "ye" has also been rendered "e" after other consonants and the vowel -y-. The "soft sign," palatalizing the preceding consonant, has not been indicated (save through -y- where immediately followed by a vowel).

Non-speakers of Russian should realize that Russian words of more than one syllable carry a single heavy stress accent that can theoretically fall on any syllable; there are few rules to provide guidance, and unfortunately it is not usually indicated orthographically. The vowel -yo- however is always stressed.

Russian personal names always have three components: (1) the first or proper name (*imya*); (2) the patronymic (*otchestvo*), derived from one's father's first name with the termination -ovich, -evich or -ich (masculine), -ovna, -evna, -ishna (feminine); (3) the surname *familiya*), that arrived in Russian society later than the others, and generally ends in -ov, -ev, -yn, -in, -sky (masculine), -ova, -eva, -yna, -ina, -skaya (feminine). A normal polite form of address is by the first name and patronymic "Familiar" forms of first names are common: e.g. Kolya from Nikolai, Sasha from Aleksandr(a), Vanya from Ivan, Masha from Mariya etc.

It is interesting to know the national origins of some other common types of surname in the region. The ending -enko is originally Ukrainian; -ko, Belarusian. Georgian names commonly end with -shvili, -dze, -ia. The great majority of Armenian names end in -yan (-ian). Latvian names often end in -s, Lithuanian ones in -is. Many Turkic names have been "Russianized" by the addition of the termination -ov to their original form. The surname endings -ovich, -evich are of West Russian or Polish origin; so, often, are -ovsky, -evsky (if stressed on the penultimate syllable).

In rendering personal and place names for the purposes of this volume we have permitted ourselves some inconsistencies where a common English usage has become so normal that strict transliteration might cause confusion or irritation. Thus we use the following forms (correct transliteration and stress in brackets): Potemkin (Potyómkin), Gorbachev (Gorbachóv), Khrushchev (Khrushchóv), Alexander (Aleksándr), Peter (Pyotr), Tsar Nicholas (Nikolái in other cases), Tsar Paul (Pável in other cases), St Sergius (Sergéy or Sérgiy), St Stephen (Stepán), Sophia (Sofiya). Some late 19th-and early 20th-century public figures had a preferred Western spelling of their names which we follow: e.g. Diaghilev (Dyágilev); Ehrenburg (Erenbúrg); Benois (Benuá); Tchaikovsky (Chaykóvsky); Nijinsky (Nizhínsky); Chagall (Shagál); Meyerhold (Meyerkhóld); Eisenstein (Eyzenshtéyn); Witte (Vitte). Moscow (Moskvá), St Petersburg (Sankt-Peterbúrg), Archangel (Arkhángelsk), Dnieper (Dnepr), Pripet (Pripyát), Crimea (Krym), Caucasus (Kavkáz), White Lake (Beloózero).

Many non-Russian names are also spelt conventionally (e.g. those of most Union Republics). In other cases the *Times Atlas* spelling is normally followed. A few other Russian words well known in English are also affected: taiga, soviet (taygá, sovét—each of two syllables); rouble (rubl—one syllable); chernozem (chernozyom).

The rendering of names in an atlas such as this has unavoidably become a more complex matter than it was in 1989. Then, it was normal simply to transliterate from the Cyrillic forms given in Soviet reference-works according to a consistent system, using conventional English forms where they existed (and the Roman spelling of Baltic names in Lithuania, Latvia and Estonia). With the dissolution of the Soviet Union into independent Republics the following processes have complicated the issue. (1) Many place-names have been changed, usually to a pre-Soviet form: it is not always easy to establish when this has officially taken place, and it can lead to odd results (e.g. there is still a "Leningrad Province" whose capital is now St. Petersburg). (2) A Latin alphabet, with its own norms, has replaced Cyrillic in official use in some of the republics. (3) In Ukraine and Belarus, where Slav languages closely related to Russian and using the Cyrillic alphabet have official status as "first languages", many changes reflecting the modern pronnunication of these languages have modified the accepted orthography. These changes are reflected in many modern English language atlases and we have followed this in the third part ("Regions and Republics") of this volume. Since the reader may well wonder, e.g., if "Kyyiv" is the same as the more familiar "Kiev", or "Bukhoro" the same as "Bukhara" (they are), we have put the familiar forms in brackets where appropriate. In the first two parts we have retained earlier spellings. We are aware that no solution to the problem of rendering names in English is perfect, but trust we have struck an acceptable balance in our new edition.

LIST OF ILLUSTRATIONS

Abbreviations: t = top, tl = top left, tr = top right,
c = center, b = bottom etc.

Equinox acknowledge the assistance of Malcolm Day, London, Nichlas Harris, Oxford, Andras Bereznay, London, and Zoë Goodwin, London, in preparing maps. Maps were drafted by Euromap, Pangbourne, Alan Mais, Hornchurch, and Lovell Johns, Oxford.

GAZETTEER

An entry which is not in Russia or its neighboring republics includes its country name and a descriptive term if a physical feature, e.g. Cerigo (*isl*), (*Greece*).
An entry followed by an asterisk indicates a territorial unit,e.g. country (for former Soviet Republics), county, province, region.

Abast'umani, 41°44'N 42°51'E, 198
Åbo (*Finland*), 60°27'N 22°15'E, 60, 67
Achinsk, 56°20'N 90°33'E, 204
Adrianople (*Turkey*), 41°40'N 26°34'E, 35, 38, 41, 125, 127
Aegviidu, 59°18'N 25°57'E, 192
Afghan Dominions*, 104
Agçabadi, 40°05'N 47°27'E, 199
Agdash, 40°38'N 47°29'E, 199
Agdham, 39°59'N 48°57'E, 199
Agstafa, 41°07'N 45°27'E, 198
Ainazi, 57°50'N 24°29'E, 192
Ain Jalut (*Israel*), 31°52'N 35°50'E, 50
Aizpute, 56°42'N 21°49'E, 192
Akhalkalaki, 41°26'N 43°29'E, 198
Akhalts'ikhe (Akhaltsikhe), 41°37'N 25°59'E, 125, 198
Akkerman, 46°10'N 30°19'E, 125
Akmolinsk, 51°10'N 71°28'E, 172
Aksay, 51°24'N 52°11'E, 216
Alapayevsk, 57°55'N 61°42'E, 204
Älät, 39°57'N 49°25'E, 199
Alatyr, 54°51'N 46°35'E, 109
Alaverdi, 41°08'N 44°40'E, 198
Aldan, 58°44'N 125°22'E, 205
Aleutian Is (*USA*), 57°00'N 175°00'W, 129
Alexandria (*Egypt*), 31°13'N 29°55'E, 50, 115
Algiers (*Algeria*), 36°50'N 3°00'E, 115
Almaty (Alma-Ata), 43°19'N 76°55'E, 12, 172, 217
Altagaç, 40°50'N 48°54'E, 199
Altay Mts, 48°00'N 90°00'E, 12
Aluksne, 57°22'N 27°00'E, 192
Alytus, 54°22'N 24°08'E, 192
Amasia (*Turkey*), 40°37'N 35°50'E, 38
Amastris (*Turkey*), 42°01'N 32°22'E, 38
Ambarchik, 69°39'N 162°27'E, 172
Ambrolauri, 42°32'N 43°12'E, 198
Amderma, 69°44'N 61°35'E, 172
Amorion (*Greece*), 41°18'N 26°26'E, 38
Amsterdam (*Netherlands*), 52°21'N 4°54'E, 12, 91, 115
Amur*, 129
Anadyr' (Anadyr), 64°41'N 177°32'E, 13, 173, 205
Anatolia*, 127
Anazarbos (*Turkey*), 37°25'N 35°32'E. 38
Ancona (*Italy*), 43°37'N 13°31'E, 115
Andrusovo, 54°40'N 31°51'E, 79
Angekhakot, 39°34'N 45°55'E, 198
Ankara (Angora), (*Turkey*), 39°55'N 32°50'E, 28, 38, 152, 172, 174, 176
Annam*, 50
Antioch (*Turkey*), 36°12'N 36°10'E, 38
Antiochia (*Turkey*), 38°05'N 30°45'E, 38
Antivari (*Yugoslavia*), 42°05'N 19°06'E, 38
Anyksciai, 55°35'N 25°07'E, 192
Aqmola, 51°10'N 71°30'E, 12, 22, 23, 26, 216
Aqtau, 56°07'N 98°28'E, 12, 216
Aqtöbe, 50°16'N 57°13'E, 12, 216
Aquileia (*Italy*), 45°47'N 13°22'E, 38
Aragats (*mt*), 40°32'N 44°11'E, 198
Aral, 46°56'N 61°43'E, 216
Ararat, 39°47'N 44°46'E, 198
Ararat, Mt, (*Turkey*), 39°44'N 44°15'E, 12
Arkhangel'sk (Archangel), 64°32'N 40°40'E, 12, 74, 128, 148, 152, 172, 174, 204
Armavir, 44°59'N 41°10'E, 152
Armenia*, 12, 22, 23, 26, 38, 125, 148, 157, 198
Arqalyq, 50°17'N 66°51'E, 216
Artemovsk, 48°35'N 38°00'N, 187
Art'ik, 40°40'N 43°56'E, 198
Arys, 42°26'N 68°49'E, 216
Arzamas, 55°24'N 43°48'E, 207
Ashchsay, 43°15'N 68°53'E, 216
Ashgabat (Ashkhabad), 37°58'N 58°24'E, 12, 22, 26, 128, 172, 216
Ashtarak, 40°19'N 44°23'E, 198
Astara, 38°27'N 48°53'E, 199
Astrakhan' (Astrakhan, Itil), 46°22'N 48°04'E, 12, 35, 36, 41,55, 60, 67, 74, 79, 104, 108, 109, 111, 128, 148, 152, 157, 172, 174, 204
Astrakhan*, 55
Atbasar, 51°49'N 68°18'E, 216
Athens (*Greece*), 38°00'N 23°44'E, 35, 38, 115, 127, 128, 147, 148, 174, 176
Atyrau (Guryev), 47°08'N 51°59'E, 12, 79, 108, 109, 111, 172, 216
Austerlitz (*Czech Rep*), 49°10'N 16°53'E, 115
Avzyan-Petrovsk, 35°26'N 57°10'E, 108, 109
Ayaguz, 47°59'N 80°27'E, 217
Azerbaijan (Azerbayjan)*, 12, 22, 23, 26, 148, 157, 198, 199
Azizbekov, 39°38'N 45°30'E, 198
Azov, 47°06'N 39°26'E, 74, 91, 104, 108, 109, 111, 125, 128

Babruysk, 53°08'N 29°10'E, 186
Baghdad (*Iraq*), 33°20'N 44°26'E, 50
Bagrationovsk, 54°26'N 20°38'E, 192
Bakanas, 44°50'N 76°13'E, 217
Bakchisarai, 44°56'N 33°58'E, 125
Bakharden, 38°25'N 57°24'E, 216
Bakhmach, 51°10'N 32°48'E, 186
Baku, 40°22'N 49°53'E, 12, 22, 26, 36, 104, 108, 109, 128, 148, 152, 157, 172, 174, 199
Bakuriani, 41°45'N 43°31'E, 198
Balakän, 41°44'N 46°24'E, 199
Balaklava, 44°31'N 33°35'E, 125
Balqash, 46°51'N 75°00'E, 217
Balta, 47°58'N 29°39'E, 186
Balti, 47°44'N 27°51'E, 186
Baltiysk, 54°41'N 19°59'E, 192
Bank, 39°26'N 49°15'E, 199
Baranavichy, 53°09'N 26°00'E, 186
Barda, 40°23'N 47°08'E, 199
Barnaul, 53°12'N 83°50'E, 12, 105, 204
Barysaw (Borisov), 54°09'N 28°30'E, 79, 115, 186
Bashkend, 40°39'N 45°31'E, 198
Batumi (Bat'umi), 41°37'N 41°36'E, 125, 148, 152, 198
Bauska, 56°22'N 26°50'E, 192
Bayqongyr, 47°46'N 66°01'E, 216
Bayramaly, 37°44'N 62°13'E, 216
Beijing (Peking), (*China*), 39°55'N 116°25'E, 13, 50, 129, 172
Bei Shan (*mts*), (*China*), 41°00'N 95°00'E, 12/13
Belarus (Belorussia)*, 12, 22, 23, 26, 28, 74, 148, 176, 186
Belgorod, 50°38'N 36°36'E, 60, 67, 152
Belgrade (*Yugoslavia*), 44°50'N 20°30'E, 28, 60, 91, 115, 127, 128, 147, 148, 152, 157, 174, 176
Belogorsk, 50°55'N 128°26'E, 205
Beloozero *see* Belozersk
Belorussia* see Belarus*
Belovo, 54°27'N 86°19'E, 204
Belovodskoye, 42°52'N 74°28'E, 217
Belozersk (Beloozero), 60°00'N 37°49'E, 41, 55, 56, 67, 206
Belucha, Mt, 49°58'N 86°11'E, 12
Berdyans'k (Berdyansk), 46°45'N 36°47'E, 125, 186
Berdychiv, 49°54'N 28°39'E, 186
Berezan I, 46°32'N 31°57'E, 36
Berlin (*Germany*), 52°32'N 13°25'E, 12, 28, 91, 115, 128, 147, 157, 172, 174, 176
Berrhoia (*Greece*), 40°42'N 22°29'E, 38
Bessarabia*, 115, 125, 127, 128, 148, 152, 157, 174
Bezhetsk, 57°49'N 36°40'E, 56
Bialystok (*Poland*), 53°09'N 23°10'E, 28, 41, 115, 148, 176
Bila Tserkva, 49°49'N 30°10'E, 186
Bilhorod-Dnistrovs'kyy, 46°10'N 30°19'E, 186
Birzai, 56°10'N 24°48'E, 192
Bishkek (Frunze), 42°53'N 74°46'E, 12, 22, 26, 172, 217
Blagoveshchensk, 50°19'N 127°30'E, 13
Bodaybo, 57°52'N 114°05'E, 205
Boksitogorsk, 59°28'N 33°49'E, 204, 206
Bolnisi, 41°28'N 44°33'E, 198
Bologna (*Italy*), 44°30'N 11°20'E, 115
Bologoye, 56°28'N 30°07'E, 206
Bolshevik Russia*, 152
Bonn (*Germany*), 50°44'N 7°06'E, 176
Bordeaux (*France*), 44°50'N 0°34'W, 115
Borisov *see* Barysaw
Borisovka, 43°15'N 68°12'E, 216
Borjomi, 41°49'N 43°23'E, 198
Borodino, 55°01'N 37°19'E, 115
Borovichi, 58°22'N 34°00'E, 55, 206
Borovsky Pafnutiev, 55°11'N 30°19'E, 55
Boryspil, 50°21'N 30°59'E, 186
Bosnia*, 127, 147
Bratislava (*Slovakia*), 48°10'N 17°08'E, 12, 28, 176
Bratsk, 56°20'N 101°50'E, 13, 205
Bremen (*Germany*), 53°05'N 8°48'E, 60
Breslau (*Poland*), 51°05'N 17°00'E, 60, 115
Brest (Brest-Litovsk), 52°08'N 23°40'E, 28, 58, 79, 148, 152, 186
Brody, 50°05'N 25°08'E, 186
Brunswick (*Germany*), 52°15'N l0°30'E, 60
Bryansk, 53°15'N 34°09'E, 56, 58, 67, 111, 174, 204
Bucharest (*Romania*), 44°25'N 26°07'E, 28, 115, 127, 128, 147, 148, 152, 157, 172, 174, 176
Budapest (Buda, Pest), (*Hungary*), 47°30'N 19°03'E, 28, 50, 60, 127, 128, 147, 148, 152, 157, 174, 176
Bukhoro, 39°47'N 64°26'E, 104, 128, 216
Bulgar, 55°02'N 49°57'E, 35, 41, 45, 50, 55, 60
Burgas (*Bulgaria*), 42°30'N 27°29'E, 127
Byaroza, 50°23'N 31°32'E, 186

Caesarea (*Turkey*), 38°42'N 35°28'E, 38
Cairo (*Egypt*), 30°03'N 31°15'E, 50, 115
Carpathian Mts, 47°32'N 24°45'E, 12, 36
Carpatho-Ukraine*, 176
Catalonia*, 115
Cattaro (*Yugoslavia*), 42°52'N 18°16'E, 50, 127, 128
Caucasus Mts, 12, 22, 23, 26, 35, 36, 104, 111, 128, 148, 172, 198
Cerigo (*isl*), *(Greece)*, 36°09'N 24°35'E, 115
Cesis, 57°18'N 25°18'E, 192
Cetinje (*Yugoslavia*), 42°23'N 18°55'E, 127
Ceuta (*Spain*), 35°53'N 5°19'W, 115
Chagatay*, 50
Chalcedon (*Turkey*), 40°59'N 29°02'E, 38
Chardara, 41°18'N 67°56'E, 216
Chärjew, 39°09'N 63°34'E, 12, 216
Charsk, 49°37'N 81°02'E, 217
Cheleken (Krasnovodsk), 40°01'N 53°00'E, 12, 152, 216
Chelyabinsk, 55°12'N 61°25'E, 12, 104, 109, 172, 204
Cheremkhovo, 53°04'N 103°00'E, 172
Cherepovets, 59°05'N 37°57'E, 204, 206
Cherkassk, 46°52'N 40°00'E, 104, 108, 109, 111
Cherkasy, 49°27'N 32°04'E, 186
Chernigov*, 41, 45
Chernihiv (Chernigov), 51°30'N 31°18'E, 35, 41, 45, 50, 55, 56, 58, 67, 186
Chernivtsi (Chernovtsy, Czernowitz), 48°19'N 25°52'E, 148, 176, 186
Chernyakovsk, 54°36'N 21°48'E, 192
Cherny-Yar, 48°04'N 46°06'E, 108
Cherskiy, 68°45'N 161°15'E, 13, 205
Chersky Mts, 65°02'N 144°32'E, 13, 22, 23, 26
Cherson, 44°52'N 33°28'E, 35, 36, 41, 55, 58
Cherven, 53°40'N 28°28'E, 35
Chiat'ura, 42°15'N 43°17'E, 198
Chiili, 44°10'N 66°37'E, 216
Chilik, 43°37'N 78°16'E, 217
Chios (*isl*), (*Greece*), 38°27'N 26°09'E, 127
Chirchik, 41°28'N 69°31'E, 216
Chisinau (Kishinev), 47°00'N 28°50'E, 12, 22, 26, 28, 111, 148, 152, 176, 186
Chita, 52°03'N 113°35'E, 13, 172, 205
Chonai (*Turkey*), 37°25'N 30°10'E, 38
Chorgun, 44°53'N 33°56'E, 125
Chornobyl', 51°16'N 30°15'E, 186
Chotin *see* Khotin
Christiania *see* Oslo
Chudovo, 59°10'N 31°41'E, 206
Chuguyev, 49°51'N 36°44'E, 79
Chukchi Mts, 68°30'N 176°30'E, 13
Chust, 40°59'N 71°14'E, 216
Claudiopolis (*Turkey*), 40°45'N 31°33'E, 38
Cologne (*Germany*), 50°56'N 6°57'E, 60
Colonia (*Turkey*), 40°19'N 37°58'E, 38
Commander Is, 55°00'N 167°00'E, 13
Communism Peak (*mt*), 38°59'N 72°01'E, 12, 217
Comrat, 46°18'N 28°40'E, 186
Constanta (*Romania*), 44°10'N 28°40'E, 127, 176
Constantinople *see* Istanbul
Copenhagen (*Denmark*), 55°43'N 12°34'E, 12, 28, 91, 115, 128, 172, 176
Corfu (*isl*), (*Greece*), 39°38'N 19°57'E, 115, 127
Corinth (*Greece*), 37°56'N 22°55'E, 38
Corsica (*isl*), (*France*), 42°00'N 9°00'E, 115, 147
Cottbus (*Germany*), 51°43'N 14°21'E, 28
Courland*, 104, 148
Crete (*isl*), (*Greece*), 35°15'N 25°00'E, 35, 38, 127, 147, 174
Crimea*, 45, 55, 56, 58, 60, 67, 79, 104, 108, 109, 125, 128, 148, 174, 186
Croatia*, 174
Cyprus (*isl*), 35°15'N 32°36'E, 35, 38, 147
Cyrene (*Libya*), 32°48'N 21°53'E, 115
Czernowitz *see* Chernivtsi

Dagestan*, 128
Dalmatia*, 127
Damascus (*Syria*), 33°30'N 36°19'E, 50
Danzig *see* Gdansk
Dashhowuz, 40°40'N 71°45'E, 216
Daugavpils (Dvinsk), 55°52'N 26°31'E, 148, 152, 192
Däväçi, 41°12'N 49°02'E, 199
Davyd Haradok, 52°04'N 27°10'E, 186
Delhi*, 50
Deptford (*UK*), 51°29'N 0°03'W, 91
Derbent, 42°03'N 48°18'E, 36, 41, 104, 108, 109
Deulino, 56°30'N 37°43'E, 67
Dickson, 74°30'N 81°03'E, 204
Dilijan, 40°45'N 44°52'E, 198
Dniprodzherzhyns'k (Dneprodzerzhinsk), 48°30'N 34°37'E, 186
Dnipropetrovs'k (Dnepropetrovsk), 48°29'N 35°00'E, 12, 28, 172, 174, 186
Dobruja*, 127
Dodecanese (*isls*), (*Greece*), 36°30'N 27°00'E, 127
Dolyns'ka, 48°06'N 32°46'E, 186
Donbass*, 186
Donets'k, 48°00'N 37°50'E, 12, 187
Dorostol, 44°02'N 27°28'E, 35, 41
Dorpat, 58°20'N 26°44'E, 60, 152
Dortmund (*Germany*), 51°32'N 7°27'E, 60
Dresden (*Germany*), 51°03'N 13°45'E, 91, 115, 176
Druskininkai, 54°00'N 23°58'E, 192
Dudinka, 69°27'N 86°13'E, 172
Durazzo (*Albania*), 41°18'N 19°28'E, 38, 127
Dushanbe, 38°38'N 68°51'E, 12, 22, 26, 216
Dushet'i, 42°05'N 44°42'E, 198
Dvinsk *see* Daugavpils
Dzerzhinsk, 56°15'N 43°30'E, 207
Dzhambeyty, 50°16'N 52°33'E, 216
Dzhankoy, 45°42'N 34°23'E, 186
Dzhetygara, 52°14'N 61°10'E, 216
Dzhugdzhur Mts, 58°00'N 138°00'E, 13
Dzhusaly, 45°47'N 64°18'E, 216

Ekibastuz, 51°45'N 75°22'E, 217
Elba (*isl*), (*Italy*), 42°48'N 10°15'E, 115
Elbing (*Poland*), 54°10'N 19°25'E, 60, 148
El'brus, Mt, 43°21'N 42°29'E, 12
Embi, 48°47'N 58°05'E, 216
Ephesos (*Turkey*), 37°41'N 27°31'E, 38
Epirus*, 127
Erfurt *(Germany)*, 50°58'N 11°02'E, 115, 176
Ergli, 56°50'N 25°33'E, 192
Ersingian (*Turkey*), 39°58'N 39°57'E, 38
Erzurum (*Turkey*), 39°57'N 41°17'E, 125, 148
Esenguly, 37°31'N 53°59'E, 216
Estonia*, 12, 22, 23, 26, 28, 104, 148, 152, 157, 172, 174, 176, 192
Esztergom (*Hungary*), 47°46'N 18°44'E, 38
Euchaita (*Turkey*), 40°29'N 34°50'E, 38
Eupatoria *see* Yevpatoriya
Eylau (*Poland*), 54°11'N 19°32'E, 115

Farghona, 40°23'N 71°19'E, 216
Feodosiya, 45°03'N 35°23'E, 152, 186
Ferahabad (*Iran*), 36°10'N 53°49'E, 108, 109
Ferapontov, 60°02'N 34°32'E, 55
Fetisovo, 42°46'N 52°38'E, 216
Fort Ross (*USA*), 38°36'N 123°12'W, 129
Fort Shevchenko, 44°31'N 50°15'E, 216
Fort Wrangel (*USA*), 56°32'N 131°12'W, 129
Frankfurt (*Germany*), 50°06'N 8°41'E, 60
Franz Josef Land (*isl*), 12, 22, 23, 26, 128, 172
Friedland, 54°30'N 20°18'E, 115
Frunze *see* Bishkek
Füzuli, 39°35'N 47°07'E, 199

Gagra, 43°21'N 40°16'E, 198
Galatz (*Romania*), 45°27'N 28°02'E, 127
Gali, 42°37'N 41°46'E, 198
Galich, 58°20'N 42°12'E, 38, 41, 45, 55, 56, 58
Galich*, 41
Galicia*, 45, 148
Gallipoli (*Turkey*), 40°25'N 26°41'E, 125, 127, 147
Gallipoli Peninsula, 40°01'N 25°46'E, 148
Gänçä, 40°39'N 46°20'E, 199
Gangra (*Turkey*), 40°35'N 33°37'E, 38
Ganyushkino, 46°38'N 49°12'E, 216
Gdansk (Danzig), (*Poland*), 54°22'N 18°38'E, 55, 58, 60, 115, 148, 152, 157, 174, 176
Georgia*, 12, 22, 23, 26, 38, 55, 104, 125, 148, 157, 198
Gibraltar (*UK*), 36°09'N 5°21'W, 115
Gizhduvan, 40°07'N 64°15'E, 216
Glasov, 58°09'N 52°42'E, 152
Glubokoye, 50°06'N 82°15'E, 217
Gnesen *(Poland)*, 52°55'N 15°01'E, 58
Gniezno (*Poland*), 52°32'N 17°32'E, 38
Golden Horde*, 50, 55
Gomel see Homyel'
Gorgan, 37°31'N 53°59'E, 108, 109
Gori, 41°59'N 44°05'E, 198
Goris, 39°31'N 46°22'E, 199
Gorky *see* Nizhniy Novgorod
Gortyne (*Greece*), 35°01'N 24°59'E, 38
Goslar (*Germany*), 51°55'N 10°25'E, 60
Gotland (*isl*), (*Sweden*), 57°50'N 18°52'E, 41, 60, 67
Goyçay, 40°38'N 47°43'E, 199
Greater Khingan Mts (*China*), 48°00'N 121°30'E, 13
Grebenka, 50°10'N 32°45'E, 186
Greifswald (*Germany*), 54°06'N 13°24'E, 60
Grodno *see* Hrodna
Groznyy (Grozny), 43°21'N 45°42'E, 12, 174, 204
Gudaut'a, 43°08'N 40°10'E, 198
Gulbene, 57°10'N 26°42'E, 192
Guliston, 40°30'N 68°52'E, 216
Gumbinnen, 55°30'N 23°03'E, 148
Guryev *see* Atyrau
Gusev, 54°48'N 22°10'E, 192
Gushgy, 35°18'N 62°22'E, 216
Gyamysh *(mt)*, 40°16'N 46°21'E, 199
Gyulafehérvár (*Romania*), 46°12'N 23°42'E, 35
Gyumri, 40°47'N 43°49'E, 198
Gyzylarbat, 39°00'N 56°23'E, 216

Haapsalu, 58°58'N 23°32'E, 192
Halle (*Germany*), 51°28'N 11°58'E, 60
Hamburg (*Germany*), 53°33'N 10°00'E, 60, 115
Hanau (*Germany*), 50°08'N 8°56'E, 115
Hangay Mts (*Mongolia*), 48°00'N 97°00'E, 13
Hangö (*Finland*), 59°50'N 23°00'E, 152
Hanover (*Germany*), 52°23'N 9°44'E, 60, 91
Harbin (*China*), 45°45'N 126°41'E, 172
Hasankale (*Turkey*), 39°56'N 42°11'E, 125
Hawaiian Is (*USA*), 19°30'N 155°30'W, 129
Helsinki (Helsingfors), (*Finland*), 60°08'N 25°00'E, 12, 28, 79, 115, 128, 148, 152, 172, 174, 176
Helvetia*, 115
Heracleia (*Turkey*), 41°02'N 27°59'E, 38
Herat (*Afghanistan*), 34°20'N 62°10'E, 50
Herford (*Germany*), 52°07'N 8°40'E, 60
Herzegovina*, 147
Hierapolis (*Turkey*), 37°57'N 28°50'E, 38
Hiiumaa (*isl*), 58°50'N 22°40'E, 192
Hildesheim (*Germany*), 52°09'N 9°58'E, 60
Hindu Kush (*mts*), (*Pakistan*), 36°00'N 71°00'E, 12
Hokkaido (*isl*), (*Japan*), 43°00'N 142°00'E, 13
Holowczyn, 54°09'N 28°29'E, 91
Homyel' (Gomel), 52°25'N 31°00'E, 12, 56, 67, 79, 152, 174, 186
Honshu (*isl*), (*Japan*), 36°00'N 138°00'E, 13
Horlivka, 48°17'N 38°05'E, 187
Höxter (*Germany*), 51°47'N 9°22'E, 60
Hrodna (Grodno), 53°40'N 23°50'E, 28, 35, 41, 58, 67, 79, 186

Iconium (*Turkey*), 37°51'N 32°30'E, 38
Igarka, 67°31'N 86°33'E, 172, 204
Iisaku, 59°09'N 27°28'E, 192
Ijevan, 40°54'N 45°06'E, 198
Iletskaya Zaschita, 51°39'N 54°58'E, 104
Ili, 43°51'N 77°14'E, 217
Illyrian Provinces*, 115
Ilyinskaya, 51°14'N 57°10'E, 109
Imishli, 39°50'N 48°03'E, 199
Inderborskiy, 48°32'N 51°44'E, 216
Ingria*, 67
Inkerman, 44°35'N 33°34'E, 125
Ionian Is (*Greece*), 38°30'N 21°00'E, 115, 127, 128
Irgiz, 48°36'N 61°14'E, 216
Irkeshtam, 39°40'N 73°59'E, 217
Irkutsk, 52°15'N 104°17'E, 13, 74, 129, 172, 205
Irtyshk, 53°22'N 75°30'E, 217
Ishikhly (*mt*), 39°36'N 46°12'E, 199
Istanbul (Constantinople), (*Turkey*), 41°02'N 28°57'E, 35, 36, 38, 41, 50, 104, 115, 125, 127, 128, 147, 148, 152, 157, 172, 174, 176
Itil *see* Astrakhan'
Ivangorod, 48°54'N 32°14'E, 67
Ivano-Frankivs'k (Stanislau), 49°00'N 24°40'E, 148, 186
Ivanovo, 52°10'N 25°31'E, 152, 206
Izborsk, 57°12'N 28°05'E, 41, 60
lzhevsk, 56°49'N 53°11'E, 12, 108, 109, 204
Izmayil (Izmail), 45°20'N 28°48'E, 115, 148, 186
Izyum, 49°12'N 37°19'E, 56, 67, 187

Jassy (*Romania*), 47°09'N 27°38'E, 115, 148, 176
Jaunjelgava, 56°34'N 25°02'E, 192
Jekabpils, 56°28'N 25°58'E, 192
Jelgava, 56°39'N 23°40'E, 192
Jizzakh, 40°05'N 67°58'E, 216
Jonava, 55°04'N 24°19'E, 192
Jurmala, 56°02'N 22°46'E, 192

K2 (*mt*), (*Pakistan*), 35°54'N 76°30'E, 12
Kabarda*, 125
Kabul (*Afghanistan*), 34°30'N 69°10'E, 12, 50, 128, 172
Kachuga, 53°58'N 105°55'E, 172
Kaffa, 44°59'N 35°45'E, 5, 60
Kagan, 39°45'N 64°32'E, 216
Kalinin *see* Tver'
Kaliningrad (Königsberg), 54°40'N 20°30'E, 12, 28, 58, 60, 91, 147, 148, 152, 176, 192
Kaliningrad*, 192
Kalisz (*Poland*), 51°46'N 18°02'E, 115, 148
Kalka, 47°52'N 39°57'E, 50
Kalocsa (*Hungary*), 46°31'N 19°00'E, 38
Kaluga, 54°31'N 36°16'E, 56, 58, 67, 79, 152
Kamachos (*Turkey*), 39°20'N 39°01'E, 38
Kamenets see Kam'yanets-Podils'kyy
Kamich, 44°54'N 33°23'E, 125
Kamo, 40°49'N 43°57'E, 198
Kam'yanets-Podils'kyy (Kamenets), 48°40'N 26°36'E, 67, 79, 115, 186
Kam'yanka-Dniprovs'ka, 47°29'N 34°25'E, 186
Kamyshin, 50°05'N 45°24'E, 108, 109
Kandalaksha, 67°09'N 32°31'E, 12, 204
Kandava, 57°00'N 22°42'E, 192
Kanibadam, 40°20'N 70°18'E, 216
Kansk, 56°10'N 95°55'E, 205
Kant, 42°51'N 74°45'E, 217
Kapan, 39°11'N 46°22'E, 199
Kara-Bogaz-Gol, 41°04'N 52°58'E, 216
Karaganda *see* Qaraghandy
Karakol, 42°30'N 78°23'E, 217
Karakoram (*mts*), (*Pakistan*), 35°50'N 76°00'E, 12
Karakorum (*Mongolia*), 47°30'N 102°20'E, 50
Kara Su, 40°44'N 72°58'E, 217
Kardis (*Sweden*), 66°58'N 23°45'E, 67
Karelia*, 67
Kargopol, 61°32'N 38°59'E, 79
Kars (*Turkey*), 40°35'N 43°05'E, 125, 128, 148, 152
Kasbek (*mt*), 42°42'N 44°30'E, 198
Kashgar (*China*), 39°29'N 76°02'E, 50
Kashmir*, 105
Kaspi, 41°56'N 44°25'E, 198
Kaunas (Kovno), 54°52'N 23°55'E, 35, 41, 58, 60, 79, 115, 148, 152, 157, 172, 192
Kavalla (*Greece*), 40°56'N 24°24'E, 127
Kaynar, 49°13'N 77°26'E, 217
Kazach'ye, 70°46'N 136°15'E, 205
Kazakhstan*, 12, 22, 23, 26, 29, 128, 216
Kazan' (Kazan), 55°45'N 49°10'E, 12, 29, 45, 55, 56, 60, 67, 74, 79, 104, 108, 109, 111, 128, 152, 174, 204
Kazan*, 55, 56, 60
Kazanlinsk, 45°45'N 62°01'E, 216
Kedabek, 40°34'N 45°46'E, 198
Kedainiai, 55°18'N 23°59'E, 192
Kelme, 55°38'N 22°50'E, 192
Kem', 64°58'N 34°39'E, 204
Kerch, 45°22'N 36°27'E, 125, 172, 186
Kerki, 37°53'N 65°11'E, 216
Khabarovsk, 48°30'N 135°06'E, 13, 172, 205
Kharkiv (Kharkov), 50°00'N 36°15'E, 12, 28, 58, 104, 111, 115, 148, 152, 157, 172, 174, 186
Khashuri, 41°58'N 43°35'E, 198
Khatanga, 71°59'N 102°31'E, 205
Khazaria*, 35
Kherson, 46°39'N 32°28'E, 125, 174, 186
Khiva, 41°25'N 60°49'E, 104, 128, 216
Khmel'nyts'kyy, 49°25'N 26°59'E, 186
Kholmogory, 64°45'N 42°10'E, 60
Khorugh, 37°32'N 71°32'E, 216
Khotyn (Chotin), 48°30'N 26°31'E, 115, 186
Khujand, 40°14'N 69°40'E, 216
Khulo, 41°39'N 42°15'E, 198
Kiel (*Germany*), 54°20'N 10°08'E, 60
Kiev *see* Kyyiv
Kiev*, 41, 45
Kievan Rus*, 35, 41
Kihnu (*isl*), 58°09'N 24°01'E, 192
Kineshma, 57°28'N 42°08'E, 206

Kirishi, 59°30′N 32°02′E, 204, 206
Kirov *see* Vyatka
Kirovohrad (Kirovograd), 48°31′N 32°15′E, 28, 186
Kishinev *see* Chisinau
Klaipeda (Memel), 55°40′N 21°08′E, 58, 148, 176, 192
Klyuchevskaya (*mt*), 56°03′N 160°38′E, 13
K'obulet'i, 41°49′N 41°46′E, 198
Kodiak (*USA*), 57°49′N 152°30′W, 129
Kodzheyli, 42°10′N 68°58′E, 216
Kohila, 59°09′N 24°48′E, 192
Kohtla Järve, 59°28′N 27°20′E, 192
Kokpekty, 48°47′N 82°26′E, 217
Kolguyev Is, 68°40′N 49°50′E, 12
Kolomna, 55°05′N 38°45′E, 206
Kolomyya, 48°31′N 25°00′E, 186
Kolpashevo, 58°21′N 82°59′E, 204
Kolyma Mts, 64°00′N 159°00′E, 13, 23, 27
Komarov (*Czech Rep*), 49°55′N 17°58′E, 148
Komsomolets, 53°47′N 62°01′E, 216
Komsomolsk, 50°31′N 137°00′E, 13, 172, 205
Komunars'k, 48°30′N 38°45′E, 187
Konakhkend, 41°04′N 48°36′E, 199
Konevitsky Rozhdestvensk, 60°58′N 30°12′E, 55
Konigsberg *see* Kaliningrad
Konotop, 51°15′N 33°14′E, 186
Kopet Mts, 37°50′N 58°00′E, 12
Kornilev, 58°35′N 39°56′E, 55
Korosten, 51°00′N 28°30′E, 186
Koryak Mts, 62°30′N 171°00′E, 13
Koschagyl, 47°05′N 54°09′E, 216
Köshetau, 53°18′N 69°25′E, 216
Koslov, 52°54′N 40°30′E, 111
Kostroma, 57°46′N 40°59′E, 55, 56, 67, 152, 206
Kostyantynivka, 48°33′N 37°45′E, 187
Kotlas, 61°15′N 46°35′E, 174
Kotyaion (*Turkey*), 39°35′N 29°52′E, 38
Kovel, 51°12′N 24°48′E, 186
Kovno *see* Kaunas
Kovrov, 56°23′N 41°21′E, 206
Kozelsk, 54°02′N 35°48′E, 50, 55, 67, 79
Kozlov, 52°58′N 40°18′E, 79
Kozyatyn, 49°41′N 28°49′E, 186
Krakow (*Poland*), 50°04′N 19°57′E, 28, 35, 41, 58, 60, 91, 147, 148, 152, 176
Kramatorsk, 48°43′N 37°33′E, 187
Krasnik (*Poland*), 50°56′N 22°14′E, 148
Krasnodar, 45°02′N 39°00′E, 204
Krasnohrad, 49°22′N 35°28′E, 186
Krasnotur'insk, 59°46′N 60°10′E, 204
Krasnovodsk *see* Cheleken
Krasnoy, 54°42′N 31°58′E, 115
Krasnoyarsk, 56°10′N 93°00′E, 13, 74, 105, 172, 204
Krasny Kholm, 58°24′N 37°26′E, 55
Krasny-Yar, 46°32′N 48°21′E, 108
Kremenchuk, 49°03′N 33°25′E, 186
Kretinga, 55°52′N 21°12′E, 192
Krevo, 54°19′N 26°17′E, 58, 148
Krivoy Rog see Kryvyy Rih
Kronshtadt, 60°00′N 29°40′E, 148, 152
Kronstadt (*Romania*), 45°21′N 24°11′E, 127
Krustpils, 56°29′N 25°58′E, 192
Krychaw, 53°40′N 31°44′E, 186
Kryvyy Rih (Krivoy Rog), 47°55′N 33°24′E, 172, 174, 186
Kuldiga, 56°58′N 21°58′E, 192
Kuldzha*, 128
Kulebaki, 55°25′N 42°31′E, 204, 206
Kulikovo, 54°49′N 38°20′E, 50
Kulm (*Poland*), 58°11′N 18°42′E, 55
Kulob, 37°55′N 69°47′E, 216
Kulsary, 46°59′N 54°02′E, 216
Kultay, 45°20′N 51°19′E, 216
Kunda, 59°30′N 26°28′E, 192
Kungur, 57°52′N 56°44′E, 111
Kuolayarvi, 66°58′N 29°10′E, 176
Kup'yans'k, 49°41′N 37°37′E, 187
Kurchum, 48°33′N 83°40′E, 217
Kürdämir, 40°21′N 48°09′E, 199
Kuressaare, 58°12′N 22°30′E, 192
Kurgan, 55°30′N 65°20′E, 109, 204
Kuril Is, 47°00′N 152°00′E, 13, 22, 23, 27, 129, 173
Kursenai, 56°01′N 23°03′E, 192
Kursk, 51°45′N 36°14′E, 41, 58, 67, 79, 174
Kushensk, 60°37′N 40°15′E, 55
Kushmurun, 52°30′N 64°37′E, 216
K'ut'aisi (Kutaisi), 42°15′N 42°44′E, 125, 198
Kutkashen, 40°59′N 47°50′E, 199
Kuybyshev *see* Samara
Kuzbass*, 204
Kuznetsk, 53°08′N 46°05′E, 172
Kuznetsk, 53°36′N 87°01′E, 74, 105
Kyrgyzstan*, 12, 22, 23, 26, 217
Kyvrak, 39°23′N 45°08′E, 198
Kyyiv (Kiev), 50°28′N 30°29′E, 12, 22, 26, 28, 35, 36, 38, 41, 45, 50, 55, 56, 58, 60, 67, 74, 79, 104, 108, 109, 111, 115, 125, 128, 148, 152, 157, 172, 174, 176, 186
Kyzikos (*Turkey*), 40°13′N 27°54′E, 38
Kyzyl, 51°42′N 94°31′E, 13, 204
Kyzyl-Buran, 41°05′N 49°01′E, 199
Kyzyl-Kyya, 40°11′N 72°08′E, 217

Laçyn, 39°38′N 46°33′E, 199
Ladoga, 59°59′N 32°11′E, 41, 55, 60, 67
Lahiç, 40°49′N 48°23′E, 199
Länkäran, 38°45′N 48°50′E, 199
Laodicea (*Turkey*), 37°46′N 29°02′E, 38
Larissa (*Greece*), 39°38′N 22°28′E, 38
Latvia*, 12, 22, 23, 26, 28, 152, 157, 172, 174, 176, 192
Leipzig (*Germany*), 51°20′N 12°20′E, 91, 115
Lemberg (*Austria*), 49°28′N 24°47′E, 147, 148
Lemgo (*Germany*), 52°02′N 8°54′E, 60
Lemnos (*isl*), (*Greece*), 39°50′N 25°05′E, 127
Leningrad *see* St Petersburg
Leninogor, 50°23′N 83°37′E, 217
Lenin Peak (*mt*), 39°18′N 73°25′E, 217
Lentvaris, 54°37′N 25°02′E, 192
Lerik, 38°45′N 48°24′E, 199
Lesbos (*isl*), (*Greece*), 39°00′N 26°20′E, 127
Lesnaya, 53°32′N 30°55′E, 91
Liangchow (*China*), 38°00′N 102°54′E, 50
Libau *see* Liepaja
Lida, 53°50′N 25°19′E, 186
Liegnitz (*Poland*), 51°12′N 16°10′E, 50
Liepaja (Libau), 56°30′N 21°00′E, 152, 192
Lippstadt (*Germany*), 51°41′N 8°20′E, 60
Lisbon (*Portugal*), 38°41′N 9°08′W, 115147
Lithuania*, 12, 22, 23, 26, 28, 38, 56, 58, 60, 67, 79, 104, 148, 152, 157, 172, 174, 176, 192
Livonia*, 74, 104, 148
Ljubljana (*Slovenia*), 46°04′N 14°30′E, 28
Lodz (*Poland*), 51°49′N 19°28′E, 148, 152
London (*UK*), 51°30′N 0°10′W, 91, 115, 147
Lübeck (*Germany*), 53°52′N 10°40′E, 60
Lublin (*Poland*), 51°18′N 22°31′E, 148, 152
Lubny, 50°01′N 33°00′E, 186
Ludza, 56°30′N 27°41′E, 192
Luga, 58°42′N 29°49′E, 206
Lugovoy, 43°00′N 72°20′E, 217
Luhans'k (Lugansk, Voroshilovgrad), 48°35′N 39°20′E, 111, 174, 187
Lüneburg (*Germany*), 52°15′N 10°24′E, 60
Luts'k (Lutsk), 50°42′N 25°15′E, 18, 58, 186
L'viv (Lvov), 49°50′N 24°00′E, 12, 28, 55, 58, 60, 67, 79, 152, 174, 176, 186
Lyakhov Is, 73°30′N 142°00′E, 13
Lyon (*France*), 45°46′N 4°50′E, 115
Lyepyel, 54°48′N 28°40′E, 186

Macedonia*, 127
Madona, 56°54′N 26°10′E, 192
Madrid (*Spain*), 40°25′N 3°43′W, 115, 147
Magadan, 59°38′N 150°50′E, 13, 173, 205
Magdagachi, 53°27′N 125°44′E, 205
Magdeburg (*Germany*), 52°08′N 11°37′E, 38, 60
Magnitogorsk, 53°28′N 59°06′E, 172, 204
Mahilyow (Mogilev), 53°54′N 30°20′E, 67, 148, 152, 186
Maikop, 44°35′N 40°25′E, 152
Makarev, 57°33′N 44°15′E, 55
Makat, 47°38′N 53°16′E, 216
Makhachkala, 42°59′N 47°30′E, 204
Makinsk, 52°40′N 70°28′E, 216
Makiyivka, 48°01′N 38°00′E, 187
Maklakovo, 58°13′N 92°30′E, 172
Maladzyechna, 54°16′N 26°50′E, 186
Maloyaroslavets, 55°00′N 36°28′E, 115
Maloya Vishera, 58°55′N 32°25′E, 152
Mamanove, 54°51′N 19°58′E, 192
Manchuria*, 129
Manfredonia (Siponto), (*Italy*), 41°37′N 15°55′E, 38, 115
Mangyshlak (*pen*), 44°11′N 52°00′E, 216
Mardakert, 40°14′N 46°46′E, 199
Marijampole, 54°31′N 23°20′E, 192
Mariupol, 47°05′N 37°34′E, 125, 152, 172, 187
Marseille, 43°18′N 5°22′E, 115
Martuni, 40°09′N 45°10′E, 198
Mary, 37°42′N 61°54′E, 216
Masalli, 39°03′N 48°40′E, 199
Mashtaga, 40°33′N 50°00′E, 199
Masovia*, 58
Maykain, 51°28′N 75°46′E, 217
Mazeikiai, 56°19′N 22°21′E, 192
Mazirbe, 57°40′N 22°21′E, 192
Mazyr (Mozyr), 52°02′N 29°10′E, 79, 186
Melitene (*Turkey*), 38°22′N 38°18′E, 38
Melitopol, 46°51′N 35°22′E, 125, 186
Melilla (*Spain*), 35°20′N 3°00′W,115
Memel *see* Klaipeda
Mesembria (*Bulgaria*), 45°51′N 27°05′E, 36
Messina (*Italy*), 38°13′N 15°33′E, 115
Mestia, 43°04′N 42°46′E, 198
Mikhailo-Archangelsk, 61°05′N 45°47′E, 55
Milan (*Italy*), 45°28′N 9°12′E, 115, 147
Minden (*Germany*), 52°18′N 8°54′E, 60
Mineralnye Vody, 44°14′N 43°10′E, 152
Mingaçevir, 40°45′N 47°03′E, 199
Minsk, 53°51′N 27°30′E, 12, 22, 26, 28, 35, 41, 45, 55, 58, 67, 79, 104, 111, 128, 148, 152, 174, 176, 186
Minusinsk, 53°30′N 91°50′E, 105
Mirnyy, 62°40′N 113°32′E, 205
Mittau, 56°51′N 24°01′E, 104
Mlawa (*Poland*), 53°08′N 20°20′E, 148
Mogilev *see* Mahilyow
Mogocha, 53°44′N 119°45′E, 205
Mohi (*Hungary*), 47°52′N 19°57′E, 50
Mohyliv Podil's'kyy, 48°29′N 27°49′E, 186
Moisaküla, 58°02′N 25°12′E, 192
Moldova (Moldavia)*, 12, 22, 23, 26, 28, 58, 125, 127, 128, 148, 176, 186
Mollakend, 40°08′N 48°06′E, 199
Molotov *see* Perm
Molotovo, 41°30′N 44°00′E, 198
Montenegro*, 115, 124, 127, 128, 147, 148
Moscow, 55°45′N 37°42′E, 12, 22, 23, 26, 28, 41, 45, 50, 55, 56, 58, 60, 67, 74, 79, 91, 104, 108, 109, 111, 115, 128, 148, 152, 157, 172, 174, 176, 204, 206
Moscow*, 56, 58, 60
Mosul (*Iraq*), 36°21′N 43°08′E, 148
Mozhaisk, 55°29′N 36°02′E, 55
Mozyr *see* Mazyr
Mtskheta, 41°46′N 44°42′E, 198
Muhu (*isl*), 58°40′N 23°20′E, 192
Munich (*Germany*), 48°08′N 11°35′E, 91, 115, 147, 176
Münster (*Germany*), 50°22′N 8°16′E, 60
Murghob, 38°12′N 74°01′E, 217
Murmansk, 68°59′N 33°08′E, 12, 148, 152, 172, 174, 176, 204
Murom, 55°04′N 42°04′E, 35, 41, 55, 56, 67, 206
Murom-Ryazan*, 41
Mustvee*, 58°51′N 26°59′E, 192
Muynoq, 43°46′N 59°00′E, 216
Mykolayiv (Nikolayev), 46°57′N 32°00′E, 148, 152, 174, 186
Myra (*Turkey*), 36°17′N 29°58′E, 38
Mytilene (*Greece*), 39°06′N 26°34′E, 38

Nagornyy, 55°57′N 124°54′E, 205
Naissaar (*isl*), 59°35′N 24°37′E, 192
Namangan, 40°59′N 71°41′E, 216
Naples (*Italy*), 40°50′N 14°15′E, 115
Naples*, 115
Narodnaya, Mt, 65°02′N 60°01′E, 12
Narva, 59°22′N 28°17′E, 58, 60, 91, 152, 192
Nar'yan Mar, 67°37′N 53°02′E, 12, 204
Naryn, 41°24′N 76°00′E, 217
Naumiestis, 54°34′N 22°56′E, 192
Naupaktos (*Greece*), 38°23′N 21°50′E, 38
Naxçivan, 39°12′N 45°24′E, 198
Nazarovo, 56°02′N 90°30′E, 204
Neai Patrai (*Greece*), 38°22′N 22°45′E, 38
Nebitdag, 39°31′N 54°24′E, 216
Neftechala, 39°23′N 49°14′E, 199
Nelidovo, 56°13′N 32°46′E, 206
Neocaesarea (*Turkey*), 40°35′N 36°59′E, 38
Nerchinsk, 51°57′N 116°29′E, 74
Neringa, 55°21′N 21°05′E, 192
Nevel, 56°00′N 29°59′E, 67, 79
New Archangel *see* Sitka
New Saray *see* Saray
New Siberian Is, 13, 22, 23, 26, 129, 172
Nicaea (*Turkey*), 40°27′N 29°43′E, 38
Nicholas II Land *(isl) see* Severnaya Zemlya
Nicomedia (*Turkey*), 40°47′N 29°55′E, 38
Nikitsk, 59°43′N 38°19′E, 55
Nikolayev *see* Mykolayiv
Nikolayevsk, 53°10′N 140°44′E, 13, 205
Nikopol, 47°34′N 34°25′E, 186
Niš (Nish), (*Yugoslavia*), 43°20′N 21°54′E, 127, 176
Nizhneudinsk, 55°00′N 99°00′E, 105
Nizhniy Novgorod (Gorky), 56°20′N 41°00′E, 12, 29, 41, 55, 56, 60, 67, 79, 104, 108, 109, 148, 152, 172, 174, 204, 207
Nizhniy Tagil, 58°00′N 59°58′E, 204
Nizhyn, 51°03′N 31°34′E, 186
Noginsk, 55°52′N 38°29′E, 206
Norak, 38°24′N 69°15′E, 216
Nordvik, 74°01′N 111°30′E, 13, 172, 205
Noril'sk (Norilsk), 69°21′N 88°02′E, 13, 172, 204
Novaya Kazanka, 49°00′N 49°36′E, 216
Novaya Zemlya (*isl*), 75°00′N 56°00′E, 12, 22, 23, 26, 74, 128, 172
Novgorod, 58°30′N 31°20′E, 12, 36, 41, 45, 50, 55, 56, 58, 60, 67, 79, 91, 104, 108, 109, 111, 128, 152, 174, 204, 206
Novgorod*, 41, 45, 56, 58, 60
Novgorod-Seversk*, 41, 45
Novgorod-Seversky, 52°00′N 33°15′E, 41, 45
Novibazar (*Yugoslavia*), 43°19′N 21°32′E, 127
Novibazar*, 127
Novocherkassk, 47°25′N 40°05′E, 152
Novohrad Volyns'kyy, 50°34′N 27°32′E, 186
Novokuznetsk (Stalinsk), 53°45′N 87°12′E, 12, 172
Novorossisk, 44°44′N 37°46′E, 111, 125, 148, 152, 204
Novosibirsk, 55°00′N 83°00′E, 12, 128, 172, 204
Novy Port, 64°40′N 72°30′E, 172
Nukus, 42°28′N 59°07′E, 216
Nuremberg (*Germany*), 49°27′N 11°05′E, 60, 176

Ochakov, 46°37′N 31°33′E, 104, 125
Ochamchira, 42°44′N 41°30′E, 198
Odesa (Odessa), 46°30′N 30°46′E, 12, 28, 104, 111, 125, 128, 147, 148, 152, 157, 172, 174, 176, 186
Ogodzha, 52°48′N 132°42′E, 205
Ogre, 56°50′N 24°31′E, 192
Okhotsk, 59°20′N 143°15′E, 75, 129, 172, 205
Oktyabr'sk, 49°30′N 57°22′E, 216
Old Saray see Saray
Olekminsk, 60°25′N 120°25′E, 205
Olonets, 61°00′N 32°59′E, 60, 79
Omsk, 55°00′N 73°22′E, 12, 104, 128, 172, 204
Onega, 63°57′N 38°11′E, 12
Oni, 42°34′N 43°26′E, 198
Oral, 51°19′N 51°20′E, 12, 111, 216
Ordubad, 38°54′N 46°00′E, 198
Orel, 52°57′N 36°03′E, 45, 67, 79, 148, 152
Orenburg, 51°50′N 55°00′E, 104, 128, 152
Oreshek, 60°00′N 31°55′E, 60
Orsha, 54°30′N 30°23′E, 79, 186, 206
Orsk, 51°13′N 58°35′E, 104, 109, 174, 204
Ösel (*isl*), 58°20′N 22°30′E, 67
Osh, 40°37′N 72°49′E, 12, 217
Öskemen, 49°56′N 82°38′E, 217
Oslo (Christiania), (*Norway*), 59°56′N 10°45′E, 12, 28, 91, 115, 128, 148, 172, 176
Osnabrück (*Germany*), 52°17′N 8°03′E, 60
Özgon, 40°48′N 73°14′E, 217
Ozurget'i, 41°55′N 42°02′E, 198

Pabrade, 55°00′N 25°56′E, 192
Paderborn (*Germany*), 51°43′N 8°44′E, 60
Paide, 58°58′N 25°32′E, 192
Paldiski, 59°22′N 24°08′E, 192
Palermo (*Italy*), 38°08′N 13°23′E, 115
Pamirs (*mts*), 38°00′N 73°00′E, 12, 22, 23, 26, 217
Panevežys, 50°44′N 24°24′E, 192
Panfilov, 44°11′N 80°00′E, 217
Papal States*, 91, 115
Paris (*France*), 48°52′N 2°20′E, 91, 115, 147
Pärnu, 58°28′N 24°30′E, 192
Patrai (*Greece*), 38°02′N 21°51′E, 38
Pavlodar, 52°21′N 76°59′E, 104, 217
Pavlohrad, 48°34′N 35°50′E, 186
Pechenga (Petsamo), 69°28′N 31°04′E, 152, 176
Pechora, 65°14′N 57°18′E, 204
Peking *see* Beijing
Penza, 53°11′N 45°00′E, 55, 56, 67, 79, 108, 109, 111, 152
Perekop, 46°10′N 33°42′E, 67, 79, 125, 186
Peresechen, 47°45′N 28°56′E, 41
Pereslavl, 56°12′N 38°31′E, 55, 91
Pereyaslavets, 45°04′N 28°43′E, 35, 36, 41
Pereyaslavl, 50°05′N 31°28′E, 35, 41, 45, 79
Pereyaslavl*, 41, 45
Pereyaslavl Ryazansky, 54°55′N 39°50′E, 67
Perm' (Molotov, Perm), 58°01′N 56°10′E, 12, 104, 108, 109, 152, 172, 174, 204
Persia*, 74, 104, 108, 109, 125, 128, 148, 152, 172, 174
Pervomaysk, 48°03′N 30°50′E, 186
Pessinus(*Turkey*), 39°17′N 31°32′E, 38
Pest *see* Budapest
Petrograd *see* St Petersburg
Petropavl, 54°53′N 69°13′E, 12, 216
Petropavlovsk Kamchatskiy, 53°03′N 158°43′E, 13, 173, 205
Petrovsk, 52°20′N 45°24′E, 205
Petrozavodsk, 61°46′N 34°19′E, 152, 204
Petsamo *see* Pechenga
Pevek, 69°41′N 170°19′E, 13, 205
Philippi (*Greece*), 41°05′N 24°19′E, 38
Philippopolis (*Bulgaria*), 42°08′N 24°45′E, 35, 127
Piacenza (*Italy*), 45°03′N 9°41′E, 115
Piatigorsk, 44°02′N 43°00′E, 152
Pinsk, 52°08′N 26°01′E, 41, 45, 58, 79, 148, 174, 176, 186
Piotrkow (*Poland*), 51°23′N 19°43′E, 148
Plevna (*Bulgaria*), 43°26′N 24°37′E, 127
Plotsk (*Poland*), 52°32′N 19°55′E, 148
Pobeda, Mt, 65°10′N 146°00′E, 13
Pobedy Peak (*mt*), 42°05′N 80°04′E, 12, 217
Podolia*, 58
Podol'sk, 55°23′N 37°32′E, 206
Pogost-na-more, 64°02′N 38°05′E, 60
Poland-Lithuania*, 55, 74
Polatsk (Polotsk), 55°30′N 28°43′E, 35, 36, 41, 45, 55, 58, 60, 67, 79, 186
Polessk, 54°51′N 21°09′E, 192
Polevskoy, 56°28′N 60°15′E, 204
Pology, 47°30′N 36°18′E, 186
Polotsk *see* Polatsk
Polotsk*, 41, 45
Poltava, 49°35′N 34°35′E, 56, 58, 67, 79, 91, 152, 186
Pomerania*, 58
Port Arthur, 38°16′N 122°06′E, 129
Port Iliç, 38°55′N 48°47′E, 199
Posen (*Poland*), 52°25′N 16°53′E, 58
P'ot'i (Poti), 42°11′N 41°41′E, 125, 198
Prague *(Czech Rep*), 50°05′N 14°25′E, 12, 28, 38, 60, 147, 157, 176
Predivinsk, 57°04′N 93°29′E, 172
Preili, 56°16′N 26°50′E, 192
Preslav (*Bulgaria*), 43°09′N 26°50′E, 35, 41
Prishib, 39°09′N 48°34′E, 199
Propoysk, 53°35′N 31°28′E, 67
Prussia*, 58, 74, 79, 91, 104, 115
Prussia, East*, 148, 157, 176
Pryluky, 50°35′N 32°24′E, 186
Przemysl (*Poland*), 49°48′N 22°48′E, 35, 41, 58, 176
Pskov, 57°48′N 28°26′E, 36, 41, 45, 55, 56, 58, 60, 67, 79, 91, 104, 128, 152, 174, 176
Pskov*, 56, 58, 60
Pudozhskoi, 62°11′N 37°08′E, 60
Pushkin, 39°28′N 48°34′E, 199
Pustynsk, 54°25′N 26°44′E, 55
Putivl, 51°21′N 33°53′E, 67
Pyongyang (*N Korea*), 39°00′N 125°47′E, 13

Qaraghandy (Karaganda), 49°55′N 73°11′E, 12, 172, 217
Qaratau, 43°10′N 70°28′E, 216
Qarqaraly, 49°25′N 75°28′E, 217
Qarshi, 39°00′N 65°55′E, 216
Qazax, 41°05′N 45°22′E, 198
Qazimämmäd, 40°03′N 48°56′E, 199
Qostanay, 53°15′N 63°40′E, 12, 216
Quba, 41°23′N 48°33′E, 199
Qünghirot, 43°05′N 58°23′E, 216
Qüqon, 40°33′N 70°55′E, 216
Qurghonteppa, 37°52′N 68°47′E, 216
Qusar, 41°27′N 48°27′E, 199
Qvareli, 41°27′N 45°47′E, 198
Qyzylorda, 44°50′N 65°10′E, 216
Ragachow, 53°04′N 30°00′E, 186
Ragusa (*Croatia*), 42°40′N 18°07′E, 38, 127
Rakvere, 59°22′N 26°28′E, 192
Raseiniai, 55°28′N 23°02′E, 192
Rasht (*Iran*), 37°18′N 49°38′E, 108, 109
Rawa (*Poland*), 51°46′N 20°12′E, 91
Rechytsa, 52°21′N 30°24′E, 186
Reval *see* Tallinn
Rezekne, 56°30′N 27°22′E, 192
Rhodes (*Greece*), 36°26′N 28°14′E, 38
Rhodes (*isl*), (*Greece*), 36°20′N 27°59′E, 35, 127
Riga, 56°53′N 24°08′E, 12, 22, 26, 28, 41, 45, 55, 58, 60, 67, 74, 79, 91, 104, 111, 115, 128, 147, 148, 152, 157, 172, 174, 176, 192
Rivne (Rovno), 50°39′N 26°10′E, 152, 186
Roja, 57°30′N 22°46′E, 192
Rokiskis, 55°59′N 25°32′E, 192
Rome (*Italy*), 41°53′N 12°30′E, 38, 115, 147, 176
Rostock (*Germany*), 54°06′N 12°09′E, 60
Rostov, 57°11′N 39°23′E, 12, 29, 41, 45, 55, 56, 79, 147, 148, 152, 157, 172, 204, 206
Rovno *see* Rivne
Ruhnu (*isl*), 56°51′N 23°25′E, 192
Rumelia, East*, 127
Ruschuk (*Bulgaria*), 43°50′N 25°59′E, 115
Russia*, 12/13, 22, 23, 26, 28, 29, 67, 74/75, 79, 91, 104/105, 108, 109, 111, 115, 125, 127, 128, 129, 147, 148, 152, 157, 174, 204, 205
Rust'avi, 41°34′N 45°03′E, 198
Ruzayevka, 52°48′N 66°55′E, 216
Ryazan' (Ryazan), 54°37′N 39°43′E, 12, 35, 41, 45, 50, 55, 56, 104, 111, 204, 206
Ryazan*, 45, 56, 58, 60
Rybinsk, 58°01′N 38°52′E, 206
Rzhev, 56°15′N 34°18′E, 56, 79, 206

Saaremaa (*isl*), 58°40′N 22°50′E, 192
Sabirabad, 40°00′N 48°28′E, 199
Sadon, 42°50′N 44°03′E, 204
St Lawrence I (*USA*), 63°00′N 170°00′W, 13, 129
St Petersburg (Leningrad, Petrograd), 59°55′N 30°25′E, 12, 28, 91, 104, 109, 111, 115, 128, 147, 148, 152, 157, 172, 174, 176, 204, 206
Sakar, 38°57′N 63°45′E, 216
Sakhalin (*isl*), 51°00′N 143°00′E, 13, 23, 27, 75, 129, 173
Saki, 41°12′N 47°10′E, 199
Salavat, 53°22′N 55°50′E, 204
Saldus, 56°38′N 22°30′E, 192
Salekhard, 66°33′N 66°35′E, 12, 204
Salerno (*Italy*), 40°40′N 14°46′E, 38
Salihorsk, 52°45′N 27°39′E, 186
Salyan, 39°36′N 48°59′E, 199
Salzburg (*Austria*), 47°54′N 13°03′E, 38
Samara (Kuybyshev), 53°10′N 50°10′E, 12, 67, 79, 104, 108, 109, 111, 128, 152, 172, 174, 204
Samarqand, 39°40′N 66°57′E, 12, 50, 104, 128, 172, 216
Samaxi, 40°38′N 48°37′E, 199
Samogitia*, 58
Samos (*isl*), (*Greece*), 37°45′N 26°58′E, 127
Samtredia, 42°10′N 42°22′E, 198
San Francisco (*USA*), 37°45′N 122°27′W, 129
Sangaçaly, 40°15′N 49°25′E, 199
San Stefano (*Turkey*), 41°00′N 28°55′E, 127
Saragt, 36°34′N 61°32′E, 216
Sarajevo (*Bosnia Herzegovina*), 43°52′N 18°26′E, 28, 127, 147
Saratov, 51°30′N 45°55′E, 12, 29, 67, 74, 79, 104, 108, 109, 111, 152, 172, 174, 204
Saray (New Saray), 48°21′N 45°08′E, 50, 55
Saray (Old Saray), 47°48′N 47°54′E, 55, 60
Sardes (*Turkey*), 38°28′N 28°02′E, 38
Sardinia (*isl*), (*Italy*), 39°57′N 9°00′E, 115, 147
Sarkel, 47°53′N 42°51′E, 35, 36, 38, 41
Sarny, 51°21′N 26°31′E, 186
Sarysu, 48°29′N 70°19′E, 216
Saulkrasti, 57°20′N 24°28′E, 192
Sayan Mts, 53°50′N 97°30′E, 13, 22, 23, 26
Scutari (*Albania*), 42°06′N 19°19′E, 125, 127
Sebastia (*Turkey*), 39°44′N 37°01′E, 38
Sech, 47°53′N 34°11′E, 55, 67, 79, 111
Seleukia (*Turkey*), 36°22′N 33°57′E, 38
Semey (Semipalatinsk), 50°26′N 80°16′E, 12, l04, 217
Senaki, 42°16′N 41°59′E, 198
Seoul (*S Korea*), 37°30′N 127°00′E, 13, 129, 172
Serbia*, 124, 127, 128, 147, 148, 174
Sergiyev, 56°20′N 38°10′E, 206
Serpukov, 54°53′N 37°25′E, 55, 206
Sevan, 40°33′N 44°56′E, 198
Sevastopol' (Sevastopol), 44°36′N 33°31′E, 12, 28, 104, 111, 115, 125, 128, 148, 152, 157, 174, 186
Severnaya Zemlya (Nicholas II Land), (*isl*), 79°00′N 95°00′E, 13, 22, 23, 26, 129, 172
Shakhty, 47°43′N 40°16′E, 204
Shalqar, 47°48′N 59°39′E, 216
Shaumyani, 41°22′N 44°46′E, 198
Shaumyanovsk, 40°24′N 46°33′E, 199
Shaviklde (*mt*), 42°14′N 45°35′E, 198
Shchuch'insk, 52°59′N 70°14′E, 216
Shebelinka, 49°27′N 36°31′E, 186
Shenkursk, 62°05′N 42°58′E, 148, 152
Shepetivka, 50°12′N 27°01′E, 186
Shikoku (*isl*), (*Japan*), 33°00′N 133°00′E, 13
Shipka Pass (*Bulgaria*), 42°46′N 25°33′E, 127
Shostka, 53°51′N 24°45′E, 186
Shü, 43°40′N 73°47′E, 217
Shubarkuduk, 49°08′N 56°30′E, 216
Shusha, 39°44′N 46°45′E, 199
Shuya, 56°49′N 41°23′E, 206
Shymkent, 42°16′N 69°05′E, 12, 216

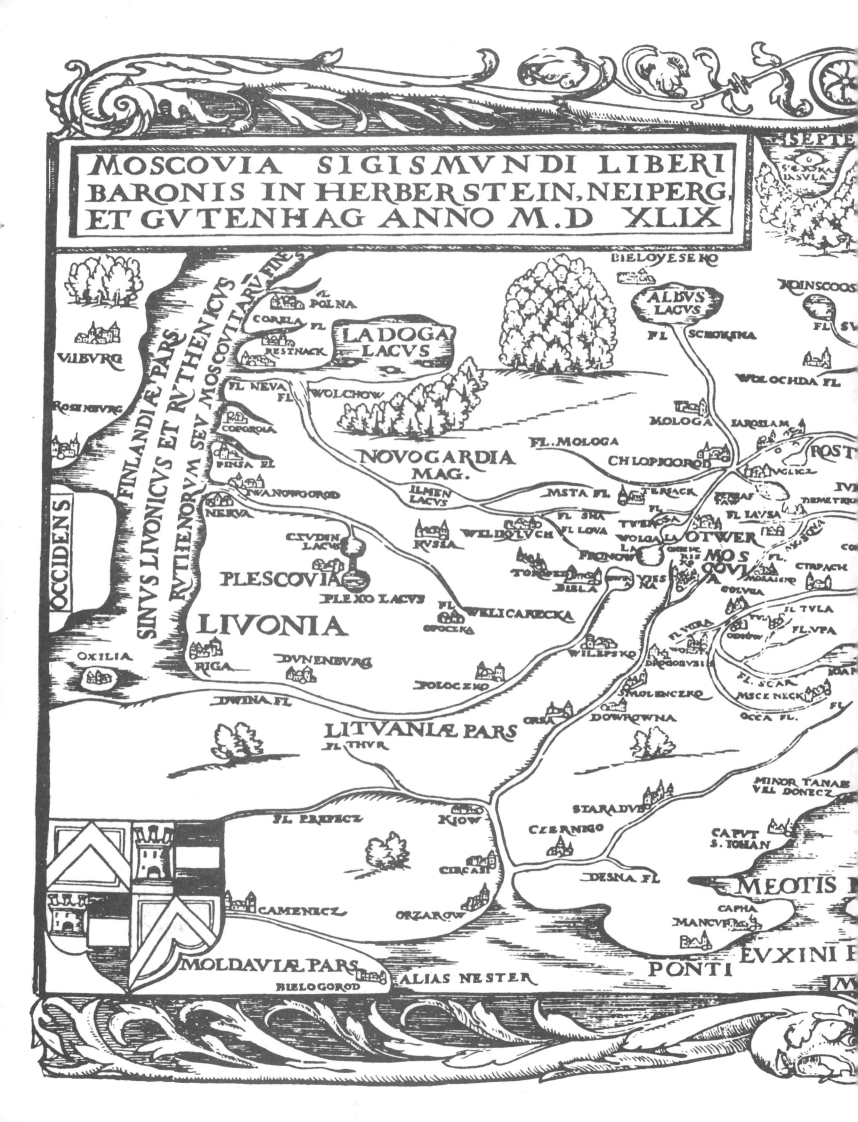

MOSCOVIA SIGISMVNDI LIBERI
BARONIS IN HERBERSTEIN, NEIPERG,
ET GVTENHAG ANNO M.D XLIX